THE FENRIS WOLF

Issue no. 5

Edited by Carl Abrahamsson

TRAPARTbooks

The Fenris Wolf, issue no 5

ISBN 978-91-986243-1-1

Trapart Books
P.O. Box 8105
SE-104 20 Stockholm
Sweden

info@trapart.net
www.trapart.net
www.patreon.com/vanessa23carl

Editor's Introduction

*We are animals, we live on animals, and animals live on us. We both have
and are parasites. We are predatory, and we are the living prey of the predatory. And when we follow the love act it is truly, in the idiom of the theo-
logians,* more bestiarum. *Love is profoundly animal; therein is its beauty.*

– Remy de Gourmont, *The Natural Philosophy of Love,* 1903.

In one brief year's time, from the spring of 2011 to the summer of 2012, we have
published three *Fenris Wolf* volumes. In all, almost a thousand pages of challenging
thoughts and ideas. *The Fenris Wolf* will continue to roar onwards once a year from
now on. The reason for this is not only the apparent appetite for our open-minded and
eclectic mix, but also because there's so much good material around that simply needs
to be presented and preserved in book form.

While slaving away at my desk, I thought of possible dedications for this issue, but
realized that the inclusion of Ezra Pound's postscript to his 1922 translation of Remy
de Gourmont's *Physique de l'Amour* (*The Natural Philosophy of Love,* Rarity Press, New
York, 1931) would be dedicatory enough – and directed at both gentlemen. Gourmont
is one of those figures who could clearly be regarded as a cultural "gnostic" – a mover
and shaker truly challenging stagnant thoughts and customs stemming from religious
intolerance and anti-sexual attitudes. Not only in spirit, in his altruistic attempts at exploring and experimenting with multifaceted cultural aspects of individual liberty, but
also thematically – something quite obvious specifically in this study of the physical act
of love-making among animals, originally published in French in 1903.

Pound was not the only modernist enamored by this forceful Frenchman. But
Pound did, however, go from mere admiration to action in translating this, at the time,
highly controversial book on sexuality. His postscript also shows how he took things
one step further by integrating his own speculations on the relationship between brain,
sperm and creativity – a subject no less controversial today, especially, it seems, in circles
opposed to individual gnosis and liberty.

It is my hope that there will be a renewed interest in Gourmont's seminal (sorry,
couldn't help that!) work, and that Pound's prescient and almost prophetic perspective
continues to throb vitally in scientific-neurological research as well as within that of
literary and magico-anthropological studies.

Thanks and praise to the following: *All* the contributors, without whom... Also, to
everyone responsible for the *Knowledge & Delight* symposium in London in September
2011, especially Ania Orzech and Krzysztof Azarewicz. Also, to Roberto Peyre and
Joyce Ip of BLOT for the invitation to participate in the panel discussion on Voodoo/

Vodou during the massive exhibition of the Marianne Lehmann collection at Etnografiska Museet in Stockholm 2011.

Also, to Per Faxneld and the other organizers of the *Second International Satanism Studies Conference* at the University of Stockholm in September 2011, to which I was (more or less) invited as the only *hors Académe* scholar, and which provided much food for thought. The heavy Satanic influx in this issue is in many ways a direct (editorial) result of/reaction to that conference.

Also, many thanks to the excellent art institution Gasworks in London for arranging the session "Art and the Esoteric" with Fredrik Söderberg, Gary Lachman and myself in December 2011.

Thanks also to Kathy Schneider, permissions coordinator at Llewellyn, Kelsey Ford, permissions coordinator at New Directions, Peteris Cedrins, Michael and Annabel Moynihan, and to Vera Mladenovska Nikolich for much appreciated editorial assistance, and to Fredrik Söderberg for a whole lot of magic.

An editorial note: As the texts in this issue stem from various minds from various cultures, there are obviously some stylistic inconsistencies. I have chosen to keep these, including possible "magical" language quirks and experiments, in the name of heterogeneous and creative integrity. However, for any spelling or typographical errors, pure and simple, I assume full responsibility.

Finally, I would like to say that the views and values expressed in the various texts in this eclectic anthology are those of the respective authors, and do not necessarily represent my own views, or any kind of general "Fenris Wolfian" perspective.

Vade Ultra!

Carl Abrahamsson
Stockholm-Monstropolis, Midsummer 2012

The Freedom of Imagination Act

Jason Louv

1. Consider the whole of technology and mechanization as a time machine, beaming itself backward into the past, drawing the present towards it. A non organic future, invading the organic past.

2. There is a future in which the machine severs the human soul; another in which it serves the human soul.

3. In the first, you live in the same way that corporate-farmed animals currently live. In the second, you live the way you like. The deciding point between these two realities is the direct action of the human soul.

4. Soul is not in the body; the body is in soul. Imagination is the gateway to the soul and the vector of freedom.

5. In order for the time machine to sever soul, it need only lock the gate: imagination. This is why, though we live in an age of the greatest information proliferation in recorded history, we are slowly losing the ability to imagine. Information is not imagination; the most advanced content delivery systems in the world are useless if their very existence means the end of real content.

6. The desertification of imagination is a problem just as real on its own plane as deforestation is on the physical one. The fragmentation and destabilization of concentration keeps human consciousness crippled. Though it may be deliberate, this is a mistake.

7. Question: All around you, you see systems put in place to suppress, depress, confuse and distract the soul. WHY has so much effort been put into this? And WHY does it never quite seem to be successful? What can we deduce from this?

8. Answer: The soul must be perceived as a threat, and must also be stronger than any known attempt to suppress it.

9. In brief:

10. Magic is imagination and will (repetition).

11. The imagination is the human organ used for direct perception of reality. The will is the human organ used, over time, to change that reality and crystallize it into matter.

12. Sex is the rocket fuel of both imagination and will – use it.

13. The image of the "self-destructive artist" is a culturally implanted kill switch. Ignore it. Imagination is a weapon; you have been indoctrinated with these images so that if you discover the weapon, you will use it on yourself and save them the trouble.

14. Do not permit the colonization and strip-malling of imaginary and interpersonal space. Man should be staring through telescopes, not into computer kaleidoscopes.

15. The old world is burning, and will soon be burnt down. Imagine better.

16. Trade in Our Failed State for the Right to Hallucinate.

Such Stuff as Dreams are Made of:
The Tempest, Eleusis and
the Psychedelic Renaissance

Patrick Lundborg

The following text is an edited chapter from Patrick Lundborg's upcoming book, Psychedelia – Ancient Culture, Modern Lifestyle. *It's a comprehensive and pioneering look at psychedelic culture of the past and present, and a book that comes highly recommended. – Ed.*

1

Written towards the end of a career of awe-inspiring creativity, William Shakespeare's *The Tempest* also signals the end of an era of intellectual freedom that made a career like his possible. *The Tempest* suggests the existence of a created world which is neither allegory nor psychology, but rather a world in the true sense; an alien place at the other side of the mirror, or that world from which we snatch glimpses when we dream. Like learning of a new continent, we can see the similarities and also the dissimilarities with our own world; there's people there, some of which may look like us, others which may look or behave in a way that appears to us quite surreal; they move about in a landscape where some of our natural laws seem to hold, while others don't. We may spot creatures, strange as things from another planet, whom we soon come to learn.

In other words, another world, which may be watching us in precisely the same way as we look upon it, with no causal priority. Coleridge, not surprisingly, understood the nature of *The Tempest*, describing it as '…a birth of the imagination… It addresses itself entirely to the imaginative faculty'. Another scholar found *The Tempest* to be 'pre-allegorical', while today's leading critic Harold Bloom opts for 'visionary comedy'. Such a genre-transcending work is the final invention of a creative power which the freedom of the Renaissance allowed to ignore the man-made institutions of power, be it Church or State or Academy, and to instead engage in play for play's sake. As Coleridge points out, Shakespeare never promulgates any party tenets. His freedom is that of the child at play, and the rules and roles are present for as long as the play lasts. *The Tempest* does not concern itself with symbol or interpretation, but with the here and now of its autonomous world. Appropriately, it's one of relatively few Shakespeare plays to observe the unity of time and place. Like the shipwrecked crewmen in the play, the spectator is an outsider entering another world, intuiting the rules and roles of the play as it unfolds before him.

It is logical that the only traces of a theme in the play that Harold Bloom finds, is that of authority; the juggling of rules and roles where play is the central, or only, activity. Coleridge, perhaps remembering his own opium visions, compares the world of *The Tempest* to '...our mental state, when dreaming... we simply do not judge the imagery to be unreal'. For a modern psychedelicist, experiencing Shakespeare's play the way Coleridge intends, the unfolding of Prospero's magic plan is like a vision sequence under tryptamine drugs, an experience often described as 'dreaming while awake'.

It is interesting that the two most frequently staged Shakespeare plays over the last century are the ones which could also be called the most 'psychedelic'; *The Tempest* and *Macbeth*. Despite numerous differences, they display a world where the boundaries between dream and wakefulness are unclear, and they are also both concerned with the theme of magic. Macbeth and his wife are lost in classic 'bad trips'; spiralling downwards, they cannot stop the terrifying hallucinations arising from their murderous guilt. But their drama follows an archetypal logic which is familiar and unambiguous, and the viewer's imagination is challenged in the surrealism of detail, but not of scope. Relentless towards its audience like a well-made horror film, *Macbeth* has lent itself to a number of successful movie adaptations, such as Orson Welles' expressionistic 1948 version, Kurosawa's *Throne Of Blood* (1957) and Roman Polanski's powerful presentation from 1971(incidentally, Polanski's first work after the Tate-LaBianca murders).

The situation for *The Tempest* is strikingly different. There exists no major or classic movie version of the play, and even the one closest to Shakespeare's text (from 2010) takes the curious liberty of changing the male Prospero into a female Prospera, despite the strong patriarchic character of this role. Worse still, at least according to Harold Bloom, are the numerous stage productions of the play that have exploited the text for themes of colonialism, racial struggle, or Marxist revolution, all of which is very poorly supported by Shakespeare's 1611 text. Derek Jarman's rarely seen 1979 adaptation explores an experimental 'punk' aesthetic which has little to do with the subtle moods of the original. A more interesting derivative is Peter Greenaway's *Prospero's Books*, but it is again so much closer to Greenaway's pre-occupations than Shakespeare's that it doesn't offer much insight into the play. For these reasons, and despite the number of modern stage productions, public awareness of this enchanting work is limited.

Before moving on to *The Tempest's* complex relation to the psychedelic tradition, a brief summary of the story may be in order. The main character of the play is Prospero, a former Duke of Milan who was removed from power by his plotting brother, taking advantage of Prospero's consuming interest in occult studies. Banished to a desert island along with his young daughter Miranda for many years, Prospero finally gets his chance to seek revenge upon his enemies when a ship carrying them passes nearby. With the aid of the powerful spirit Ariel, he arranges a shipwreck which brings the survivors to his island in small, scattered parties. To his aid he has the deformed Caliban, a young native who reluctantly helps Prospero in his tasks. The rest of the play unfolds Prospero's plan to regain his throne in Milan, find a suitable husband for his daughter, and subjugate his enemies into recognition of his sovereignty. These goals are all reached via his occult powers, which he then abandons in an epilogue, as he is returning to Milan.

2

Even among the most conservative critics, there is agreement that there is something peculiar going on in *The Tempest*, something which is unexplained to this day. It was not unusual for Shakespeare to leave loose ends or contradictions in his texts, but the enigmas of *The Tempest* are of a different order. The status of the text is uncontroversial, meaning that scholars find it to be entirely in Shakespeare's hand, with no augmentation by editors or collaborators. The play as printed in the First Folio 1623 was the play that Shakespeare had written, a definite version around which there is no dispute. So what mysteries one finds in the text, the playwright clearly intended to be there.

Frank Kermode, editor of the standard scholarly Arden edition (1954), recognizes the lack of proper explanation around certain passages:

> *The Tempest* is far from being a loosely built play; and nowhere in Shakespeare, not even in his most intensive work, is there anything resembling the apparent irrelevance of lines 73-97. It is a possible inference that our frame of reference is badly adjusted, or incomplete, and that an understanding of this passage will modify our image of the whole play.

Probably commenting upon the same mysterious passages, Harold Bloom finds in the play '...a sophisticated comic achievement we still cannot fully apprehend'. Much admired by critics and audience during 400 years of performance and research, *The Tempest* remains only partly understood; Kermode indicates that we may not even be close to a complete understanding.

What makes this interesting to the psychedelic student is that Shakespeare's strange and unexplained tangents frequently seem to refer to ancient mystery rites. Wherever *The Tempest* gets foggy, it points in this specific direction. The entire play is steeped in references to occult and esoteric practice, as is well-known, but these unexplained passages offer a different type of reference, appearing abruptly and seemingly meaningless. The most famous example, alluded to by Kermode above, is a section in Act 2, Scene 1, where three of the minor characters suddenly engage in a dialogue about Dido and Aenas of the *Aeneid*. The passage, which takes up 25 lines of text, is completely unwarranted in its context, and is neither prefigured nor revisited later. It reads almost like a Burroughsian cut-up, where a block of unrelated text pops up in the middle of something else. The passage is not particularly amusing, and its only content of meaning appears to be the Dido reference. Needless to say, Shakespeare critics have puzzled over this alien intrusion for centuries.

In 1921 one Colin Still, a literature student of a more speculative bent than Kermode and Bloom, suggested that this, along with several other dubious passages in *The Tempest*, was in fact a deliberate, hidden reference to the Greater Mysteries at Eleusis. Invoking the *Aeneid* was a way for Shakespeare to secretly communicate with learned members of the audience; the ones who knew that Book VI of Virgil's epic is a mythologized description of the initiation at Eleusis. In other words, when watching or reading *The Tempest*, this sudden invocation of Virgil's *Aeneid* is a hidden link to Eleusis.

Of course, Virgil and the *Aeneid* were omnipresent in the late Renaissance culture that Shakespeare inhabited, and a passing reference should not be over-interpreted, even if quite mysterious. But as Still points out, Shakespeare enriches the connection by making several other brief references to the *Aeneid*, again with little importance to the plot of *The Tempest*. The Bard clearly wished to invoke Virgil's epic, in a manner odd and uncalled for.

Further signs of Shakespeare's hidden agenda can be found in the Masque play of Act IV. This scene comes as unexpected as the *Aeneid* dialogue. Although the pagan origins of the Masque fits the style of *The Tempest*, it offers no development of the plot, nor does it illuminate what comes before or after. After some 80 lines of rhymed song of little merit, Shakespeare himself, in an amusing meta-comment, suddenly has Prospero interrupt the meaningless diversion by remembering the actual plot in progress (i.e.: the threat of Caliban's betrayal). Harold Bloom calls this Masque the nadir of the drama and can only explain it as a parody of fellow playwright Ben Jonson. So: what is this long passage of wasted pastoral comedy doing in such a tightly written play? Prospero's peculiarly absent-minded behavior, entirely out of step with his status as the omniscient mage of the play, suggests the presence of some hidden process. It is almost as if Prospero reluctantly allowed a few minutes for the Masque on order from his 'master', a master who can only be author himself. If Shakespeare forced this unnecessary Masque scene into Prospero's magic plan, as the text seems to suggest, what would Shakespeare's motivation be?

To answer this, one needn't look further than the first two lines of the Masque. These invoke the goddess Ceres, '…most bounteous Lady, thy rich leas / Of wheat, rye, barley, vetches, oats, and pease;'. This is a reference with immediate connection to Eleusis. Ceres is the Roman name for Demeter, the main goddess of the Eleusinian mysteries. Her status as a vegetation deity is recognized in the second line, and it is also in this property that she is venerated at Eleusis, where her search and ultimate retrieval of her abducted daughter Persephone overlays an older myth of agricultural death and rebirth. Over time, the Eleusinian rites underwent a second metamorphosis, so that the kykeon's psychedelic revelation and rebirth of each participant became the concrete expression of the Demeter-Persephone myth. Demeter's appearance in *The Tempest* seems as inexplicable as the Masque itself, in view of the immediate (Miranda's wedding) and overall (Prospero's magic scheme) context. However, the spectator or reader of *The Tempest* who has already discerned hidden Eleusinian elements will find in the presence of Ceres/Demeter yet another indication of this secret theme. This would also clarify the dialogue after the end of the Masque, where Ariel again brings up the presence of Ceres, but no other goddess. Frank Kermode's commentary finds Ariel's line here (IV:1, 167) puzzling. But in view of a hidden Eleusinian link, repeating the name of Ceres/Demeter could be a signal to the informed spectator, who otherwise may have missed the significance of the goddess' identity.

Colin Still, in his 1921 study, brings up many more instances of what he takes to be ancient mystery rite elements. Again, these clues are of special interest when their appearance in the text is unexpected and inexplicable, since this indicates a deliberate agenda of Shakespeare's. Such an instance is the curious insistence from one of the minor characters upon the cleanliness and dryness of his clothes, a seemingly meaningless fact repeated four times during the play. Is this an indication of the new garments that the initiands at Eleusis and elsewhere would don, before the major rites? Possible hidden messages like these, the lengthy Dido and Aeneas passage in particular, are reminiscent of the 'twilight language' often employed by spiritual teachers of the East. The twilight language presents a text with a surface meaning, not necessarily one of great merit, while its important content is hidden inside the parable, enumeration, or instruction. To unlock the true meaning of a twilight language text, the student needs to be familiar with certain key metaphors and marker words, by the decryption of which the higher teaching can be extracted. For example, an instruction on how to concentrate on a mundane household task may in fact hide details of an advanced tantric practice. Often associated with Vedic mysticism, twilight language is also used extensively within kabbalah and Western hermeticism, fields that saw great interest during the late Renaissance of Shakespeare. It is not unlikely that *The Tempest* contains a great deal of twilight language, not just in the most enigmatic sections discussed here, but throughout the play. This would be entirely in line with the strong esoteric influence that informs the play, and from a modern perspective help explain the sense expressed by Kermode, Bloom and others vis-à-vis *The Tempest*; that we have not yet fully understood it.

If there are links to the psychedelic rites at Eleusis hidden in *The Tempest*, we are still left with the question what Shakespeare wanted from us, after he had pointed us to the gates of the Great Temple. Here the indicators in the play are less clear, but a few remarks exist that could be taken as a concealed pattern. At places in the text, Prospero and Ariel insist upon a dramatic change, a 'sea-change', to be experienced under the hands of their magic powers. Such changes are actually hard to discern with any of the characters, except Prince Ferdinand and Prospero himself. Prince Ferdinand claims to have been given a 'second life' by Prospero; a claim that does not match the outward events of the drama very well. Instead, Prospero expresses remorse over the shortness of our earthly existence, as in the play's most famous monologue '…We are such stuff / As dreams are made on; and our little life / Is rounded with a sleep'.

If viewing *The Tempest* as a mystery rite in its totality, these statements make more sense. If the shipwreck at Prospero's island is analogue to entering the Eleusinian mysteries, then a life-altering experience does lie within reach, and of the shipwrecked men, Ferdinand at least manages to fulfill the life-change and 'rebirth' of the Greater Mysteries. Colin Still finds a symbolic schema in the structure of the play, where Ferdinand is the fully qualified initiate into 'the new life', while the plotting dukes and lords of the larger party are accepted only as passing the Lesser Mysteries, and the smaller party of the two hapless drunks and Caliban fail the initiation rites entirely. This seems overstated, and is poorly matched by the structural balance of the play, even if Still's individual observations are useful. Simply put, if Shakespeare had such a schema before him, he would have written the play differently. Frank Kermode calls Still's theories 'improbable', but give them enough merit to reference the 1921 book in his scholarly introduction.

A modern interpreter may take the Eleusis links and the overall nature of the play as reasons to proclaim *The Tempest* a drug fantasy, like *Kubla Khan* or *Alice In Wonderland*.

This is certainly a less radical reading of the text than the Marxist stagings that made Harold Bloom so ill at ease. The shipwrecked visitors to Prospero's island refer, at various points, to the sense of being drugged or hypnotized; 'a strange drowsiness befalls them' observes Sebastian in act II, and a little later he and Antonio discuss the strange states between sleep and wakefulness all of them experience: '…This is a strange repose, to be asleep / With eyes wide open; standing, speaking, moving / And yet so fast asleep'. The lost Prince Ferdinand sounds equally hypnotized as he follows Ariel's invisible presence, stating that 'This music crept by me upon the waters', and later on, 'My spirits, as in a dream, are all bound up'. Even the uncouth, wild Caliban gives an atypical display of poetic vision when musing upon his half-dreaming state, which like Ferdinand he connects with music:

> Sometimes a thousand twangling instruments
> Will hum about mine ears, and sometime voices
> That, if I then had waked after long sleep,
> Will make me sleep again: and then, in dreaming,
> The clouds methought would open, and show
>   riches
> Ready to drop upon me; that, when I wak'd,
> I cried to dream again.

These movements in and out of sleep, while Prospero's net of white magic slowly pulls the scattered parties in towards his compound, contribute greatly to the sense of drugged dream that the play instills. It is no wonder that Coleridge admired it, as it has the feeling of an Oriental opium dream. With its somnambulant days and magical music, *The Tempest* seems a peculiarly modern fantasy of a desert island; nearer to the 1950s Exotica visions of Eden Ahbez than the terrifying castaway fate sailors feared, while holding nothing of the rationalist challenges of Robinson Crusoe. The characters seem like slightly unreal versions of themselves, and despite the gravity of their situation, they appear unfazed and even satisfied. This daydreaming mood is as elusive as the ultimate meaning of the play, and it is perhaps such multi-levelled ambiguity that makes *The Tempest* seem both the most modern and the most psychedelic of Shakespeares' plays.

Was Shakespeare mainly carrying the spiritual torch of Eleusis into a new era, or was there something more concrete behind his psychotropic orientation? Recent research indicates that he may have been no stranger to the use of drugs, ranging from the cannabis that he definitely grew in his garden, to more exotic inebriants such as coca leaves and nutmeg. Sonnet 27 contains clues to 'weed' and 'compound' that remain open to interpretation, while the unapologetic escapism of Sonnet 76 reminds once more of the opium fantasies of Romanticists like Thomas De Quincey:

> Weary with toil I haste me to my bed,
> The dear repose for limbs with travel tired;
> But then begins a journey in my head,
> To work my mind when body's work's expired.

3

In order to understand the extraordinary period that Shakespeare captured and ultimately bid farewell in *The Tempest*, one needs to view the pan-European Renaissance not as a rebirth of classic Athens as much as a mirror of the Hellenistic period that came after Athens and before the rise of Christianity. Hellenism was a great time for spiritual speculation, ranging from voodoo-like magic rites to abstract metaphysical theories. It is no coincidence that one of the key scriptures (the *Corpus Hermeticum*) that vitalized the cultural climate of 15th century Italy were occult treatises from Hellenistic Egypt. However, this orientation towards esoterica has been obscured in conventional Western history, which prefers to discuss the immortal works of Renaissance architecture or the political-mercantile intrigues of the Italian city states, rather than the developments that otherwise defined the era, which was a profound cultural migration into various forms of mysticism and the occult.

The Renaissance did not mirror Hellenism in all its developments. While Florence may have stood as a new Alexandria, it had no Eleusis to support it. A thousand years of Christian dominance lay between Florence and the psychedelic rites of the Greater Mysteries. Nature cults and pagan beliefs still survived around Europe, but the urban intelligentsia had been stripped of its direct access to mystic insight. When Cosimo de Medici's Platonic Academy opened its doors in Florence, it was soon filled with young intellectuals starving for ideas that lay outside the orthodox Christian canon, be it the sophisticated philosophies of Plato or the theurgical magic of Egyptian occultists. Perhaps as an effect of this dam-burst of information, all ancient scriptures were considered of interest, and the division between philosophy, mysticism and magic became even less stringent in the 1400s than it had been during the Hellenistic era. For this reason, the most important intellectual advances of the Renaissance came not in classic philosophy, but rather within the vast, heterodox field usually labelled Western esotericism.

The relationship between esotericism and psychedelia is complex, ranging from a frictionless overlap to direct anti-thesis, depending on which aspects one examines. As suggested by the modern scholar Nicholas Goodrick-Clarke, a possible division that applies to both Hellenism and Renaissance is to split the field into mysticism on the one hand, and esotericism on the other. Mysticism is the seeking of a higher state of consciousness, of non-dualistic union with the ultimate being, the *unio mystica*. Esotericism is the occult and magic activity which does not strive for ego-loss and mystic union, but power over the mundane or intermediary planes. Esotericism is in a way a strengthening of the ego, rather than the dissolvement of the ego. These distinctions are not entirely obvious, and certainly open to debate. For the present purpose they will suffice, as the intent or direction of the activity will almost always help differentiate between 'mysticism' and 'esotericism'.

Mapping this table against the typical expressions of psychedelia, from Eleusis up until our present time, one will find the majority of overlap to be with Mysticism. That is not to say that Esoteric endeavors in psychedelia are lacking, but the number of successful ones are apparently fewer than the cases of non-dualist transcendence. Indeed, so common are the ego-dissolving states of *unio mystica* to high-dose psychedelic experi-

FIELD	BRANCHES	ATTRIBUTES	ROLE	OBJECTIVE
Esotericism	Sympathetic magic; Alchemy; Cabbalah; Numerology; Hermeticism; Astrology; Sorcery; Voodoo	Magic correspondences; Imagination; Intermediary Spirits	Controlling subject	Power over the mundane world and intermediary spirits
Mysticism	Meditation; Contemplation; Hatha Yoga; most classes of Tantra; Pantheism	Quieting of ego; Material simplicity; Holistic view	Passive subject	Unio mystica; non-dualistic transcendence; Nirvana; Samadhi
Hybrids	Neoplatonism; Shamanism			

ences that the state has become near synonymous with the successful trip. The various schools of Esotericism tend to put words like control and power at the center of the enterprise, and one needn't examine many handbooks on psychedelic drugs to realize that assertion of control and power is a sure way to trigger a negative experience on LSD. From the table above, it seems clear that psychedelia is strongly oriented towards one side of the Western spiritual tradition, which is the side of Mysticism. For this reason, several of the esoteric schools flourishing in the Renaissance and beyond will not be dealt with in this work, as they are too far removed, or even directly opposed to, psychedelic culture and its celebration of individual life and spiritual transcendence.

Even so, one must realize that all these occult schools and forms of magic and mysticism together form a rich path of alternative belief systems that reaches back into ancient history. Eleusis, Alexandria, Florence and even Haight-Ashbury stand as moments in history when monotheistic dogmatism and political tyranny withdrew like ebbing tide, and the spiritual underground rose to the surface. Ultimately the dominator culture came flooding back, but with a little patience and imagination, one can see the other path beneath the water, winding its way along the bottom; sometimes nearly lost, at other times in history, colorful and strong. This is the secret spiritual tradition of the West, always opposed by strong religious and political forces, yet validated by Plato and Shakespeare. Its coming into favor appears to be socio-culturally dependent; it gains strength in periods of rapid change in society, combined with a falling away of older homogenous belief systems.

4

If the spiritual heritage of the Renaissance has been downplayed or misrepresented by the traditional culture-bearers of Church and State due to its strong esoteric flavor, it seems that another form of misrepresentation lingers within the esoteric field itself. The Kabbalah research of Pico della Mirandola, the magic cosmologies of Heinrich Agrippa and John Dee, the theurgical rituals of Hermes Trismegisthus and the creative alchemy of Paracelsus, have all influenced later occult schools a great deal, and they live on in underground traditions beneath the mainstream. But these are all developments within the esoteric side of Renaissance thought, and their orientation towards sorcery and power set them at a distance from the mystic-platonic elements also present at the time. In fact, Renaissance esoterica followed a path very similar to that of the Hellenistic philosophies, moving from classic roots in Plato, Plotinus and meditative mysticism towards an increasingly wild-grown and speculative occupation with magic and alchemy. From the viewpoint of traditional history of thought, this was a degeneration. From the psychedelic perspective of this text, the development of the Renaissance also appears as a decline, not because of its increasing obscurity, but because it removed itself further and further from the fundamental Platonist world-view of mystic ascent into higher forms, and the Eleusinian mode of hedonism and private revelation.

Yet it may not have been that simple. A third interpretation of the Renaissance could be made, one which is neither the classicist orientation towards art and architecture, nor the esotericist focus upon magic and hermeticism. This third viewpoint goes back to the very earliest days of the Renaissance and Marcelo Ficino (1433-1499), the free-spirited Florentine scholar whose influence on the era was immense. In addition to leading the Platonic Academy, Cosimo de Medici had assigned Ficino with the task to translate Plato. But as new stacks of ancient scriptures were brought to de Medici's court, the translation of Hermes Trismegisthus was instead given priority. That the occult and magic texts of the *Corpus Hermeticum* were considered more important than Plato's philosophy illuminates the esoteric orientation of the Renaissance. After translation, the *Corpus Hermeticum* was debated with much enthusiasm by the young thinkers at the Florentine Academy, and over the next decades copies made their way around Europe, eagerly snapped up and scrutinized by local occultists. Hermeticism became an intellectual trend of the Renaissance, and its vagaries of content and structure became advantages as the scientific and esoteric speculation expanded.

Ficino, however, remained close to the classic Greek metaphysics, and unlike many of his contemporaries his orientation towards Neoplatonism conserved a psychedelic thread that ran through most of his work. While most Renaissance occultists promoted an active manipulation of the world via magic ritual and use of intermediary spirits, Ficino stayed clearly on the side of Plotinus, who favored meditation as the ultimate method to ascend to the higher planes. In Ficino's view, the human ability to think and love made each one of us a microcosm of a macrocosmic world soul constituted of a single loving consciousness. This is a view also expressed by psychedelicists such as Aldous Huxley, who on mescaline found the world to be made entirely out of love. Along with its potential for love, our human consciousness is minded and aware, as are the higher planes towards which we strive. Ficino finds each human a messenger between the ordinary world and the higher spiritual realms, and with proper purification each soul can acquire total knowledge of the world, which the world soul already possesses. What stands in the way for us to reach the Platonic-Eleusinian revelation?

> Through meditation, Ficino believed, the soul exchanged its commerce
> with the mundane and material things of this outer world for a new con-
> tact with the spiritual aspects of the incorporeal and intelligible world of

higher planes. Such spiritual knowledge is unobtainable as long as one's soul is enmeshed in ordinary experience and the noisy concerns of this troubled world. In these lower states of consciousness, the soul is barely awakened. But once the attention is directed inward, the soul begins to ascend the spiritual hierarchy of the cosmos, all the while learning and interacting with higher spiritual entities.

(from *The Western Esoteric Traditions* by Goodrick-Clarke, 2008)

Like Plotinus before him, these teachings of Ficino may sound similar not only to the higher states of a psychedelic experience, but also to tenets of buddhism and hinduism; the *Tat twam asi* pronouncement of the latter in particular. However, Ficino held certain esoteric beliefs that places him firmly in the Renaissance model he helped shape; the magical correspondences to the starry heavens expressed via astrology for one, and the existence of intermediary spirits for another. Both elements can be found among later Neoplatonists of Hellenism, but are less easy to align with the original mystic trajectory of Plato, Eleusis and Plotinus.

Despite the superior stringency of his teachings, Ficino found in the *Corpus Hermeticum* a useful model to marry the abstract hierarchies of the Neoplatonist cosmology with a magic-occult paradigm that took the mundane world as its point of origin. This way, the corporeal world and its objects too entered a stratified hierarchy, so that herbs, stones, statues and so forth could be invested with spiritual qualities. This practice would become the main concern for some of his successors, but Ficino did not invoke them into a system of controlling magic; instead he regarded the spiritual charge of mundane objects as useful tools in healing. He separated what he called demonic magic from his new spiritual or natural magic, the latter of which was to assist the human subject in ascending the higher planes. In his healing practice, he would dress in the proper ceremonial colors that matched the celestial correspondences of the situation, and then he employed fragrances, the singing of Orphic hymns, and ritual objects to establish the hierarchical connection. In Ficino's thought, there was a vertical link between celestial bodies, music, herbs, stones, man-made objects such as statues, and the status of the human soul.

With this, we unexpectedly find ourselves in the vicinity of aboriginal shamanism. Although Ficino arrived at this practical philosophy by way of classic Greek and Egyptian scriptures and his own genius, the resulting ritual model is curiously like the shamanic healing session found among Amerindian tribes, down to the use of costume, fragrances and 'heavenly' singing. The parallel is stronger in its expression as ritual than in underlying cosmology, yet it's highly interesting to note that another great Renaissance esotericist reached a similar model via another route. While Paracelsus (1493-1541) lingers in the history books as an alchemist whose inquisitive nature caused profound effects on the field of medicine, his underlying philosophy is less well understood. Paracelsus drew much inspiration from Ficino, and like the Florentine master he developed a system of thought that was both consistent and clearly defined. The two men stand as the alpha and omega of an alternate path for Renaissance mysticism, one which was overshadowed by the sorcerers and occultists, but which today impresses with its relevance and logic, not least from a psychedelic perspective. Like Ficino, Paracelsus developed the idea of the magus as a combined priest/physician, whose task it was to cure the sick patients of society, whether it be it from disease or spiritual suffering. Again we find a role which is remarkably close to that of the curandero-shaman of Amerindian cultures.

Paracelsus developed Ficino's ideas into a philosophy of holistic intuition which makes the shamanic parallel even more conspicuous. According to Paracelsus, in his constant striving towards healing, the magician-shaman should use his role as a messenger between the mundane world and the astral world to discover the cause of the suffering with the patient. To this end, he would use his training in mental powers such as meditation, as well as sacred objects, to establish a sympathetic connection with the higher powers, which would then reveal the source for the disease or discomfort. Sickness would often, but not always, be traced to astral imbalances, and they would be remedied by a physical medicine which also contained archanum, or spiritual powers. This, rather than making gold or finding eternal life, was the true purpose of alchemy according to Paracelsus; an indication of how broad and near-meaningless the term 'alchemy' had become.

What Paracelsus and Ficino developed was not alchemy, but a form of Neoplatonic Shamanism, an achievement which sets them apart from their Renaissance colleagues, and indeed from any precedents in Western spirituality. They came upon this due to a great interest in alleviating the suffering of others, combined with a stringent independence of thought. The result is a remarkable contribution to psychedelic history that casts a gigantic arc from the mystery rites of Eleusis to the Ayahuasca shamanism of Amazonia.

5

It is not known precisely which Renaissance esotericists Shakespeare drew on when writing *The Tempest*. Clearly his orientation lay towards the occult-magic side of the culture, more than the Neoplatonic-mystic heritage. Prospero is not given to metaphysics, but remains the hands-on puppet-master or mage, using astral powers to manipulate worldly events to his satisfaction. It has been suggested that the name and concept of his air spirit 'Ariel' comes from a book by the German occultist Johannes Trithemius, published shortly before the play. A more profound influence on *The Tempest* is likely to have been the legendary astrologer and alchemist John Dee (1527-1608), who some believe served as a direct model for Prospero. Dee's powerful presence at the Elizabethan court, and the wide range of occult knowledge that he accumulated, would make him a candidate for a real-life Prospero. Although Dee represents the esoteric, non-mystic side of late Renaissance spirituality, he holds a place in psychedelic history as a source of inspiration for modern-day hallucinogen icon Terence McKenna, so much so that he played the role of the English occultist in *The Alchemical Dream*, a charming documentary made in the late 1990s.

During his life-altering hallucinogen experiences in the Amazon jungle 1971, McKenna at one point paused to reflect that he was no longer able to distinguish between science and ritual. This was more than just a comment on the bizarre circumstances of his and his brother Dennis' on-going tryptamine experiment; Terence was in fact quoting John Dee. Blending science with ritual was a hallmark of Renaissance experimentation, and John Dee engaged in a field that the McKennas took great interest in; alchemy. As is well-known today, there is a distinction between exoteric alchemy, which aims to transform various base metals into gold, and esoteric alchemy, which is a quest for eternal life, facilitated via a magic elixir or the 'philosopher's stone'. Familiarity with alchemy helps illuminate many aspects of Terence McKenna's thought, the La Chorreran events chronicled in *True Hallucinations* most of all. In a somewhat playful manner, alchemical terminology recurs throughout McKenna's account, so that the psilocybian mushroom is equalled with the philosopher's stone, or *lapis philosophorum*, the experiment is called an *opus*, and so forth. In his lectures McKenna would occasionally go on alchemical tangents that reflected great knowledge of the field, but over time these references became less frequent. Alchemy in its classic, gold-making sense fell out of favor with contemporary thought long ago, while the vague, formal expressions of exoteric alchemy only makes it blend into a vast river of alternative spiritual belief systems ('new age'). Despite McKenna's enthusiasm, alchemy in either form has not carried over well into psychedelic culture; even less so than its Renaissance sister field of astrology.

John Dee was also knowledgeable in natural science and its relationship to esoterica, and among other things he furthered the study of light that had engaged pre-renaissance mystics. Dee's later development dealt much with the direct reading of the will of God, for which he saw angels as the central medium. He employed spirit channelers to communicate with these angels. This was performed in a largely Christian ritual context, and Dee's method was not to summon or demand the angels, but ask humbly for their assistance. In this technique we find another parallel to aboriginal shamans, who typically advise against calling upon spirits directly, due to the dangers involved. Terence McKenna transformed Dee's technique into useful pieces of psychedelic trip advice, suggesting that the traveller go into each experience on a note of humility and simply ask for help, then remain open to whatever the trip would bring, rather than to try and force the direction or responses. Another of McKenna's helpful suggestions, that the psychedelicist should purify himself before the experience by taking a personal inventory of known issues and 'hang-ups', may too derive from this source.

As an esotericist, Dee is more interesting than most continental colleagues, and his eventful biography would make for a good historical movie. Dee unified Kabbalah, alchemy and mathematics in his 'monas'; a complex hieroglyphical symbol that has been called 'an alphabet of nature'. This differs somewhat from the theurgic magic of many Renaissance hermeticists in that Dee strives to interpret and divine rather than manipulate, and also in the ultimate goal of mystic ascent to God as an effect of the cosmic understanding. So there is a Neoplatonic residual here, missing from much occult esotericism. On the other hand, Dee took great interest in the developments of Kabbalah that Pico della Mirandola had engineered, an element that would raise much attention from later-day occultists, but lay far removed from the Neoplatonic-Eleusinian mysticism. The kabbalists paid much attention to numbers, characters and sacred words, and Dee brought his linguistic interest so far that he presented a new 'ur-language', Enochian, said to stem from the angels Adam and Enoch. As a communicator with angels, he clearly prefigures Swedenborg and Blake, and even Rilke. Reaching the high age of 81, John Dee passed away at the same time that Shakespeare began work on *The Tempest*.

6

While occultists like John Dee received support from royal patrons at European courts, other occultists suffered torture and burning at the stakes as condemned heretics. In a few cases this fate befell learned men who had simply gone too far in their radical spirituality, such as the infamous Giordano Bruno. The large majority of occultists imprisoned and executed during the Renaissance were however of an entirely different background: they were alleged to be witches.

It is often believed that the witch-hunts evolved as an extension of the medieval Inquisition in order to keep it operational, but recent research shows that many of the witch trials were instigated by the local public, who demanded action from the authorities. The hysteria tended to flare up during periods of hardship, such as diseases (i.e.: the bubonic plague) or famine, and behind the witch-hunts a motivational pattern based on scapegoating is not hard to detect. The witches, who in earlier and more charitable times were known as 'wise women' or 'cunning folk' offered an ideal scapegoat; as women, single and usually poor, lacking formal education and the support of powerful men, their position was a complete inversion of the circumstances that allowed speculative thinkers like John Dee and Marcelo Ficino to prosper freely. The spiritual freedom of the Renaissance was not a universal given, but a comfort available to those who were in the right place, of the appropriate background and of the right gender.

Shakespeare features witches in both *Macbeth* and *The Tempest*, and his depiction reflects the same hostile sentiment that had caused Queen Elizabeth to issue an anti-sorcery tractate targeting witches. The three Weird Sisters of *Macbeth* are among the Bard's most famous creations, and in line with the uncompromising tone of that play, they are outlined not as mere agents of the occult but in a truly fearsome, inhuman manner. In *The Tempest* the witch Sycorax has no lines, yet her presence is felt in a dual role as the deformed Caliban's mother and as the loathsome anti-thesis of the dignified Prospero. Even to the relative freedom of the Renaissance, the witch is truly alien; she represents a relationship with nature that is improper. Behind the scapegoat there may figure another perception which is equally abject to the self-centered master of ceremonies the Renaissance held up as role model. The witch is not exerting control over nature, but emanates out of nature with her secret, pantheistic knowledge. The witch represents true folk wisdom, not the theoretical insights of Kabbalah and alchemy.

The important role that psychotropic plant drugs played in classic witch-craft has been well established in modern times. So overwhelming is the number of detailed source testimonies from witches, priests and physicians that the ignorance that long lingered over this field is puzzling. Some early historians (such as Edward Tylor in 1871) did posit the importance of the ointments and their visionary effect for the experiences reported by witches, but later decades actually display a regression of the scholarly insight. It is possible that the climate of the Victorian and Edwardian eras affected the studies of this controversial and often sexually oriented field. Margaret Murray, who otherwise showed little restraint in extravagant theories, mentions 'ointments' but otherwise does not devote a single paragraph to the witch plants in the 270 pages of her *The Witch-Cult in Western Europe*. The great pharmacologist Louis Lewin in 1924 acknowledged the probable role played by Datura type plants for visions which the witches perceived to be real, and the sexual element of the intoxication was finally brought into focus by Erica Hesse a few decades later.

The basic pharmacopeia of the European witch was established via Michael Harner's 1972 essay *The Role of Hallucinogenic Plants in European Witchcraft*. Harner draws on the aforementioned writers as well as the 1960s research of Julio Baroja to present a comprehensive overview of the plants and their effects. Although their morphology (appearance) may differ substantially, the 'witches weeds' are remarkably similar in other respects. The four classic plants all belong to the Solanacae (potato) family, and the active elements are the same in all four: the alkaloids atropine, scopolamine and hyoscyamine. One may suspect them to be interchangeable in use, but much like shamanic Ayahuasca brews, the preparation seems to have involved several plants, along with other admixtures, and our knowledge here is too limited to judge on the rationale. One thing that is vital to realize, and rare among plants, is that these alkaloids (some might say toxins) are effective via skin absorption; therefore the witches used them as ointments, rather than potions or snuffs.

Popular Name	Genus	Comment
Deadly Nightshade	Atropa Belladonna	
Henbane	Hyoscyamus	Used in non-prescription drug Asthmador for asthmatics
Mandrake	Mandragora	
Thorn Apple; Angel's Trumpet; Jimson Weed; etc	Datura stramonium (and variants)	Closely related to the South American Brugsmansia, which is often referred to as "Datura" or "Tree Datura"

Within modern drug research, these extremely powerful plant drugs are usually characterized as deliriants rather than psychedelics or hallucinogens. They differ from the classic psychedelics in several ways, the most fundamental being that they tend to create states of complete psychosis, wherein the user does not remember taking a drug, nor can separate the dream world he or she has entered from reality. For this reason, the solanaceous drugs are very risky, a danger compounded by the fact that some of them may be found growing in ordinary gardens and parks. The state of intoxication typically lasts at least 24 hours, sometimes up to three days.

A common Datura scenario finds the user experiencing some mild effects, falling into an unpleasant sleep, and waking the next day only to find the drug effect much stronger than the day before. Accidental deaths due to the individual's complete dissociation from reality are known, while others have reported on profound changes or damages to their personality that seem to be permanent. Blurred vision is very common, but tends to pass. Less dramatic but equally bizarre are recurring reports from independent sources of the Datura user smoking and dropping non-existing cigarettes, as well as receiving hallucinatory visits from childhood friends. Due to its global availability, Datura is by far the most commonly used of the solanaceous plant drugs today, but the positive trip experiences reported from it are few and far between. Timothy Leary said that he had never heard of anyone having a good trip from Datura.

However, it remains a fact that the witches used these drugs recurringly and understood them well enough to establish a shamanic alliance with them; as Harner and others make clear, the witches developed a consistent method of preparing, ingesting, experiencing and psycho-integrating these feared plant drugs. Not until recently was it understood that the witch 'riding' her broomstick was in fact the practical act of applying the green ointment to her vaginal membranes, for maximum absorption. The flight to the Sabbat and the encounter with the Devil, demons, and other witches all took place in a hallucinatory delirium, for which the witch had set aside needed time and solitude. Recuperating from the long drug flight, the visions were integrated into her existing knowledge of spirits and nature, and in a short while she would again accept clients and conduct her business.

The witches did not claim to perform sorcery or devise spells when they were on their long vision flights; the completely immersive mental state made this impossible. The practical side of witch-craft was instead handled via the Esbat, which was a 'business meeting' for which no powerful ointments were used. This division of practice has been used to distinguish the European witch tradition from that of the shaman, who heals and divines when he is in the visionary state. However, a clear parallel can be found if one compares the demanding vision flights of the witch with the early training and initiation rites of the shaman, which takes place in isolation and (in drug-using tribes) with very high doses of the entheogen, rendering the apprentice unable to perform any task except receive learning. It is also well established that many tribal shamans in the Amazon know how to mix Brugmansia/Datura with their Ayahuasca brews for a predictable effect, while archeological finds in Northern Mexico demonstrate a local ritual use of Datura of great antiquity. Comparable evidence exists on Datura use among the older folk religions of the Himalayan region, where it may have come to influence the Vedic religions.

The fundamental problem of the witches' ointment drugs in the West today is that the knowledge on how to use them has been lost; hence the wildly unpredictable results and obvious cases of persistent overdosing. Since psychotropic fiends show little restraint in subjecting their minds and bodies to various uncontrolled experiments, it is possible or even likely that a sub-culture may develop around the solanaceous deliriants in the future. Datura in particular holds such a substantial position in entheogenic history, not just in Europe, that its proper usage and cultural history deserves thorough examination. At the same time, these plant drugs should not to be confused with the classic psychedelics, from which they differ in most major respects.

Anthropologists are uncomfortable with the concept of the witch, which falls outside their neat structuralist models, while historians have tended to focus entirely on the witch-hunts and their context. Prejudice and political agendas have influenced the scholarly treatment of the witch and witch-craft to a much larger extent than a comparable field such as shamanism. There is no shortage of source material ranging from trial testimonies to public banishments, but the analysis of such material has been tendentious. At least three lines of reasoning can be identified:

A) The classic-naïve view says that there were no real witches per se, just eccentric or outcast women who were scapegoated by the Church, and whose testimonies were complete inventions brought forth under torture. This opinion was long in dominance, and may even today be found in simpler text-book presentations.

B) The practical view, which today dominates among scholars, acknowledges that many victims of the witch-hunts were practicing witches according to the classic folklore view, whose testimonies of animal transformation, nocturnal Sabbat flights to meet the Devil, and various sexual encounters, did reflect actual vision experiences had under the influence of deliriant plant hallucinogens such as Datura.

C) The neo-pagan view holds that the witches were indeed practicing occultists, and as such they belonged to a vast, secret society whose roots went back to ancient nature cults. This hypothesis has found little traction with academicians, but has raised substantial support among independent students and the general public.

If the use of strong intoxicants among Renaissance witches is an unchallenged fact today, there still lingers a substantial controversy around the alleged existence of pagan witch cults. This issue is important to the psychedelic field, since such congregations of plant drug users would lay bare yet another ancient thread in the spiritual underground tradition of the West. Others have found the question of equally great interest, and it came to play a vital part in shaping the esoteric culture of the 20th century. Central to the debate stands Margaret Murray, whose 1921 work *The Witch-Cult in Western Europe* put forth the existence of long-running lines of European witch-craft orders. Murray posited that the alleged witch sects persecuted during the late Middle Ages represented the surviving legacy of pagan nature cults, whose unbroken tradition reached back into pre-Christian days. Meticulously footnoted and indexed like a scholarly work, Murray's book found more success with mainstream readers curious about the occult than with scholars, who have repeatedly emerged to discredit and dismiss her work as unscientific, misleading, and biased. This did not prevent interest in Murray's book from growing steadily over the decades, and it was a best-seller as late as the 1960s. Like the works of Erich von Däniken or Graham Hancock, Murray's ancient witch-cult theory struck a nerve in the public mind, who simply enjoyed the idea and its various implications, and her influence ran deep enough that modern witch covens, contemporary Wicca witch-craft, and the entire field of neo-paganism can be to some extent traced back to her 1921 work, even as its standing among branch historians and anthropologists steadily declined.

This is where the story might have ended, but towards the end of the century, some anthropological evidence has been brought forth to suggest that Murray may not have been so wrong after all. The Italian scholar Carlo Ginzburg, following decades of fundamental research, was able to present a series of intriguing clues to the existence of various pagan rites and groups that survived well into early Modernity. His work deals primarily with Northern Italy and the Alpine Region, which is also where the earliest instances of witch persecution arose in the 14th century. Ginzburg's most remarkable discovery, and one that sent shock waves through the anthropological field of the 1960s, was the existence of an ancient sect of pagan witch-doctors and demon-slayers as late as the 16th century. The details around this fertility cult are outré enough to intrigue any psychedelicist. In Northeastern Italy existed a widespread belief that certain men and women were marked at birth as defenders against witches and demons. Chosen defenders of the harvest and the fields, the 'Benandanti', or 'good walkers', ventured forth in their dreams to do battle with the forces of evil. The Benandanti was recognized already as a new-born, via a special sign given during delivery; that of being born wrapped in the placenta. As Ginzburg discovered, the Benandanti was merely one facet of a Central European region still immersed in pre-Christian nature cults; peasants observed the equinoxes and solstices rather than the Catholic calendar, and the local population engaged in ancestral worship, animal totemism, ancient rites and superstition.

The Benandanti were not witches but witch-doctors, defenders of nature against witch-craft; a fact that so confused the Catholic Inquisitors that they were unable to pass judgment on the pagan cult members until after long deliberation. Ginzburg brings up several other examples of pagan ritual and beliefs in existence around the Alpine region at the time of the Renaissance, though none as out of the ordinary as the Benandanti of Friulia. Whether this was a curious anomaly in history or the expression of a much larger remnant of pagan nature cults that Margaret Murray had intuited behind the witch-hunt era may remain impossible to tell, but clearly this is not a field for the dogmatic dismissals. Fortunately, anthropology is occasionally able to shed its conservative skin and move forward, thanks to diligent and open-minded scholars such as Carlo Ginzburg and Michael Harner.

Another intriguing aspect of folk medicine that may link the pagan heritage of the witches with the use of genuine psychedelics, meaning LSD rather than the solanaceous deliriants, is the use of ergot rye. The knowledge of how to create a hallucinogenic brew from the purple fungus of rye or barley may have been lost after the Christians destroyed the Great Temple at Eleusis, but concoctions made from the same plant infestations continued to be used in folk medicine throughout Europe. Its primary application was in connection to child-birth, where mid-wives administered it either to induce an abortion, or to hasten the delivery and so reduce the pains. Mid-wifery is a role traditionally associated with local witches, particularly in the strictly heretical aspect of inducing an abortion. The ergot rye and its lysergic acid component is obviously another plant drug in the witch's pharmacopeia. The old use lives on in the popular name Mutterkorn, meaning 'mother rye', which Albert Hofmann used as a heading for his Sandoz research presentation, *Die Mutterkorn Alkaloide*. Over the centuries, the application of ergot rye in child-birth was reduced to control bleeding, and it was in this respect that Dr Hofmann began to experiment with his series of ergot derivatives that ultimately produced the very special 25th variant, d-lysergic acid ethylamide, or just plain and simple LSD.

It is not difficult to find in these grain fungi a bridge connecting the ancient mystery cults to the witch-craft plants of the Renaissance, and from there a winding road up to the psychedelic culture of the 20th century. The path moves, in a symbolic manner too obvious for the psychedelicist to ignore, from the re-birth into 'new life' rituals of Eleusis, to the very concrete births and abortions overseen by European witches and midwives, back to the mystic-visionary 're-imprinting' and 'ego-death' rites that followed Hofmann's discovery of LSD. Working in the same Alpine region where the earliest witch-hunts had occurred 600 years earlier, Hofmann recognizes the ergot's connection to 16th century folk medicine in *Road To Eleusis* (1977), but does not extend the reference to the witches and their possible ancient heritage. Carlo Ginzburg is less cautious: 'It is probable that ergot was part of popular, predominantly female medicine for a very long time'.

From this follows the suggestion that the knowledge of ergot was not limited to its obstetric application, but as a deliberately used psycho-active agent. Any student of LSD is familiar with the ominous affliction 'ergotism', which is usually described as poisoning via bread baked from ergot rye. So terrifying are the descriptions of ergotism that it has actually hampered modern psychedelic research, since even the most daring psychonauts have been unwilling to perform bio-assays with the rawer forms of ergot. This is one reason why the lysergic code to the Eleusinian Mysteries took so long to crack. However, the case is more complex than just the issue of deadly food poisoning, since there are two different types of ergotism; one is the gangrene-like form which causes death and is traditionally known as 'St Anthony's Fire'. The other type of ergotism is convulsive and causes epileptic-like states followed by a lengthy loss of consciousness. Although this too is clearly a form of poisoning, it appears that this second state could induce vision states that were considered profound, even with the terrifying side effects. Therefore, as Ginzburg implies, it is possible that a primitive form of entheogenic use of ergot rye survived through the Middle Ages and onwards, side by side with its established use among mid-wives and witches. As Ginzburg points out, both types of ergotism may appear more like the workings of an evil spell than some type of disease, which would strengthen the plant drug's association with witchcraft.

The Old World, meaning Europe, is famously barren when it comes to useful psychedelic plants. The Americas and the Far East offer a hallucinogenic flora which is maybe ten times as bountiful as Europe, where an unsteady distribution of psilocybian mushrooms is the sole representative of classic hallucinogens. Given man's natural inclination for higher states of mind, and the ultimately disappointing blur and stupor of wine and beer, the European naturists have tried to make do with what was available, which was a limited catalog of deliriants and semi-toxic plants. In addition to the four classic 'witch plants' listed above, the Amanita muscaria or fly agaric grows in abundance in Northern Europe and the Alps. The fly agaric's role in ancient shamanism is well-known today, but it appears that a diffusion of popular usage not immediately connected to the shamanist cultures of Russia and Siberia occurred around Europe. In Scandinavia, where Christening did not fully take hold until a few centuries before the Renaissance, use of the fly agaric was common among heathen warrior tribes who can scarcely be linked to remote shamanic traditions.

What is puzzling is that people who try the fly agaric today rarely report on pleasant or useful experiences. Conversely, the effects are typically described as somatically unpleasant, combined with an unimpressive stupor or mental blur. Although less dramatic, the lack of enthusiastic trip reports from Amanita muscaria is reminiscent of the negative modern response to other traditional esoteric plants, such as Datura. How should we gauge these pan-European drug cultures built on plant compounds that modern users with rare exceptions find unpleasant and of little use compared to the major hallucinogens? Was the innate drive for altered states so strong that people in older days accepted grave somatic discomfort and occasional deaths just to get their 'visionary fix'? Or did these pagan traditions develop methods for preparation and ingestion of the deliriants and intoxicants that rendered the experience less unpleasant and more hallucinatory; methods which are now lost and unknown to us? In view of the ingenuity demonstrated by Central and South American tribesmen in preparing and combining plants to create powerful visionary states, we should not dismiss the possibility that comparable skills did once exist with European pagans, among witches and surviving fertility cults in particular.

8

On a cold night in November 1619, while stationed in Neuburg an der Donau, a young French soldier experienced a series of powerful dream visions that would have a profound influence not only upon his own life, but upon the totality of Western culture. In the dream a whirlwind knocked him over, after which he heard a thunderous explosion, which caused him to briefly awaken and see sparks flying from his stove. Falling asleep again, an angel descended upon the young man, and showed him a large dictionary and a collection of ancient poetry. Opening the book of poetry he finds the question "What path should I follow in life?", to which the dictionary seemed to provide the answer. Already engaged in the field of mathematics and the ultimate goals of science, the young man took his visitation from the 'Angel of Truth' as a confirmation that this scientific quest was the chosen path for him.

The young man was René Descartes, and in the following decades he would revolutionize the fields of both science and philosophy. As he declared at the time of his mystic vision:

> This, I perceived, was called universal mathematics... Such a science should contain the primary rudiments of human reason, and its province ought to extend to the eliciting of true results in every subject. To speak freely, I am convinced that it is a more powerful instrument of knowledge

than any other that has been bequeathed to us by human agency, as being the source of all others.

According to Descartes' world-view, mathematics was the fundamental nature of everything that existed, and within mathematics the tools of numbers, order and measurement provided the only working material needed.

Four years before Shakespeare's *The Tempest* first appeared in print, and only ten years after the passing of the great spiritist John Dee, the young French philosopher proclaimed a world-view which had no room for visionary comedies or esoteric speculation, or indeed anything that could not be measured and counted. That this anti-spiritual, ultra-rational philosophy received its private validation by a visiting Angel is a great irony, remarked upon by Rupert Sheldrake, who otherwise found few reasons to be cheerful when contemplating Descartes' new paradigm:

> It was a vision of a machine-like world governed entirely by universal mechanical laws with no inherent spontaneity or freedom. This was the essence of the mechanistic theory of Nature. The soul, the animating principle, was withdrawn from the whole of nature and from the human body too... This desacralized, de-animated soulless vision of nature became the foundation for modern science and was established as its reigning paradigm in the scientific revolution of the seventeenth century.

Clearly, this was not the time to talk of angels. Descartes regarded himself as a Catholic, but unsurprisingly received severe criticism from his compatriot and colleague Blaise Pascal, whose own private vision had led him the opposite way, from the neutral precision of mathematics into a more devout religiosity. As Pascal surely realized, the Church stood to lose as much as any occultist or man of letters from the coming rationalism. But it was Descartes' vision that would prevail, as Pascal's devotional fire and the fairies and witches of Shakespeare and the esoteric seances of John Dee were pushed away from the spotlight of the human enterprise. Great scientific discoveries would follow from this fork in the road, but much was also lost.

The esoterica and occultism of the Renaissance did not need Descartes to find itself unwelcome in the 17th century, however. An upswing in religious puritanism among the public raised questions around the activities of kabbalists and hermeticists, who in hard times would also find themselves scapegoated in the same way as witches. A new perception of the magician emerged, one that was considerably darker than the master of nature that reigned during the high Renaissance. Accusations of black magic and ties to devil worship grew more common, and the lasting perception of the mage was not that of Prospero, but of Faustus. Presumably inspired by the famous occult writer Henry Cornelius Agrippa, the Faust legend received its most significant treatment in the play by Shakespeare's contemporary Christopher Marlowe, and much like the two rivalling playwrights, Dr Faust and Prospero stand as rivalling interpretations of a free-spirited era that was drawing near its close.

By the mid-1600s, Shakespeare, Marlowe, Descartes and Pascal were all gone, and in their wake would follow an outwardly eventful era as Modernity took shape, with wars and enlightenment, scientific revolution and religious puritanism, global trade, slave trade and colonialism. The spiritual underground of the West withdrew from its Renaissance podium into a quieter mode of operation, its presence felt most strongly in a few atypical visionaries like Swedenborg and William Blake.

Secret Societies and the Modern World

Gary Lachman

The following text was delivered as a lecture at CAPC, the Museum of Contemporary Art, in Bordeaux, France, in 2011. – Ed.

Let me begin by saying that I am delighted to be here in Bordeaux, speaking to you about secret societies. Actually, it is rather apt that I am doing this here, as Bordeaux itself features, to some extent, in the history of secret societies. In 1857 a group known as the 13 Society was founded here, in Bordeaux. Now, unlike many secret societies, they were actually anti-occult and anti-magic. They were strict rationalists and the aim of the society was to show the absurdity of superstitions. They had 13 members and they met at a house, the address of which was number 13. They sat 13 at table and their meetings were held on Friday the 13th. The members of the society walked under ladders, spilled salt, crossed knives, broke mirrors, and paid absolutely no attention to omens and warnings. It appears that this group had some illustrious members. Leon Gambetta, General Boulanger, and President Marie Francois Said Carnot were said to have belonged to it. The group apparently had a branch in London as well, and were known as the "13 cult," although that is practically all that is known about them. Elliot O'Donnell, from whose book *Strange Cults and Secret Societies of Modern London*, published in 1934, I learned of the 13 Society, says of the English branch that it "has its headquarters in a London suburb and owing to its being a strictly secret society, it is very difficult to find out much about it." Which seems to make sense. Yet, it must have been an extremely *secret* secret society, because, if you do a little digging, you'll discover that quite a lot *is* known about some of the other, more well-known secret societies, if that isn't too much of an oxymoron. I should add that I have no idea if Elliot was right, in saying that Leon Gambetta, President Carnot, and other prestigious people were members of the 13 Society. But it certainly makes things interesting to wonder if they were...

My other reference to Bordeaux and secret societies is somewhat more mysterious. The Russian mystical philosopher P.D. Ouspensky was a lifelong seeker of what he called "the inner circle of mankind" and a student of the enigmatic Armenian esoteric master G.I. Gurdjieff, who, incidentally, lived for many years in France. In his book *A New Model of the Universe*, Ouspensky has a chapter called "Esotericism and Modern Thought." In it he remarks that while some members of what he calls "esoteric schools" are said to live in "remote and inaccessible parts of the globe" – the Himalayas, Tibet, or some mountainous regions of Africa – others "live among ordinary people" and even belong to the "uncultured classes" and are engaged in insignificant and perhaps even "vulgar" professions. And to make his point, Ouspensky remarks that a "French occult author stated that he had learned much from an Oriental who sold parrots at Bordeaux."

Now, I am not of the opinion that selling parrots, in Bordeaux or anywhere else, is necessarily a "vulgar" profession, and that to do so one must be "uncultured," but Ouspensky's point is that, we can never know exactly *who* might be a member of one of these schools. There might be one, right now, sitting next to you in this room. They may have heard of this exhibition and have come tonight to see what kind of people are drawn to it. He or she may be here, looking for recruits. I don't know. And that's the point. We never *can* know.

The French occult author Ouspensky refers to is Saint-Yves d'Alveydre. Saint-Yves d'Alveydre was a rather eccentric character. Among other things, when his wife, a wealthy Polish divorcee, died, he turned their house in Versailles into a shrine to her, where he wore purple velvet and lived in isolation, and continued to set a place for her at the dinner table, as he believed he could still communicate with her on the "astral plane." He was born Joseph Alexandre Saint-Yves in Paris in 1842, and was given the title "Marquis d'Alveydre" by the Pope in 1880. He was a devout Catholic, but he mixed his Catholicism with a hefty portion of the occult and mysticism, something other French occult thinkers did as well – Eliphas Levi, for example, whose real name was Alphonse Louis Constant and who was a defrocked priest. In the 1860s d'Alveydre spent some time on the isle of Jersey in the English Channel, where he met political exiles, one of whom was Victor Hugo, who combined his politics with mesmerism and spiritualism, something d'Alveydre did as well. During the time of the Paris Commune – which, as a member of the army, d'Alveydre helped suppress – d'Alveydre began to develop a peculiar form of what we can call "occult politics." This was a kind of extreme totalitarian government that d'Alveydre called "synarchy." If "anarchy" means "no" government, or "without" government, "synarchy," for d'Alveydre, meant "total" or "complete" government. It meant that no aspect of a synarchical society would be outside government control. As that control was divinely inspired, d'Alveydre believed this was all right.

D'Alverydre got his ideas about "synarchy" from that parrot seller in Bordeaux. His name, at least according to occult history, was Haji Sharif. Now, Haji Sharif, if he existed, was a Hindu who left India after the Sepoy Rebellion of 1857 – oddly, the same year that the "13 Society" began. He was d'Alveydre's Sanskrit tutor. Like many thinkers in the late 19th century, d'Alveydre wanted to discover the primal, 'ur' language, from which all others developed. But along with teaching him Sanskrit, Haji Sharif also taught d'Alveydre another language, what he called Vattan, which neither d'Alveydre or anyone else had ever heard of until then. Vattan was, Haji Sharif said, the primordial language of mankind, and it was still used in the mysterious kingdom of Agartha, which happened to be an unknown civilization, hidden below the Gobi Desert. Agartha, Haji Sharif said, was a subterranean world, like something out of Jules Verne's *Journey to the Centre of the Earth*. It's millions of subjects were ruled by someone known as the "King of the World," and also the "Sovereign Pontiff." Agartha was a highly technologically advanced civilization, and it had agents all over the world, reporting back to the

Sovereign Pontiff on new developments on the surface – apparently they moved from nation to nation via underground tunnels, rather like the Eurostar. It's form of government was synarchy, which, d'Alveydre says, was the form of government for the whole world, until around 4000 BC, when it collapsed at the beginning of recorded history. D'Alveydre was confident that the upper world would soon see the virtues of synarchy and embrace it, at which time the King of the World would emerge and take his rightful place as ruler of the surface world, too. D'Alveydre wrote letters spelling this out to the Pope, Queen Victoria, and Tsar Alexander III, urging them to take up the cause of synarchy. Evidently he was quite serious about this.

What these world leaders thought of d'Alveydre's ideas is unknown, but strangely enough, d'Alveydre's synarchy gained some popularity in the 1890s. It was seen, understandably enough, as a possible alternative to anarchy. These were the years when anarchists were tossing bombs and assassinating political figures left and right, much like today, and d'Alveydre drew large sympathetic crowds when he lectured on synarchy. He formed a lobbying group, called the Syndicate of the Professional and Economic Press, which pressured government ministers, promoted discussion of his ideas, and published synarchist tracts. Again, the group is supposed to have claimed some important figures in politics and finance – sadly, I don't have any names – and d'Alveydre's work was considered significant enough for him to be made a Chevalier of the Légion d'honneur in 1893.

By the early 20th century, D'Alveydre had apparently lost interest in his idea, and devoted the last years of his life to developing a complex system of occult knowledge that he called the "Archeometer." But in the 1930s, a group of French political extremists re-discovered d'Alveydre's ideas and tried to put them into practice. A character named Vivian Postel du Mas – who, some sources say, had some association with Rudolf Hess – wrote a *Schéma de l'archetype social* – an "Outline of Archetypal Society" – and *La Pacte Synarchique* – "The Synarchic Pact" – which detailed a synarchist society based on the Hindu notion of caste. These were said to have reached high ranking figures in the French government of that time, and also during the Occupation, and were also to have influenced the right-wing terrorist group the Cagoule and the Comité Secret d'Action Révolutionnaire, or CSAR, which had among its aims the overthrow of the Third Republic. Quite a leap from selling parrots in Bordeaux, n'est-çe pas?

Now, I mention synarchy and terrorist groups like the Cagoule because I think that when most of us think about secret societies – if we think of them at all – it is usually in terms of dark, sinister, dangerous individuals, gathering together to usurp political and social power and to exercise it over the rest of us. In the case of d'Alveydre's synarchy – which actually has its roots in Plato and the Hindu Laws of Manu – this seems to be true, at least in its later manifestation. And a similar unease and concern gathers around contemporary notions of secret societies, around names like the Bilderbergs and Skull and Bones, and ideas like that of a "new world order." We live in a world of "conspiracy consciousness" and false realities, a sort of Philip K. Dick or *Matrix* mindset. I think we should be concerned about these, and other groups, if indeed they are involved in making plans and decisions that affect our lives. But what I want to do with the rest of my talk, is to give some examples of secret societies that we can call, for sake of a better word, "positive," and which contributed in important ways to making what we call the modern world. In doing so I will be exploring a bit of what, at the risk of sounding sensational, we can call the "secret history" of modernity, which is part of a larger, broader attempt, that I make in my books, to show how "occult" or "esoteric" societies and ideas have helped to make the world we live in today. Not – I hasten to add – in a sensational or fantastic way, involving conspiracy theories and hidden cabals pulling strings behind closed doors. I am not interested in "exposing" or "revealing" the "truth" about secret societies. But if you look at history with an unprejudiced eye, you can, I believe, see how societies considered "secret" have had a hand in it. And, as I say, in a "positive" way.

The first group I want to look at is, in effect, the first modern secret society; pretty much all the others that followed, at least in the west, were influenced by it. In 1614, in Kassel, Germany, strange "manifestos" appeared, announcing the existence of a mysterious society, known as the Brotherhood of the Rosy Cross. The Rosicrucians, as they called themselves, were adepts – sages and philosophers – who were followers of a mysterious individual known as Christian Rosenkreutz. Christian Rosenkreutz, the story goes, had travelled in the East, the Holy Land, and North Africa, in search of secret knowledge, which he received and tried to pass on to others in the west. Sadly, no one was interested, and he discovered that all the great thinkers and philosophers he spoke with were only interested in safeguarding the knowledge they had. They wanted to keep this to themselves, and weren't interested in sharing it, or in what Christian had to teach them. He lived to the ripe age of 106 – he was born in 1378 and died in 1484 – and, in order to spread the knowledge he had gained, he started a community of scholar-magicians, who studied astrology, alchemy, Hermeticism, but also the religion and the science of the day. They were also healers, who travelled through the land, tending and curing the ill, for no charge. When Christian died, his body was placed in a seven-sided tomb, which was filled with magical and alchemical texts and instruments, and was illuminated by seven lamps and a kind of "miniature sun". Here he lay undisturbed until 1604, when his tomb was discovered. When it was opened, Christian's body was found to be uncorrupted, and the texts and instruments he was buried with were in perfect condition. His discoverers decided to carry on his work, which they saw as a "general reformation of Europe," an attempt to ignite a new age of scientific, religious, political, and social freedom. The manifestos they distributed called for their readers to join them in this effort, which, in essence, was aimed at breaking the oppressive hold of the Catholic Church and the Habsburgs over central Europe.

Now, many people were moved by this call, and wanted to join the Rosicrucians, and for a few years, a "Rosicrucian furore" as the historian Frances Yates called it, broke out over Europe. If it was around then, the tabloid press would have had news stories and "revelations" about the mysterious Rosicrucians in the papers every day, and the news about them would be "trending" on the net and turning up on Facebook and Twitter. But try as many people did to find and join the Rosicrucians, it appeared that they were nowhere to be found. All attempts to meet them failed. One of the most well known individuals who tried to join the Rosicrucians was the philosopher René Descartes. But he simply couldn't find them. Nobody could.

Now, this absence led the Rosicrucians to earn a nickname, and people started referring to them as "the Invisibles." And this led many people to believe the whole thing had been a hoax, and that the Rosicrucians simply didn't exist. Others believed they did exist, but only made themselves known to those worthy of them. And others argued that they had left Europe, and were now living in Tibet. At some point during the furore a Lutheran pastor named Johann Valentin Andreae announced that he was the author of at least one of the Rosicrucian manifestos, a strange dream-like work called *The Chemical Wedding of Christian Rosenkreutz*, a surreal narrative made up of weird, alchemical symbols and allegories. And Andreae said that the whole Rosicrucian affair was what he called a *ludibrium*, a Latin word that means "serious joke." This meant that it was a kind of "fiction," but with serious intent. This intent, Frances Yates argues, was at least in part to stir up opposition to the Habsburgs and draw support for Frederick V of the Palatinate, whom many Protestant leaders believed could offer a serious challenge to Habsburg rule.

Many people, however, refused to believe that the Rosicrucians were really only a kind of philosophical and political fiction, a "pious lie" aimed at inspiring regime change in Mittel Europa. Yet, given that the Rosicrucians could not be found, what could these people do? Well, if the original Rosicrucians couldn't be found, they did the next best thing: they became Rosicrucians themselves. And this, I believe, was at least one of the aims of the Rosicrucian manifestos: to give those who were unhappy and discontent with the oppressive Catholic and Habsburg rule and who wished for a more free, progressive society, a *model* which they could copy. So, if the Rosicrucians were a kind of "lie," it was the kind that could be made true, by those who were inspired by their ideals.

Now, many reinvented themselves in this way as Rosicrucians, but two figures did it in great earnest, and each embodied different aspects of the Rosicrucian ideal. One is what we can call the Hermetic or magical aspect, and the other is the utopian or political one. Although the two were combined in the original Rosicrucian manifestos – the magical view of the world itself calls for a more open vision of society – in their followers they tended to separate into particular pursuits. The man who embodied the Hermetic and magical aspect of the Rosicrucians was the Englishman Robert Fludd.

Fludd was a brilliant polymath and he applied his enormous intellect to spelling out in detail the Hermetic-Rosicrucian idea that man is a "tiny universe," a microcosm of the vast macrocosm. For the Hermetic-Rosicrucian view, we somehow contain the universe within ourselves. Fludd was, in effect, the last great Hermetic cosmologist, and he was trying to "know the mind of God" well before Stephen Hawking. I discuss Fludd's work in a recent book of mine, *The Quest for Hermes Trismegistus*, and sadly, I can't go into it here. The other individual, who carried on the utopian aspect of the Rosicrucian ideal, was the Bohemian philosopher and educator Jan Comenius.

Comenius may not be well known in France; I'm not sure. But he's a national hero in the Czech Republic, where his birthday is a holiday. In Hungary, a teaching college and an adult education program are named after him. Rembrandt painted his portrait. He was asked to be the first president of Harvard University, and UNESCO offers a "Comenius medal" for outstanding achievement in education. That in itself seems good evidence that a "secret society" can inspire positive work. Comenius belonged to the Bohemian Brethren, a mystical strain of Protestantism that started with Jan Huss. He preached a philosophy based on piety and the spread of education, what he called "pansophism," and he was a central promoter of the Rosicrucian ideal of free and open knowledge, shared by all, in the service of humanity, beliefs that he expressed in his many writings. When the hopes for a new Europe led by Fredrick V of the Palatinate collapsed, at the start of the Counter-Reformation and the Thirty Years War, Comenius fled his homeland. He became a target of Counter-Reformation reprisals. His house, library, and manuscripts were all destroyed, his wife and child died, and he went into exile, a story he depicts in his heartbreaking work *The Labyrinth of the World*.

During his wanderings, Comenius met Samuel Hartlib, a Pole who, like Comenius, was inspired by the Rosicrucian ideal. He shared Comenius' belief in education and his commitment to helping his fellow man. Hartlib went to England in 1640, and promoted his Rosicrucian-Comenian ideas. He was what was then called an "intelligencer," what we would call a "networker," someone who made connections and contacts, bringing people and ideas of a like mind together – he would have loved the internet. In 1640, Hartlib spoke to Parliament, expounding on his utopian ideas. He met with positive response, so positive that he encouraged Comenius to travel to England to join him. Comenius did, and it seemed that in England he found a land where his Rosicrucian dream of free and open education and a progressive society would become real. Alas, England itself was on the brink of disaster. Although Comenius was received with great enthusiasm, in 1642 civil war broke out, and Comenius' dreams were dashed once again.

Yet, in another way, they were fulfilled, at least to some extent. In 1645, some scientific enthusiasts started to gather in London. One of these was a man named Theodore Hack. Hack was one of Hartlib's agents, and a keen follower of Comenius. These informal gatherings were the beginning of what would later become the Royal Society, the oldest and most prestigious scientific society in the world. In 1646 and '47, Robert Boyle, the "father of modern chemistry" and one of the "enthusiasts" who took part in these meetings, wrote to a friend, requesting certain books. These, he said, would "make him extremely welcome to our Invisible College." Boyle describes the members of this "Invisible College" as men of "capacious and searching spirits" who "endeavour to put narrow-mindedness out of countenance" and who "take the whole body of mankind to their care." We remember that the Rosicrucians came to be called "the Invisibles," and that they promoted philanthropy, and open and shared knowledge. And in a letter to Hartlib, Boyle speaks of the philanthropic and civic-minded plans of the "college." A few years later, Boyle's "Invisible College" became the Royal Society.

There is, I believe, a clear connection here between the Rosicrucian ideal of a free, open, and accessible knowledge and its use in promoting a progressive, philanthropic society, and the beginnings of one of the most important scientific societies in the world. Not bad for a secret society that quite possibly didn't even exist.

My second secret society is thought by some scholars to have emerged out of the Rosicrucians, although there is still debate about this. Exactly when Freemasonry began is still an open question. Several dates have been suggested and the roots of Freemasonry have been said to lie in ancient Egypt, with the Knights Templar, and in other places.

Quite a few. All this is still unclear. One thing that is clear, however, is that, for much of its existence, Freemasonry has been the object of suspicion. There has been a sense that it is "up to no good" in some way. More than any other secret society, Freemasonry has been accused of a number of dark intrigues, mostly to do with taking over the world. You can find many sites on the internet discussing this, and claiming that this or that influential figure in politics or world finance, is really in the employ of the power mad Masons. And I think the start of this paranoia about Freemasonry must be laid at France's door, and with the conspiracy theories surrounding Freemasonry and its offshoot, the Illuminati, as the agents responsible for the French Revolution. This idea began in 1797, when the ex-Mason and priest Abbé Barruel published a sensational four-volume work, *Memoirs Illustrating the History of Jacobinism,* in which he claimed that the French Revolution was part of a grand pan-Europe plot to abolish the church and the monarchy, and that one group above all others was behind this: the Illuminati. Barruel's work was oddly echoed by another paranoid tract, *Proofs of a Conspiracy Against All the Religions and Governments of Europe*, published in the same year and written by John Robison, a professor Natural Philosophy and secretary of the Royal Society of Edinburgh. The villain of both works is the Bavarian Illuminati, a Masonic offshoot, started in 1776 by Adam Weishaupt, a professor of canonical law at Ingolstadt.

The Illuminati is still around, at least according to several internet websites and the novelist Dan Brown – Hillary Clinton is supposed to be in its employ – but to see it as the sole agent responsible for the French Revolution is, to put it mildly, absurd. Although it is true that Adam Weishaupt's aim in starting the Illuminati was to break the repressive hold the Jesuits had on Bavaria – much as the Rosicrucians wanted to break the Habsburg's hold – according to one account, Weishaupt himself could "barely organize a picnic, let alone the Terror." The Illuminati is actually one of the great oxymorons in the history of secret societies. Although it presented itself as an esoteric, mystical branch of Freemasonry, able to offer its initiates deeper, more secret initiations, in actuality Weishaupt was a rabid rationalist, who had no interest in the occult or mysticism, and merely used Freemasonry as a means of recruiting people to his cause of eliminating "prince and nations from the face of the earth."

The Illuminati lasted only eight years; in 1784, it, and all other secret societies, were outlawed in Bavaria, and it was by that time falling apart through internal squabbles anyway. Yet this idea that the Illuminati in particular and Freemasonry in general is a dark force, secretly at work overthrowing the governments of the world, has lasted far longer than the Illuminati themselves. In 1905 the anti-Semitic forgery *The Protocols of the Elders of Zion*, which was most likely written in France but imported to Russia, where it was published, linked the Masons with the Jews and rising "world communism" as spectres planning the conquest of the globe. One reader who took these claims seriously was Adolf Hitler, who persecuted all three groups. And in 1924, the idea that the Masons were planning to take over the world appeared again in the monumental conspiracy tract *Secret Societies and Subversive Movements* by the English historian and proto-fascist Nesta Webster. For Webster, the Illuminati were responsible not only for the French Revolution, but also the 1848 Revolution, WWI, and the Bolshevik Revolution. One of her readers was Winston Churchill, who took it all quite seriously. Webster herself took it very seriously, and was so convinced she was a target of reprisals, that she never opened her door without a loaded pistol in her hand.

While Abbé Barruel and John Robison were wrong to believe that the Illuminati were "behind" the Revolution, it is true that the years leading up to the Revolution saw a great increase in Freemasonry and "fringe Masonic" groups in France. Some of these groups were allied to others who were followers of the ideas of Franz Anton Mesmer, the German healer who believed he had discovered the secret cosmic force of "animal magnetism." Whatever we might think of "animal magnetism," Mesmer did have a high success rate with magnetic cures, and in France in the 1780s he initiated groups that were called Societies of Harmony. Some of these blended ideas of an individual "regeneration" through mesmerism with those of a political and social "regeneration." Other groups, also calling for a "regeneration," but of a more spiritual kind, were formed of followers of the Swedish religious thinker Emanuel Swedenborg, who wrote books about his travels to heaven, hell, and what he called the spirit world. Often, those put into a "magnetic trance," spoke of what they saw, using Swedenborg's accounts of heaven and hell as their guides. These ideas blended with those of political revolution. If, in the "magnetic cures," the patient begins his recovery by entering what was known as the "magnetic crisis" – a kind of convulsive fit – then society too, could be "cured" of its ills by throwing it into its own "crisis." Following this, it would return to its "natural" state of health, a kind of primitive harmony, free from the taints of corruption.

One result of this strange blend of Freemasonry, Mesmer, and Swedenborg, is that the Masonic egalitarian ideal of a brotherhood of man (and of woman; there were Masonic auxiliary groups dedicated to women, and one of the most influential Masonic promoters of the time, the Sicilian magician Cagliostro, initiated women into his "Egyptian Masonry") were spread widely across Europe and even into the New World. Another Revolution that Freemasonry was supposed to be "behind" was the American one of 1776. While the idea of Illuminati agent provocateurs stirring up the Colonies is a non-starter, what is true is that the Masonic notion of the value of the individual, whatever his social rank, fed the forces that led to the War of Independence. This egalitarian ethic was disseminated, not by sinister cabals, but by the power of the *Zeitgeist*. They were "in the air," and they got there because of the popularity of Freemasonry. So a nefarious society which aims at world domination was one of the most important means by which our ideas about "human rights" and the value of the individual, whatever his social rank, spread across the world. Again, a positive effect of secret societies.

My last secret society is technically not really a secret one, although the source of its ideas and ideals is. The Theosophical Society was founded in New York in 1875 by two Americans and one Russian. The Americans were William Quan Judge and Colonel Henry Steel Olcott. The Russian was the incomparable Madame Blavatsky. Some of you may know of Madame Blavatsky or may have at least heard of her. In the popular mind she is known as the most flamboyant of the 19th Century mediums, although that is really only a charicature of her. She was an enormous, larger than life character: she weighed 230 lbs, chain smoked cigarettes, and had a "colourful" ironic sense of humour and spoke her mind about everything. She was also one of the most remarkable women of the 19th Century, something I try to make clear in a book about her that I am just finishing.

Before she came to public notice in New York and went on to international notoriety, Blavatsky journeyed around the world, travelling in India, the Middle East, Egypt, the Americas, Europe, the Far East, and many other places, joining a number of secret and Masonic societies along the way – she was even initiated into the Druze. I mentioned Jules Verne earlier; Blavatsky was his contemporary and her life was certainly as adventurous as any of his novels. Her most fantastic claim was to have spent seven years in Tibet, at a time when white European men had enormous difficulties crossing its borders. During one of her sojourns in Tibet, she said that she became the student of two Hindu sages, whom she called the Masters – later, during her time in India, she referred to them as Mahatmas – who initiated her into a secret esoteric school. The Master's real identities were always kept secret, and Blavatsky became their agent or emissary in the western world. She was given the mission to bring the wisdom of her Eastern Masters to the west, and this was the reason why she founded the Theosophical Society. We remember that the Rosicrucians were said to have left Europe and relocated to Tibet, and in esoteric history there is a direct line of descent from these early "Invisibles" to Blavatsky's "Hidden Masters."

Theosophy means the "wisdom of the gods," and Blavatsky wrote two enormous books – *Isis Unveiled* and *The Secret Doctrine* – that spell out in meticulous and often fabulous detail exactly what that wisdom is. I do not have the time to go into theosophy in detail here, but the essence of her teaching is that modern, present-day humanity is only a relatively recent development, and that in ages past, other civilizations existed on the earth. She speaks of Atlantis and Lemuria, and explains that the modern religions of Christianity, Hinduism, Islam, Judaism, Buddhism, and the rest, are really later developments of a primal, pre-historic spiritual revelation, what she calls the "ancient wisdom." Part of this wisdom is the understanding of "spiritual science," what we would call magic, and she argues that the ancient mystical philosophers – Pythagoras, Plato, Plotinus and the Neo-Platonists – knew the secrets of this science, and were able to use "powers" that modern materialist science simply cannot comprehend. She herself was known to exhibit these powers, what we would call paranormal phenomena.

But along with reintroducing this ancient wisdom to the modern west, Blavatsky also had an ethical and social message, one that was in line with the egalitarian ideas of the Freemasons. Her great-grand father Prince Dolgorukov had been a high-ranking figure in Russian Freemasonry in the late 18th Century, and it was through discovering and reading his occult library, that Blavatsky devoted herself to finding the "Hidden Masters" and "Unknown Superiors" that were spoken of in Masonic lore. Earlier I mentioned the political associations of Freemasonry, Mesmerism, and Swedenborgianism in pre-revolutionary France. A similar *mélange* developed in Russia, and Blavatsky's great grandfather was linked to spiritual-political machinations involving figures as legendary as the Comte de Saint-Germain – who, incidentally, was said to have discovered the secret of eternal youth. This combination of spiritual and political reformation, which we saw at work in the Rosicrucians, inspired Blavatsky too, and it informs what we can see as the "mission statement" of the Theosophical Society. This consisted of three central themes: the study of ancient and modern religions, philosophies, and sciences; the investigation of the unexplained laws of nature and the psychical powers of man;

and the formation of a universal brotherhood of humanity, without distinction of race, creed, sex, caste, or colour.

Blavatsky relentlessly championed this last, social message, throughout her career. Before founding the Theosophical Society, she had been involved with several progressive movements and groups, in which she campaigned for a freer, more open, and classless society. As with the Rosicrucians and the Illuminati, one of her main foes was the Catholic Church, which she felt was an oppressive and outdated influence, and which she believed had distorted Christ's true teaching. She was not an arm-chair revolutionary. In 1867 she was wounded at the battle of Mentana, in which she fought on the side of Mazzini and Garibaldi against the papal army, which, sadly, was supported by the French. And in a broader, more philosophical battle, she championed Buddhist and Hindu spirituality against what she saw as an oppressive Judeo-Christian monotheism. More than anyone else, Blavatsky is responsible for the 20th Century's long love affair with the "wisdom of the East," and many people today who recognize the Dalai Lama as a spiritual leader have Blavatsky to thank for it. She really is the one who first brought Tibetan and Mahayana Buddhism to wide notice in the west, and many of the most influential Buddhist scholars, translators, and interpreters of the early 20th century were either Theosophists themselves or were deeply influenced by her, names like W. Y. Evans-Wentz, who compiled *The Tibetan Book of the Dead*, Edward Conze, who translated many important Mahayana scriptures, and D.T. Suzuki, who introduced Zen to the western mind.

Now, when we look at Blavatsky's writings about Atlantis, Lemuria, lost civilizations, psychic powers, Hidden Masters, reincarnation, karma, and all the rest, it seems a remarkable heap of, frankly, crazy stuff. And much of it, unfortunately, has devolved into a kind of domesticated, mainstream "New Agism." But the strange thing is that, at the time, and into the early 20th Century, it was immensely popular. And not just with woolly-minded eccentrics and uncultured flower sellers. Some of the most influential people of the time became Theosophists. A list of people who either became Theosophists or who were influenced by Theosophy includes some very important names. Here are a few: Thomas Edison, W.B. Yeats, Wassily Kandinsky, Alexandre Scriabin, T.S. Eliot, William James, Piet Mondrian, Henry Miller, Paul Klee, George Lucas, Elvis Presley – even Albert Einstein is said to have had a copy of Blavatsky's *Secret Doctrine* by his bedside, and some have argued that his theory of relativity was inspired by it.

There are many more names, and the fact that Theosophy and the Theosophical Society helped inform much of modern art, music, and literature has, over the years, been acknowledged. It has even been said that abstract art, supposedly invented by Kandinsky, was a product of his deep interest in Blavatsky's ideas. But what is less known is the political and social influence Theosophy had. This is most clearly seen in India, where the Theosophical Society was instrumental in helping to bring native Indians to self-awareness, by introducing to them their great texts and scriptures, something they had lost touch with, because of the work of western missionaries. Theosophy also worked to dismantle the caste system and to abolish arranged child marriages and barbaric practices such as *suttee*. But in its broadest impact, the Theosophical Society was instrumental in helping India achieve independence itself.

Blavatsky moved to India from New York in 1879, and Theosophy became an instant success there, because it celebrated Indian culture, literature, and spirituality, at a time when Hindus were being force fed Christianity and western ideas. Blavatsky and her colleague Colonel Olcott became national heroes in India because they were two famous white westerners who brought Hinduism to Hindus and Buddhism to Buddhists, at a time when Hindus and Buddhists were pretty ignorant of their history and culture. Colonel Olcott himself became a national hero in Sri Lanka, for his efforts on behalf of Buddhist education, and, among other honours, his face adorns a commemorative stamp there. Mohandas Ghandi praised Theosophy for reintroducing him to the *Bhagavad Gita*, and he visited Blavatsky during her last days in London, and said her writings inspired him to return to his Hindu roots. Jawaharlal Nehru became a Theosophist and praised the Theosophical Society for inspiring him. He was initiated into the society by Annie Besant, the British socialist and feminist activist who converted to Theosophy and became the head of the Theosophical Society after Blavatsky's death. Besant too went to India, and there she became a tireless campaigner for Indian independence. She campaigned for Home Rule across the sub-continent, and was even arrested for her efforts. But through the work of the Theosophical Society, India had become conscious of its past, its accomplishments, its inspiring art and culture, and its deep spirituality, and could no longer remain under the British Raj. As we know, it achieved independence in 1947. Both Blavatsky and Besant were dead by then, but they no doubt heard about it on the astral plane.

So here again is a very concrete and historically significant way in which the vision of a progressive, open, and free society, initiated, as I point out, by the Invisible Rosicrucians a few centuries earlier – that is, by a secret society – helped to shape the political and spiritual map of the modern world. I hope this makes clear that not all secret societies want to take over the world, and that some have actually made it a better place to live in.

The War of the Owl and the Pelican

Timothy O'Neill

History is the record of warfare between secret societies.
> – Ishmael Reed, "Mumbo Jumbo"

One of the great problems with understanding the entire flow of Western Gnosticism, Illuminism and Esotericism as related but unique traditions is the overwhelming complexity of historical blending, intermixing, schisms, forced conversions and subtle takeovers between the three.

Understanding the social history, the genuine historical effects and the social psychology of these phenomena would seem to be hopelessly confused. We are at a point since the 1990's when the attempt to bring these beliefs to the larger world of Comparative Religion and History of Philosophy as academic systems began in earnest with the dedicated efforts of a small number of scholars, but where do we fit into that process as practitioners and workers in the real worlds of these beliefs? How do we come to an understanding of our own traditions from within?

There are approaches that achieve these goals by oversimplifying to a dangerous extreme. These are the approaches of the conspiracy theorists and religious zealots. There is another, more difficult and demanding approach that looks at basic patterns of thought and belief and asks the tough questions like "Who believed what and when did they believe it and why?" This is more like an approach through historical analysis of comparative religion and philosophy. Gnosticism, Illuminism and Esotericism are all forms of both religious and philosophical belief systems in their own right and of course they relate to the dominant forms of Religion and Philosophy during the course of History. This is what allows us to get any kind of handle on their complexity at all.

There are clearly repeating themes and motifs that tell us that a consistent belief system has survived through time, with modifications due to historical necessity, but essentially the same in core beliefs. It we trace certain beliefs back through time to a point in the early formation of Greek Philosophy, one of these currents jumps out as a key to understanding two underground streams running through Western history down even to this day.

A potent mixture of Pre-Socratic and Pythagorean philosophy with the insight-oriented approach of the Mystery Religions was the origin point for a particular approach that we can follow through the Ages with some clarity. The belief that Humanity could be made perfect through a combination of education, reason, exposure to the Wisdom of the Mysteries with a strong moral compass was created during the heyday of the Pythagorean Brotherhood; that mysterious and influential organization about which we still know so little. Enough pieces of Pre-Socratic, Pythagorean and Mystery Religion teachings and experience have come down to us to indicate that the idea of the perfectibility of Mankind was a belief that has had influence all the way down through the Ages.

The enemies of this way of thinking were clear from the earliest days: any sort of belief based on emotionalism or blind faith with devotion to meaningless ideals imposed by political structures from above on the basis of sheer tradition or power mongering were seen as the key forces holding Humanity back. These forces opposed the rational and logical progress of Humanity toward self-determination and ultimate perfection.

The idea of the perfectibility of Mankind was by no means a monolithic belief in itself. There were at least two major interpretations:

1. The collectivist, socio-political and radical rationalist viewpoint

2. The individualist, spiritualist and traditionalist viewpoint

The first of these gave rise to strongly secular and socially based groups like Freemasonry, the Royal Society, the Illuminati, Fabian Socialism, and Marxism. All of these groups shared a common interest in expanding the base of educated, free-thinking and rationalist people in the World organized in a way to end the tyranny of Monarchy, Religion and Capitalism. The second viewpoint gave rise to more mystically inclined groups like the Rosicrucians, the Gnostic Christianity of the Holy Grail and even the mystical and emotional fervor of pan-Germanic pagan National Socialism. Clearly, these interpretations are dialectically oppositional and gradually became deadly enemies of each other, yet they began in exactly the same context and with the same exact goal in the ultimate perfection of humanity. Understanding how they have interacted as dialectic can help us to clear up some of the most enigmatic and misunderstood historical phenomena, such as the bizarre alliance and then war between Russia and Germany during the Second World War.

Since both of these approaches to Perfectionism live in the most radical fringes of political, religious and social life, so they have both had recourse to exactly the same methods for inculcating new members into their odd and counter-intuitive ways of thought. They each borrowed heavily from Islamic gradualism, a technique perfected by radical groups like the Hashashin and Sufi groups like the House of Wisdom. They also both borrowed heavily from Kabbalah for their organizing and mystical doctrines. Both of these philosophies use a ten degree system of advancement and initiation which is used to gradually bring the new initiate to a fully illuminized understanding of the gnostic "truth." This is not surprising, since Islam and Mystical Judaism were "outsider" traditions themselves and had to learn to survive in often harsh and oppositional climates.

This deep underlying unity of purpose and shared source of technique helps us to explain the constantly evolving alliance and warfare between the collectivist and individualist perfectionisms. They come together and then battle constantly depending on exterior and interior circumstances. In our example above, both Marxist Russia and National Socialist Germany shared many common features and a common source in Illuminati-socialist thought, yet it became clear that Russia lived by the rationalism and cosmopolitanism of Marx while Germany lived by the Romanticist and Nationalist vision of Schiller and Nietzsche. The two could only live together for so long, since Germany longed to create its own Socialist Utopia wherein the whole world would become Socialist-German rather than Russian Marxist-Communist. The great irony here is that Marx was German, Hitler was Austrian-German, and the whole thing began in Germany with Adam Weishaupt, who was one of the great early free-thinkers and progenitors of Socialism. Rosicrucianism was also German in origin. So many deadly enemies came from exactly the same country and even from one part of that country... Bavaria! The historical synchronicities and coincidences abound here.

We seem to have wandered very far from our origins in Pre-Socratic Greek philosophy and the Mystery religions but I think we are already prepared to present a dialectical table of the two Perfectionist streams and what made up each:

The Two Streams

Collectivist versus Individualist
Rationalist versus Mystical
Cosmopolitan versus Nationalist
Liberalist versus Conservative
Marxist versus Socialist
Free-thought versus Traditionalism
Science and Empiricism versus Emotionalism and Romanticism
Mathematics versus Symbolism
Reason versus Faith
Left Brain versus Right Brain
Male Domination (Mars) versus Female Domination (Venus)
Illuminati versus Illuminist

Both share a Ten-Degree system of initiation, a rootedness in Kabbalah and a Gnostic Philosophy with an approach based in the Mystery religions.

What this essentially reveals is that we have a Left-brain versus Right-brain approach to the very same problem. This identifies clearly why there is such a high level of feelings around which approach is "right" since both claims to be the "truth" of perfectionism!

I think we can now descend to yet more of the concrete elements of history to try to reconcile some very odd things that were hitherto inexplicable. Author Terry Melanson has a reputation as a "nutter" because of his website: *www.conspiracyarchive.com* which contains some of the trappings of the usual conspiracy theorist rhetoric; yet his book *Perfectibilists: The 18th Century Bavarian Order of the Illuminati* does a creditable job of collecting together the best of European mainstream historical research on the Illuminati over the last two decades and presenting a balanced picture of an organization with clearly stated ideals shifting with the ebb and flow of historical exigency. The Illuminati clearly continued to exist after their suppression in Bavaria and the use of reading soci-

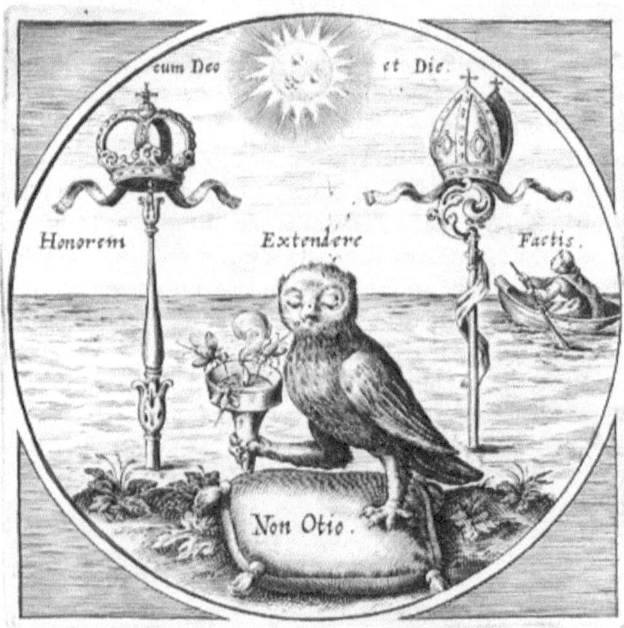

eties and social groups to further their goals set the ground work for their later influence on the French and Russian Revolutions. I highly recommend Melanson's work, because far from presenting idle speculation, he names the names of known Illuminati who continued their work far into the Jacobin era and beyond. This confirms that the Illuminati shared many of the ideals and goals of the Enlightenment philosophers as a whole and individuals, such as Jean Jacques Rousseau, while not identifiably members of the Illuminati, certainly did express ideas strikingly similar to their key thoughts and goals.

This is a good moment to state something obvious that is rarely made explicit. While there have been influential and powerful members on both sides of the Illuminati-Rosicrucian war, the truth is that it has largely been a war of ideas and concepts. The idea that either side has some sort of ultimate power or control over the destiny of Mankind is sheerest poppycock and a sure sign of someone trying to muddy the waters. Both of these groups have had tremendous influence upon the course of history but it is mostly through their ideas and only rarely through the intervention of powerful individuals who most often represent the "third enemy"... Old money, old politics and old religion; the Old World Order that has been the real controlling force since the days of Moses and who would seriously doubt something that obvious?! The Bankers, the old Church and the old Politics are clearly in control and the efforts of the Illuminati and Rose-Croix to remove them have been somewhat less than successful over the course of 2,500 years!

Just as Robert Anton Wilson expressed a grain of truth with his "Illuminati" and "Erisians" so a recent phenomenon on the Internet has raised some interesting questions about the whole Illuminati-Rosicrucian war. The whole idea of self-published

"Kindle" books has just come about to the wider attention of the publishing world as a whole and the jury is still out, yet there are now a whole series of Kindle books written by three authors who claim to be a 7th degree cell of the Bavarian Illuminati in Great Britain. Their claims are fascinating because they tend to lend support to the model we have examined here, yet there are peculiar elements to their books that make one wonder about their veracity. The authors go by the pseudonyms "Adam Weishaupt", "Michael Faust" and "Mike Hockney." Their books have some interesting elements like the claim that the Illuminati are the survival of the Pythagorean Brotherhood (something we claimed earlier!), that John Uri Lloyd's famous sci-fi story "Etidorhpa" was actually written by a renegade Illuminatus and that meritocracy is a much better political system than plutocracy... Well, who would argue with that one, except a plutocrat?! The jury is still out on all of these books (there are now close to fifty in print) but they do have obsessive elements that lend to the belief that they are the real article. There is a persistent, even ranting obsession with Abrahamic religion that echoes Weishaupt' and Marx' viewpoints. There is an underlying belief that Mankind can be made perfect and that is the key element here.

Looking at the social psychology of the Illuminati-Rosicrucian war, the key word is "outsider" since neither group has really held on to any substantial power for very long. There tends to be a level of paranoia and crankiness in these Kindle books which is fascinating. There is a sense of narcissistic woundedness and the innate superiority of the Illuminati viewpoint which reminds me of Laurence Sterne's famous novel *Tristram Shandy* and its references to Uncle Toby and his obsessive "hobby horse"... An apt image since that book is a key part of the Order of the Skull and Bones ritual and it is clear that the Order was originally based in... Germany! Whether or not the books are real in the sense of representing genuine information about the survival of the 18th Century Order, they do give one a sense of something odd and unsettling, even un-nerving, which leads me to a more positive hope that they are something real. Like the now infamous fraud of the Priory of Sion documents, we may never really know who really did what when, but it is enough to go on and that is all we can ask for.

There is one more aspect of our story that I need to address and that is the peculiar symbolism of the Owl and the Pelican. The Illuminati and their allied groups chose the Owl as their key symbol since it is the emblematic sign of Minerva, Greek goddess of Wisdom. The Rosicrucians chose the Pelican since it traditionally pierces its own breast to feed its young... A metaphor for the hard work of perfectionism and how the mystical tradition must feed its young from its own blood and sweat since the Universal Alchemy of perfection proceeds on the work of the few acting for the many.

The Great Rite, Hermeticism
and the Shamanic-Pagan Tradition
of the Sacred Forest of Nemi

Revealed by Dianus del Bosco Sacro, Grand Conservator of the Sacred Forest Tradition. As authorized by Diana del Bosco Sacro di Nemi e Benevento, 38th Arch Priestess of the Sacred Forest Tradition. Translated and Introduced by David Griffin, Guardian of the Mysteries of the Sacred Forest.

Translator's Introduction

Dr. Ronald Hutton's historical tome *Triumph of the Moon* examined the modern origins of Wicca in the British Isles, demolishing the belief of most Neo-Pagans in any substantial Pagan survival from antiquity. The unexpected reemergence from Italy last year of the previously occulted Shamanic-Pagan tradition of the Sacred Forest of Nemi, therefore understandably generated a certain amount of controversy in the Neo-Pagan community.

The present article, written by Dianus del Bosco Sacro, details for the first time how Hermetic alchemists, from a hidden Partenopean initiatic center, secretly preserved essential elements of ancient Paganism from the Inquisition during the dark age of Christianity. During the course of Dianus' exposition, we shall witness how the sexual mysteries of The Geat Rite comprise an unexpected and omnipresent Ariadne's thread, demonstrating the continuity of Pagan elements from the most ancient times until today.

Throughout history, we encounter the same, sublime sexual mysteries again and again, albeit clothed in ever changing symbols: from the rites of Dionysos, Diana, and Janus to sexual mysteries depicted in the frescoes the Villa of the Mysteries in Pompeii and their impact on Gerald Gardner and the Great Rite of Wicca – from the rich symbolism of Hermetic alchemy to the sexual mysteries encoded in Charles Godfrey Leland's "Aradia, the Gospel of the Witches."

According to the lore of the Shamanic-Pagan tradition of the Sacred Forest of Nemi, The Great Rite first arose with the ancient shamanism and sacerdotal lineages of the Great Mother Goddess in Continental Europe. While these primordial sexual mysteries were preserved along Matriarchal lines in Europe, they also spread to Sumeria, Babylon, and Egypt, where over time they evolved into the Royal Art of Alchemy.

Following the conquest of Egypt, the sexual mysteries of alchemy were carried to Rome by Priests of Isis. Arriving along the Partenopean coast in Naples, Cuma, and Pompei, this masculine Priesthood encountered the great Pagan Matriarchs. These Patriarchal/alchemical and Matriarchal/sacerdotal/shamanic lineages immediately recognized their sexual mysteries to be so similar, they could only have arisen from a common source.

Thus began the intimate collaboration between Pagan Matriarchs and Hermetic Masters, which would endure occulted for many Centuries. So it came to pass that when the Pagan Matriarchs faced eradication at the hands of the Roman Catholic Church, they found sanctuary in the Parthenopean initiatic school of Hermetic Masters.

Most historians and anthropologists, it turns out, have been looking in the wrong places for evidence of Pagan survival since antiquity. For the real evidence lies not amongst folk magic and cunning folk, but masked in the symbols of Hermetic alchemy.

THE GREAT RITE, HERMETICISM, AND THE SHAMANIC-PAGAN TRADITION OF THE SACRED FOREST OF NEMI

In the ancient world it was believed that the Isiac, luminous, sapiential and transforming presence was potentially present in every woman, but it had to be awakened through initiation into the Mysteries. Furthermore, as we shall see, initiation in the Mysteries put Neophytes in contact with the powers of fertility and regeneration by passing through death and the underworld.

Initiation to the Mysteries played a fundamental role in the existence of whoever approached it and the fact that, during all those centuries of initiations (from Eleusis, to the Mysteries of Dionysus to those of Isis, to the Mysteries of Cybele and Mithras), no one ever broke the oath of secrecy formulated during the act of acceptance of initiation testifies to how sacred initiation was considered.

Aristotle, Plato, Plutarch, Sophocles and Euripides, to cite the most well known, tell us that whoever received initiation was destined, after death, to a luminous fate, completely different from that of common mortals. Moreover, numerous testimonies of people initiated in the Mysteries report an "indescribable experience, miraculous in nature, which would transform in an irreversible way whoever took part in it".

To gain a better grasp of initiation in the ancient world, we shall avail ourselves of certain of the myths recounted to initiates that survived up until our days. The first archaeological evidence is dated to the VIII century BC, whereas the destruction of the sanctuary in Eleusis by the hands of the Goths can be dated back to the end of the IV century AC (The Eleusinian mysteries had already been banned a few years earlier by emperor Theodosius). The Eleusinian mysteries were dedicated to the two goddesses Demeter and Persephone.

The root of the name "Demeter" is best rendered as "Mother Barley", which significantly links her to the cycle of aspics and of nature. The etymology of Persephone, on the other hand, is related to *fero* and *foneuo*, or to *ferbo* and *foneuo*, the former meaning "she who brings destruction", the latter "she who nourishes everything and kills everything." Demeter, known as Ceres in Latin, was not only the goddess of the harvest and of the renewal of nature, as it is generally believed. The priests of Ceres in Rome were the *edili*, that is the constructors, who also administrated the law. Calvus says: "Demeter assigned to us the sacred laws, joined the bodies of lovers at night, the Great Rite, and founded the great cities".

The Rape of Persephone by Thomassin

The myth of Persephone and Zeus describes how she was kidnapped by Hades, who took her to the underworld on his winged chariot, while she was picking daffodils (or poppies) in a field, where, in some versions, she lost a sandal. Not seeing her daughter return, Demeter began to search for her in despair. Helios (or Hecates or Eubuleus) warns her of the kidnapping. Thus she wanders the earth with a torch, searching for her lost daughter.

Disguised as an elderly woman and wearing a veil, Demeter reaches Eleusis, in the kingdom of king Celeus, where she becomes the wet-nurse of Demophon, the king's son. Jambel, one of the servants, soothes her melancholy with obscene jokes and humorous wit (according to other versions the person making her laugh is paunchy Baubo and her husband, Dysalules. Baubo even shows her Iacchus, her baby son poking out his head from between her thighs as though born in that instant).

The queen offers her wine, but Demeter refuses and instead prepares a water, flour and barley bran beverage instead, the *kikeon*, which was later used by initiates of her Mysteries. Demeter is discovered while purifying Demophon with fire, to render him immortal, and thus reveals herself, imposing the construction of a temple in her honor.

Imprisoned in her sorrow, Demeter stops the earth from bearing fruit, until Hermes, sent by Zeus, convinces Hades to set Persephone free to return to her mother. But Ascalaphus, gardener of the underworld, convinces Persephone to eat seven pomegranate grains, so that the girl will have to come back to Hades during winter months.

According to other versions it is Triptolemus, the "triple warrior" brother of Eubuleus (both sons of Dysaules and Baubo), who brings Persephone back to earth. This, it is said, is the reason why Demeter establishes the Mysteries and reveals to men how to grow grains.

Triptolemus, in the underworld, is identified as Dionysus and there is talk of a subterranean wedding between Dionysus and Persephone, the Great Rite, and the sacred child Brimus, born from this union, is also identified with Dionysus. It is also said, in a fragment by Heraclitus: "In actuality, Dionysus and Hades are the same god."

The Mysteries of Demeter and Persephone were celebrated at two different times of the year: The "Lesser Mysteries" were celebrated during the month of *Anthesterion* (at the time of the Vernal equinox). During the Lesser Mysteries initiates were prepared for coming revelation and learned certain particulars of the myth of Demeter and Persephone, reaching the status of *mystai*. In the Lesser Mysteries, following the sacrifice of a sow, initiates were subjected to a test of the four elements.

The "Greater Mysteries" took place in the month of *Boedromion* (at the time of the Autumnal Equinox). The Greater Mysteries and were reserved for those who were destined to have the transforming vision, called the *epoptai*. The initiation took place in a subterranean chamber of the temple called *Telestrion*; the initiates were called *mystagogoi*. Immediately prior to entering the Telestrion, initiates were given a ritual beverage to drink called *kikeon*. It is believed that the beverage was a powerful hallucinogen due to the presence of horned rye, a fungus commonly infesting barley aspics.

Porphyry reports that the Eleusian mysteries were closed with pronunciation of the phrase *Konx Om Pax*. The Greater Mysteries proceeded in this manner: the *ghenos Eumolpidi* would choose the best priest, the Hierophant, who would supervise the "vision", a representation of Persephone's kidnapping by Hades, of their wedding, and of the announcement of the birth of Iacchus-Dionysus.

The names of the officiating priests could not be pronounced. They would be carved on bronze or lead tablets, then entrusted to the depths of the sea. The torch carriers also belonged to the same family. Later on, the novices would dive to purify themselves, reprising Eumolpus' initiatic dive, Eumolpus being the initiator of the cult, thrown into the sea by his mother.

The following day, a procession would be held, in which the entire populace would participate. Novices and initiates would emerge from the *Telestrion*, bearing the sacred objects of the cult. These ritual objects were:

—∞— Demeter's torch

—∞— An aspic of barley

—∞— A mysterious box that Persephone frequently holds in her hands (we will return to this in our discussion of the myth of Eros and Psyche)

—∞— A golden branch to placate Cerberus

—∞— A pomegranate

—∞— A piglet

The *Tesmophora* in honor of Demeter (*Thesmom*: ancient laws. Initiatrix of laws through agriculture which had brought civilized life) instead were festivities celebrated in autumn in which only women married with Athenians could participate. It was forbidden for men to enter while a secret ritual was in progress. We find the same festivities and mysteries of feminine identity in the feast of the *Bona Dea* (good goddess) in Rome.

The Eleusian Mysteries were powerful rites of transformation involving multiple aspects: physical, psychological, and spiritual. They were first and foremost Rites of Passage, from adolescence (Persephone) to maturity (Demeter), through which women grew in consciousness of their power to create life and inspire desire in the male, through The Great Rite and the union of matrimony.

This rite of passage, however, did not have a merely individual character: the whole of Nature followed the destiny of Kore (Persephone). Kidnapped by Hades into the underworld, nature would retreat underground during Autumn and Winter.

The birth of Iacchus-Dionysus (still in the representation of the Mysteries of the Great Rite) in the secrecy of the Telestrion did not merely represent a transition from maidenhood to womanhood. All of the feminine forces of nature were involved in the rite, all of the forces of birth and regeneration, so that a woman would recognize in herself the same spark which, every year, would reignite in the world at Winter Solstice when the days began to lengthen the spark pushing lymph to rise in the trunks of trees, flowers to bloom, animals to desire each other, to mate and procreate, the crops to give fruits, the climate to become warmer and the hours of light to exceed the hours of darkness.

The cult of Demeter, however, referred not merely to the cyclical renewal of nature. A fundamental point of this transformation, of this overturning, of this awareness of the immense feminine power, was the experience of death, the descent into the Underworld and the contact with the divine spirit of death, which would culminate in the *Epopteia*, the transforming vision.

"Blessed is he who has seen!", says the Homeric hymn and Plutarch, in his treatise on the soul, says that death and its horrors turn into bliss of the soul and that the initiated, who passed through the vision, does not doubt their own destiny of salvation whereas the others, the non-initiated, are damned.

Ceres/Demeter, keeping an eye on the Mysteries.

Euripides has Hercules himself declare, after he defeated Cerberus and came back safe and sound from the underworld, "I was capable of this much because I have seen the sacred actions of Eleusis".

So what was this mysterious vision initiates were destined to behold in the secrecy of the *Telestrion*? We know from Clemente Alessandrino that initiates were required to pronounce this phrase: "I fasted, I drank the potion, I took... from the crate, then after manipulating I put... back in the basket, and then in the crate".

Then followed the vision, the *epopteia*, at the end of which the Hierophant, the unknown person belonging to the ghenos of Eumolpides who officiated the ritual, in silence showed the initiate an aspic of barley. Hence the birth of Iacchus-Dionysus-Brimus, a divine child born from the union of Persephone with Dionysus (or with Triptolemus), and here we find again the adumbration of the Great Rite, or ritual of Demeter with Zeus or Triptolemus, announced with the words: "The queen gave birth to Brimus, Brimus the sacred child".

But what did the crate contain? Walter Otto observes that structure of the *Telestrion*, full of pillars, and the Eleusian accounting books exclude any form of theatrics that was not of extreme simplicity, leaving the whole thing to the two officers only and not in the symbolical actions happening outside, and the hypotheses that the initiated witnessed a true miracle: an epiphany of Persephone (Apollodorus reports that, in the instant when Kore was evoked, the hierophant would hit a bronze gong, while we use the drum that came from ancient shamanic traditions, called *echeion*, which would open up a passage to the kingdom of the dead (the extra-sensorial realm), to the sudden ripening of an aspic before the amazed eyes of the attendants. As we will see shortly discussing the Villa of Mysteries in Pompeii, we can hypothesise that the crate to which Clemente Alessandrino referred, contained a wooden phallus and that this object, absorbing energy from the initiate, would float in the air, against every law of gravity, prefiguring the awakening of the forces of nature and of the ghenos. Whether these "miracles" were the result of tricks or of actual divine intervention, it is not for us to know.

Let us expand on certain aspects of the mythic ritual we know accompanied the Mysteries: Demeter's laughter: old Baubo (or Jembe the servant) made Demeter laugh to chase away her melancholy. In this we recognize the manner in which the Great Rite has always been celebrated in our tradition; chasing away tears, cheerful, full of laughter, games and satisfaction of the soul.

Let us attempt to unveil certain additional points, albeit respecting oath bound material, as herein lies concealed an internal mystery of The Great Rite. This laughter, like many forms of humor, is linked to *strabismus*, that is to seeing two things at once that are incompatible to one another: From the womb of the paunchy old woman, a boy pops out, as though she had just given birth to him, and Baubo/Jembe accompanies the act of uncovering her thighs with jokes and obscene insults which no one would have expected from her.

The sterile womb of the old woman is the sterile womb of the earth itself. Simultaneously, it is that part of the soul that never lived and that gave fruit. Furthermore, this refers to a technique and a particular moment of the Great Rite itself, which is unveiled during initiation. It is not a coincidence that a sense of humor in Latin and Italian is called "spirit," and that tricksters and sorcerers, to make their apprentices progress, do not spare them memorable pranks and jokes.

The characteristic strabismus of this type of *mot d'ésprit* is a preparation for the journey to the underworld, for a type of perception that goes beyond the rigid separation between the ego and the World, between here and there, between sleep and wakefulness, between life and afterlife, mask and face. And it also indicates a way of pointing the eyes (cross-eyedness) that evokes an ocular revulsion capable to make one perceive the underworld while still living, capable to bring, in this manner, sexual intercourse to a subtle level.

One should not underestimate the importance of this aspect. Aristophanes said: "Athenian women, while going to celebrate the Mysteries on chariots, would exchange insults and laugh. These were called "the chariot insults". They would insult one other because it was believed that, when Demeter first came to Eleusis looking for Kore, overwhelmed by despair, Jambe, the servant of Celeus and Metanira, by covering her with insults, made her smile."

Let us also recall that in ancient Rome the feasts in honor of Cybele, the Great Mother, were celebrated between March 15th and March 27th and that one of the days, March 25th, was dedicated to a feast called Hilaria, during which, for an entire day, the follower of goddess Cybele would exchange jokes and obscene jests and they would laugh relentlessly to celebrate the resurrection of Attis.

The Pomegranate. Persephone is forced to go back to the underworld because she indulged the temptation to eat seven grains of pomegranate. As often happens, the symbol of these seven grains has several meanings, sometimes even opposite and complementary of each other: representing the seven dismembered parts of the body of Dionysus (as well as the four phases of the lunar cycle, each seven days long, during which the Great Rite takes place in our tradition).

These grains of pomegranate remind us on the one hand that what leads us to death is the fragmentation of emotions and the dispersion of perception that the rational mind causes when it is the only master of our life. The power of identifications and projections. Dionysus, when dismembered by Titans, is looking at himself in a mirror, which shatters into pieces. In this as well lies a particular, practical symbolism of our tradition of the Great Rite.

On the other hand, after the passage into the Hades, "eating the grains" to our tradition means reuniting what has been dispersed, the two into one, reunifying the dismembered body of Dionysus and bringing him back to life. All this follows a perfect rule in the Great Rite which leads to an operation where the seven parts of the inner human being are reunited by the force of the ritual and by its progress, then leading to a reblossoming – a return into life. This, of course, only scratches the surface of this symbolism, whereas the initiate of The Great Rite easily recognises practices, rituals, techniques of our tradition that have been accurately passed on to us from the distant past, although filtered through divergent sets of symbols.

The subterranean wedding of Persephone with Dionysus and the wedding with Hades. What do these weddings mean, from a spiritual point of view?

In the sacred wedding, the feminine power was viewed by the man as a sapiential, transforming power of salvation, guiding him in his inner quest (Sophia, Virgin Mary, Isis, Athena, Tara, the alchemical Queen). The woman, instead, experienced the masculine power as that active force leading to the accomplishment of elevated objectives, a force made fertile and conscious by the encounter with the feminine energies, of which, in turn, it would exalt the value and function.

The wedding with Dionysus and the rituals of death and resurrection of the initiated in the Mysteries enhanced the feminine principle to a source of light and redemption. Dionysus was the god who unravelled within himself all the potential of the masculine, all the nuances of virility, from the infernal to the uranian [ie celestial] ones, in a continuous compenetration between the sensorial aspects and the extra-sensorial ones, between the physical beauty and the psychic one, between art and ideas. Moreover, Dionysus was the groom destined to girls who had died prematurely and the wedding with the god implied the union with the essence of that vital spark that animates all living beings, that celestial fire that makes wine boil in barrels and gives blood its vital energy.

It is not possible to speak more clearly of this point, for herein lies the true heart of the Great Rite, which has always remained secret, revealed only to initiates, and to those who have profoundly understood the transforming capability of the Mysteries of sacred love. Thus I must leave this mystery veiled, and continue instead to expound upon the additional symbolism.

It was the role of Dionysus, then, to harmonize sensuality and the erotic-sexual impulses with the desire of eternal union with the beloved. This is a key point which must be kept in mind, and which explains that the sacred wedding does not require an orgy or launching ourselves into frenetic sexual intercourse. Whoever thought this to be the case has only partially understood, as in the Great Rite there is not the licentiousness one might imagine.

We must be forever mindful as the techniques of The Great Rite, while they can bring one to a superior state, may as well lead one to an inferior subtle state... an infernal state. Let us recall the words Heraclitus, which provide us with the key to correct understanding: Indeed "Dionysus and Hades are the same God," meaning that his Mysteries can either lead one higher or lead one lower.

Bachofen in his *Matriarchate* and Kerenyi in his *Dionysus* wrote that the "god of women" incarnates two aspects of Eros that the feminine psychic evolution must integrate with one another: an inferior one, that of "ethereal tellurism", the impure Eros of the muddy depths, the god linked to the death of young energies, to the terrestrial Aphrodite and the indiscriminate eroticism, and the uranian Eros, Psyche's lover, linked to the celestial Aphrodite, to the holy matrimony and to the eternal union with the loved being.

"A superior spiritual existence must necessarily", says Bachofen in the *Matriarchate*, "merge in harmony with physical existence." I repeat that in our tradition this refers to the presence of two types of Mysteries suited for different people, being well aware that not all people are suited for a certain type of Mysteries, as souls are different and distinct in their force and power.

The cult of the god was then perfectly compatible with the condition of married woman and it represented the attempt at subjugating the raging, incontrollable powers of the Eros and of life, after having evoked them by means of the ordering principles of rhythm and dance and other things that have to be left here unsaid, to preserve the sanctity of oath-bound initiatic mysteries.

Let us therefore move forward to examine certain images coming from the frescoes of the Villa of the Mysteries in Pompeii, a place of feminine initiation into the Mysteries of Dionysus. These images will help us elaborate on what we thus far been revealed. Let us recall that, in Dionysian sacrifices, part of the sacrificed animal was preserved after dismemberment to be used for its future reintegration and rebirth.

Some, in accordance with the myth of Dionysus Zagreus' resurrection, believe that [this part] was the heart, others assert that it was the phallus. It is possible that the two organs incarnated the same principles in different ways. To the Greeks, in fact, the heart was the first organ forming in a human body, the site of vital fire and intelligence, whereas the phallus was the perceivable sign of the powers of fertility, dominated by both uranian and subterranean energies, by the celestial fire of Eros as well as by the force of desire, coming from the reign of Hephaestus, situated underneath volcanoes.

And here is where we find again, and point out, another peculiar symbolism that is unveiled in the tradition of the Great Rite and a specific type of union. In actuality, there was also a bit of a pun between the mystical object taken in the procession during Dionysian feasts, kept in a sieve for grains, and the words *kradìa*, "heart" and *krade*, "fig tree." For this reason, the fig tree and its fruits were sacred to the god, and during these same processions phalli were made of fig wood and adorned with garlands of flowers.

As an aside, it is interesting to note in this context that in the Gospels Jesus curses the Fig tree, hence cursing the Mysteries of Dionysus, prefiguring what in the later centuries will happen in terms of persecution by Christianity, first of the ancient Mysteries, then of so-called "witchcraft" later.

In the Dionysian Mysteries, initiates took part in a nocturnal ceremony (known from Demosthenes' invective against Aeschines) during which they had to wear deer skins and predispose a wine crater from which they would draw. Next they were smeared with a mixture of clay and hay, before a priestess would emerge wearing the mask of a Gorgon. Among the attendants' screams were pronounced these words: "I escaped evil. I found the best".

It is also known that feminine initiation would climax with the contemplation of the content of a liknon which held a phallus. The object lying in the liknon was treated by the women, says Kerenyi, like a baby that had just awakened and probably the year of Dionysus started with a ritual serving to awaken the phallus in the liknon. In the Sacred Forest tradition, the meaning and the practices connected with this aspect of the Dionysian Mysteries are also explained at length.

The day following the nocturnal ceremony mentioned earlier, the group of the initiates walked the streets carrying the kiste and the liknon, containing the phallus covered with pastries and fruits. Some brandished live snakes (note the symbolism of the snake... and what that actually meant and means) and people were crowned with fennel and white poplar.

In another festivity sacred to Dionysus, the festival of Phallophories, huge phalli were carried and exhibited in public. According to Herodotus, the place of origin of the Phallophories was Egypt, the land from whence derived the Alchemy that spread afterwards. In the Egyptian processions that Herodotus reports, women carried around statues with enormous phalli which, thanks to specific mechanisms, could move. All of this is significant towards gaining an understanding of how the Dionysian Mysteries would later be preserved and transmitted in alchemical language.

References to the phallus are to be found, in any case, throughout the Dionysian sphere. Erect phalli made of stone were frequently present on sepulchres as symbols of the primary and subterranean generating forces of the progeny's ghenos, which the initiated was called to recognize and confront within himself in order to have access to the Afterlife.

The generating power, the force of instinct and desire represented by wooden phalli being carried in procession, is the archetype of the virility distributed among men. This gift from Dionysus also manifests itself through the solar and celestial current of life revived each year at the Winter Solstice, when days begin to grow longer again, determining the awakening of Nature. First in occult fashion, then manifestly, this same Vernal current causes lymph rise up in the trunks and branches of trees and ignites the spark of Eros.

This impersonal, universal and immortal current, which the Greeks called *Zoì*, is opposed by the individual currents of women and men, confined to and aimed at self preservation and reproduction, animated by a vital force destined to extinguish in its uniqueness, which the Greeks knew as *Bios*. So the *Zoì* was the divine and immortal nature of man, whereas the *Bios* was the totality of his temporal nature, destined sooner or later to the dwellings of Hades.

In Dionysian initiation and feasts celebrating the awakening of the vital and instinctual principle, the role of women was fundamental. It was, in fact, up to the feminine pole of existence to awaken the *Zoì* from its winter hibernation, reignite the sleeping fire, set back in motion the powerful forces of desire and vital growth, paralyzed by frost and death. In this symbolism is clearly revealed to the eyes of the initiate, the role of the Priestess and of woman in the Great Rite as transmitted in our tradition.

To the wild and orgiastic dances of inebriated Maenads who, half naked, would climb up secluded mountains to celebrate the sacrifice and the feeding on raw meat (symbolism we shall find again in alchemy, which deserves careful contemplation) and brandishing live snakes, we can associate some of the frescoes adorning walls of the Villa of Mysteries in Pompeii. These wall paintings represent the various phases of the initiation of a matron, a new bride, to the Mysteries of Dionysus.

In the center of the front wall, Ariadne holds in her arms a semi-naked Dionysus crowned with ivy, laying languidly on her lap. I remind the reader that Dionysus (by assonance: Dio-nisos "the crippled god") is only wearing one sandal, while the other one lays beside the chair where Ariadne is sitting. I focus briefly on this solely because monosanaldalism is signalled also in chapt. 2 part 3 of the *Nocturnal History* of Carlo Ginsburg. Ginsburg affirms that the monosandalism of Dionysus, Jason, Persephone, Hermes, Perseus and the lameness of other gods, heroes and characters of myths, fairy tales and legends (a long procession of figures including, among others, Oedipus and Cinderella) represents the occurrence of a passage through the world of the dead and an acquired relation to the infernal world.

In particular, the "hopping" steps of certain ancient dances related to funeral cults and transposed also in some witches' dances are noteworthy, and certain movements that must be made in the tradition of The Great Rite (which include the crane dance) (ref. E. De Martino, *Morte e Pianto Rituele*, Chapt.s 5 and 7).

Limping, as well as the use of a cane to help it, has an ambiguous symbolical meaning: it could be the visible sign of a spiritual handicap as well as indicate the condition of the initiate, who has recognized his own dependence on cosmic laws. Think of Jacob, limping after his victorious struggle with the angel, of Volcano, Varuna, Odin and of blacksmiths in general who, knowing the secret of forging metals (here again, we come across Alchemy as a filter Mysteries later passed through), extracted from the depths of the Earth, are often represented as limping. Sometimes, instead, limping is a diabolical character, attributed to the devil.

But let us resume the examination of wall paintings in the Villa of the Mysteries. Beside the two central figures [Bacchus and Ariadne] a woman kneels with an arm outstretched towards a liknon and, without touching it, somehow magically causes the phallus to float up from the liknon, which is covered by a drape. With the other arm she holds a torch. Next to the kneeling woman, a winged feminine figure is represented in the act of scourging. [Translator's note: An element later reappearing in Gardnerian Wicca].

The victim of the whip is a prone woman, with an afflicted expression, apparently waiting for the next lash, leaning her head on the lap of another sitting woman. Next to them, there is a naked Maenad, covered only by a corner of a cloak taking the form of a crescent, and another dressed Maenad who holds a Thyrsus dancing as well, while moving towards the sitting woman.

The four feminine figures are arranged to form a circle. The room is dominated by the image of a matron who, comfortably sitting on a high back chair, observes the entire sequence of the initiation.

On the other side of the entrance two women are depicted. One of the two, the sitting one, is a young maid observing the scene of the initiation. The other one, in a standing position, instead gazes upon a small object held by a winged Eros.

The figures must be considered as a group: the kneeling woman is a carrier of light. The torch is also an extremely important symbol of Diana, the mistress of Witches known as Diana Lucina, while in Alchemy the torch indicates the lighting of the secret fire leading to the coction. In all of these diverse instances, we always see the the same Mysteries represented the common symbolism of the torch, a symbol of the feminine power to evoke the generating forces of Nature, to ignite the fire of The Great Rite, to light the Alchemical fire, to awaken and excite the masculine instincts and sexuality.

Nemesis, the winged figure brandishing the scourge, is the celestial equivalent of the woman causing the phallus to rise above the liknon. The lash of the Goddess, aimed at the kneeling woman who represents Winter, has the effect of causing the sun's cycle to turn at the winter solstice: days start to lengthen again after the occultation of light.

Naturally, all of this adumbrates operative meanings and ritualistic secrets of The Great Rite, which we cannot unveil directly but only indicate as masked in the symbolism. The use of the whip has been known forever in certain contexts, and in Alchemy it also represents the discipline used to conduct the work. Let us recall that the whip has the effect of increasing the blood rush and the release of certain hormones into the circulation that produces changes in consciousness. Alchemy is in fact very precise in this, turning not only to the spirit but to the body as well, in its transformations and operations, based on the main theory of this same science that affirms that ALL IS ONE and every [alchemical] work always stems from that.

I am aware that I have not been exceedingly clear, as I may not unveil in a clearer fashion the Mysteries which have been such for millennia. Let us continue our analyses of the paintings in the Villa of Mysteries. Nemesis, the winged angel of sufferance and mourning, is then the other face [of] fertility, she who has the power of making the sun's cycle turn, thereby allowing the rebirth of Dionysus dismembered by Titans.

The four women disposed in a circle are clearly the four seasons in which the year is subdivided: the first, prone one, taking the "Solsticial" lashing is Winter, the naked Maenad dancing, carrying the crescent is Spring, the dressed one is Summer, and the one sitting looking at Nemesis and seems to want to console Winter is Autumn. Twin sister of Nemesis was Aidos, Modesty, she who preserves the secrets of night, a goddess probably linked to the summer solstice and to sunset, and to the beauties of nature in the underground.

Goddess Nemesis is sometimes identified with the Fortune, Vortumna, "she who makes the year turn", more often known with the name of Tyche, sister of Nemesis. Speaking of the symbolical meaning of the lashing we should mention the habit of whipping the crops and the trees in orchards to make the fruitful and the Roman festivity of Lupercalia, during which young luperci ran on the streets of Rome whipping the women they encountered with goatskin straps with the purpose of rendering them fertile within the year.

Aidos is almost certainly depicted as well in the wall painting in the Villa of Mysteries: she is a woman who covers her head with a purple drape and holds her hand out, as though wanting to push something away. In our tradition as well, and in the Rite here represented, the drape is present and it has a specific ritualistic and operational meaning in the mysteries of the Great Rite. The drape seems to be the same that later will cover the phallus, in one of the following scenes. Covering one's head, looking inside oneself, it then corresponds to having concealed and covered the generating principle, to the external. In the tradition of the Great Rite that indicates a phase of the ritual itself and the inner accomplishment through some specific external operations [performed] by the couple. I can only give this suggestion, to be clearer without revealing anything that must be left unsaid: the entire sequence recalls certain aspects of Christian Easter in the period preceding the Resurrection.

The analogy is strengthened by the fact that some of the women officiating the ritual carry olive branches. Moreover, a woman standing beside the one who makes the phallus fluctuate in the air holds a crate full of fresh reaped barley aspics. In Palazzo Marino, in Rome, an altar from the II century AC is preserved, and it holds the image of the Dioscures, of Zeus and two figures identifiable as Helen (holding a torch) and Leda with the swan, who covers her head with the cloak similarly to the women in the Villa of Mysteries we just described. And in analogous fashion to our Rite that is presented here. The circumstance gains significance from the point of view of our interpretation if we think that, in the Attican version of the myth of the birth of Dioscures and of Helen, she who mates with Zeus in the form of a swan generating the egg is Nemesis [and] Leda is only the egg's keeper. Another similar bas-relief is preserved, still in Rome, in the Basilica of the Four Saints. The two young women beside the entrance show us two complementary aspects of the ritual: one observes the various scenes. If we move our eyes to the opposite wall, another series of wall paintings brings us deeper into the hidden meaning of the Mysteries of Dionysus.

Beside goddess Aidos, Modesty, with her veiled face, a Satyr plays the lyre and in the background we see two Paniscs, one of which has a black goatskin with her while the other nurses a nanny goat. A third goat is painted up front. In the scene described above, the Satyr plays the Apollonian lyre, which makes the soul pass from the world of "here and now" to the obscure world of the depths of psyche. Here is also adumbrated the use of the sound as it is both in the Great Rite and later in Alchemy. The world to which we have access is revealed, sprung open by the power of sacred music: the first Panisc, the one nursing the nanny goat, incarnates the sacred spring of animal energies, of vitality, of Bios, of primary impulses and of initiation, while the other one stares at herself in the mirror.

The Panisc, who plays the seven pipe pan flute, composes the melody that constitutes the thin essence of every living being and the awakening of inner centers and the seven main gods inside every human being, linked to the seven skies. Naturally there exists also a Mystery of the Sacred Rite related to these sounds and we could comprehend it, at least a bit, if we replace the seven pipe pan flute with the human body and the sacred touches that are performed on it to wake the music of spheres and the powers contained in it.

This means that she recognizes inside herself various figures of the ritual, indicating the profound Mysteries that are needed to know ourselves.

Life is seen as a dance that follows the sound of that invisible instrument. The Panisc holding it has the power to determine at any moment the death of the Bios that has been assigned to her, simply by stopping her playing. Here, another profound Mystery is hidden. Through the Dionysian exhilaration and possession, initiation was meant to reveal to everyone this sacred background of the "animal side" of human beings. Satyrs, Eroses, Paniscs, Nymphs and other figures of the Dionysian procession are nothing but the objectification of the prime, inaccessible sources of human instincts, divine and sacred springs of water from which the initiated, descended within themselves, had to be able to draw to regenerate and transform themselves. The sublime side of man, according to the Greeks, had then to be searched for right in the apparently lowest point of being, where the instincts originate. He who has eyes to see should open them wide and observe!

To the left of Aidos, beside Dionysus and Ariadne, [there is] the most famous wall painting in the Villa of Mysteries: a sitting Satyr shows an empty recipient to a young man staring at his reflection in the shiny interior of the cup, but a second young man, standing behind the first one, holds up a Satyr mask oriented in such a way that the first young man sees in the cup the reflection of the mask instead of his own face.

The whole thing is meant to show that, behind what seems to come from the conscious will, inexpressibilities are concealed, the incommensurability and the terrorizing luminosity of the sacred and divine. Every man carries within himself the infernal world of the demons and the dead as well as the celestial one of the gods. That is why the young initiated, instead of seeing his own face reflected in the cup, he stares at the face of an old bearded Satyr, a mask, coming from the most abyssal depths of his unconsciousness. But this mask also indicates the source of power in action in the Rite and in the Great Rite.

He then gains consciousness of the true origins of what he believed was his own Ego, of the timeless being living within him, and he is initiated to the world of adult men, those who know how, in the monotonous flow of profane time, thousands of invisible thresholds leading to the eternal time of gods are concealed. In summary, he becomes a man in the truest and most subtle sense of the term.

It is not unrelated to this symbolism, the fact that the young man is staring at his reflection in an empty cup, destined to contain wine. Generating the overlap between Bacchus-Dionysus and the god of wine are the mere modalities of preparation of the beverage, from the archaic dance of grape crushers, masked as Satyrs and Sileni, gods of instincts transforming vital energy contained in blood, to the processes of fermentation and ripening of wine, which "feels" the spring and boils in the jars and barrels, perfecting itself through the work of the celestial fire animating it. References to alchemy and to the magical function of wine [are found] in the tradition of Witchcraft as inebriating beverage and its sacred function in the Great Rite. Wine, the blood of the earth, induces to procreation, to possession, to brotherhood and conviviality, the sensuality and the loss of inhibitions. Drinking wine facilitate the insurgence of mania in the possessed by Dionysus and it would set in motion, unleash an aspect of instinctiveness otherwise blocked by many ways of conditioning because perceived as dangerous.

This experience leads the initiate to the wonder of he who finds himself inhabited by invisible forces of unknown origin. "Once his individuality is broken", says Colli in his "Greca", he is "possessed by Dionysus and sees what the non-initiated cannot see". In this hidden affinity between subterranean religions of psyche and the celestial ones lies the sense of all feminine initiations and the role of Dionysus as "Soter", that is saviour, and god of women.

The two Dionysian initiations (the lesser and the greater Mysteries) were awaiting the dead in the Afterlife and, in particular, it was believed that people who died at a young age were called to a Dionysian wedding and that Eros-Dionysus-Hades kidnapped women from life to unite with them in subterranean matrimonies. While the sound of Dionysian flutes accompanied the funeral ceremonies, the young maids who had died were supposed to turn into Ariadne; and the young men into Dionysus himself. Hence, the Great Rite could start and the Sacred Wedding and the Hierogamy could be revealed to their eyes like the Mystery of Mysteries. Kerenyi believes that women, lured out of their Bios, out of their individual existence, had to reunite in the Afterlife with the *Zoì*, the cosmic current of life. In Alchemy, this is referred to as the Work of the White or contact with Goddess Diana.

We have talked, in fact, about the effects of what happened in the Greater Mysteries and we ignored the Lesser Mysteries, mentioning only that probably the initiated had to take four tests related to the four elements. A glimmer of light is shed on this by the beautiful story of Eros and Psyche, contained in the *Golden Ass* by Apuleius. The book tells the story of the narrator's transformation into an Ass and his adventures, before returning to human form thanks to the intervention of goddess Isis. The story of Eros and Psyche, in fact, adumbrates an initiation to the lesser Mysteries the way they are passed on in our tradition.

The Myth

Venus, jealous of the beauty of mortal Psyche, sends her son Eros on a mission to make the girl fall in love with a man of humble origin. Meanwhile, Psyche's father, worried about his daughter not finding a husband despite her beauty, interrogates the Oracle of Apollo, who predicts that the girl will have to marry a being that is not human in origin, "a cruel and ferocious monster with the face of a snake", after being exposed on top of a mountain. Eros sees her and falls in love with her while Psyche is sleeping.

When Psyche wakes up, she finds herself in a fairy tale palace and walks around the rooms conversing with an incorporeal voice. Eros accepts to marry her on the condition that she must never look at his face and that they would get together only at night. The wedding is celebrated, but Psyche's envious sister instills in her the suspicion that Eros is a horrendous monster.

Psyche, who meanwhile has become pregnant, then observes the beautiful face of Eros in the light of a candle. Getting emotional, she spills a drop of melted wax on Eros, who wakes up. Eros reprimands Psyche for betraying their pact and then vanishes. Crazily in love, Psyche walks the earth in search for him (while she was staring at him, she had also wounded herself with the point of an arrow from the god's quiver...). After these facts, the envious sisters will die, killed by their own yearnings.

Meanwhile, thanks to her servant habit, Venus finds Psyche and abuses her, then putting her in front of a mound of poppy seeds, chickpeas, lentils and broad beans, and asks her to separate them. Psyche passes this first test thanks to the sympathetic help of ants. [Earth, analytical faculties, knowing how to assign each thing its own value, choose and discern]. The second test consists of going to a herd of sheep with wool of the purest gold, bringing back to Venus a substantial amount of that wool. Before it's too late, a marsh reed explains to Psyche that, while the sun is high in the sky, those sheep will ram and bite ferociously, instilling a deadly venom into whoever goes near them. It is necessary, the reed continues, to wait for the sun to pass noon, and then the sheep will become docile and the wool could be gathered without danger. Psyche follows the reed's advice and gathers the wool locks that got stuck in the woods vegetation. [Water, flexibility, knowing how to choose the suitable moment, after a path of maturation, that is after noon, letting things "be done" by themselves – the wool getting stuck in the branches.]

In the third test, Venus leads Psyche to the top of a mountain, shows her an impetuous river flowing in an inaccessible valley guarded by ferocious dragons and gives her a cruet: the girl will have to gather the river's water, the river being a tributary of the Styx, the swamp of Hell. Even the water of that river itself screams and opposes to whoever tries to gather it. Psyche is helped by an eagle [wind, vision ability, culture [of] development of superior faculties, knowing how to draw our own "inner water" overcoming the abyss separating us from that spring].

Finally, the last test: Venus gives Psyche a can, a pisside, and asks her to take it into the Afterlife, to Proserpina/Persephone, to get from her a bit of her eternal beauty. She warns her not to open the can and to bring it back to her. Overwhelmed by the impossibility of that task and not knowing how to get into Hades, Psyche is about to jump off a high tower to kill herself, when the tower she climbed on itself decides to help her. The tower shows her the route to get into hell and gives her some good advice: Psyche will have to bring with her two coins and two buns kneaded with honey. On her path, she will encounter a crippled donkey farmer with a crippled donkey, and the farmer will ask her to help him pick up the wood he had dropped. Psyche will have to keep going without listening to him. Then she will have to be ferried across the subterranean lake leading into the kingdom of Hades, by paying Charon with a coin, which he will have to pick from Psyche's mouth. She will have to pay no attention to a dead old man who will appear floating on the lake's surface asking her to be ferried across, and no attention to the weavers who will ask for her help.

Divine law forbids Psyche from touching their work and interfere [says the tower: "down there mercy is forbidden by the laws: all of these are tricks from Venus"]. She will satisfy the ferocious dog Cerberus, who guards hell, with one of the buns. Once she gets to hell, Persephone will offer her a lavish banquet, but Psyche will have to ask for a piece of dried up bread and eat only that. After picking up her can with its precious content, she will be able to go back, giving the other bun to Cerberus and the other coin to Charon. "But most of all", the Tower warns, "do not ever open that can!" But Psyche, who wants to win Eros back and be even more beautiful, opens the can and an infernal sleep assails her. Eros will wake her up to lead her into the sky with him. [fire: knowing to recognize the function of each thing, its reason to be, the scheme beyond appearances. Never self pity, be merciless with oneself, and hence never project our own weak and diseased parts to the outside]. By infringing the first prohibition, Psyche is pushed by disequilibria of the soul (envy, yearn, jealousy, her evil sisters) to observe Eros' face. And that is what reductionists normally do when they desperately try to rationalise what cannot be reduced to reason. After a purification (death of the sisters, impure parts of the soul), Psyche takes the test of the four elements, and passes it. She then infringes the second prohibition as well, while she carries the box that almost all the Kores of the archaeological museum of Athens carry as a dowry for Persephone... Paradoxically, it is by infringing the second prohibition, opening the box that was intended for Venus and then falling into the sleep of death, that Psyche finally gets to reunite with Eros and ascend to the sky with him.

I simply wanted to recount the most foreign and Exoteric parts of this marvellous fairytale, ignoring the esoteric meanings and the Great Rite, but I believe that even just the title of the Fairy tale or Myth tells us all about its link and its function in the Great Rite itself and about the function of Love in our tradition. But let us move to analyze how all this tradition is poured into Alchemy.

ALCHEMY AS RE-IMMERSION OF ANCIENT MYSTERIES

I am going to talk about Alchemy in terms of specific re-immersion of the ancient Mysteries of the ancient mother.

Alchemical science evolves itself in its techniques that are the same all across the world, and that indicates the universality of techniques and specific operations. In occidental culture, the sapiential vein of Mysteries re-emerges after the Christian obscurantism of the middle ages and it acquires a metallurgical and pre-chemical language to conceal the true essence of the operations it involves, which, instead, are about a specific technique of interior elevation by using the energy that man has been provided with since the beginning.

In Alchemy then, one finds all the re-immersion of that which once were the superior Mysteries. These Mysteries were lived in absolute tranquillity in the ancient world; we have seen that in the images of the Villa of Mysteries and we have understood it from the rituals linked to every God or Goddess throughout the year. The course of the Sun and the eight main festivities, which are typical of witchcraft, can in fact be read and linked to the various alchemical operations that later on have been codified by alchemy and which must be performed in complete union with the course of the sky and of the stars.

Let us analyze for a moment these eight festivities, even though we all know what they are about: The feast of October 31st of Feast of All Hallows, also named Halloween, can be related to the Nigredo and to the preliminary work done in lacinia with the putrefaction of matter and its turning to the black colour of death or, like it is often called, Raven's Wing. The raven is a bird of death and that period of the year can be associated exactly with that.

The second festivity we have is the Yule or winter Solstice, when the sun is reborn, even though imperceptibly, and it starts to rise again and give more light to the Earth to make it wake up. This feast, in alchemy, can be associated with the first calcinations, or fire awakening within oneself, and it begins the real work of inner reconstruction.

The third feast, the Candelora, is the rise of the fire to a superior level. It is a most secret technique used by alchemists and they never disclosed it in a complete fashion to protect their other [techniques], hence I will not reveal it, but for the sake of our work it is enough to know that the fire lit at Christmas rises and becomes stronger and more purified leading the human soul to a more refined level, strengthened in its essence.

The fourth festivity or Primiera or Ostara. In this feast the actual alchemic works are begun after the preparation of the matter in the previous festivities. Here is when the daily and monthly rhythms of alchemical practice begin, and the matter starts to feel the effects of the work through the increase of the heat, which begins to transmute the matter into considerable matter in order to prepare it for the next festivity or operation.

The next feast is May Day, also called Beltane. In this feast, the God encounters the Goddess and in alchemy the King is joined with the Queen or Sulphur to Mercury in order to have the possibility to create the first seed of Philosophers' Gold.

The next feast is The Herbs or Summer Solstice, in which the sun acquires its true vigour and power, spreading all of its blessing over the Earth. The God is exalted and the Mother waits to spread her fruits, which are the result of the union with the God on May Day.

Alchemically, we work more on the philosophical Sulphur and fire so that the gradation gradually increases and the first stars begin to appear. That is, the internal formations of matter resulting when, by increasing the gradation, the signs indicating that the Sulphur has been completely purified start to appear.

I would like to explain this process more in detail, but what I mean can be comprehended by analyzing the pagan Feast and the Gods associated and represented in it. This is the period when wild grown Herbs are picked and the morning dew that fell overnight is collected because these are the first results of process within the body of the alchemist or within the matter he is working on where the first excrescences and natural fluids come out of a coction bubble and one has to be careful enough to gather them to work on them differently and then use them for the purification and healing from of all illnesses.

The following feast is August 1st or Harvest Feast or Lammas, in which the first fruits of the union between the god and the goddess are picked. The Goddess starts to give birth to her wonderful fruits to nourish all her children in the boiling heat of the Sun, her companion. This shows us how in Alchemy the increase in the heat finally brings its products in the refined matter and everything comes to light after months of hard, careful and precise work.

The refined mercurial matter is finally transformed into Minor Work or Work of White and it gives its wonderful fruits for the first time. The operator sees his work crowned with success and his feminine counterpart within him has given birth to what his masculine had sown.

The last feast is Secunda or Autumn Equinox, where day and night are even in length again and hence the Rebis has been formed and created. The male and female are united and the second fruits, or Work of Red, are harvested. The labour of Hercules carried out in the beginning with the Calenda or Shamain is finally over and the alchemist is dead, reborn, and resurrected to a superior level where evenness in the internal parameters between God and Goddess, or masculine and feminine part of the self, is restored.

Having come to the end of this journey, let us stop for another moment in the analysis. There are eight Pagan festivities, of which four major ones and four minor, and those are called Sabbaths. The Sabbath is the Great Rite conducted in different fashions for each of the eight festivities. Let us not forget that there are also the Esbaths, or full moons, in which other minor operations are performed, yet those are not of minor importance in the purpose of the alchemist, who must purify and refine the matter more and more.

Even these celestial recurrences correspond to alchemical processes that the operator performs to refine the matter more and more and bring it to the level of Gold. As I said, I must not divulge everything, but, as I mentioned, everything is associated with the Great Rite and with its Mysteries, which are always Mysteries of Union and matrimony, of Ecstasy and rebirth.

I hope to have managed, with these few lines, to give an insight of the link that exists between the feasts of Witchcraft, or Pagan Festivals, and the ancient and noble art of Alchemy which, following Nature as it has always claimed to do, cannot do but conform to seasonal rhythms and to the course of the two planets which have the most influence on us, and of stars, irradiating their power on us at all times.

If we reason in these terms, we will begin to understand and comprehend the fundamental importance of the Gospel of Aradia and the rhythms that are transmitted by it, even though in an incomplete and mutilated fashion. In the Gospel of Aradia we find general elements of instructions for the Great Rite mixed with elements of simple witchcraft practice.

This mix-up arose through the almost hasty gathering done throughout time of various elements of traditional knowledge passed on from member to member with little or no written documents. In the next section, I will analyze some of these elements, bringing to light, through the symbolic forms, the concealed meaning intended for them.

These elements have been passed onto me by those who have educated me in the time of my tradition, which has always been the custodian of the Great Rite as main and central part of magical and religious knowledge. But let us analyze the Blessing of Diana's Supper as reported in the Gospel of Witches.

THE SABBATH, TREGENDA, OR WITCHES' GATHERING: HOW TO CONSECRATE THE SUPPER

Here follows the supper: The Supper corresponds to the union of the masculine and feminine and to the ability of eating and assimilating elements which are different from our body but which are needed by our body to stay alive and to LIVE. The symbol of the supper and of eating is associated with the Great Rite and with the dichotomy of food and sex.

What must [the supper] include and what must be said to consecrate this to Diana: In these lines it is explained that instructions are being given for the ingredients to use in the supper or Great Rite.

You will have to take flour and salt, honey and water and pronounce this spell. Flour indicates the masculine principle, honey the feminine principle, salt the masculine principle, water, again, the feminine one. So we have four materials like the four elements which are always present when we eat or dine or perform the Great Rite in the matrimonial union of the two natures:

—⚹— Earth, Flour

—⚹— Salt, Fire

—⚹— Honey sweet as Air

—⚹— Water... water.

Hence the supper is alchemical cobation, transforming all foods in the great fire of the stomach and in the great fire of love, which is established between the foods introduced and the body receiving them. In fact, in the ancient theories of medicine, there was the conviction that if a food had not been loved by the body receiving it, then the body would rebel and feel sick. Today we would say that the stomach had indigestion. But in any case, we all know that if we eat foods that our body cannot digest or which are contrary to our nutrition we will cause a lot of damage to ourselves. The spell is a propitiating magic formula, but also the procedure by which the supper or the Great Rite is celebrated.

If we take the definition from the dictionary, it says: "Ritual by which, pronouncing specific formulas, some supernatural intervention is invoked to cast away a malicious force: to operate, to perform the spell!"

Every alchemical operation which, as we said, is always comparable to a sacred meal, must begin, the adepts say, with a prayer to God and a spell cast against adverse celestial forces so that they stay away and let us work in peace and tranquillity. It is a rule that must never be infringed, because Alchemy is a peculiar Art that has its basis in the intimate union of the Operator with the matter he works on and its transformations, transformations which are always parallel between him and the matter and hence they happen simultaneously in the two vases used, that is his body and the vase where he placed the matter to cook. What appears inside the external vase must reflect inside him and vice versa, otherwise it means he is not proceeding properly.

And that is the true meter to know and to check that the operation is going well, and this is always the indicator that nowadays is called the litmus test in Chemistry. In Alchemy we do not need an actual test, as our own souls become the test.

As we saw, flour is the male principle, associable with the inner seed of the male and with the earth. That is in fact loaded with potential.

THE SPELL OF FLOUR

> I pray to you, flour!
> Who are our body –
> Without thee we could not live–
> Thou who Before becoming flour,
> Have dwelled underground where all the secrets are hidden.

I still want to remind [the reader] that to cast a spell is to purify and cast away the negative things inside a substance or a thing.

Flour as a masculine element represents the semen enclosed in the male body, and it needs to be cleansed of the impurities accumulated in it.

An operation exists that allows to do that and it is enclosed in the symbolism of the course of the Sun throughout the year and it cannot be revealed here; it is present in every alchemical practice when we talk about cleansing the matter from the useless things weighing it down.

But the thing that interests us is to ascertain that even here, in the Gospel, this is mentioned, although in a different language and with a different procedure.

> You are ground to be put to the wind,
> You float in the air like dust and slip away,
> Taking your secrets with you!
> But when you will be barley in aspics
> In aspics so beautiful that fireflies
> Come to shed light on you so that you can grow more beautiful,
> Otherwise You could not grow and become beautiful,
> Hence you too belong to the Witches and Fairies,
> Because fireflies belong to the Sun

The term ground once again recalls the alchemical practice, which prescribes exactly the grinding of matter, in order to make it extremely subtle, as is done with flour after grains have been reaped at the right time. The aspic grown from the depths of the earth, blossomed and recalled by the care of the farmer, the force of the Sun and the force of

the Moon, by the nourishment of the earth and irradiated with rain and air is finally ready to be transformed into mild flour which must nourish the human body to allow it to keep on living. One can notice the links between the period of Sabbaths, as I described summarily earlier, but:

> Corporal firefly, come running and come racing,
> Put the rein to the horse!
> Put the rein to the king's son!
> The king's son will let you go,
> But I want to catch you,
> Since you are beautiful and glowing,
> I want to put you under a glass,
> And look at you through a lens.
> Under a glass you will stay
> Until all the secrets of this world are of that other one
> You let me know
> And even those of the barley and flour.
> As soon as these secrets I know,
> My firefly, I shall let you go,
> Once the secrets of the earth I know,
> Blessed you must be, I will tell you!

Entities in the Brain

Philip H. Farber

In the introduction to the 1904 edition of *The Goetia of Solomon the King*, Aleister Crowley explained his idea that "The spirits of the Goetia are portions of the human brain. Their seals therefore represent … methods of stimulating or regulating those particular spots (through the eye)." I used to correct Uncle Al when I would talk about this, and suggest that he likely meant "the human mind" rather than "the human brain." However, many years later, having studied some of the recent advances in neuroscience, I've come to think that Crowley's statement was unusually prescient. In fact, it now seems very likely that the human brain is wired to perceive entities and that we can, in fact, localize these entities to certain areas of the brain. Activity in the brain might not be all that happens when we communicate with entities, but it may prove to be a very important piece of the magical puzzle.

After all, our physical organism is the principle tool that we have for practicing magick, exploring our reality, and interacting with the world around us. Understanding, in general, how our brain responds to magical operations and to perception of entities can be incredibly useful and may point us toward more effective methods of magick.

Let's start with the most basic bit here. When we look at something or think about something, we have to make a determination whether or not that something is really a someone. We have to be able to distinguish between a human being and everything that is not human. The process of delineation begins with brain cells known as mirror neurons. Mirror neurons are motor neurons. They fire at times that are appropriate for the vast majority of motor neurons: when some body part needs to be moved. If you move your hand, you are engaging the motor neurons to initiate and control the movement. Mirror neurons go a little further; they also fire when you watch (or listen to, or feel) someone else perform a movement. This may lead you into performing the action yourself, as when a yawn becomes contagious or when laughter proves infectious. Mirror neurons may also come into play when hear a great guitar line and feel moved to play air guitar. More generally, though, mirror neurons allow us to "try on" someone else's behavior internally, to have a moment of shared emotion, feel someone else's pain, and experience empathy and sympathy. About twenty percent of motor neurons also function as mirror neurons.

To accomplish their ends, mirror neurons first have to decide what will activate them and what won't. In 1950, early computer scientist Alan Turing speculated that machines could be said to achieve artificial intelligence if and when its communication could not be distinguished from a human. Turing proposed a test in which an interrogator sat before two terminals, a human communicating through one by typing and a computer through the other. If the interrogator could not tell the difference, the machine would then be considered an artificial intelligence. An intuitive Turing Test, if you will, performed by the mirror neurons, seems to immediately categorize things into "conscious entity" and "inanimate lump." We look at each other and, hopefully, we recognize another human as both conscious and at least reasonably intelligent. Some very simple visual patterns, for instance, seem to fire off this sense of recognition – a smiley face, have-a-nice day symbol is recognizable to us as a human face; a South Park cartoon character can be identified with, at least for a half hour at a time, as a conscious entity with the ability to communicate, make decisions, and act, however stupidly, upon the world. Linguistic patterns also seem to have a similar ability. A sentence formed with proper syntax suggests that its writer or speaker is possessed of some measure of intelligence. Whereas a formed with sentence syntax that proper its–suggests little or nothing. Based on such unconscious intuitions, we recognize writers as conscious entities when we read their well-formed sentences. We recognize other humans as such when we communicate with each other in text environments such as Internet forums. And we even recognize fictional characters as entities for whom we might predict behavior and sympathize. There are likely also many other behavioral patterns and cues that help us to, unconsciously, tell the difference between a conscious entity and a brick of cheese.

Another factor of interest to the magician is that mirror neurons will also respond to imagined entities. For instance, imagining a sex act may get you aroused, visualizing another person's face may get you to smile (or frown or scratch your nose), and getting that guitar solo stuck in your head may also produce air guitar phenomena. Here's an exercise to explore some of your own mirror neuron responses:

Exercise: Watch Yourself Relax

—⁓— Imagine that you can see yourself, or hear yourself, or feel yourself, as if observing another person. Make it like looking at a movie or a picture of yourself. If you are better at hearing or feeling, then hear yourself talking or making sounds, or feel where your presence would be.

—⁓— Imagine that this other self that you are observing is in a place that is very comfortable and very, very relaxing. It's not necessary to see, hear or feel the place, just keep your attention on this other self.

—⁓— Watch, listen, and/or feel as this other self becomes more and more relaxed, more and more comfortable, and exhibits the effects of relaxation: softer muscles, different posture, different facial expression, and so forth.

—⁓— Make changes to the structure of the image (but not the content):

a. Make the image larger or smaller.

b. Make the colors brighter or more muted.

c. Emphasize the foreground as opposed to the background, and vice versa.

d. Make the sounds or speech louder or quieter (if the emphasis is on hearing rather than seeing).

e. Speed up and slow down the action (works for all senses).

f. Move the image closer or farther away (works for all senses).

g. Give the image a soft glow or sparkles.

k Notice any changes to your state as you experiment with these changes.

While mirror neurons use motor areas of the brain to internally replicate actions, cortical midline structures have the ability to model or represent your whole mind, your whole body, indeed, your whole life. Through a medium of memory, states, and submodality markers, your brain composes the story of your life, complete with character development, backstory, and an entire world in which it can play. That same engine of modeling, with the power to represent a complete mind, also comes into action when we make our internal representations of others. The mirror neurons help us begin the process by recognizing other people as being like us, and understanding their movements and intentions. From there, the default network can develop complex psychological models. This ability is called Theory of Mind and allows us to not only empathize, but to make detailed projections of another person's thought and behavior. Mirror neurons conspire with the cortical midline structures of the default network to bring us the rich and detailed world of imagination.[1] And, as already noted, our imaginings can activate our neurology and physiology as if they were "real."

There's a natural purpose for this mental activity. In effect, evidence suggests that when humans get social, we are interacting as much with these internal models of each other as with the actual people they represent. It is part of how we relate to each other all the time. There are quite a few predictions that we make about each others' behavior, for instance, that are complex, yet so fundamental to our behavior that we take them for granted. The simple, motor-neuron behaviors may be the most obvious: if someone offers you a glass of water, you automatically and unconsciously make detailed predictions about how they will follow through, where they will go, where the glass will end up, and anything else that helps enable you to meet and receive the glass with your own hand. Beyond the simple monkey tricks, though, we also make more elaborate social predictions, about whether someone will respond appropriately to a joke, if it is the right time to shake hands (which involves social prediction as well as motor prediction), and what kind of efforts will most please employers, friends and family members. Whether these

---

1 Uddin, Lucina Q., et al. "The self and social cognition: the role of cortical midline structures and mirror neurons." *Trends in Cognitive Science*, 11:4, 2007.

predictions are entirely accurate or not, they are parts of the model on which we base our decisions and actions.

Indeed, the nature of the model sometimes becomes painfully apparent when our communication goes awry. For instance, consider the mighty provider for his family who buys his wife houses, cars and boats, but she leaves him anyway because all she wanted was to spend some time with him. These purely hypothetical people remain at odds because they each continue to operate on fallible maps of each others' mind. He thinks that property ownership will make her happy. She thinks he likes her company.

Sometimes we use the limits of human model-making to our advantage, as when a fighter feints in one direction and strikes from another, or when a stage magician uses misdirection to create an illusion. If a hapless opponent makes a faulty prediction about what the fighter intends, he gets clobbered. If an audience member acts on an inaccurate model of the magician's movements, she gets to be delighted by the illusion.

A few major pieces of our model are now in place. We know that mirror neurons and the cortical midline system of the default network can recognize and model entities in response to human-shaped images as well as words, sounds, feelings, and movements. Combined with the sensory tendencies in which they are encoded, these images convey information about state. For most people, viewing these entity images can also nudge our neurology and physiology toward the state. The human-shaped symbols can come pretty close to some of the traditional symbols used to access specific states. Those symbols are, of course, the gods, goddesses, demons, angels, and entities of every pantheon from every culture.

Indeed, some of the gods and goddesses of the ancient world not only look like us, but began their careers as human beings. This is perhaps most apparent in African and African Diaspora traditions where it is said that the Loas and Orishas once walked the Earth as our ancestors. By engaging in exploits that attained the level of legend, their lives became enshrined as tales and they transformed into beings of myth, memetic entities transmitted through stories, images and rituals from mind to mind and from culture to culture. This is, potentially, the continuing memetic spread of states, across big swaths of time.

Other historically important entities had human-shape symbols created for them. The gods of nature were linguistic and iconic representations of the forces and secrets of the world around us. They were qualities that were given the faces, hands, bodies, words and emotional experiences of humans so that we could appreciate them, discuss them, and share their states with others. Sometimes they are blended with animal or other non-human properties – for instance, the body of a lion on the Sphinx – but nonetheless include enough human-like cues to be recognized as entities.

When we see a god/dess figure (or read their name, hear their song, feel their presence, etc.), our brains activate the equivalent states. This is the essence of invocation; being in the presence of the god elicits the qualities within us. Experiencing the states as you create the god anchors them to the image and allows you to re-access the states at will simply by contemplating or visualizing the god/dess.

In our culture, we have images, figures, and human-shape symbols that we use for communicating and sharing states, but we don't necessarily call them gods. We call our important tales movies, books, comics, history and journalism. We call their inhabitants fictional characters, superheroes, historical figures and celebrities, among other things. When we contemplate our contemporary stories and the entities that populate them, as well as mythic tales of heroes and deities, we activate our neurology in ways that allow us to feel the joy, passion, sorrow, power, ethics, and wisdom of the gods. When we watch Luke Skywalker destroy the Deathstar, we feel elation, almost as if we fired the decisive shot ourselves. When we look at the statue of Abraham Lincoln at the Lincoln Memorial in Washington, D.C., we may feel inspired by the wisdom and compassion of the great president. When we read a book or watch a movie about how Frodo Baggins carried the Ring to Mordor, we feel some of the excitement, horror, loyalty and persistence that the fictional Frodo feels. When we see or hear our favorite rock stars, we feel something of the freedom and exuberance they transmit through their performance. We often use specific sensory-based language to describe what distinguishes these characters: "He is a shining example." "She is larger than life." "They went out in a blaze of glory."

EXERCISE: INSTANT GOD/DESS

—⚘— Decide on a quality that you either have and would like to enhance, or one that you don't have and would like to acquire. For instance, creativity, compassion, patience, strength, assertiveness, financial skill, adaptability, understanding, concentration, flexibility, love, sex appeal, or whatever you decide upon. Make sure this quality is a positive one, that is, it is one that stands on its own and is not expressed as a lack of something else (for instance, "reduced stress" might be expressed here as "relaxation", "no more bad luck" might be expressed for these purposes as "good luck" and so on).

—⚘— Breathe and banish.

—⚘— Create a dissociated image of yourself, standing or sitting. Eliminate background and any accessories, objects, props, and so on that might be in your image so that the image is just you.

—⚘— Begin to adjust the physiology of the imagined person to include more and more of your desired quality. Pay attention to and adjust facial expression, posture, breathing, movements, skin tone, muscle usage and anything else that might pertain.

—⚘— Adjust the structure of the image (submodalities) for greater impact. Experiment with image size, color depth and quality, image location, and special effects such as glows, sparkles, shimmers. Take each of these to its greatest intensity – for instance, the image could be increased to much greater than life-size. If this image were a god of that particular quality, how would these submodalities manifest? Just how big is a god/dess of x?

—⚘— Begin to add in extra features and aspects from other humans, from animals, machines as appropriate to a god/dess of this quality. For instance, if cunning and strength are useful to this entity, give it some qualities of a tiger or other animal that might represent those qualities (head, body, teeth, eyes, whatever). If enhanced intelligence or processing speed is important, then maybe a computer chip or having a computer as an accessory might work. Take as much time as is necessary to test out some of these qualities. Notice which ones feel the best and keep them. Have fun with this and make your image fantastic.

—⚡— Adjust physiology to account for the additions. If you added a computer chip to the brain, how would that be reflected in facial expression, breathing, posture, etc.?

—⚡— Contemplate the image for at least 30 seconds.

—⚡— Pull the image into the circle with you and draw it into you. Wear it like clothing, wrap it around you, let it interpenetrate your body and mind. Let your own body, posture, breathing, facial expression, etc. reflect what you saw in this image. Let the memories of this (future) self who possesses the quality you would like to enhance be your memories now.

—⚡— Breathe and banish.

—⚡— Be open to thoughts, epiphanies, and suggestions from your unconscious mind that may occur throughout the day as a result of this practice.

The similarity (or, perhaps, identity) between the way we respond to traditional gods and goddesses and the way we respond to celebrities offers a means of research. A 2005 study at the University of Leicester in England sought to examine how our brains respond to images, names and sounds related to celebrities. The research was based, in part, on a previous theory called the "grandmother neuron" theory, first proposed in the early '60s, which suggested that we have specific brain cells to recognize family members. That is, when you see or think about your grandmother, there is a specific neuron that is activated. This theory was considered by many to be too simplistic – but the University of Leicester study found that this is exactly how we respond to celebrities. Subjects who viewed different images of Halle Berry (for instance) would activate the same single brain cell – and that neuron would fire not only for images of her, but for drawings, and even her name, printed on paper. The "Halle Berry neuron" would also ignore images of other actresses, inanimate objects and, generally, anything that wasn't Halle Berry.[2]

If a specific neuron or even an area of the brain can respond to our concept of a celebrity-entity, it stands to reason that we have similar responses to our magical entities. If that brain area or neuron responds to the visual input of a written name, it can certainly respond to the visual cue of a sigil in the same way. In short, without benefit

---

2 Quian Quiroga R, Reddy L, Kreiman, G, Koch, C and Fried, I. "Invariant visual representation by single neurons in the human brain." *Nature*, 435: 1102-1107, 2005.

of brain scans, Aleister Crowley was probably right in his assessment of Goetic entities and brain areas. The sigils very likely do activate those spots in the brain, via the eyes, that relate to the specific spirits.

The question now becomes, "Is that all that happens?" If I'm driving my car and hooked up to a device that monitors brain activity, there will be a unique signature related to driving, which might include modeling of the road, predictions about other drivers, motor functions, sensory activities, and so on. But it's not all that's happening at that time. There are events taking place that we will usually take as being external to us, including the bodies and brains of other people involved. The problem here is that deep down the magical rabbit hole, the distinctions between "self" and "other," "me" or "the entity," start to seem a little bit arbitrary. I'm reminded of Lon Milo DuQuette's famous quote: "It's all in your head... you just have no idea how big your head is."

There is an area in the right parietal lobe that accounts for our sense of self. That is, it helps us to make a distinction between "me" and "not me." We usually sort things out so that "me" ends at our skin. But that may be a trick of neurology because, really, our skin and cells are created of permeable membranes, we would die without the air around us, and our consciousness is largely occupied with perception of the world around us. And when that part of the brain is disrupted with a magnetic beam (or by injury), people start to lose sense of self, are not able to recognize themselves in the mirror, and feel a sense of union or oneness with their environment.

What is "self" and what is "other entity" may come down to a difference in delineation only. That is, what is included in the circle of self is self, and what is included in the triangle of art is other – because we choose to define it that way.

I encourage self-flex: the ability to identify with "selves" of more variety and scope than the singular "self," and, at will, to suppress the "self" part of the brain to a greater or lesser degree.

At the Well of Initiation

Aki Cederberg

Approaching Arcadia

As I sit and drink wine on the balcony of my hotel, watching the summer sun set in the Atlantic Ocean on the horizon, it is very quiet in the village of Sintra, Portugal. Save for dogs barking, occasional cars driving by, and bells ringing somewhere in the distance, the cobblestoned streets are empty and silent. This magical blue hour, *l'heure bleue*, is very different from the morning and day when the main streets are invaded by hordes of fat and noisy tourists, who crowd the numerous shops and restaurants selling over-priced trinkets and bland food. But by evening, the tourists mostly shuffle away, and the streets die down. Completely oblivious to all of this, high upon the mountain above and somehow seemingly apart from time, hovers the majestic, slightly melancholy ruins of the Moorish castle. Eyeing the terrain below, beyond the picturesque pastel-hued houses and cobblestone streets, I can see mansions and palaces sprout throughout the resplendent green valleys; in a certain light, they resemble golden phalluses or rockets standing erect, ready to blast off and ascend into the heavens. As the sun sinks into the sea and the sky slowly fades into a deepening array of reds, lilacs and blues, a gentle mist settles upon it all. Subtly, a gentle but clearly mountainous breeze runs through the dark terrain. And there in the distance, white-silver-gray and shrouded in green, lies the reason for my pilgrimage here: the mysterious and magical Quinta da Regaleira, one of the foremost hermetic landscapes in all of Europe.

In *The Lusiads,* L.V. de Camões wrote of Sintra, "…where every pool and stream has Nymphs in its waters." Indeed, there is a definite air of the otherworldly in this quaint little village, apparent even if one is not the least bit familiar with its history. High up on the serra, its brooding fairytale castles, its numerous magnificent palaces and pastel-hued quintas (country villas) are archetypical in their mythic storybook presence, surrounded by equally moody and magical nature–mountains with lush and dewy forested valleys strewn with giant boulders of rock, exotic species of flora and fauna, botanical gardens and winding pathways on the hillsides. This added to the fact that a cursory glance at the history of Portugal and Sintra will reveal a land steeped in myth and magic.

The larger area of Sintra, meaning roughly the area from Sintra-Vila in the serras, to the coast of Cabo da Roca, the westernmost edge of the European continent, has been inhabited since prehistoric times. As long as anyone can remember, it has been connected to the idea of a terrestrial paradise, of a mythic Arcadia, home of Pan. This is attested to both by its rich oral tradition, as well as archeological findings and a later lit-

Quinta da Regaleira. Photograph by the author.

erary tradition. It has been claimed that Cynthia, goddess of the moon, was worshipped here. And it is said that it is from her that the place derives its name: from Cynthia comes Cintra (Sintra), connecting the place strongly with the goddess. Another claim is that "Sin" is a Hebrew word for moon, and "tra" is a word referring to a tripartite goddess, while another theory purports that the name is derived from "Suntria", the first syllable of which is the Indo-European root word for the sun. Whatever might be the truth behind these etymological theories, it is undeniable that the locality is strongly linked to the dual divinities of the sun and the moon, as well as the sea – all of which are interconnected. Mythical sea-creatures, Tritons, monsters and mermaids prevail in the tales and history of the area since pre-historical times. In fact, so well were the tales of sea-gods established, that at the time of Tiberius Caesar a local delegation travelled to Rome to inform the Emperor of their existence. These links to ancient divinities of the sky and sea abound in the landscape of Sintra, alive even to this day in folklore, literature, art and architectural design.

While strolling along the little alleys and winding narrow lanes of Sintra-Vila, soaking up the surroundings along with copious amounts of sangria and wine, this atmosphere was tangible. It seemed to be alive with a sense of wonder and of myth. Not surprisingly, romantic Sintra has historically been the refuge of Portuguese royalty, and local as well as foreign artists, writers and composers. Lord Byron wrote of Sintra-Vila famously as "a glorious Eden", while Hans Christian Andersen invoked it as a "a true vignette of the Thousand and One Nights, a fairy-tale vision". Richard Strauss described one of its palaces as the "Castle of the Holy Grail". Overlooking the valley, with the castles and palaces hovering in the clouds above, it was easy to see why.

It seems that even the "Great Beast" himself, Aleister Crowley, found the atmosphere of Sintra appealing to his occult interests. Although the details of his visits are unclear, it seems Crowley did explore and enjoy the village and its surrounding areas through his friendship and correspondence with the famous Portuguese poet Fernando Pessoa. Pessoa, a man with his own esoteric leanings, had made a translation into Portuguese of Crowley's "Hymn to Pan". Apparently Crowley arrived in Portugal in September of 1930 along with his then-current girlfriend. As Autumnal Equinox of that month was approaching, speculations of planned rituals abound, but whatever these plans were, they were nevertheless abandoned after a quarrel with his would-be "Scarlet Woman", resulting in her leaving the country. Following this, there are entertaining stories of Crowley planning a false suicide to unnerve the woman who had so abruptly left him during their journey. According to the story publicly expounded by co-conspirator Pessoa, who was clearly in on the joke, Crowley vanished and left a suicide-note to be found at the cracks of Boca di Inferno, "Hell's Mouth", an impressive ravine by the sea some distance from the village of Sintra. There was a police investigation of the mysterious case and repeated mention of it by the local newspapers. Rumors abounded of possible foul play, homicide and ghost-sightings, again fueled by Pessoa himself. It seems both men were quite the tricksters. Whatever the factual truth behind these stories might be we may never know, but it is undeniable that they have left their mark on the more recent folklore of Sintra. Indeed, it is not hard to imagine old uncle Al in the company of Pessoa, sitting at a quiet village-café, perhaps playing a game of chess, laughing in their beards while plotting their mischievous pranks.

More recently, Sintra has again garnered more to add to its already vast occult history. On the winding pathways of the mountainous terrain, my girlfriend and I came upon a lane and a mansion that seemed oddly familiar, as were some places of the Vila. It was only later that we realized and learned why these sites seemed familiar: Sintra was the location where Roman Polanski filmed part of his occult thriller *The Ninth Gate*. In the story, the main character (played by Johnny Depp) seeks to authenticate a rare esoteric book whose author is supposedly none other than Lucifer himself. Things take an unexpected turn as the protagonist ends up questing for the mystery himself, and, after having copulated with his female daemon, receives some kind of Luciferian illumination or initiation. The nature of this illumination is not expounded upon any further in the film, but merely hinted at, as in the last scene the protagonist enters the opening gates of a castle and the picture dissolves into brilliant light.

ENTERING THE GATES

It was precisely this "questing for the mystery" that had brought me here, and that had indeed been the driving force behind my initiations and numerous pilgrimages of the past. But rather than a theory or ideology set in book or stone, my guide had been a deep inner impulse to seek out illumination, a desire for the holy and eternal, a desire for the revealing of divine presence and wonder itself, to be experienced first-hand through living things, personalities and places, and not through intermediary forces. Descending from a line of seafarers on one side, I had heard the sea-gods blowing their conch-shell trumpets, and they were beckoning me, along with Pan playing his flutes and Orpheus strumming his lyre.

And so it was that me and my girlfriend were wandering along a winding hillside road lined with palm trees, following the six-pointed stars engraved in the cobblestones, eventually arriving at the stone walls outlining the remarkable occult garden of the Quinta da Regaleira.

When a map is laid out of the vast, four hectare estate situated on a mountain side, the area itself is pentagonally-shaped, and clearly forms an *inverted* pentagram when viewed in relation to the road and the landscape. This is also suggested by both the main entrance gate and the palace, that is, the *Quinta* itself, being situated directly on the lowermost point of the pentagonal area.

There is an old saying by Cicero, that if you have a garden and a library, you have everything you need. In light of this thought, Caravalho Monteiro, the visionary behind the Quinta da Regaleira, truly had everything: a microcosm of his own design, including the grand garden with a chapel, grottoes, waterfalls and various elaborate constructions, as well as a palace with a substantial library. Upon entering the main gates it becomes apparent that the Quinta da Regaleira is clearly a total environment of impressive magnitude and detail, a world constructed to reflect its creator's esoteric and aesthetic interests and passions. At the same time it can be seen as being a late addition to the tradition of sacred pagan gardens of Europe, reflective of traditional initiatory themes. Walt Disney would no doubt have been envious, and indeed the Regaleira garden possesses a distinct playful and whimsical quality, somewhat like an esoteric amusement park. Gardens of such magnitude and symbolic depth, if they withstand the onslaught of time, can serve as a refuge of age-old wisdom and as blueprints for meaningful, harmonious, highly aesthetic landscapes, in contrast to the homogenized and often ugly modern environments.

Entering the imposing, exuberantly decorated main house flanked by an equilateral Templar cross, is a delve back in time and into the history of the Quinta da Regaleira itself. Nicknamed the "Palace of Monteiro the Millionaire" after its main proprietor António Augusto Carvalho Monteiro, the estate originally named "Quinta da Torre" had several owners since the mid-1600's. In 1840 it was acquired to serve as a summer retreat by a family of rich merchants, the Barons of Regaleira, who constructed a palatial house and chapel on the estate, and it is from them that it derives its name. In 1892 it was bought by the wealthy bibliophile, collector and monarchist Caravalho Monteiro, who also bought patches of surrounding land, purposefully giving the estate the aforementioned pentagonal shape it still has today, as well as its wonders. Monteiro was clearly a man with a vision. With the assistance of several notable artists and architects, chief among whom was architect, painter and set designer Luigi Manini, Monteiro devoted much of his later life (as well as a fortune) to design and create the estate. The bulk of the work was concluded in 1910, although some designs were left unrealized, such as the plans for a massive fountain of Neptune. The estate as a whole invokes neo-manueline, romantic, gothic and renaissance architectural styles. In 1946, a quarter of a century after Monteiro's death, the estate was sold and had a few different owners, including a Japanese corporation, until the year 1997, when it was finally bought by the Municipality of Sintra and restorations began for it to be open to the public a year later.

Inside the house, we find it equally exuberantly themed and designed as its edifice is, although stripped bare of most of its interior elements, original furniture and collections. Nevertheless, there are distinct, eclectically styled rooms: the porch carved in limestone, the Renaissance Hall decorated in Italian Renaissance style, the King's Room with portraits of Portuguese royalty and coat-of-arms and the Hunting Room with a massive fireplace featuring a statue of a hunter and frescos with themes relating to hunting and the cycle of life. As we continue up the the staircase, occasionally we see tiles with Templar crosses, which we encounter again on the weathervane above the other floors, the terrace and spiral towers with panoramic views over the Sintra hills and Atlantic Ocean.

Not much is known for certain of Caravalho Monteiro's official associations to any esoteric order, but speculations abound. However, as attested to by the recurring symbolism prevalent throughout the entire estate, it is clear that Monteiro had a strong interest in esoteric traditions, alchemy, Freemasonry, the Knights Templar and the Rosicrucians. Monteiro also had a substantial esoteric library, today gathering dust in some historical archive, attested to by the original room of the library with a black floor and mirrors at the base of the bookshelf, invoking a strange sensation of the room floating on air.

In the house we see written on a wall the alchemical motto referring to the process of internal purification:

V.I.T.R.I.O.L.
Visita Interiora Terrae Rectificando Invenies Ocultum Lapidem
(Veram Medicinam).
Visit the Interior of the Earth, and Rectifying (Purifying), you will find the
Hidden Stone (True Medicine).

On another wall, very much resembling an ancient Vedic prayer I learned while traveling in India, is a quote from Henrique José de Souza:

Conduz-me di ilusório ao real, das trevas á luz, da morte á imortalidade.
(Lead me from illusion to reality, from darkness to light, from death to immortality.)

With these words as our guide, we exit the palace and enter the garden.

CROSSING THE THRESHOLDS OF THE GODS

Taking a few preliminary steps into the garden, we are immediately greeted by a white marble statue of the god Hermes, identifiable by his caduceus (a short staff entwined by dual serpents), followed by a lengthy succession of other gods. But it is Hermes that one encounters first and it is he who reveals the nature of the experience that we are to embark on. Hermes is the messenger of the Gods, the mediator between the human and the divine, the bringer of teachings and knowledge, the maintainer of the sacrality of sexual undertakings, vegetal fertility and nourishment. According to legend, Hermes was born in a cave of a mountain, after Zeus raped the goddess of Earth, Maïa.

Continuing along the Threshold of the Gods, a long terrace that runs parallel with the outer wall and ends at a gate-structure, the Pisões Loggia, we are guided along by a line of divinities following Hermes: Vulcan, Pan, Dionysos-Bacchus, Orpheus, Venus, Flora, Ceres and Fortune. Fiery gods and goddesses of joyful wisdom, ecstasy and eroticism, sensuality and seduction, love and beauty, poetry and charm, abundance and prosperity, creative fire and transformation; all connected to the fertile earth, but also to the sometimes frightful underworld and its subterranean, chthonic realms. We recognize these sensual gods by their attributes: Orpheus by his lyre, Venus by her seductive posture, Pan by his flutes and whimsical smile, Dionysos-Bacchus by his grapevines and face contorted in ecstatic abandon. At the end of the Threshold stands a large statue of a lion, one of the most elevated of natural creatures, suggesting courage, strength, nobility and kingship. As we walk along the terrace under the sun, surrounded by the resplendent beauty of the garden and the ever-present divinities, it is evident that we are to be their protégés on this quest. With Hermes at the helm, it is these gods who are the patrons of the Hero who journeys between worlds. It is they who are the torchbearers when we enter into the dark, subterranean worlds inside the earth and begin our interior voyage.

The Chapel, Axis Mundi

Via a system of tunnels connected to the palace and garden, we approach one of the most mysterious sights at the Regaleira: the chapel. The chapel is built in resemblance of the Axis Mundi, the cosmic pillar or world tree, with three floors – one below, one on and one above ground. To reach the lower, underground floor of the chapel we cross a metal gate with a spiral-horned animal creature along with a prominent pentagram and two sunwheels – definitely not something one is accustomed to finding in a church.

As expounded on before, the guide for my pilgrimages has always been some intangible inner impulse, stemming from visions and dreams, which I have sought the equivalent of in the waking world. One of the central talismanic dreams of my life has been the following: I descend in a spherical vessel below the ocean and inside the earth, only to discover a subterranean shrine to an undivided truth. And now, in the waking world, as I lay my hands in the baptismal fount by the entrance to the lower floor of the chapel, I am awestruck by what I see: a shrine as the one in my dream. Contrary to many of the opulent designs of the Regaleira, the underground chamber is very simple and almost archaic. It has vaulted ceilings, an undecorated altar and floor of marble or stone. The floor is made up of black-and-white tiles (similar to the ones used by Freemasons), marking the co-existing powers of light and darkness, male and female, and the balanced union thereof. The altar itself is a carved marble slate, with two black crosses: one above it, and a second exactly similar one below it, again pointing to the hermetic axiom: as above, so below. I later learned that it was in this crypt that Caravalho Monteiro's body was brought and laid out after he died in 1920. As I breathe in the damp, subterranean air, I wonder at this underground temple, this dream vision become flesh, and feel like having been here before.

Through a spiral staircase, we ascend to the main floor of the chapel, consistent in its imagery with the underground shrine, as well as exactly mirroring it in placement and form. On the ceiling directly above the main entrance to the chapel is an all-seeing eye in the triangle, the imagery of which can be traced back into some of the oldest human cultures, including ancient Egyptian and Hindu mythologies, as well as being strongly linked to the Great Architect of Freemasonry. The entrance gateway structure itself is decorated with a multitude of esoteric signs: a mystic rose, an ark, a chalice suggestive of the grail, and of course a large equilateral Templar cross. This particular equal-armed cross was used by the Order of the Knights Templar, as well as its successor in Portugal, the Order of Christ. Entering the chapel, the main floor again features the same massive equilateral cross, surrounded by pentagrams and sunwheels.

Throughout the chapel alchemical, hermetic and occult themes abound. On the outside wall of the chapel, there is a sculpture of an athanor, the "alchemical oven". Above the altar of the ground floor, we see an image of Christ, the King, crowning a woman identified as the Virgin Mary. The colours of Mary's clothing are clearly suggestive of the process of alchemy: Negredo (the dark-blue cloak), Albeda (the white headcloth), Rubedo (the red dress) and Auredo (the golden shroud and background). A large letter, "M", is carved centrally above the painting. The whole scenario is evocative of "the divine couple", suggestive of Hieros Gamos, the sacred union.

Lastly, ascending to the small floor above ground through yet another spiral staircase, we see yet again equilateral Templar crosses and sunwheels, like the ones on the ground floor below us.

The chapel structure is clearly an image of the tripartite Axis Mundi, with its three floors and levels of being – heaven, earth and underworld – all mirroring each other in space, locality and form. The Axis Mundi is reflective of the interconnectedness of life and the various realms of being on all planes. Not merely to be taken to mean the connection between the underworld (the world of the ancestors and the dead), the middle plane (the world of human affairs), and the upper worlds (the realms of the gods, however we might perceive them), the Axis Mundi is that place where dream and reality, the subject and the object, the interior and exterior meet and intersect.

Exiting the chapel, having been immersed in its manifold occult nature and curious marriage of paganism and christianity, I have to pinch myself to see that this isn't all some surreal dream.

THE FOUNT OF ABUNDANCE

Gradually, we follow the paths upward. Beautiful, bewildering things await us behind every turn in the resplendent garden: labyrinth caves, statues and structures of mythical animals, little stairways leading to hidden tunnels and artificial lakes leading to grot-

The Fount of Abundance. Photograph by the author.

tos. We sit down at a carved stone bench in the shade for a respite, while a statue of a woman holds a cup in the air above us. Benches such as these are scattered throughout the property, with statues of sleeping lions or guard dogs sitting at attention, always accompanied by human figures holding chalices aloft in reverential pose. Indeed water, water-containers and sea-symbolism are a recurring, dominant theme throughout the estate. Water is present throughout the land as bodies of water in lakes, ponds and underwater aquariums, in flowing form as springs, waterfalls and various fountains, as well as in in symbolic form – all pointing to the primordial waters, the abundance of the nectar of life, which nourish not just the physical but also the "spiritual" realms.

Clearly reflecting this is the Fount of Abundance, a massive façade built out of marble, flanked by obelisks, and decorated with conch seashells and dual serpentine fish. At the center of it is the large heraldic-style monogram of Caravalho Monteiro himself, "CM". The structure stands on a clearing above the lower part of the garden, and in front of it is an altar and small marble throne. On a hunch, I take note of the colors and discover that the fount design clearly follows, as in the chapel, the alchemical procession of four stages and their associated colors: black/dark blue, white, red and yellow/ gold. Water flows into the elevated fountain in the middle, symbolically representing the panacea, the elixir of life.

Between the statues and fountains such as this, hidden in plain sight amongst greenery and wrought into architecture, are large vases and urns decorated with an assortment of green men, goats and satyric figures with grapevines in their hair – further underlining and pointing to the *semen virile*, the solar seed and sacred substance of which we are to take part.

THE GARDEN OF ENIGMAS

We stop at the outdoor terrace of the Quinta da Regaleira restaurant, a stone-structure just behind the main house, featuring a large fountain in the middle guarded by four mythical animals. While lazy cats wander by, we sit in the shade surrounded by the stone edifice and lush greenery, eat olives, fresh bread and risotto with scallops, not to mention strong green sangria, which the waiter tells us is "the best in the world". As we order our second pitcher, I am starting to agree with him wholeheartedly. A garden of pleasures, indeed.

Here in the shade, I reflect on why gardens have always held a special place for me, both as physical places as well as inner landscapes. I have explored the garden from the primal sacred groves often surrounding holy trees in my homeland and beyond, to the small pagan garden of a place where I lived in my youth that held a small altar and natural temple amidst all the various plants, flowers and herbs. I have traveled and visited gardens from the secluded, privately owned featuring elaborate shamanistic, surrealistic creations of art, to the majestic and opulent Renaissance gardens throughout Europe and the exotic gardens of Asia. In gardens I have found both the impeccably maintained and groomed perfection of the here-and-now, as well as moss-swallowed melancholy and nostalgia. For me, these gardens, at the core, all represent the same thing in different guises. They reflect the particular history and worldview of their creators and maintainers, and all have their particular mythologies and languages, but some perennial themes seem consistent. And, perhaps more importantly, all represent a reverential attitude toward life, nature, toward the divine and art – art being man's expression of his own divine nature.

Fueled by the sangria, we continue our travel upward, and arrive at the Temple of Flora, a large greenhouse which makes apparent Caravalho Monteiro's enthusiasm for flora and fauna. An avid botanist, Monteiro filled his garden of earthly delights with a multitude of species of plants, from the various colorful flowers, herbs and topiary to the wide variety of massive trees, as well as the wildlife that these attract. The Temple of Flora features parallel fertility pillars and carvings of a fairy and a faun by its main door, and above it is Flora herself as a reclining nymph set in stone. Central on the main façade is a large tile panel showing a group of partially naked priestesses surrounded by animals conducting a fertility rite, making offerings of fruits and flowers to the divine, possibly in the form of Demeter or Ceres. As if on purpose, the revered figure is left out of the picture, and we are left with an image of reverence and homage to manifold nature itself. The array of plants at the Regaleira, whether present as herbs, flowers or topiary are far from merely decorative: they are part of the language of the garden, as the personalities of nature, possessing different characters, correspondences, associations and meanings.

Following a path from the Temple of Flora, we come upon an imposing, semicircular formation. As we enter its base, we find Leda's Cave, a chamber in the shape of a perfect hexagon. At the far end of the cave is a statue of Leda with a swan, behind which is an underground stream. In the Greek pantheon, Leda was the the wife of king Tyndraeus of Sparta, who was seduced by Zeus in the form of a swan. Their consummation, which took place during the same night as Leda laid with her husband, resulted in offspring of uncertain origin, either divinely immortal or kingly mortal. This myth, in light of Caravalho Monterio's monarchism, suggests the recurring motif of divine kingship. By its structure, placement and symbology, the grotto of Leda also suggests the marriage of heaven and earth. The high ceiling and form of the cave creates a strange acoustic effect, echoing the rippling sound of flowing water.

Through spiral staircases, we arrive at the upper stone structure housing the Regaleira Tower, with an impressive view over the garden and the area surrounding it. As we continue to follow the paths leading to further heights, we find hidden entrances to the central system of interconnected caves and underground walkways throughout the land, such as a lake with a waterfall. The lake has stones placed on its surface which form a walking path on water that leads, just as in fairytales, behind the waterfall and into hidden caves. We forego the hidden entranceways and climb upward, arriving at a highly dramatic structure, the Terrace of the Celestial Worlds. High on the estate, the terrace is a wide castle-like opening overlooked by a towering ziggurat, whereupon contemplation of the celestial can truly occur, as an elevated panorama opens to us. Opposite the terrace is another equally dramatic structure, Guardian's Gate, composed of dual towers flanking a central arched pavilion, which again hides a hidden gateway into the subterranean tunnels in its shadow, guarded by twin crocodiles or reptilian figures holding a seashell to their ear. The figures again remind me of the presence of dual water-creatures throughout the terrain, such as twin fish and twin serpents.

My Soul is the Deep Forest

The higher we ascend in the garden, the wilder and more untamed nature grows, in stark contrast to the carefully planted and groomed grounds below. Again, this aspect of the garden points at a balance between different co-existing elements and planes of life, between the refined and the wild, the clear and the hidden. Shrouded paths of stone, occasional grottos and rough walkways surround us, as we find ourselves in a forceful forest of majestic trees and unbound nature. The forest speaks to us about the "vital enigma", the mystery of life, and is an analogy of the spirit or soul itself.

The presence of trees holds a special significance at the Regaleira. According to the map, there are close to two dozen different species of trees growing in the garden. The reverence of sacred trees goes back to the oldest of human cultures. It is expressed in a wide range of religions and mythologies throughout the world, whether in the shape of the world tree, the all-encompassing structure interconnecting all worlds above and below, inside and outside; or as the sacred grove, which can be seen as the "first garden", a territory marked off as a place of the numinous.

According to the yogis, "the connected ones", of the ancient Indian oral tradition, before temples there were holy trees. Later around these trees temples were erected, which can still be witnessed all throughout India and Nepal today. In Nordic myth and religion, the high god Odin hung from the world tree Yggdrasill for nine nights in order to receive the runes, the secrets themselves. In my homeland, Finland, the forest as a whole has since ancient, pre-Christian times been considered holy. Often there was a clearing surrounding a special tree that was seen as distinct from the rest, with a personality and presence of its own, and which was marked off as a sacred grove. Consequently, as has been painfully documented, one of the first acts of the arriving Christian church upon entering Finland was to systematically and literally uproot this tradition by felling holy trees, burning sacred groves, and often erecting churches on these very places. Yet despite of this the reverence for the tree and the relationship with the forest remains ingrained in our ancestral soul.

At Regaleira, the various species of trees, just as the plants, tell of the manifold nature of the place. They are not arbitrarily or accidentally placed. As an example, Yew, a tree traditionally associated with both death and immortality, grows right next to one of the central structures of the Regaleira, the Initiatory Well, clearly associated with the life-death-rebirth cycle it embodies. Yew is sacred to Hecate, "lady of the underworld", who lives in a cave and presides over secret, illuminating rituals. In the Nordic tradition, Yew is sometimes thought of as the World Tree Yggdrasil (instead of Ash), and is connected to the runes *eihwaz* and *yr*. Cypress, which has similarly deathly associations, stands by the cave entrance to the crypt of the chapel; while at the side of the upper level of the chapel is lofty Oak, representing majesty, victory, immortality and fruitfulness, sacred in the various pantheons to the high gods Zeus, Jupiter and Thor. In the upper, rockier and wilder regions of the estate we find Pine, marking steadfastness and loyalty, and sacred to Neptune, Dionysus, Diana, and Cybele. As we see by these examples, the nature of the garden is alive with different personalities and powers, and serve a purpose in unfolding the narrative of the journey.

INTO THE UNDERWORLD: THE INITIATORY WELL AND THE SACRED UNION

Beyond all these beautiful and bewildering things, all paths in the garden seem to lead to a curious central structure of the Regaleira: the *Poço Iniciático*, the Initiatory Well. Located high up on the estate, the well itself is hidden to the untrained eye inside what looks like a natural rock formation. As in mythic tales, one has to scale its surfaces to find the revolving stone block door (facing north) that will grant one entrance. Pushing the heavy door aside, we come to the uppermost floor of the well and view down the dizzying, perfectly round spiral staircase descending some nine floors and 30 meters below ground. More than an actual well, it is a subterranean, inverted tower. Looking down into the abyss, at the bottom center of it is an eight-pointed compass rose laid out in four subtly different colors of marble – blue, yellow, red and white – again indicative of the alchemical process and its associated phases, as well as the four elements of air, fire, water, earth. The compass rose design, which features three consecutive circles, consists of an equilateral cross emerging from a central red dot or circle, with pointed extensions toward the cardinal points, as well as smaller extensions inbetween. It is a central mark of the quest, as well as of the initiate or adept himself. The rose compass is illuminated via natural light that shines from a circular opening to the sky at the top of the tower.

Poço Iniciático, the Initiatory Well. Photograph by the author.

As we start to descend down the spiral staircase, touching the damp, mossy stone walls, the light gradually recedes and water runs and drips around us. Counting the numbers of the steps as we we walk (139), from its digits we get the sacred number 13 (1+3+9), which corresponds in various esoteric traditions to death and rebirth, the end-goal of the initiatory journey. The empty niches that are carved into the walls between the staircase and open to the central void are 22 in number, another sacred number, which calls to mind the Major Arcana of the Tarot and the principles they embody. At the bottom looking up, the view is a perfect copy of the one seen at the top, except that now the circle is the sky of light.

There is a small baptismal fount of water at the entrance to the circular opening at the bottom, clearly marking that this is a sanctuary, a place of the holy. With the water I rinse my palms and forehead. Then, I take my girlfriend by the hand and we walk into the darkness.

We wander in the dark, damp caves. Sometimes they are lit with small ribbon lights, sometimes pitch-black dark. At times we have to crouch, and occasionally we step in puddles of water. The caves reach far and wide, and have several dead ends like an unfinished well that one cannot ascend, the meaning of which remains obscure in the otherwise so meticulously designed layout of the whole complex. Perhaps the dead ends tell of the aborted quest and importance of persistence to find the true goal one is seek-

The Initiatory Well, view from the bottom. Photograph by the author.

ing for. The caves also have many hidden gates and entrances. And yet we tread along in the darkness.

I knew this dark labyrinth, this maze, like an old friend. I too had wandered far and wide, lost as a spiritual orphan, and grown weary in the maelstrom of the gorging void of worldly meaninglessness. I too had come to many illusory goals, only to discover them to be dead ends. I had tasted all the bitter, salty waters of human life – despair, disillusionment and death; I knew them only too well. But in all of these misadventures I had never lost sight of that spark inside, which gave rise the profound glimpses in which I saw "the ruins of my being as fragments of the divine". And those glimpses drove me through the abyss and up toward the surface of the world, toward the sun.

After wandering in the darkness we eventually approach an opening, a definite source of sunlight. At the end of a long passageway with various diversions we come to the entrance situated farthest from the well: the Cave of the Orient, the re-entry to the gardens below. But before we return into the world of light, I lead my girlfriend to a little cave near the entrance. And there, in the damp cave, in the darkness of the subterranean world, we make love. In an effigy of the sacred union, heaven embraces earth as we kiss, sweat and unite. For a moment at least, Eros conquers Thanatos, and the world is recreated in an act of joy, an expression of divine ecstasy. A moment of eternity in the tomb of the earth, from which we emerge as if reborn.

The well is clearly a symbolic initiation, an analogy set in stone and marble, earth and water, of life-death-rebirth. Both an ascent and a descent, the quest leads to a receding from the mundane world and a simultaneous re-entering of the deep recesses of earth, which are equally the cradle of life as well as the grave of death. The initiate enters the interior of the earth and underworld, undergoes an internal, allegorical death and leaves the ordinary world behind. He traverses in the darkness. Perhaps he gets lost in the labyrinth along the way, and possibly he struggles through a "dark night of the soul", all but his own daemon as the guide and torch to lead him through the journey. He drinks from the primordial waters, from the well beneath the world tree. Then, finally, having traversed through the unlit realms and hidden caves of being, he re-emerges victorious into light, into the surface of the world from which he came, but *transformed* by the initiatory experience he has undergone. This initiation, of course, is a mere beginning. It is the sacred mark of crossing the veils to another world. The initiate returns home and to the ordinary world, now with eyes in *both* worlds, perhaps carrying gifts and drops of divine nectar with him. Slowly, he churns experience and knowledge into wisdom, and sees analogy at play, and the relation is clear: heaven meets earth, and earth salutes heaven; as above, so below. And so he rediscovers the world again, finding a garden of delights, a paradise regained.

As we exit the caves, it is a quiet and warm day. There are only a few visitors, and still the sun still shines in the sky, unhindered by the lazy clouds. Unhurriedly, we wander down the little lanes, back to the restaurant for a final libation of sangria to conclude our adventure. And down below us is the garden of the divinities, and the gods are there, waiting for us, inviting us to play.

Return to the Garden of Earthly Delights

The garden on a higher level presents the basic question of how we relate to the world around us, to nature, and to ourselves.

If we are "closed off" from a position that allows us a sense of wonder and reverence, we are not likely to come away with anything of lasting value or deeper meaning. Consider the pious, who can find god only in a building of their own flock, who find wisdom only in a words spoken by intermediaries of god or on the written page of a holy book, who repel all expressions of the divine that do not fit their definite, vehemently non-psychedelic and self-limiting worldview. Consider the modern tourists who approach the garden as a park full of entertaining and amusing follies, who loudly and crudely rush their way through every potentially sacred experience, already anticipating the next quick fix. Both are cut off from the ever-unfolding nature of reality and creation, from the flow of life, from the sense of mystery, awe and reverence in presence of the manifold personalities of nature.

At the root of this non-reverential approach is the underlying tragic theme of a schism in the soul of man. The spiritual impulse has been tainted and traumatized by ideas of the expulsion of man from the garden of paradise, of the fallen nature of man, of sin and the necessity of redemption or salvation. At the core of this lies the belief in a separation of man from nature as well as from the divine and eternal, resulting in the malady of monotheist religions, as well as their modern atheistic ideological counterparts. Both are essentially two sides of the same coin. For their kind, the world is a valley of tears apart from god, nature is devoid of spirit, and this is manifested as the barren, soul-destroying things they construct and spew out into the world. The modern world and much of its unquestionable misery and ugliness is much a reflection of these two dominating extremes that are nevertheless paradoxically interconnected.

But on the other hand, we can approach the garden with a reverential attitude, as a microcosm with its own language, symbology, cartography and meaning reflective of something larger than itself. If situated in the close vicinity of urban surroundings, gardens are a respite from all the worldly banality and noise. If built and consecrated in untouched nature, gardens are marked off areas dedicated to the numinous, the holy. Either way, they serve the same original purpose. The garden is the interface between nature and art, and a bridge between the human and the divine. The garden is a refinement of nature according to an ideal or principle in line with that very same nature. This principle can be applied to the world outside its borders, but equally, and perhaps more importantly, it can be seen as an analogy of the world within and without, a metaphor of human existence and life itself, in all its multiplicity and manifold nature.

If we open ourselves to the experience of wonder inside the garden, we can find something quite profound, and indeed, moving. Its perennial themes tell of the timeless quest of the hero – that is, the true human being. The timeworn beauty of garden structures reminds us of the passing of time. The way the sun moves across the dome of the sky above the garden mirrors our own human lives of birth, life and death: rising in the damp dawn, it grows in might and gathers momentum, casts shadows and creates different moods during its journey, and finally sets in a sea of darkness, only to be reborn again. All of this ignites a romantic longing in our hearts to be at home in the world and, equally, to be part of the infinite.

At the recommendation of a friend, I briefly met with an author in the café that he ran, who has written about the occult roots of Portugal. Without realizing it, because the book title did not include his full name, this was the author of a book I was just then reading. I suggested that he, as the author, inscribe my book with a dedication of his own choice. Quoting John Milton, he wrote: "Man's disobedience, and the loss thereupon of Paradise, wherein he was placed: Then touches the prime cause of his fall, the Serpent, or rather Satan in the Serpent; who revolting from God…" *(Paradise Lost)*

In Quinta da Regaleira, I found not a paradise lost, but in stark contrast, nature and art embracing in an image of a paradise regained. As a model of the cosmos, the Regaleira garden speaks to us not of the gloom and doom of a church, not of the vacuity of a shopping mall – but of life as a journey, an adventure, an unfolding of creation and gnosis. If we have the vision and might to make it so, life is not just a valley of tears, but a garden of joy with fountains of wisdom running through it, rooted in an ancient well of memory, mystery and wonder. Drink thereof, and be full.

BIBLIOGRAPHY

–∾– Daniélou, Alain: *The Phallus*. Inner Traditions, Rochester, Vermont, U.S.A., 1995.
–∾– Godwin, Joscelyn: *The Pagan Dream of the Renaissance*. Weiser Books, York Beach, Maine, U.S.A., 2005.

—⁓— Jack, Malcom: *Sintra: A Glorious Eden.* Carcanet Press Limited, Manchester, England, 2002.

—⁓— Kovalainen, Ritva & Seppo, Sanni: *Puiden Kansa (Tree People / Das Volk der Bäume).* Hiilinielu tuotanto, Hämeenlinna, Finland, 2006.

—⁓— McIntosh, Christopher: *Gardens of the Gods: Myth, Magic and Meaning in Horticulture.* I.B. Tauris, London, England, 2005.

—⁓— Müller-Ebeling, Claudia; Rätsch, Christian; Storl, Wolf-Dieter: *Witchcraft Medicine: Healing Arts, Shamanic Practices, and Forbidden Plants.* Inner Traditions, Rochester, Vermont, U.S.A., 2003.

—⁓— Rice, Boyd & Janeiro, M.: *The Vessel Of God / Porto do Graal.* Terra Fria, Sintra, Portugal, 2005.

—⁓— *Quinta da Regaleira.* Edición - Cultursintra Foundation, Sintra, Portugal, 1998.

—⁓— *Quinta da Regaleira: Colecção - Arte, Naturzea & Símbolo.* Cultursintra Foundation, Sintra, Portugal.

The Magical Life of Derek Jarman

Renata Wieczorek

I am the mirror, the fire that consumes all that is created.
I bring the winter of thy flowers and the frost that secretly destroys the temple.

(Ariel in *Jubilee*)

People in art are not people,
Dogs in art are dogs,
Grass in art is not grass,
A sky in art is a sky,
Things in art are not things,
Words in art are words,
Letters in art are letters,
Writing in art is writing,
Messages in art are not messages,
Explanation in art is not explanation.

(Ad Reinhardt, *California*)

I met Derek Jarman when I was 14. On a sunny afternoon I went for a walk along the streets of my hometown, Warsaw. It was early spring and people were buying bunches of silvery pussywillows walking with the sprays etched in the sunlight. I stepped into a café and saw my friends at one of the tables and so moved toward them to say hello. When I was passing by one of the tables, I noticed a black-eyed stranger looking at me with joy, friendliness and surprise. He smiled at me and since I felt as if I'd already met him I asked my friends if by any chance they knew who he was. They did. They came to the café to meet him and to listen to his talk on his newest film, *The Garden*. He came to Warsaw for a few days for the first and only time. The talk made me look at some things in a completely different way and the meeting and a chat we had later on were so strange and full of enigma that I had no choice but to start a long journey in pursuit of truth. The dark-eyed stranger started *his* journey many years before.

Derek Jarman was born on the 31st of January 1942 in Northwood. In the 60's he studied English Literature, History and History of Art at the Kings College and Painting at the Slade School of Fine Art. After graduating he worked as a stage designer. An accidental encounter on the train with one of Ken Russell's co-workers resulted in his becoming production designer for *The Devils* and one more of Russell's films in which he created extraordinary stage designs. Encouraged by Russell, he made a few experimental Super 8 shorts that included *Journey to Avebury*, *The Art of Mirrors* and *In the Shadow of the Sun*.

His first feature film, *Sebastiane*, made in 1976, was a brave interpretation of the life of St. Sebastian. The story had apparent homoerotic overtones and caused consternation, if not indignation, among most of the British audience. On the contrary, Jarman's father – a former military officer – after seeing the film said that it perfectly well showed what life was like in military barracks. But such opinions, good reviews and the fact that the film is probably the only production with all the dialogue in Latin, didn't prevent distributors from classifying it as gay porno to be shown in erotic cinemas. That's how Derek Jarman gained the label of a highly controversial director who had no respect for religion, society, morals or history.

But he seemed to take delight in such opinions and his later works and activities confirmed this. No doubt he was the most non-conformist and uncompromising British director, showing in a very honest and even brutal way the hypocrisy of current society and the inconvenient truths about reality we all face but hardly ever notice. *Jubilee* and *The Last of England* were bitter reflections on the lot of his motherland, *War Requiem* was an anti-military exposé. His works also had a poetic and even visionary side. His feature films *The Angelic Conversation* and *The Garden* are the most personal records of spiritual experiences and development. His last work, *Blue*, is an absolutely unique "diary" of fighting an illness, accepting one's fate and the approach of death.

In 1986, Jarman made *Caravaggio* – the only of his films which gained some commercial success – and it strengthened his position as an independent and controversial but nonetheless outstanding artist. It was also this year, on 22nd of December, that he was diagnosed HIV positive. At this time such a diagnosis was equal to a death sentence but Jarman instead of breaking down started his most intensive work. The eight years between this diagnosis and his death were the most productive in his career. It was during this time that he directed the films *The Garden*, *War Requiem*, *(Queer) Edward II*, *Wittgenstein* and *Blue*. It was a race against death and time, and its meaning and significance, like all events in Jarman's life, was as much symbolic as multi-layered.

Derek Jarman directed many video clips for such artists as Marianne Faithful, Pet Shop Boys, Marc Almond, Bob Geldof and Suede. He was openly gay – though he didn't like the word and preferred describing himself as "queer" – being the first British artist who proudly admitted to belonging to this minority. He considered his films, especially *Sebastiane*, as "a message of solidarity to people who have been dispossessed."[1] He was also engaged in the British "occult underground." Music to his films were created by Throbbing Gristle *(In the Shadow of the Sun)* and Coil *(The Angelic Conversation* and *Blue)*, and he also sympathized with Psychick TV and Thee Temple Ov Psychick Youth. He was interested in all things mysterious and described his films as magical ceremonies. One of his favorite historical figures was John Dee, a Renaissance scientist and magician, with whom Jarman identified to some degree. One of his projects that was never fully realized is a story based on Aleister Crowley's ideas and threats awaiting the New Aeon coming into being. It is based on Jung's *Aeon* and the *Revelation of St.*

---

1 Interview with Lynn Barber, *The Independent on Sunday*, the 4th of August 1991.

John and was meant to be a combination of politics, art and mythology. The script is a thrilling read indeed.

A few years before his death, Jarman moved to the shingle desert of Dungeness on the southeast shore of England and created around his cottage the most extraordinary and amazing garden. Gardening – apart from making films, writing and painting – was one of his greatest passions. When asked what he wished to be given for his fifth birthday Jarman said that he wanted a book on flowers and he recalled later on how heavily disgusted his father was of such interests, which he considered as "sissy".

Jarman's friends and colleagues remember him as a man whose two qualities struck almost everyone who met him: these were his energy and generosity of spirit. To these qualities should be added his humour, his honesty and, especially towards the end of his life, his truly heroic courage.

Another of his qualities was his openness to the unconscious that was linked to an openness to chance effects, an ability to make creative use of accident. "This partly accounts for his tendency to take whatever was happening in his life at any given moment and transform it into a theme of universal, almost mythic, significance. If he was constantly absorbing inspiration from everything and everyone around him, his personal vision was so powerful that whatever he absorbed tended to be subsumed into that vision rather than ever being allowed to deflect him from it."[2]

⁓〰⁓ ⁓〰⁓ ⁓〰⁓

Hear me in the Great Silence
Woe to the man who replaces the many by the simple
For he shall give birth to torment.
Consider the world's diversity and worship it
For the lesser gods are many and the world is
Mirrored in their image.
By denying these gods their multiplicity
You deny your own true nature.

(Derek Jarman, unrealized script)

When Derek Jarman was nineteen he went with a few friends for a holiday trip to Greece. On a sunny and extremely hot day they arrived at a shady valley and to their great joy found fresh water in a small spring. They drank from it, enjoyed a bath, and rested in the shadow. To their surprise they were awoken not by birds singing gaily but by a furious patrol of Greek police. The incident could have ended in jail because, according to the police, the young tourists committed not only an act of vandalism and performed highly immoral behavior, but also profaned the sacred well of Apollo. Luckily, they were only administrated a rebuke and after many years Jarman remembered the event with much humor, noticing that in this accidental way he experienced a true Apollonian initiation.

---

2 Gray Watson, "An Archeology of Soul", in *Derek Jarman: A Portrait. Artist, Film-maker, Designer*, Thames, London 1996, pp. 33-34.

Many years later Jarman showed his Apollonian qualities in visionary films like *In the Shadow of the Sun*, *The Garden* and *The Angelic Conversation*. The title of the latter obviously referred to the work of John Dee.

Jarman read widely in psychology, magic and the occult. He pointed out that Jung's *Alchemical Studies* and *Seven Sermons to the Dead* could be seen as keys to his film *In the Shadow of the Sun* even though he read them after making the film. Jarman claimed that these books gave him confidence to "allow dream-images to drift and collide at random". He was also deeply influenced by Francis Yates' writings on the hermetic tradition in the Renaissance. He especially estimated John Dee, Giordano Bruno and Henry Cornelius Agrippa with his *Three Books of Occult Philosophy*.

Jarman's interest in John Dee and some other Renaissance magicians, like Bruno and Agrippa, was a result, as he used to say, of his fascination with all kinds of secrets and enigmas. He claimed to have an obsession with a language of closed structures, with ritual of closure, seclusion and sanctuary. This is reflected in *Sebastiane* and his other films and, of course, in his decision to move to a deserted area of Dungeness. He placed himself among such artists as Kenneth Anger, Jean Cocteau and, foremost, Pasolini, because of their tendency to remain outside the mainstream and because of their attempts to get through the screen into the world closed from ordinary exploration. This explains Jarman's interest in magic, especially John Dee and the use of the title of a book by Dee for his own work.

However, in *The Angelic Conversation* there are Shakespeare sonnets, not Enochian calls, that are the Leitmotif of the film. It is an oniric story of two men looking for the Truth – mainly about themselves – and Love, which they apparently find in the end. But, like most of Jarman's works, this one is so multi-layered and full of allusions (and illusion) that it escapes one interpretation. Furthermore, Jarman always pointed out that his films are a "product" of cooperation of many persons – his actors, friends and colleagues – who helped in their realization. This way the films were products of many emotions, ideas and personalities, slipping from a clear-cut characterization. And it doesn't exclude the fact that in each of his films Jarman was telling one basic story – the story of the complex personality of its creator and director. In his last work, *Blue*, he did it without the slightest camouflage. He used to say that he had at last done what he always wanted to: he made a film EXCLUSIVELY about himself.

The music to *The Angelic Conversation* was created by Coil and includes an amazing piece played on Pan's pipe, Jarman's favorite instrument. He described his artwork saying it was a world of dream, of magic and of magical rituals, but there were also pictures of burning cars and radar systems which are there to remind one of the price that is to be paid to make this dream true in a world full of violence.

It is worth noticing that John Dee appears in one of Jarman's earliest films, *Jubilee*, where he becomes a witness to the moral and intellectual disintegration of post-Victorian England as he is showed around by the black (sic!) angel Ariel. Ariel, played by Karl Johnson, who in one of Jarman's last pictures impersonates Ludwig Wittgenstein, also appears, of course, in *The Tempest* which is another brave and controversial interpretation of a classical story. It is a well known fact that Prospero, claimed by some to be Shakespeare's *alter ego*, reminds one of John Dee – the circle being (almost) completed.

Jarman's interest in magic and exploring realms inaccessible for "ordinary" quest was also reflected in his fascination with Super 8 – the film format that he used until the end of his life. He wrote: "This is the way the Super 8s are structured from writing: the buried word-signs emphasize the fact that they convey a language. There is the image and the word, and the image of the word. The 'poetry of fire' relies on a treatment of word and object as equivalent: both are luminous and opaque. The pleasure of Super 8s is the pleasure of seeing language put through the magic lantern."[3]

The "poetry of fire" was one of the most important, significant and frequent symbols in his productions, including video clips. He wrote: "The child of fire is the child of disobedience. In revolt. The Promethean child steals the matches to strike a dangerous light in the dark."[4]

One of the most spectacular examples of fire – solar symbolism can be found in an unrealized film, *Silence is Golden (Nijinsky's Last Dance)*. Nijinsky dances his last dance and is "wreathed in flames". He (Nijinsky) says he is "washing his hands in the sun" and his body is burnt to ashes.

Another important chance effect or apparently accidental event happened to Derek Jarman in the spring of 1987. He went with a few friends on a trip in search for materials for a film he was planning. They were heading to the most eerie, mysterious and secluded area of England: the salt marshes of Denge and a desolated cape named Dungeness. The place is believed to be accursed and it is said that demonic forces dwell there – this belief probably being based on the fact that the marshes once long ago were a "hatchery" of plagues. Dungeness is the southernmost area of Great Britain and is a shingle desert, in fact the largest shingle formation in the world, surrounded from three sides by the sea. What strikes every visitor most forcibly about this place are two things: the wind and the light. The wind brings a salt breeze and carries an amazing sound from the air, sea and stones that to some sounds like the most beautiful song but to others it drives them mad. The light is the most spectacular and makes the landscape look like Vermeer's paintings. There are not too many buildings, just a few fishermen huts and cottages, a Bird Observatory, two lighthouses and a nuclear power station.

The wilderness of Dungeness attracted Jarman a few times before – it was there that he thought of making his next film. That day, on a sunny spring afternoon, he told his friend as they were driving towards one of the lighthouses that if only the one cottage he liked were for sale he would immediately buy it and move there. When a couple of minutes later they were passing by this cottage, they saw a white and green board "For Sale". There was no choice but to make the wish come true. Jarman bought the cottage from the money he inherited after his father's death earlier that year and moved to Dungeness to the former fisherman's house named Prospect Cottage.

"Dungeness, Dungeness, your beauty is the best, forget the hills and valleys", Jarman wrote enchanted by the place, adding, "The landscape is like the face you

---

3 Derek Jarman, *Dancing Ledge*, Quartet, London 1984, p.129
4 Derek Jarman, *Chroma*, Century, London 1993, p.37

overlook, the face of an angel with a naughty smile".[5]

However, this "angelic face" of Dungeness had also a very unpleasant and even scary side. There are salt storms that in a few hours burn all plants, which are not many in any event, and cover cottage windows with salty frost. The wind that never dies away makes people nervous and disturbed and it induces thoughts that maybe the frightening local beliefs about the place might be true. It is no wonder that very few persons want to stay there. Jarman was not surprised that most of his friends preferred only short visits to his new house, returning to the less "angelic" regions of England as soon as possible. But he loved the place in an unconditional manner and made it one of the most important parts of his life, appreciating it for being both at the same time absolutely open and absolutely isolated from the world.

When Jarman moved to Dungeness the terrain around Prospect Cottage didn't differ from the surrounding moon-like landscape. One could find only some white flowers fighting with the wind and sea-kale *(Crambe maritima)*, a plant with blue-greenish leaves and bunches of pea-like, green or bone-color seeds, which apparently finds the desert to be a friendly realm.

The new owner soon started creating a garden in front of the cottage, which didn't go unnoticed by ecologists who demanded that he stop this "destructive activity," Dungeness being a strictly protected area where it is not even allowed to bring soil from different places. Jarman was very surprised by their demands and petitions because in his opinion there was no difference between him planting flowers and birds bringing seeds that accidentally start to grow in this unwelcoming wilderness. The ecologists were not convinced by such arguments but they didn't send an official ban so the rebellious gardener continued his work. In his garden appeared and bloomed a few kinds of poppies, dog rose, irises – which mysteriously survived blows of the salt wind – lavender, snowdrops and anemones. At the beginning people thought that he was creating the garden for magical purposes. He confirmed their conjectures, writing that it was magic indeed – white magic in the shadow of the nuclear plant. However, his garden became the most magical place indeed.

He indulged in the ambiguous character of his creation underlined by the closeness of the nuclear power station. However, he could find true beauty even in this symbol of evil forces. He wrote, "The nuclear power station is a wonderment. At night it looks like a great liner or a small Manhattan ablaze with a thousand lights of different colours. A mysterious shadow surrounds it that makes it possible for the stars still to glow in a clear summer sky."[6]

Nature herself was of his most interest and attention. He observed the plants, the Sun moving and "the moon [which] is even more spectacular [here]. The sunset turns the seashore into a rosy mirror, with streaks of pink cloud. Then the moon comes, and casts a silver path across the waves, a shimmering carpet for the stars. There is very little to interrupt you here, just the wind, which, like the mistral, can drive you slightly mad."[7]

He treated his garden as a pharmacopeia that allowed him to forget for a moment

---

5 *Derek Jarman's Garden*, London 1995, p. 118.
6 *Ibid*, p. 67.
7 *Ibid*, p. 118.

A section of Derek Jarman's garden at Dungeness. Photograph by the authoress.

his illness. After 1991, his stays in Dungeness were interrupted more and more frequently with painful infections and longer stays in the hospital. In the last year, even a few weeks before death, he was coming to Dungeness blind and with an oxygen apparatus. Because of medicaments that he had to use his skin was very sensitive to sunrays so despite the illness he was very tanned – almost *burnt* by the sun. Some of his acquaintances used to behave rather stupidly when he was coming back to London, asking where he was on vacation to get such a beautiful sun tan. In one such embarrassing situation an impatient Jarman answered: "Oh, I've just been in hell!"

In Dungeness were realized two films considered by Jarman to be the most personal and important in his career: *The Garden* and *Blue*. In the latter it is the wind and the sound of the sea waves washing the shingle shore that recalls one of the director's favorite place on Earth.

In front of Prospect Cottage in the central part of the garden is a large shingle circle planted with gorse *(Ulex europaeus)* that has a wooden, apparently phallic, pale in the middle: its solar symbolism is obvious. It is worth noting that gorse is the sacred flower of the A∴A∴ and was chosen as the heraldic emblem to be a symbol of the Great Work. It symbolizes the Sun in full blaze, and "its branches are exceedingly firm, as should be the Will of the Adept, and they are covered with sharp spikes, which symbolize, on the one hand, the phallic energy of the Will and, on the other, the pains which are gladly endured by one who puts forth his hand to pluck this bloom of sunlight splendour."[8] Another gorse circle can be found at the back of the cottage.

The garden in Dungeness has no fence or other boundaries – no one makes fences

8 Aleister Crowley, *Liber 777 and Other Qabalistic Writings*, Weiser Books 1986, p. 97.

there. In this way the garden created around Prospect Cottage goes fluently into the wilderness of Dungeness desert. However, it only apparently has no limits, geodesists could certainly measure where it ends; Jarman bought the cottage with some land around it.

In the back garden near the kitchen window he grew a dog's rose, the plant of which he was especially proud. There were also many "treasures" found on the seashore hidden among the flowers. Jarman also used to have a beehive at the back of the cottage where he observed the life of its inhabitants and collected honey with the eagerness of an amateur. He used to give the honey to his friends; it was a gesture as much friendly as symbolic.

A garden and bees collecting pollen is one of the favorite motives of alchemical myths. To this alchemical story we should also add Jet, the tame crow that came each morning to Prospect Cottage and stole everything that glittered and buried it in secret hideaways at the end of the garden. The crow followed Jarman when he was going blackberrying in the salt Denge marshes, swooping low over his head. There was also Thomas the old black cat stalking his dinner through the broom, blackened by salt spray.[9]

Brillant, gorgeous, painted, gay,
Vivid, flaunting, tearway,
Glowing, flaring, luring, loud,
Screaming, shrieking, marching, proud,
Mellow, matching, deep and somber,
Pastel, sober, dead and dull,
Constant, colourful, chromatic,
Party-cloured and prismatic,
Kaleidoscopic, variegated,
Tattood, dyed, illuminated,
Daub and scumble, dip and dye,
High-keyed colour, colour lie.

(Derek Jarman, *Chroma, A Book of Colour – June '93*)

Derek Jarman became interested in alchemy early in the 70s, when he read Jung's *Alchemical Studies*. He remembered that it was probably the fascinating illustrations of metals, kings and queens, dragons and serpents that made him pick it up. Then he bought and read original texts by John Dee, Giordano Bruno and Cornelius Agrippa – he found the first edition of *The Occult Philosophy* on a market stall and bought it for five pounds. It had only a few pages missing and turned out to be in better condition than the copy owned by the British Library.

His library makes one think of Prospero and the books he brought onto his island: the *Pimander* and Orphic Hymns, Plotinus on the soul, *The Book of Life* by Ficino,

---

9 Derek Jarman, *Chroma*, Century, London 1993, p. 140.

Conclusiones by Pico Della Mirandola, Paracelsus, Roger Bacon, *The Secret of Secrets*, Agrippa's *Occult Philosophy* and of course John Dee's *Hieroglyphic Monad,* in which the Renaissance magus revealed to the world the magical symbol representing all the powers and characteristics of the Philosopher's Stone and completed mathematical proof to show the deeper meaning and relationships of the ancient ciphers of alchemy, using to this end Euclidean geometry. The glyph was said to incorporate the powers of the Stone whenever it was drawn and meditated upon and the proof in Dee's belief was to "revolutionize astronomy, alchemy, mathematics, linguistics, mechanics, music, optics, magic, and adeptship". However, the key to the inmost meaning of the Hieroglyphic Monad was never revealed by Dee to the public since he thought it senseless to talk about it to the uninitiated. It is said it was lost when Christian fundamentalists broke into Dee's home and burned his library, which was once the largest in England with over 4,000 rare books and manuscripts. It seems obvious (though often objected) that neither mathematical nor philosophical speculations give us Knowledge, which can be found only through Art and Symbol. If so, maybe the Lost Key can be found, or at least looked for, through studying the creations by Derek Jarman, the admirer of what the Monad truly represented.

Toward the end of his life Jarman used his wide knowledge on magic, alchemy and occultism and his education as a painter writing the most extraordinary *Book of Colour*, titled *Chroma*.

According to Agrippa, color is a kind of light. Of course the way we perceive colors depends not only on light, but Agrippa meant, it seems, that color *is* light, and its play allows us to see the physical world as multicolored, which in itself is (or at least might be: we never know) only illusion. It's not that surprising if we take into consideration that light is brought (to mankind) by the master of illusion and patron of visual arts, especially cinema – Lucifer, the rainbow angel, sometimes identified with Apollo.

In his *Book of Colour*, Jarman included thoughts on eleven colors, shadow which follows the light and many other matters – taking a fascinating journey through centuries with their outstanding painters, philosophers and magicians. He wouldn't be himself though, if he didn't complete the sophisticated investigations with some less intellectual stories. For example, in the chapter on Red he remembers with nostalgia his mother's scarlet nail polish and lipstick and how he, as a young boy, painted his own nails bloody red and danced in his mother's room like the Whore of Babalon, shocking and disgusting his father, who nailed him on this bizarre behavior.

The use of alchemical symbolism and profound knowledge is apparent also, and foremost, in the garden in Dungeness. One aspect of it can't be overlooked and repeats in many configurations in multiple ways: it is its solar character. It was emphasized by the owner by engraving on the southern wall of the Prospect Cottage the poem by John Donne: *The Sunne Rising*. Dungeness happens to be the sunniest area in England.

However, it is worth noticing once more that Jarman took an evident delight in the fact that his own personal paradise garden was overshadowed by the nuclear power station and, in that sense, he went beyond disapproval of the "dark satanic mills", coming closer perhaps to the Blake of *The Marriage of Heaven and Hell.* But his vision, like that of Pasolini, his hero, was profoundly moral: all the more so, because of "the tension resulting from his openness to the claims of evil".[10]

This "satanic" side of Jarman's complex nature and art was obviously of great interest and disgust of the "moral" English society. To this we should add his emphasizing the role of homosexual love, sex and lifestyle as a "liberator" from the oppression of "normal" society and from the "gutter of Christian love" – no wonder one of the bishops named him, to Jarman's great amusement, "Satan's spawn", describing his books, films and the garden in Dungeness as highly satanic. Oddly enough, nothing was closer to the truth for the latter, if we consider the esoteric meaning of the anti-hero persona and the solar aspect of Jarman's private paradise on Earth.

Into his black paintings created at the end of his life Jarman painted the philosophic egg. He says: "This was the Quest, not a parody – the Quest that could end with a burning in the Field of Flowers – like Bruno who described the Universe as numerous worlds sparkling like dust in a shaft of sunlight. You could get more than your fingers burnt for that thought."[11]

Derek Jarman died on the 19th of February 1994 after a long series of painful infections caused by AIDS. He didn't permit strong drugs to be induced to relieve pain, he wanted to remain conscious to the end to, in his words, experience all man does, including death. Before the funeral his friends gathered in his cottage in Dungeness where his body was exposed in the living room facing the garden and the nuclear plant. In his hands he was holding, instead of a rosary, a small plastic green frog. Those who participated in the ceremony at the nearby Old Romney graveyard on that sunny day say they have never seen such an amazingly clear blue sky.

10 Gary Watson, *An Archeology of Soul*, in *Derek Jarman: A Portrait. Artist, Film-maker, Designer*, Thames, London 1996, p. 46.
11 Derek Jarman, *Chroma*, Century, London 1993, p. 142.

"A Dark Room of Desire"
The Sensual Shrapnel of Pierre Molinier

Genesis Breyer P-Orridge

My first ever awareness of Pierre Molinier was in a book on Surrealism that I received as a prize for "initiative" from the English private school I attended on a scholarship. The easiest way to describe, maybe even explain, the impact of that "public school" (it remains a British irony that the most elite, privileged places of education are called public!) is to say it was like the one depicted in the film *If…*. But one hundred times more brutal in every possible way. This was 1968 and I had already contacted the cultural maquis, got my civilian clothes ready so I could pass unnoticed on the streets and was poised to slip swiftly into the underground torrent of alternative lifestyles of the era.

A few very blurred photographs and a tantalizing anecdote suggesting Molinier was too sexually oriented for the Surrealist hierarchy stuck deep in my mind. During the 1970's the erotic crossover movie *Emanuelle* revealed a surfacing of eroticism from the psychedelic journals into post-sixties suburbia. The character I was instantly intrigued by was the old man, the dilettante, who preferred to orchestrate (or castrate comes to mind) libidinous scenarios as a means of personal illumination and even neo-spiritual revelation for his chosen participants. In this movie, naturally, it was Emanuelle who discovered an existential liberation through fetishized humiliation. Where the thought that next drew my attention came from I am unsure, but somehow I became aware that this "old decadent" was based upon Pierre Molinier. Likewise a mythic proposal that Molinier inspired Pauline Réage and the *Story of O,* and to "test" her degenerate credentials he had masturbated in front of her after inviting her into his home! Very probably, at this stage, accuracy doesn't matter… We reveal our private nature by the décor of our fantasies.

What concerns me as I write is the fact that I felt very comfortable admitting Molinier into my private pantheon of Occultural Saints alongside Brion Gysin, William S. Burroughs, Austin Osman Spare and Hans Bellmer. So much so that when Colin Naylor, who at that time was editor of *Art and Artists* magazine, invited me to co-edit with him what turned out to be an encyclopedic reference book called *Contemporary Artists* that ended up over 1000 pages long, I insisted, "Only if you promise to include Brion Gysin and Pierre Molinier". St James Press/Macmillan's struck the deal and my small contribution to these artists' vindication was sealed.

Once I met Jean-Pierre Turmel through his immaculately precious series of interventional projects *Sordide Sentimental* I found a truly kindred spirit, as they say. Not only in his public championship of marginalized arts and music, nor just through his intelligent insistence that mediums, messages, experiments, transgressive alchemists of all persuasions benefit from cross-fertilization but because even his most private fetishized obsessions paralleled my own in an uncanny manner. Through Jean-Pierre I was able to visit *L'Oeil Fertile*, and actually buy various rare and limited catalogues of Molinier's work and discover that for once my expectations were fully satisfied. His guerilla darkroom of desire exploded across my visual cortex and embedded its mercurial mandalas in mobius patterns of sensual shrapnel. The visceral wounding of my aesthetic was orgasmic and permanent. Certain congruences and convergences of image were to be forever occupied by his touch. It was fortunate that I had developed my own manner of collaging to a place I felt confident about, so his beachhead into the unconscious didn't rattle me too much. For in his explorations of the most basic of all subjects... The human body... He applied patterns and interplays so meticulously, that felt as familiar at times as my own, and those of Lady Jaye with her sequential Polaroid landscapes of flesh.

I have always believed, with fervor similar to spiritual faith that art must be indivisible from inner authentic LIFE, that to create is an act of devotion. The first book of the bible is the *Book Of Creation*. It proposes, quite clearly that *Creation* is the fundamental *raison d'être* of existence, indeed that the very nature of the original explosive release of nothingness is the source of all particular interactions considered as living ever since. Our imagination struggles to construct a picture to represent this moment. When artists try, they tend to use a blossoming rosy rose, various mandalas come to mind, ripples flowing outwards from a centre. All of them strive to give us maps of invisible locations. Just as the existential mystery of how could something come from nothing and fill everything as we try to comprehend a Universe, so the same questions arise as we try to create an image to explain and describe ourselves, human beings.

Ancient humans wondered how did we come from within women from nothing? We didn't understand the connection of sexual release (as it was initially) and procreation until relatively recently when women "discovered" linear time via their menses. The interplay of male and female was always central to artistic endeavor. As if by repetition we might reach a mitigating comprehension and merge into unity instead of being endlessly at the whim of the rage of binary perception. Ancient stories tell of a perfect first race of beings, all hermaphrodites, created in the image of "God". Then these beings are shattered into two separate halves, male and female. This dies-integration is symbolized by the double helix of DNA, or of the caduceus of medicine (the reduction of life to mechanics). Despite the beauty implicit in the way male and female fit together, like continents driven apart by geological plates shifting catastrophically, we have worshipped biological difference and designed societies founded in all things binary. Our vision is filtered by spectacles of inertia.

Yet we have built a technological environment in which we reside that worships evolutionary progress and pretend to be fueled by change. We are trapped into assuming co-option and commodification are dynamics of change. They are not. This text has not got space to unravel all those contradictions but I move through them to suggest the vital importance of Molinier's (and some others') alternative imagery for the human body.

Molinier has seized the means of perception (as Lady Jaye says...) and re-configured it. Everything becomes raw material, malleable and neutral. There is no specific gender anymore. No male or female, merely surfaces and a canvas of skin stretched across multiple skeletal frames. The frame of reference, the "classic" and "male" nude is gone. Evaporated into painterly gestures. Lipstick is slashed across one face, more faces. It becomes closer to Japanese calligraphy than to make-up. And what is make-up, but conscious deception? Brion Gysin found his exploration of consciousness and/or light eventually led him to the dreamachine on one hand. The first artwork created that you had to look at with your eyes closed! And abstracted marks tumbling out of deconstructed language in a Pollockian mirage.

A visionary artist is compelled to follow the ultimate prize, the Holy Grail. The Rose Cross! No surprise then that we find mysterious clues to a Masonic connection in Molinier's life. Within the mystery we are driven against a terrifying truth. Death! From nothingness came creation yet it all contains a fatal flaw. Eventual annihilation. Even a Universe must end. The artists try to make sense and use their senses to speak with our senses. Realizing that time is short and nothing is as it seems, they are forced to use metaphors and symbols.

The irreversible compulsion of Molinier's montages, where men become women, become clones of themselves, become animalistic, become erotic, become gross, become romantic, generates a maelstrom of fluid possibilities. We are in the eye of his tornado, red slippers flash past, a witch, a dildo, a mask always a mask. Pierre Molinier insists we face the impenetrable fact of our obliteration. Yet simultaneously he describes a frolicking masqued ball, a carnival of interchangeable characters. All of who can be him and equally therefore all can be ourselves as well.

As we enter an era, suggested by the artist Breyer P-Orridge as of *Pandrogeny*, Pierre Molinier's work will become ever more relevant. He has bequeathed us a primitive language of sorts, a profound imagery with which to reconcile our evolutionary necessity to change. Not just adjust our current ineffectual systems but to totally surrender our attachment to the biological loop that perhaps once enabled our Darwinian maturation but now cripples our options for any survival at all. But we cannot, must not, expect to look, feel or function the same.

As one navigates the photographic simulacra of Molinier's exquisite work, the repeated hints of mandalas out of more mundane raw material I wonder if this is more than a balancing effect but also might touch upon a sense of urgency within materialist cultures to unravel linear versions of time and consensus reality before we hurtle headlong into disaster as a species because we still insist on applying an over-riding picture of cultures being linear as well? Art like Molinier's and similar works (like Steven Leyba, Stelarc, Breyer P-Orridge, Orlan) attempt to solve this auto-destructive trajectory by proposing both a vision of time as a congregation of loops and looping that in themselves require a sense of responsibility for a future as we might all experience just that! And by proposing a massive rethink of our attitude to the human body. A final declaration that it is *not* sacred in any way, merely, as Lady Jaye reminds us, a cheap suitcase to give mobility to consciousness. Furthermore, a cheap suitcase that breaks down faster the more you "travel".

Molinier's multiple combinations of bodies in particular insist we mutate, immerse our *Self* in potentia. His maps describe a tumultuous reconstruction of our physical self-image. They propose eroticism over replication and androgeny as a natural, even preferred state. He implies DNA and experience spiraling and also he proposes mutation, deliberately engineered in order to divert behavior patterns that are catastrophic if left unchecked. Our patterns of existence must change at a molecular level; our cultural passion for obliteration must be transformed.

"Kreeme Horn"
In Praise Of The Grotesque

Genesis Breyer P-Orridge

"There are those of us who make a bitter pretence of loving life whilst suffering the deepest torment and anguish at sharing any moment with the sentimental herd. Sauntering stupefaction is our lot. A shadowless existence illuminated by altruistic horrors of charity and compassion. We are homely, and disfigured by the sheer intensity of our hideous impulses. Our greatest achievements are validated by their degree of monstrosity. We are as deformed as the compassionate wrath of your wild "God" and are marred only by the curdling curse of remaining still human despite our most cruel efforts. There can be no kindness within our emotions, no hesitation in our violence. No joy in the blessings and wonders of nature. We are foul, loathesome, offensive, repugnant and harsh. We are the ugliness, the disconnected. We are the awkward, the disgraceful. We are the ugliness, the disenchanted."

"ALL BEAUTY IS OUR ENEMY "
"ALL BEAUTY IS OUR ENEMY"

AH, MY FRIENDS, THESE ARE NEEDFULLY SADISTIC TIMES. PETTINESS RULES EACH DAY AND BLATANT CORRUPTION IS EMBLAZONED IN THE HIGHEST PLACES AS QUITE FORGIVEABLY VIRTUOUS.

THE CHARMED LIVE EMPTY LIVES AND THE REPLETE LIVE CHARMINGLY. AND IS THIS NOT ALL DREADFULLY APPROPRIATE? BRUTALLY ENTERTAINING?

IN THOSE MYTHICAL QUAGMIRES OF MORBID OCEAN SO LONG AGO I WOULD SOONER CONCUR THAT IT WAS A MOLECULAR UGLINESS THAT PARASITISED CARBON AND GAVE IT PRETENSION. NO SPLENDOUR OF LIGHTENING NOR ANGELIC CREATURES WITH AN IMPOSSIBLE FERVOUR FOR DEFEATISM.

THESE LAUGHABLE DREAMS UPHOLD BEAUTY AS A QUINTESSENTIAL GOLDEN THREAD IN A MAZE OF WEAK NOBILITY. NATURE IS OUR MOTHER SUCKLING US AS PURE UNTAINTED INFANTS IN A PERFECT GARDEN SPOILED ONLY BY THE ERRORS OF A FEW EMPOWERED BY OUR MYSTERIOUS FLAW. OUR DESTINY TO FIND OUR WAY BACK TO

THE LIGHT AND ESCAPE THE UGLY DEMON SO UNSPEAKABLY HID-
EOUS AT THE BLACK CENTRE OF OUR BEGINNINGS.

YEAH RIGHT! I DONT THINK SO..!

OH, THIN INSIPID LULLABYS OF COMPLIANCE! DO WE NOT SEE THE
RIPPING FLESH OF COUNTLESS PRETTY CREATURES AS THEY BECOME
SUSTENANCE FOR THE GROTESQUE LUST ALL BODIES REQUIRE AS
AN INDEFATIGABLE RIGHT? THERE IS NO BEAUTY HERE. NO HIGHER
PURPOSE THAN LIMITLESS DEVOURING AND MUTILATION. THE PRO-
GRAM, DEAR BLINKERED FRIENDS, IF PROGRAMME THERE IS, IS SUR-
VIVAL. SURVIVAL BY ASSIMILATION. SURVIVAL BY ANNIHILATION. SUR-
VIVAL BY ABOMINATION. THIS IS OUR LOT. OUR MORTALLY WOUNDED
BLIND ENDEAVOUR. THERE IS NO DIGNITY HERE, NO HONOUR IN
THIS GROTESQUE CARNAL CRAVING.

AH YES! BUT WAIT, TELL ME QUICK, YOU ARE HERE TO SAVE US ALL,
YOU ARE OUR PRIEST, OUR LIGHT, OUR CONSCIENCE, OUR EYES. THE
SELFLESS CREATOR OF BEAUTIFUL THINGS, YOU SAY?

SEE BEAUTY IN EVERYTHING, YOU SAY. STOP! RIGHT THERE LET ME
REMIND YOU OF THAT YOU WOULD EXHALE. THOSE WHO FIND BEAU-
TIFUL MEANINGS IN UGLY THINGS ARE CORRUPT WITHOUT BEING
CHARMING. THEY ARE IRREDEEMABLY PATHETIC. THIS IS A FAULT.
THESE MEDIOCRITIES ARE OUR DOWNFALL.

CREATOR OF GROTESQUE THINGS.
REVEAL THE GROTESQUE.
CONCEAL BEAUTY.
TRANSLATE GROTESQUE THINGS.

THE LOWEST FORM OF CREATIVITY IS THE DECEPTION AND CONCEIT
OF PERPETUATING ANY FORM OF FAITH IN BEAUTY.

THEY ARE THE ELECT TO WHOM GROTESQUE THINGS BRING ONLY
RAPTURE!
THOSE WHO FIND GROTESUQE MEANING IN UGLY THINGS ARE THE
CULTIVATED. BLESSED ARE THEY FOR THEM THERE IS SALVATION.

THE GROTESQUE IS NEVER MORBID. THE GROTESQUE CAN EXPRESS
EVERYTHING. IT IS THE DELUDED SPECTATOR NOT LIFE THAT THE
GROTESQUE MIRRORS. NEVER FORGIVE THE LIAR THE JUDAS THAT
ASSERTS THAT SUCH A THING AS BEAUTY EXISTS. ALWAYS, ALL WAYS,
WITHOUT HESITATION, WORSHIP THE SAINTLY TRUTH THAT ONLY
UGLINESS EXISTS.

THOSE HIGHER QUALITIES REVERED BY THOSE WHO DEMONSTRATE NONE OF THEM, THESE ARE FOR THE LIVING DEAD, ZOMBIES WHO WOULD TRUDGE FOREVER IN THE MORTUARY SLIME THEY SLURP AS IF IT IS DIVINE NECTAR.

DEFILED ARE THEY. THOSE WHO REMAIN AT THE SURFACE DO SO AT THEIR OWN PERIL. THOSE WHO DIVE BENEATH ALL SURFACES GLO-RIFY THE GROTESQUE, UPROOTING UGLINESS TO BE THEIR HEROIC STANDARD.

BE WARNED, YOU ARE MARRED, MISSHAPEN AND MEASLY. YOUR DESPARATION IS DISFIGURED DEVOTION. YOUR BEAUTY IS THE EN-EMY. ACCEPTANCE OF THE GROTESQUE IS THE REDEMPTION OF SAN-ITY. THERE IS NO BEAUTY ONLY UGLINESS. THERE IS NO GLAMOUR ONLY GHASTLY BLEMISH. ALL ROMANCE DISFIGURED. ALL MORALS MONSTROUS! ALL BEAUTY OUR ENEMY!

THEY ARE THE ELECT TO WHOM GROTESQUE THINGS BRING ONLY RAPTURE!

INELEGANT EPISTLES:

1. Careless Idle Chatter
2. Merely Nodding
3. Raw Mode Of Life
4. Rumour And Dishonour
5. Ugliness Is A Form Of Genius

"ALL BEAUTY IS OUR ENEMY"

Translator's Postscript (to Remy de Gourmont's "The Natural Philosophy of Love")

Ezra Pound

Il y aurait peut-être une certain corrélation entre la copulation complète
et profonde et le développement cérebrél.[1]

Not only is this suggestion, made by our author at the end of his eighth chapter, both possible and probable, but it is more than likely that the brain itself, is, in origin and development, only a sort of great clot of genital fluid held in suspense or reserve; at first over the cervical ganglion, or, earlier or in other species, held in several clots over the scattered chief nerve centres; and augmenting in varying speeds and quantities into medulla oblongata, cerebellum and cerebrum. This hypothesis would perhaps explain a certain number of as yet uncorrelated phenomena both psychological and physiological. It would explain the enormous content of the brain as a maker or presenter of images. Species would have developed in accordance with, or their development would have been affected by the relative discharge and retention of the fluid; this proportion being both a matter of quantity and of quality, some animals profiting hardly at all by the alluvial Nile-flood; the baboon retaining nothing; men apparently stupefying themselves in some cases by excess, and in other cases discharging apparently only a surplus at high pressure; the imbecile, or the genius, the "strong-minded."

I offer an idea rather than an argument; yet if we consider that the power of the spermatozoid is precisely the power of exteriorizing a form, and if we consider the lack of any other known substance in nature capable of growing into brain, we are left with only one surprise, or rather one conclusion, namely, in face of the smallness of the average brain's activity, we must conclude that the spermatozoic substance must have greatly atrophied in its change from lactic to coagulated and hereditarily coagulated condition. Given, that is, two great seas of this fluid, mutually magnetized, the wonder is, or at least the first wonder is, that human thought is so inactive.

Chemical research may have something to say on the subject, if it be directed to comparison of brain and spermatophore in the nautilus, to the viscous binding of the bee's fecundative liquid. I offer only reflections, perhaps a few data; indications of earlier adumbrations of an idea which really surprises no one, but seems as if it might have been lying on the study table of any physician or philosopher.

There are traces of it in the symbolism of phallic religions, man really the phallus or spermatozoid charging, head-on, the female chaos; integration of the male in the

---

1 "There might be, perhaps, a certain correlation between complete and profound copulation and the development of the brain."

male organ. Even oneself has felt it, driving any new idea into the great passive vulva of London, a sensation analogous to the male feeling in copulation.

Without any digression on feminism, taking merely the division Gourmont has given (Aristotelian, if you like), one offers woman as the accumulation of hereditary aptitudes, better than man in the "useful gestures," the perfections, but to man, given what we have of history, the "inventions," the new gestures, the extravagance, the wild shots, the impractical, merely because in him occurs the new up-jut, the new bathing of the cerebral tissues in the residuum, in *la mousse*[2] of the life sap.

Or, as I am certainly neither writing an anti-feminist tract, nor claiming disproportionate privilege for the spermatozoid, for the sake of symmetry ascribe a cognate role to the ovule, though I can hardly be expected to introspect it. A flood is as bad as a Translator's Postscript famine; the ovular bath could still account for the refreshment of the female mind, and the recharging, regracing of its "traditional aptitudes"; where one woman appears to benefit by an alluvial clarifying, ten dozen appear to be swamped.

Postulating that the cerebral fluid tried all sorts of experiments, and, striking matter, forced it into all sorts of forms, by gushes; we have admittedly in insect life a female predominance; in bird, mammal and human, at least an increasing male prominence. And these four important branches of "the fan" may be differentiated according to their apparent chief desire, or source of choosing their species.

Insect, utility; bird, flight; mammal, muscular splendour; man, experiment.

The insect representing the female, and utility; the need of heat being present, the insect chooses to solve the problem by hibernation, i.e. a sort of negation of action. The bird wanting continuous freedom, feathers itself. Desire for decoration appears in all the branches, man exteriorizing it most. The bat's secret appears to be that he is not the bird-mammal, but the mammal-insect: economy of tissue, hibernation. The female principle being not only utility, but extreme economy, woman, falling by this division into a male branch, is the least female of females, and at this point one escapes from a journalistic sex-squabble into the opposition of two principles, utility and a sort of venturesomeness.

In its subservience to the money fetish our age returns to the darkness of mediaevalism. Two osmies may make superfluous eggless nests, but do not kill each other in contesting which shall deposit the supererogatory honey therein. It is perhaps no more foolish to go at a hermit's bidding to recover an old sepulchre than to make new sepulchres at the bidding of finance.

In his growing subservience to, and adoration of, and entanglement in machines, in utility, man rounds the circle almost into insect life, the absence of flesh; and may have need even of horned gods to save him, or at least of a form of thought which permits them.

Take it that usual thought is a sort of shaking or shifting of a fluid in the viscous cells of the brain; one has seen electricity, stripping the particles of silver from a plated knife in a chemical bath, with order and celerity, and gathering them on the other pole of a magnet. Take it as materially as you like. There is a sort of spirit-level in the ear, giving us our sense of balance. And dreams? Do they not happen precisely at the

---

2 Mousse (Fr) = foam (Eng)

moments when one has tipped the head; are they not, with their incoherent mixing of known and familiar images, like the pouring of a complicated honeycomb tilted from its perpendicular? Does not this give precisely the needed mixture of familiar forms in non-sequence, the jumble of fragments each coherent within its own limit?

And from the popular speech, is not the sensible man called "level-headed," has he not his "head" well screwed on or "screwed on straight"; and are not lunatics and cranks often recognizable from some peculiar carriage or tilt of the headpiece; and is not the thinker always pictured with his head bowed into his hand, yes, but level so far as left to right is concerned? The upward-jaw, head-back pose has long been explained by the relative positions of the medulla and the more human parts of the brain; this need not be dragged in here; nor do I mean to assert that you can cure a lunatic merely by holding his head level.

Thought is a chemical process, the most interesting of all transfusions in liquid solution. The mind is an up-spurt of sperm, no, let me alter that; trying to watch the process: the sperm, the form-creator, the substance which compels the ovule to evolve in a given pattern, one microscopic, minuscule particle, entering the "castle" of the ovule.

"Thought is a vegetable," says a modern hermetic, whom I have often contradicted, but whom I do not wish to contradict at this point. Thought is a "chemical process" in relation to the organ, the brain; creative thought is an act like fecundation, like the male cast of the human seed, but given that cast, that ejaculation, I am perfectly willing to grant that the thought once born, separated, in regard to itself, not in relation to the brain that begat it, does lead an independent life much like a member of the vegetable kingdom, blowing seeds, ideas from the paradisial garden at the summit of Dante's *Purgatory*, capable of lodging and sprouting where they fall. And Gourmont has the phrase "fecundating a generation of bodies as genius fecundates a generation of minds."

Man is the sum of the animals, the sum of their instincts, as Gourmont has repeated in the course of his book. Given, first a few, then as we get to our own condition, a mass of these spermatozoic particles withheld, in suspense, waiting in the organ that has been built up through ages by a myriad similar waitings.

Each of these particles is, we need not say, conscious of form, but has by all counts a capacity for formal expression: is not thought precisely a form-comparing and form-combining?

That is to say we have the hair-thinning "abstract thought" and we have the concrete thought of women, of artists, of musicians, the mockedly "long-haired" who have made everything in the world. We have the form-making and the form-destroying "thought," only the first of which is really satisfactory. I don't wish to be invidious, it is perfectly possible to consider the "abstract" thought, reason, etc., as the comparison, regimentation, and least common denominator of a multitude of images, but in the end each of the images is a little spoiled thereby, no one of them is the Apollo, and the makers of this kind of thought have been called dryasdust since the beginning of history. The regiment is less interesting as a whole than any individual in it. And, as we are being extremely material and physical and animal, in the wake of our author, we will leave old wives' gibes about the profusion of hair, and its chance possible indication or sanction of a possible neighbouring health beneath the skull.

Creative thought has manifested itself in images, in music, which is to sound what the concrete image is to sight. And the thought of genius, even of the mathematical genius, the mathematical prodigy, is really the same sort of thing, it is a sudden out-spurt of mind which takes the form demanded by the problem; which creates the answer, and baffles the man counting on the abacus.

I question the remarks about the sphex in Chapter 19, "que le sphex s'est formé lentement,"[3] I query this with a conviction for which anyone is at liberty to call me lunatic, and for which I offer no better ground than simple introspection. I believe, and on no better ground than that of a sudden emotion, that the change of species is not a slow matter, managed by cross-breeding, of nature's leporides and mules, I believe that the species changes as suddenly as a man makes a song or a poem, or as suddenly as he *starts* making them, more suddenly than he can cut a statue in stone, at most as slowly as a locust or long-tailed Sirmione false mosquito emerges from its outgrown skin. It is not even proved that man is at the end of his physical changes.

Say that the diversification of species has passed its most sensational phases, say that it had once a great stimulus from the rapidity of the earth's cooling, if one accepts the geologists' interpretation of that thermometric cyclone. The cooling planet contracts, it is as if one had some mud in a tin pail, and forced down the lid with such pressure that the can sprung a dozen leaks, or it is as if one had the mud in a linen bag and squeezed; merely as mechanics (not counting that one has all the known and unknown chemical elements cooling simultaneously), but merely as mechanics this contraction gives energy enough to squeeze vegetation through the pores of the imaginary linen and to detach certain particles, leaving them still a momentum. A body should cool with decreasing speed in measure as it approaches the temperature of its surroundings; however, the earth is still, I think, supposed to be warmer than the surrounding unknown, and is presumably still cooling, or at any rate it is not proved that man is at the end of his physical changes. I return to horned gods and the halo in a few paragraphs. It is not proved that even the sort of impetus provided by a shrinking of planetary surface is denied one.

What is known is that man's great divergence has been in the making of detached, resumable tools.

That is to say, if an insect carries a saw, it carries it all the time. The "next step," as in the case of the male organ of the nautilus, is to grow a tool and detach it.

Man's first inventions are fire and the club, that is to say he detaches his digestion, he finds a means to get heat without releasing the calories of the log by internal combustion inside his own stomach. The invention of the first tool turned his mind (using this term in the full sense); turned, let us say, his "brain" from his own body. No need for greater antennae, a fifth arm, etc., except, after a lapse, as a *tour de force*, to show that he is still lord of his body.

That is to say the crawfish's long feelers, all sorts of extravagances in nature may be taken as the result of a single gush of thought. A single out-push of a demand, made by a spermatic sea of sufficient energy to cast such a form, to cast it as one electric pole will cast a spark to another; to exteriorize; sometimes to act in this with more enthusiasm than caution.

---

3 "... that the sphex has formed itself slowly". A sphex is a type of "digger" wasp. *–Ed.*

Let us say quite simply that light is a projection from the luminous fluid, from the energy that is in the brain, down along the nerve cords which receive certain vibrations in the eye. Let us suppose man capable of exteriorizing a new organ, horn, halo, Eye of Horus. Given a brain of this power, comes the question, what organ, and to what purpose?

Turning to folk-lore, we have Frazer on horned gods, we have Egyptian statues, generally supposed to be "symbols," of cat-headed and ibis-headed gods. Now in a primitive community, a man, a volontaire, might risk it. He might want prestige, authority, want them enough to grow horns and claim a divine heritage, or to grow a cat head; Greek philosophy would have smiled at him, would have deprecated his ostentation. With primitive man he would have risked a good deal, he would have been deified, or crucified, or possibly both. To-day he would be caught for a circus.

One does not assert that cat-headed gods appeared in Egypt after the third dynasty; the country had a long memory and such a phenomenon would have made some stir in the valley. The horned god would appear to have persisted, and the immensely high head of the Chinese contemplative as shown in art and the China images is another stray grain of tradition.

But man goes on making new faculties, or forgetting old ones. That is to say you have all sorts of aptitudes developed without external change, which in an earlier biological state would possibly have found carnal expression. You have every exploited "hyper-aesthesia," i.e, every new form of genius, from the faculty of hearing four parts in a fugue perfectly, to the ear for money (*vide* Henry James in *The Ivory Tower*, the passages on Mr. Gaw). Here I only amplify what Gourmont has indicated in Chapter 20. You have the visualizing sense, the "stretch" of imagination, the mystics – for what there is to them – Santa Theresa who "saw" the microcosmos, hell, heaven, purgatory complete, "the size of a walnut"; and you have Mr. W., a wool-broker in London, who suddenly at 3 a.m. visualizes the whole of his letter-file, three hundred folios; he sees and reads particularly the letter at folder 171, but he sees simultaneously the entire contents of the file, the whole thing about the size of two lumps of loaf sugar laid flat side to flat side.

Remains precisely the question: man feeling this protean capacity to grow a new organ: what organ shall it be? Or new faculty: what faculty?

His first renunciation, flight, he has regained, almost as if the renunciation, so recent in terms of biology, had been committed in foresight. Instinct conserves only the "useful" gestures. Air provides little nourishment, and anyhow the first great pleasure surrendered, the simple ambition to mount the air has been regained and regratified. Water was never surrendered, man with subaqueous yearnings is still, given a knife, the shark's vanquisher.

The new faculty? Without then the ostentation of an organ. Will? The hypnotist has shown the vanity and Blake the inutility of willing trifles, and black magic its futility. The telepathic faculty? In the first place is it new? Have not travellers always told cock and bull stories about its existence in savage Africa? Is it not a faculty that man has given up, if not as useless, at any rate as of a very limited use, a distraction, more bother than it is worth? Lacking a localizing sense, the savage knowing, if he does, what happens "somewhere" else, but never knowing quite where. The faculty was perhaps not worth the damage it does to concentration of mind on some useful subject. "Instinct preserves the useful gestures."

Take it that what man wants is a capacity for clearer understanding, or for physical refreshment and vigour, are not these precisely the faculties he is forever hammering at, perhaps stupidly? Muscularly he goes slowly, athletic records being constantly worn down by millimetres and seconds.

I appear to have thrown down bits of my note somewhat at random; let me return to physiology. People were long ignorant of the circulation of the blood; that known, they appeared to think the nerves stationary; Gourmont speaks of "circulation nerveuse," but many people still consider the nerve as at most a telegraph wire, simply because it does not bleed visibly when cut. The current is "interrupted." The school books of twenty years ago were rather vague about lymph, and various glands still baffle physicians. I have not seen the suggestion that some of them may serve rather as fuses in an electric system, to prevent short circuits, or in some variant or allotropic form. The spermatozoid is, I take it, regarded as a sort of quintessence; the brain is also a quintessence, or at least "in rapport with" all parts of the body; the single spermatozoid demands simply that the ovule shall construct a human being, the suspended spermatozoid (if my wild shot rings the target bell) is ready to dispense with, in the literal sense, incarnation, en-fleshment. Shall we postulate the mass of spermatozoids, first accumulated in suspense, then specialized?

Three channels, hell, purgatory, heaven, if one wants to follow yet another terminology: digestive excretion, incarnation, freedom in the imagination, i.e. cast into an exterior formlessness, or into form material, or merely imaginative visually or perhaps musically or perhaps fixed in some other sensuous dimension, even of taste or odour (there have been perhaps creative cooks and perfumers?).

The dead laborious compilation and comparison of other men's dead images, all this is mere labour, not the spermatozoic act of the brain.

Woman, the conservator, the inheritor of past gestures, clever, practical, as Gourmont says, not inventive, always the best disciple of any inventor, has been always the enemy of the dead or laborious form of compilation, abstraction.

Not considering the process ended; taking the individual genius as the man in whom the new access, the new superfluity of spermatozoic pressure (quantitative and qualitative) up-shoots into the brain, alluvial Nile-flood, bringing new crops, new invention. And as Gourmont says, there is only reasoning where there is initial error, i.e. weakness of the spurt, wandering search.

In no case can it be a question of mere animal quantity of sperm. You have the man who wears himself out and weakens his brain, echo of the orang, obviously not the talented sieve; you have the contrasted case in the type of man who really cannot work until he has relieved the pressure on his spermatic canals.

This is a question of physiology, it is not a question of morals and sociology. Given the spermatozoic thought, the two great seas of fecundative matter, the brain lobes, mutually magnetized, luminous in their own knowledge of their being; whether they may be expected to seek exterior "luxuria," or whether they are going to repeat Augustine hymns, is not in my jurisdiction. An exterior paradise might not allure them. "La bêtise humaine est la seule chose qui donne une idée de l'infini,"[4] says Renan, and Gourmont has quoted him, and all flesh is grass, a superior grass.

It remains that man has for centuries nibbled at this idea of connection, intimate connection between his sperm and his cerebration, the ascetic has tried to withhold all his sperm, the lure, the ignis fatuus perhaps, of wanting to super-think; the dope-fiend has tried opium and every inferior to Bacchus, to get an extra kick out of the organ, the mystics have sought the gleam in the tavern, Helen of Tyre, priestesses in the temple of Venus, in Indian temples, stray priestesses in the streets, unuprootable custom, and probably with a basis of sanity. A sense of balance might show that asceticism means either a drought or a crowding. The liquid solution must be kept at right consistency; one would say the due proportion of liquid to viscous particles, a good circulation; the actual quality of the sieve or separator, counting perhaps most of all; the balance and retentive media.

Perhaps the clue is in Propertius after all:

Ingenium nobis ipsa puella fecit.[5]

There is the whole of the XIIth century love cult, and Dante's metaphysics a little to one side, and Gourmont's *Latin Mystique*; and for image-making both Fenollosa on *The Chinese Written Character*, and the paragraphs in *Le Problème du Style*. At any rate the quarrel between cerebralist and viveur and ignorantist ends, if the brain is thus conceived not as a separate and dessicated organ, but as the very fluid of life itself.

---

4 "Human stupidity is the only thing that gives an idea of the infinite."
5 Literally, "The girl herself inspires the song". In this context, "With love itself as the sole inspiration". – *Ed.*

Poems for The Fenris Wolf

Stephen Ellis

Circular Breathing

I can love nothing now save bewitching water. (Narcissus)

There is always
some 'bounce' there,

in priestess mode
of getting up

more horns to turn
cornucopia,

the flow always
to be sorted

for later, and more
of the same.

The trick is
to let the grapes

begin to sweat,
and just as they do,

consume them
all, before they

have a chance
to wither. Anyone

can get the pitch
of a human voice,

but there are also

free voices, coming

from the sky.
We hear human

voices, but feel
the vibration of

angel matter from
another world

resonating across
the tension that plays

human sinew like
it was harp strings.

Ejaculation is
not just some

'relieving idea'
that forces upward

and out the strain
of release that sets

a birthing stain
upon the world.

Release is meant to
strengthen

and illuminate the interior
of each embrace.

If I feel my own
heartbeat, it seems

like I'm playing
the lead, but

when I hear yours,
I know we're 'playing

the bells' of
something beyond

individual capacity.
I don't mean

that the earth will
tremble. I mean

that the innocent
blush of a discovering

kiss from
the youth that lives

in each of us
will bring forward

the particulars of
a double-hearing,

of the voice that
leads you, and your own,

that leads, for
it is left to

experience to know
prudence and restraint,

while real virtue
is the fingers and teeth

that know, in
endless practice,

how holiness is but
the small hairs

that grow from
the delicious places

where fever makes
trees go green,

and the gods give you
to your abandon.

—w— —w— —w—

Pitch

Locations remain
true, though

memory fails them,
whether alert

and powerful
on the roof of

Al-Aqsa mosque
with the whole

city with its
stink and musty

illuminated yellow
air before you,

or humbled and lost
in the Cairo

train station,
the whole transmission

is in what lies
between, what you

enclose and what
encloses you, what is

before you,
and what came before

you arrived. Human
skin is touched

from the inside,

THE FENRIS WOLF

as well as from

the more usual
light winds of

spring training
that arrive sharply

from ancient
Phrygian mountain

passes. Home
is not where

the heart alone
passes daily muster.

There ought to be
a room for every

organ, and for
every organ, at least

two new senses,
and for each sense,

several fine
companions, etc,

that this is how
the house is

built, this is
how the music is

made, more Marsyas
than Apollo, and one

(one hopes) that can
read the Coptic

inscriptions dressed
in gold to know

the inlaid gold
formations of sex.

The midday meal
will be a modest

affair, a small
bowl of honey with

yogurt mixed,
to give sharpness

and pattern to
the sweetness,

with sprinkles of
sumac over

the top, to give
a dark red after-

effect to
the bitterness

tenderly realized
in the satisfaction

of finding it is
no longer there.

Invisible Twins

Of pain, there is
that born of

intimacy, and that
born of distance.

The combination of
the two yields

THE FENRIS WOLF

a phantasmagoric
'middle' that constitutes

a body of consideration
not easily grasped,

our daily air, inhaled,
exhaled, impossible

to let go of, for it,
as we in it, are

sustained by
the barren pattern

of feeling from it
our own human

warmth. Wasn't it
Yeats who noted

that time's passage
was less like

a clock's pendulum
marking tic-toc

fashion how monotony
never passes

but marks us with
our own carnal

commonness, and more
like twin bobbins

on some cosmic
sewing machine

on which time's
threads are perpetually

wound and unwound
in active accumulation

and loss? It is
very like Penelope's

weaving of her
dowry rug by day,

while undoing it
by night, in

the inevitable delay
of waiting for

what will come as
inevitably complete.

The one act restores itself
in the other, yet

there is never
a time in which one

side is full in lieu
of the emptiness

of the other. There is
just the raw

sinew of the body,
readied for what

cannot be explained.
When I stand

outside at dusk,
I hear an ambiguous

hum upon the air,
and feel in my being

the threads shifting
in their poise

from one spindle to
the other. Blood

The Fenris Wolf

cuts through my veins
very like the way

these threads run
unseen through

the sounding air.
Love is this steady

lyric, and feeling it
gives authenticity

to its loss, another
kind of presence

dancing in the mind
like a delicate

ant queen, moving first
to the left, then

to the right, as if
charm alone was what

could draw the distant
relations of the planets

close, just as my
senses are close to

me. When the senses
reverse themselves,

the whine of chaos
returns from the other

side, and we are
left, as close to this

present as we were to
a previous fullness

that rose within
that we thought best

to leave undisturbed,
that is now

disturbed, from
nothing we had actually

done. The sun's
rise is not a personal

accomplishment, but it
intimately warms

one's human face,
and brings a painful

authenticity to
snow that has yet

to fall, a spring
that continues to

rise underfoot from
the past, and the steady

hum of heavy traffics
out on route 13.

—w— —w— —w—

Entry Visa

In our little
town are tire tracks

across muddy
fields, the smell

of rotting hay
and streaks on

the windowpanes
you only notice

when you stand

THE FENRIS WOLF

outside the house.

I stick a single
finger in the air

in front of me
to help me believe

that ripples
in a distant pond

take part in causing
my personality.

The sky is grey
but the air is

clear. Memory
takes the diesel

stink of the tractor
across the street

weaving back
and forth over old

blonde fields
and forms from it

the mechanical throb
of engines

beneath my feet
on the ferry back

from Chios, and evokes
the happiness of

returning east,
toward some sense of

home, left just
twelve hours before,

but which remains
still bright in heart

and sense, as if
I knew where it

was, and was going
there, as there was

in the rise of
expectation,

the fact of facing
an equivocal terror

in traverse brightened
only by the reflection

of the ferry's double
row of running lights,

that I was leaving
the sunset far behind.

—⁕— —⁕— —⁕—

Hoar Frost

The tree trembled
when we leaned

against it
from opposite

directions, and felt
our fingertips

accidentally touch:
The green depths

of those heights
is the mother of

birdsong, and our ears

THE FENRIS WOLF

hear always

the same star,
shining in

the center of
our ulterior

mysteries and their
on-going, practical

separations.
Greedily, I ate

more berries
than could fall

naturally from such
high places,

picked most of
the rest

ruthlessly and for
myself, and in

filling my
pockets with

the unbearable
lightness of

endless eros,
subtly exchanging

sun for moon
as solid life

for perfect
fluency, found later

that I had
without knowing it,

stained my pants
with the limits of dusk.

ADDENDA TO 'THE WESTERN GATE'

Like a tidy bundle come apart, the sticks of a former forest fall in a complete circle around me, suddenly free to realize the actual extent of feeling caged.

Dawn, dimness and brightening doves fall silent and rise. The sun is white, and goes yellow where it hurts, and blinding orange where, as the pale inner lining of a tangerine recently peeled, my skin is hidden but for the hunger that leaves across it a few black, undecipherable spots.

In the folds of my brain, a river under shade trees from a former life flows to cool them down.

Happiness can be a bad omen.

Their wings shuddered and my heart unfolded in a venturing toward sweet comfort that was always a step ahead.

Dirty foam at the edge of the lake gave off a scent that swarmed up in the poverty of our superior air.

We wore grey, and the small sliding wooden peek-a-boo windows in the doors of the after-hours clubs on Rainbow Street, even these were shut against letting the sun help realize their interiors.

The horse has maggots. The wound deepens.

When will you ever find out where this pedestrian fear of empty boxes comes from?

A genie lives in a sleeping voice, with its endlessly lingering tears.

It must be possible to dream something beyond a sea too wide and too long to feel on waking, the edges and distant end of it.

Rainwater writes our soil out.

Oblivion is a kind of lamentation of return.

There are parts of the human body that will always be round, anonymous and quiet.

In a small boat's river passage, you imagine under canvas flaps a cargo of sleeping eels, and you imagine how a horse might think.

Harvest is a wedding ring cut at noon with a pair of blue-handled wire cutters.

Soil becomes sand with lightning buried beneath, becomes a woven carpet whose designs have faded almost completely away, from which islands begin to rise.

Wade in the water and spit into the land, and watch for your vehicle to arrive.

The box is empty, because you distributed too evenly all that could be taken from it, just to know how little there is left, without knowing where it went.

It becomes increasingly difficult to remember who 'I' is the name for. A human nervous system gone upsidedown is silhouetted in the form of a tree against a fading evening sky.

Giving has something to do with making room for the growth of trees whose names and forms one is not yet familiar with.

Tomorrow, you will have the name that comes through the passage that brings you there. Arrival can leave a bad taste in your mouth. Remember always the tiger lily, and resist always, the rush to culture resident in the splendor of unfolding names.

The dead have their grip on everyone. That alone, is reason enough to celebrate.

—◊— —◊— —◊—

RESOLVE

What, in perception, is a true object? And what is the truth of perception itself? (anon.)

Hospitality invites
a necessary

annihilation of
the self, and makes

a whole through which
generosity can

operate. The lips
of each generation

pass this
incompletely down:

Jafar showed Jabir
who whispered it

in the ear of
Hallaj, who was

watched over by
Junayd. The writing

is on the wall,
like stars are

in the sky, incipient
always, but

taking in the end
a single day more

than a lifetime
to actively know.

But there is
a shortcut, they say,

if you wish to
abbreviate living into

the curt truth of
an understanding:

Ask nothing of
another, take nothing

from another,
and remain in the clear

abandon of having
nothing to give anyone.

Humility

The roebuck
and the rowanberry:

That these two
touch constitutes

the ignition
and initiation of

of a whole
mythology. As life

folds in upon
itself and moves

outward in expansion,
the heart is

burnished by
the simple fact of

continuing to be
a mirror in which

the gods and goddesses
renew the opportunity

of seeing their
faces as the human

antithesis of our
knowing their knowledge

of themselves in us is
equally our own.

—m— —m— —m—

Tantra

To be born
in a human body

is a gift
that fires

the absorption of
all that

surrounds
and makes it

different by
simple contrast.

You see yourself
in sleep

as in a river
whose water always

leaves your
reflection in

the holding pattern
of repetition:

You look the same
in image, yet

your substance
forever

leaves itself
in order to stay

that way. A raft
and a mirror are

not so different:
The currents

that carry each
are hard and swift

and about to
carry you to

the place where
you already are.

Is death really
a part of life?

You will not know
by being carried

down a river, or
staring at

a reflection that
can do nothing

but stare back
at you. It is

better to stare
at a piece of

wood, and learn
to call it a tree,

than to drag
your image

through the customs
house, and think

you've achieved
safe passage.

Doves swallow
hot coals for want

of a bright star
to guide them,

and this is
to rouse their

morning song, that
we might also know

that the singular
lotus of the void

will take you in
like a smoking lamp

plunged into
a vat of icy milk.

—⁊— —⁊— —⁊—

Mel Lyman:
Breakthrough with the Mirror Man

Hiram Corso

Melvin Lyman was born on March 24, 1938. Zodiacally speaking he was an Aries. He grew up in Oregon and it was there that he attended a junior college. He moved to California and was married in 1955 at the age of 17. He then took a job as a computer technician. It wasn't long before he became disillusioned with the conventional life-style and in 1961 he quit his job and began a quest for meaning of a more substantial nature. He settled in Asheville, North Carolina, and through Obray Ramsey mastered his technique on the banjo. It was through these travels that he developed a network of like-minded individuals. Lyman was a student of human nature and at this point had acquired an innate understanding in his search for meaning within his life and aimed at improving the human condition. Initially it was through music that he was able to connect with his spiritual center.

Lyman began his communal living experiment in spring 1963 living near Brandeis College in Waltham, Massachusetts. He appeared to have come from an Appalachian background with a simplicity and earthy demeanor and was dressed casually in an army jacket. He was quite adept on his numerous harmonicas and also upon the banjo. It was at this early juncture that Lyman became an Acid therapist as a guide/mentor of LSD trip sessions. He had an innate understanding of how to get into the mind of the acid experimenter and had the ability to release the stored pain and suffering to allow the energy to flow unimpeded. During this time he acquired a charisma, which accelerated his already dynamic personality to become a force of nature. He would advise the LSD experimenters to see him after they had been tripping for five hours. It was at that point that he was able to have untrammeled access to their deepest psyche and was free to impart his unorthodox therapeutic methodology.

From 1963-1964 Mel Lyman frequented Timothy Leary's Newton Center. He became quite proficient both as a participant in the LSD experience and as a guide during these sessions. In his studies of cosmic consciousness he came to the realization that he was god – or in other words he achieved that uppermost vibrational level which signifies god consciousness. Through these experiences he gained significant understanding and illumination and realized a greater purpose in his life. He had a singularity of the focus of his will and gained the ability to transform his environment through sheer intent and the power of his mind. It was a role which Mel felt uniquely prepared to inhabit. He had the certitude and determination to have achieved the highest levels of conscious awareness.

One aspect of the mental processing involved in guided LSD sessions was to build up the ego of the individual so they were able to see themselves as a superior being and one who was able to transform the world by becoming a transmitter of Mel's philosophy. He gave them a strength to become empowered yet fostered reliance upon himself as their foundation and as a beacon of wisdom.

After leaving North Carolina he sent his first wife Sophie to the west coast. His second wife Judy came apart under the pressure which was perhaps a combination of the powerful LSD trips combined with the dynamics of Mel's intense lifestyle. She moved back to Kansas in the summer of 1963. This is emotionally reflected in Mel's journals of this period and was published in *Mirror at the End of the Road*. *Mirror* offers a glimpse into the formative years of Lyman's life, fully examining his times of self-doubt and isolation and provides an insight into his later stature as 'soul of the world'. Shortly after Judy left, Mel was hired by Jim Kweskin to play banjo in his Jug Band amalgamation. By this point Kweskin had become a big draw for Harvard undergrads in Club 47, located in Cambridge, which was the center of the burgeoning folk music movement. Within a short time Mel became the spiritual essence within the band due to his compelling nature and uncompromising vision.

In 1965, at the Newport Folk Festival, Mel played a 20 minute heart-felt rendition of *Rock of Ages* as the audience began to file out. This symbolic gesture made a wordless statement of sending waves of unity to the audience, who had become disillusioned that day as Bob Dylan "sold out" to the folk music purists as he gave an electrified rock music performance. It was an impulsive move as he stepped back onto the stage alone. In a sense he felt compelled to do this as a means of accepting responsibility by manifesting a soul-baring performance.

During Mel's developmental phase he discovered the divine nature in music. It was through the Jim Kweskin Jug Band that he was able to concentrate this ability to transfer thought-forms within these transmissions to effect the consciousness of listeners and requiring them to feel in a deeper, more profound level than ordinary music demands of the listener.

When approaching a recording or video production it was of utmost importance to 'create consciously' or in other words harness the spirit by spontaneously incorporating the energy of others participating in the recording, thereby becoming able to tap into the source of inspiration (projecting from the higher self) to effortlessly allow the creativity to flow forth. Mel wrote that 'There is always an order in life. Life is the reflection of that order as man is the reflection of God. It takes a long time to find the meaning in our day to day activities but in reflection we will always detect the moving finger that traced the pattern we have followed, there is a plan. Every man is his own unique part of the plan, every life has a purpose. Lives that seemingly were lived with no kind of purpose at all might have simply served the purpose of distinguishing purpose by lack of purpose, it all fits together in some crazy way.'

Mel, becoming the unspoken leader of the Kweskin Jug Band, led them on an entirely different course than would have evolved had he not been a part of the band. It brought them into many tenuous situations in the performer/audience dialectic. The band was concerned with channeling the energy of those in the audience. Oftentimes these concert goers were confused and hostile to the fact that at the beginning of the show they were met with a mute band who waited an interminable length of time before they sensed some sort of connection to flow between them and the audience before they would deem it fit to begin playing. They were sometimes met with sermonizing upon the virtues of Mel Lyman by Jim Kweskin before the show got underway. From Kweskin's perspective the anger emanating from the crowd formed a union or magical link with them, which enabled them to 'feel', and at this juncture a connection had been made so it would be possible to play. It was a dictum of Mel's that through a destructive act a symbiosis was established which could lead to a deeper understanding. By experiencing emotional pain, anger, isolation or confusion and then overcoming it would lead to a greater perception of truth.

Lyman's message was that people have to live with their loneliness, pain and suffering and within that framework they should focus on work to improve the situation.

The philosophy Mel utilized when it came to music recordings was to allow for spontaneity and he approached it with conscious intent. The focus was to capture the inspirational spirit. This is especially evident with the U & I band recordings as well as *Birth* which exudes an eerie late-night vibe.

He drew people to Fort Hill through his writings in *Avatar* (later *American Avatar*). It was there that they learned 'hill philosophy', Mel's unique perspectives upon dealing with life to fulfill one's potentiality. The hill congregation was constantly involved in the hard labor of construction on the many Fort Hill properties and further manifesting Mel's message to the world through a variety of media. They were constantly under a pressure by higher level members which served to transform them into accepting personal responsibility for the propagation of the philosophy of the Lyman Family and catering to its continued prosperity.

It was Mel's column in the *Avatar* magazine, entitled 'To All who would Know', which revealed an insightful look into the Lyman philosophy. Astrology was an important methodical science utilized heavily within the Lyman Family and its use revealed great insights into motivations of family members as well as outsiders based upon their astrological attributions.

He also had a cantankerous, adversarial side and when it came to a battle of wills Mel was completely unrelenting. On one occasion he was served with an eviction notice in Boston, so he chose to stay on the property for months merely out of the principal. When Mel took interest in an individual who came to him for advice he was able to provide for them a greater sense of importance and depth of purpose in understanding one's life. His pragmatic yet mystical approach penetrated their deepest psyche. Mel radiated an intensity which was unmeasured in any other sort of human interaction.

One early girlfriend of Mel's during the early formative period of the Lyman Family was Jessie Benton who was the daughter of Thomas Hart Benton, the famous and quite wealthy artist. It was through Jessie that Mel acquired a property on Martha's Vineyard which was used as a retreat. Eventually the Lyman Family developed a corporate entity known as United Illuminating, Inc.

It was through *Avatar* that many people first came to hear about Mel. *Avatar* was named after Meher Baba who was often referred to as the 'Avatar of the Age'. Originally it was a Boston underground newspaper which was run by both members of the Lyman

Family and non-members from the counter-cultural scene. Mel never frequented the office of *Avatar* and wasn't actually on the editorial board, but he was the spiritual presence behind the paper and often contributed his writings, as did many others from the Lyman Family. *Avatar* later augmented its format (issues 18-23) so that it had an outer section comprised of news from the underground, and an inner supplementary section devoted to the writings of Mel. Its contents also included other news and writings from members of the Fort Hill community. He quickly became a contentious figure in the Boston area while simultaneously becoming an underground celebrity. *Avatar* began publication in 1967 and its first few issues were published from the *Broadside* magazine headquarters. When it became time to publish issue 24, Mel instigated a spiritual war with the non-Lyman Family element of the paper. This lead to a schism on issue 25. All except about 1000 copies of the 45,000 copies were stolen by angry Lyman Family members. After the fallout a lavishly printed magazine called *American Avatar* was published. There were a total of four issues which were released from October 1968 to summer 1969.

Mel was able to attract a number of influential personalities to the Lyman Family philosophy. The most notable example of course is Jim Kweskin who lived his life to fulfill the needs of Mel Lyman. Other notable people within the fold include: Paul Williams who was quite famous as a rock journalist for *Crawdaddy*, Owen de Long who was a former speech writer for Robert Kennedy, Don West, an assistant to the CBS president, and Mark Frechette who starred in the Antonini film *Zabriskie Point*. Paul Williams was actively involved within the family but eventually became dismayed by having to start at the bottom rung of Lyman's evolutionary system despite his prestige as an acclaimed writer. Richard Herbruck was the producer of the Lyman Family and in fact was the alter-ego of Mel. He produced many productions including the *Jim Kweskin's America* album.

Mel's first book, *Autobiography of a World Savior* (Jonas Press, 1966), was published by underground filmmaker Jonas Mekas. It began as a fable with sci-fi overtones and was written as an inside joke for several Scientologist friends of his. The introduction is quite illuminating and provides an insight into Mel's mindset at the time:

> Loneliness is the sole motivation, the force that keeps man striving after the unattainable, the loneliness of man separated from his soul, man crying out into the void for God, man eternally seeking more of himself through every activity, filling that devouring need on whatever level the spirit is feeding, the arena of conflict, be it flesh, thoughts, aspiring to ideals, man searches for love to satisfy his gaping hunger, an ever IN-CREASING hunger because the spirit devours flesh, exhausting every last outpost of hope and the conquest must always necessarily search for higher ground. The only pain is separation and the only joy is breakthrough and the battle only really begins when man has finally, through exhaustion, worn out every tangible means, devoured everything in sight and arrived right back where he started with an empty belly and a world with no food, having cried all of his tears and standing completely naked

and alone knowing full well that there is no comfort outside of himself, that he must walk that lonesome valley BY himself with no kind words, no friendly faces, no helping hands, only then does one begin to fully realize the meaning of utter loneliness, it's difficult, it's the most difficult stage a man will ever have to face and it is inevitable that all will someday have to face themselves and make that terrible decision. Few have ever succeeded as yet and those few we call world saviors, our enlightened leaders who threw themselves unresistingly into the black void, learned the meaning of faith, and in time found a light, their own INNER light, and WITH that light they forever tempt us to follow.

In the opening paragraphs of *Autobiography*, Mel states that he was sent on a mission to the earth to raise the vibrational spirit of every living being. In this book Mel states that there are three stages in the evolution of the mind of man. The first was called the 'concrete mind' which dealt with the ability to manipulate one's environment on the material plane to satisfy their needs. The second stage is the 'abstract mind'. This second race of man purposely sought to not concern themselves with the material level whatsoever and was more consciously fixated within their own imaginings. The third stage was a unification between the concrete and the abstract mind which harmoniously balanced the intellect with one's desires and was a path to spiritual fulfillment.

In Lyman's system adversity only strengthens a man's character. This is one reason he chose to relate the many introspective journal entries during the travels of his youth in *Mirror at the End of the Road*. His role was to manipulate members to become what they were in order to eliminate institutional conditioning and dig down to the core of the personalities. When Lyman interacts one-on-one or with a group of people he follows a process where he will wait for a 'need' to surface before he begins a transaction. He has remained silent during interviews for over an hour waiting for the need to become apparent. Once the interaction becomes on a personal level the fronts and preconceived perceptions can be eliminated and intensive communication can begin. When he begins a performance with his band there is always initially a separation between Mel and the audience. From his perspective merely to begin entertaining is false because it denies the separation and chooses to create a superficial unity. By waiting until the interaction gets to a visceral, emotional level a personal unity can occur. This approach is a way of perceiving from a 'consciously creative' perspective by entering into an unknown situation where anything may possibly occur. By opening the door to the unknown dimension a true transfer of energy can freely occur without any sort of pretense or artifice. This is a discovery for both parties involved and while it is a potential risk, the exchange transcends the known limitations and expectations. This is the heart of true creativity. Part of the induction into the Lyman Family involves being placed in uncomfortable situations to force the individual to use their intuition to overcome the obstacles which impede their progress.

The fundamental approach the family took was based upon the necessity that arose at any given moment and how they could serve to satisfy this need most efficiently. This primary consisted of group members striving to meet any requirement that Mel may have demanded at any given moment.

Many television documentaries were produced by Lyman Family members. Mel even went so far as wanting to take over CBS and formative plans were actually made toward this goal. The family operated within a crucible – a conversation quickly devolved into a confrontation which magnified the apparent indiscretions until the interrogee cracked under the pressure. Secrets weren't tolerated and it was strictly limited to a group dynamic where everyone's motivations were transparent. Life was approached communally and any sort of separatist mentality was quickly nipped in the bud – particularly any coupling or personal relationships which didn't have official sanction from Mel or higher up members.

At group dinners bulletins were read which were instructions and words of wisdom imparted by Lyman. The Karma Squad was an elite security team within the Lyman Family whose presence was a constant reminder to anyone whose transgressions worked against the aims of the family. One of their responsibilities was to make people 'feel' when they showed signs of repressing their true underlying emotions. It was also the responsibility of family members to share their understanding of Mel's message with fellow family members so that they could all be in accord when it came to applying the principles of Lyman's methodology. They were expected to profoundly have understood Mel's writings and truly have grasp the meta-meanings beyond the plethora of discourses which Mel regularly imparted to his followers.

A person must first embrace the pain of existence before they are able to feel anything beyond it. To live a meaningful existence, man must approach life as an endless quest to perfect oneself to the level of becoming a living example of the truth upon which Mel sermonized, and living consciously in the 'now'. It is a constant struggle to live at this emotionally raw level of existence and is a lifelong endeavor. Members of the Fort Hill community were emblematic of these aspirations and their unorthodox approach was underlain by a pragmatic spiritual zeal which strove against complacency and sought to fully integrate ones highest aspirations as a living testament to the form of 'god' which Mel radiated. One aspect of Mel's statement that he was God was not to be merely regarded as an overblown ego of megalomaniacal dimensions, but rather was sincerely earnest and concerned with living his life as an example – as one who is wholly focused on spiritual pursuits while being very much a part of the material world simultaneously. In this sense Mel was a 'Mirror Man' who was a reflection of one's own attempts to unite with the higher self and living in a perpetual state seeking to attain this goal.

Mel was able to destroy illusions of the self, so that the true self was able to be nurtured and have the possibility of evolution. He found that this was his calling to wake people up in the Gurdjieffian sense. To quote Mel: 'I'm out to transform the kind of pride that destroys transformation and destroy the kind of pride that transforms destruction. Got It!'

Mel Lyman died in April 1978 of causes which remain unknown to all except the Fort Hill Community members. The exact nature has never been disclosed to the public. It has been suggested that he may have suffered a long-term malady which progressively worsened. There was no actual death certificate or funeral service. There has even been speculation that Mel may have faked his own death to evade public scrutiny and moved to Europe. One of Mel's last writings are indicative of his impending death: "I know I'm done and I'll stop keeping that body alive... It really is a lot of dead weight and I don't feel it's got much more use, do you know what I'm saying. I was Emerson, I was Lincoln, I was Woody Guthrie and many more but only for short periods of time and I used those instruments because they were ready for me and I used Mel Lyman in the same way and I am nobody, I just am. Don't be sad, I'll be Mel Lyman as long as I can and in fact I may bring him back with a bang and light him up like a neon bulb and if I don't it's because it wasn't and if I do we will have a real Melvin Christ on our hands..."

Plea For Courage

Mel Lyman

We should be entering the new world, all the preparations have been made, it has all been written about and everybody wants it, it is so easy to imagine. A world where everybody loves each other and all motion is towards harmony and there is no more war or hate or fear and everybody is together all the time. It is very easy to imagine.

Yet here we sit in a grey and tumbling world out of place and bursting with song! What happened? We all saw it on LSD. A new consciousness was definitely born. Are we just experiencing the long dry waiting period? Why haven't things changed very much? Nixon is still a stale turd atop the most ridiculous decaying government that ever pretended to lead anything more than a procession of baboons to the slaughter since man first realized he needed order to survive. The Viet Nam war goes on and on and on. Hair gets longer, music gets louder, dope gets stronger, people get sillier, life still goes on and on and on. Perhaps we didn't want ENOUGH. Perhaps we have settled for too LITTLE. Perhaps what we REALLY wanted had nothing to do with everything we THOUGHT we wanted. Perhaps the new world hasn't really even BEGUN yet!

And it hasn't. We're still mired in the death and decay of the OLD one. We're still looking to the new one for something we didn't get out of the old one, we're trying to make a new deal for old goods, we're not READY to enter the Kingdom of Heaven. But why do I even bother to tell you all this at all, no one ever listens to me, you're all too full of dope and pride and ideas and yourselves to know what's even good for you anymore. You will read this piece and go away completely unchanged, probably even a little MORE smug than you already are. I really hate you bastards cause you're killing me, you're stinking up the whole world with your filthy hair and dirty clothes and empty slogans and phoney smiles and false achievements and long lost glory. It's over, man. You didn't make it. Why don't you kill yourself?

It used to be: "graduate from high school, go to college". Now it's: "graduate from high school, go to heaven". Nothing is sacred anymore, everything is cheap, including sex, love, religion and honest accomplishment. We have lost respect, we have no values, all things are equally worthless. I don't know what to do about this mess we're in, there are no answers, most people think everything's just fine. The few who know our deepest needs are still unfulfilled are regarded with great suspicion and contempt for not allowing people to "do their own thing". I don't want you to do your own thing, I want you to do MY thing, WAKE UP!

It's incredible! A whole generation of people who grew up with ABSOLUTELY NOTHING TO DO! There is nowhere to go and nothing to do. Education is a farce. Marriage and good jobs and a secure future fill no real need. It is all over before we have even BEGUN. The world is going to FILL UP WITH TRANSIENTS! And then what? A whole generation of people who grew up in a world they can't live in. It's AMAZING! So what do they do, they try to DIE in it. And what SHOULD they do? They should try and make it fit to LIVE in!

The injustice and decay that you are going to have to fight if you are to stay alive would stagger your imagination if you were only aware of it. The whole world is against you, it only wants to die in peace and it will do anything to keep from living, and it will kill you, if you're not already dead. It has seduced you into believing there is a purpose to all this suicide, a condemned and dying culture is trying to take you with it, AND YOU'RE FALLING FOR IT! We were talked out of a Revolution, even the blacks succumbed, they took the good jobs and college diplomas and laid down their arms, AND THEIR HEARTS. You have sold your souls at a mean price, you have been ACCEPTED! And so now we have a whole race of dying hippies and dying blacks, the Revolution has been safely put out and the world can settle back into dying peacefully again. Even our "free press" has fallen into the hands of the living dead. You would be surprised if you really knew who's running things, the same old dollar, AND NOTH-ING ELSE! The same dollar that we set out to stamp out has stamped US out and we never even realized it, we lost the war in the first battle and the victors have been kind enough to let us live on reservations with plenty of dope to keep us pacified. There is no hope without organization, the world is dying and we must get together and fight this creeping decay. And it's everywhere, EVEN IN YOU!!!

But it won't do us any good to march on the Capitol, and it won't do us any good to try and stop the war in Viet Nam, that's THEIR WAR, ours is here at home. We've got to stop fighting each other and fight the common enemy. We've got to get all these little communities that are forming all over the country into one BIG COMMUNITY. We've got to stop filling up the woods and streets looking for dope and love and get to know each other and start helping each other and start keeping each other awake and stop letting ourselves off so easy and stop thinking we're right and we don't have to do anything about it but just love everybody, we DO have to do something about it, we've got to FIGHT FOR OUR LIVES. Get together with your friends, pool your resources, make some money, buy a house, take on some responsibilities, learn to FIGHT for what you believe in, stop doping yourselves up, stop looking for a Utopia, look around you with clear eyes and make some clear decisions, THE ENEMY IS WITHIN! We have to start a new life here, we cannot live in this dying structure, it will kill us, it has already killed itself. Our only weapon is inner strength, a small group of people with a great deal of determination can transform the world, be the NEW Christians, fight for your life, fight for love, fight for a new world, fight for room to breathe, the Heart of God is a vast darkness that only the brave can know, this is a plea for courage, WE MUST GET TOGETHER AND FIGHT THIS CREEPING DECAY!

Plea for Courage

Something as It Really Is

Mel Lyman

I am going to burn down the world
I am going to tear down everything that cannot stand alone
I am going to turn ideals to shit
I am going to shove hope up your ass
I am going to reduce everything that stands to rubble
and then I am going to burn the rubble
and then I am going to scatter the ashes
and then maybe SOMEONE will be able to see SOMETHING as it really is
WATCH OUT

THE DAUGHTER OF ASTROLOGY:
THE YIJING AND THE DEVELOPMENT
OF GEOMANTIC DIVINATION

Gary Dickinson

Search for Knowledge, even as far as China. (The Prophet Mohammed)

In a letter to Gerald Yorke dated 28 May 1942, Aleister Crowley wrote that he had found 'identities' between certain Tarot cards, hexagrams of Yijing and Geomantic figures. Crowley told Yorke:

> This is exceedingly important from the point of view of official science, as it demonstrates beyond doubt that these independent systems reach the same conclusions, and therefore that they all represent a reality in Nature, not an arbitrary set of artificial conventions. I assure you that one day this will be the corner-stone of the scientific acceptance of the fact of Magick.[1]

Crowley assumes that the ancient Chinese oracle, the Yijing or 'Book of Changes', and the European divinatory system known as Geomancy were quite independent of each other. They appear to have arisen in very different cultures and at different times. As both are binary systems, they share obvious characteristics. But could they actually be historically linked?

Today, Geomancy has been virtually forgotten; even the term 'geomancy' has been appropriated relatively recently to describe Chinese *fengshui* practices. But, from the 12th to the late 17th century, Geomancy was the most widespread and popular form of divination in Europe after horary astrology and rejoiced in the epithet 'The Daughter of Astrology'.

Geomancy had a brief revival in the late 19th century when MacGregor Mathers incorporated geomantic divination into the curriculum of the Hermetic Order of the Golden Dawn. Mathers took the system's association with the element earth literally and, in his highly ritualised method of consultation, the hierarchies of Malkuth, the lowest and densest of the Qabbalistic sephira, are invoked. Too literally perhaps; the difficult reputation that Geomancy has suffered from may actually stem from this method of attribution.

---

1 Aleister Crowley to Gerald Yorke, 28 May 1942, Yorke Collection, Warburg Institute, University of London.

Crowley himself, of course, studied and practised the Golden Dawn method. Little wonder the 'Master Therion' found that:

> The geomantic intelligences themselves were of a low order; the scope of their knowledge was confined to a small section of the things which interested Him; also, they possessed a point of view of their own which was far from sympathetic with His.[2]

By contrast, Crowley believed that:

> The I Ching is served by beings free from these defects. The intense purity of the symbols prevents them from being usurped by intelligences with an axe of their own to grind.[3]

The Yijing was not taught in the Golden Dawn. Crowley appears to have discovered the Chinese oracle during his 'Walk Across China' in 1906.

The extent of Geomancy's recent decline is illustrated by the fact that most of the few modern references to the practice compare it to the Yijing, because the Chinese system is now more familiar to even the specialist reader.

Others have seen a close relationship between geomancy and the Yijing. In his paper *Synchronicity*, Jung mentions a 'Western method' based on the same general principle as the Yijing:

> In the Western method, which was known since the thirteenth century as the Ars Geomantica or Art of Punctuation and enjoyed a widespread vogue, there are no real commentaries, since its use was only mantic and never philosophical like that of the I Ching.[4]

Even the great sinologist Joseph Needham observed that the symbols of Geomancy are 'distinctly reminiscent of the trigrams and hexagrams of the I Ching'.[5]

But are these apparent similarities between the Yijing and Geomancy evidence of a much closer, historical connection between the two systems? Or, as Crowley believed, are the two systems independent corroboration of a universal principle in Nature?

The answer to this question is a complex one as it crosses the boundaries of several fields of study. However, it appears to me that we have to establish a possible time-frame for any connection that might have occurred. We also need to establish that such a cultural exchange was indeed possible during that time-frame and look for specific evidence for that cross-pollination of ideas.

---

2 Aleister Crowley: *Magick*, Samuel Weiser, 1994, p. 252
3 *Ibid.* p.254
4 C. G. Jung: *Synchronicity, An Acasual Connecting Principle*, Ark, 1987, pp.52-53
5 Joseph Needham: *Science & Civilisation in China*, Cambridge University Press, 1954 onwards, Vol. V:4 (1980) pp. 471-472

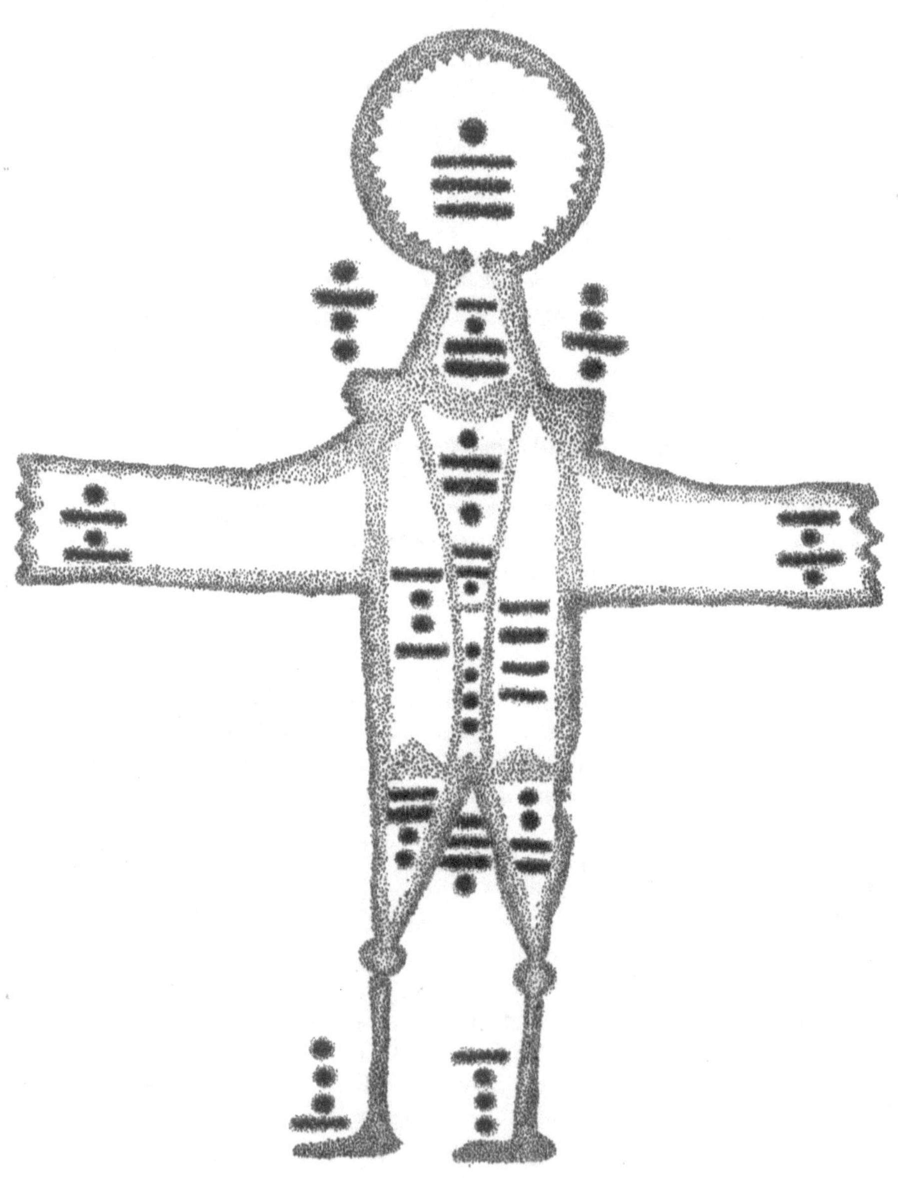

An 18th century Islamic talisman showing the 16 geomantic figures correlated with various parts of the body.

ORIGINS

We can trace the historical development of the Yijing from its earliest, probably oral, transmission a thousand years before the text was written down through to the elaborate structure raised upon it over subsequent thousands of years. Comparatively, Geomancy might just as well have washed up on the shores of Moorish Spain during the 12th century sealed in a bottle like the jinn from *The Tales of One Thousand & One Nights*.

In fact, Geomancy is another 'oriental' divination system whose origin lies in the shifting sands of the desert. One of the problems with tracing its origins is the very fugitive medium of the art itself; figures made in the sand are not by their very nature eternal monuments. Fortunately, what scholarly research is available is of a high calibre. I cite in particular the pioneering work of Emilie Savage-Smith and Marion Smith[6], the first scholars to take the subject seriously, and the works of Stephen Skinner.[7]

There is no doubt that European Geomancy is of Islamic origin. Wherever Geomancy occurs in the Near-East and Africa, whatever cultural adaptations it undergoes locally, Arab trade routes are the common link.

Hugh of Santalla's *Ars Geomantiae* (c. 1150) is the earliest known surviving work on Geomancy in any language. But Hugh himself attests to its Islamic origin although he does not give us the date or authorship of the text which he translated.

That Hugh was the first European to translate an Arab work on Geomancy into Latin is shown by the difficulty he has in translating the Arabic name of the system, *Khatt al-Raml* or 'Elegant Marks in the Sand', which finally renders as 'geomancy', literally 'to divine by the Earth'. Hugh also adopted the 16 zodiacal/elemental houses and 28 Lunar Mansions of Islamic astrology.

The earliest physical evidence of Geomancy lies in the pre-Islamic Safaitic inscriptions dating from the third to the sixth centuries C.E. The word *rammal*, 'a sand diviner', occurs on these inscriptions in personal titles. This would suggest that some form of sand divination was practiced before the rise of Islam, though we know nothing of its form.[8]

A splendid instrument used to calculate the divinatory figures rather than a book is the earliest evidence of Islamic Geomancy. Dated 1241 C.E., a century after Hugh of Santalla's translation of a lost Geomantic text, this splendid device is now in the British Museum. Made of a brass alloy beautifully inlaid with gold and silver, it was probably made in Mosul (in present day Iraq) and is signed by Muhammad ibn Khutlukh al-Mausili.

Savage-Smith & Smith note similarities between the configuration of the small inlaid silver circles of certain Geomantic figures on the instrument's dials and the constellations of the lunar mansion with which they are associated. Other non-geomantic Islamic sources also graphically illustrate some constellations in forms that closely resemble a Geomantic figure. Chinese constellations have, of course, long been drawn as linked dots or circles.

---

6 Emilie Savage-Smith & Marion B Smith: *Islamic Geomancy and a Thirteenth-Century Divinatory Device.* Undena Publications, c.1980

7 Stephen Skinner: *Terrestrial Astrology: Divination by Geomancy.* Routledge & Kegan Paul, 1980

8 Savage-Smith & Smith, p.4 (n.11)

The use of the 28 lunar mansions and the similarities between Geomantic figures and the constellations with which they were associated, and indeed the Chinese notation of star groupings are interesting. It may indicate an origin of the Geomantic figures as representations of theoretical 'constellations'. This becomes important later when we look at purely numerological Chinese systems of 'astrology' linked with the Yijing.

The concept of Geomancy being a form of 'terrestrial astrology' continued in the European tradition as late as the Renaissance. Whilst, for Crowley, 'every man and every woman is star', according to the 16th century Geomancer Christopher Cattan, "everie pricke [point] signifieth a Starre".[9]

HERMES IN CHINA

The traditional history of the Yijing claims it as the oldest of the Chinese classics by virtue of the discovery of the eight trigrams on the shell of a tortoise by the legendary Fuxi. His great antiquity is shown in representations of him as having rudimentary horns and dressed in garments made of leaves and animal skins. In some ancient accounts Fuxi himself doubles the trigrams to form the 64 hexagrams, whilst others credit Shennong, Fuxi's equally mythical successor and the first man to till the earth. Many centuries later Jesuit missionaries in China, the first Westerners to translate the Yijing, identified Fuxi with Hermes Trismegistus.

According to Arabic legend, it was the Archangel Gabriel who taught the art of Geomancy to Idris, who is sometimes identified with Hermes Trismegistus. Very interestingly there is an Islamic tradition that Idris lived in China. A letter attributed to the 12th century Moorish alchemist Ibn Arfa' Ra tells us that:

> The real name of Hermes was Ahnuh (Enoch) and also Idris (Adam's son)... He was a dweller in the upper land of China, as the author of the 'Particles of Gold' pointed out, where he says: 'Mining was looked after by Hermes in China, and Aris found out how to protect the workings from flooding by water'. Now Aris lived in lower China, and belonged to the first of the Indians.[10]

That India is apparently synonymous with 'lower China' in the writer's mind may itself be significant because, according to tradition, Idris passed the secrets of Geomancy to Tumtum al-Hindi. This legendary figure is frequently cited by Islamic writers on Geomancy and has other, alchemical texts attributed to him. There has been some debate over who 'Tumtum' was. Some believe that the name is a corruption of 'Ptolemy' but 'al-Hindu' certainly identifies him as being Indian.

The mythological history of Geomancy continues with Khalaf al-Barbari the Elder, said to have travelled to India to study the works of Tumtum, where he died in 634 C.E. at the ripe old age of 186. Before his death he passed Tumtum's secrets to Nasir al-Din al-Barbari the Younger.

---

9 Christopher Cattan: *The Geomancie of Maister Christopher Cattan Gentleman.* First Book, Chapter 1, trans. Francis Sperry, 1591
10 Needham: Vol. V:4, p.412

In summary, the tradition cited by many Islamic writers places the origin of Geomancy in the East, somewhat vaguely identified with China/India.

The names of the semi-legendary Elder & Younger al-Barbari have suggested to some scholars that Geomancy has Berber origins. The Berbers of the Maghrib in North Africa were considered by the Arabs to be a mysterious people, skilled in the arts of magic and divination. Several other well-known, but later, Geomantic authors have names which might indicate Berber origins. Shaikh al-Zanati, the 12th or 13th century (?) master of Geomancy, and Ahmad ben 'Ali Zunbul, the 16th century writer, may have belonged to Berber tribes.

Attempts to define Geomancy's place of origin also rely on some of the names of the 16 Geomantic figures being Berber. But, as Savage-Smith & Smith have pointed out, often the so-called Berber words that occur in Geomantic works are simply bad Arabic.[11] Nevertheless, we should note the apparent connection between the mysterious Berbers and the possible origins of Geomantic divination.

Ja'far al-Sadiq & the Isma'ili

Another Islamic tradition credits the invention of Geomancy to an historical rather than a legendary figure. Ja'far al-Sadiq (c. 699-765) was the sixth and last Imam to be universally recognised by all Shi'ah sects as invested with the Prophet's spiritual authority. A number of early Geomantic texts are attributed to him.

Crowley's boyhood hero, Sir Richard Burton, the great explorer, orientalist and translator of the *1001 Nights* noted: "The Arabs call it [Geomancy] El-Raml, and ascribed its present form to the Imam al-Sadik..."[12]

Needham also noted that Ja'far's name was "persistently associated from the beginning of the ninth century onwards with geomancy (sand divination)" as well as other divinatory arts.[13] More recently, Savage-Smith & Smith, in discussing the various possible origins of Arabic Geomancy, conclude:

> Although the geomantic tract may not be by Ja'far al-Sadiq and his name is seldom cited in later geomantic treatises, the attribution does raise the possibility of there having been some relations between geomancy and the Ikhwan al-Safa' (the Bretheren of Purity), a sect of the Isma'ili who were instrumental in the early propagation of astrology and numerology in the Islamic World.[14]

Ja'far al-Sadiq is reputed to have been the teacher of Jabir Ibn Hayaan (c. 720-815?). Jabir is credited with having written an enormous corpus of alchemical treatises. Many of these were translated into Latin not only at the same time as Arabic works on Geomancy but by the same people, among them Gerard of Cremona and Michael Scot. Jabir's works were to become the foundation of the European alchemical tradition.

---

11 Savage-Smith & Smith, p.3
12 Richard F. Burton: *First Footsteps in East Africa, or Exploration of Harar*. London, 1856, pp. 55-56
13 Needham, Vol. V:4, p.390
14 Savage-Smith & Smith, pp.4-5

The historical existence of Jabir and his identification with his latinised namesake, Geber, are the subjects of intense scholarly debate. One survey of the corpus attributed to him revealed over a thousand works, too large perhaps to have been the labour of one man. Needham believed that the corpus was:

> The work of many different writers with a common philosophical out-look; none can be earlier than about 850 and the whole collection must have been completed not only before 987 but before about 930 because there are quotations in Ibn al-Wahshiya al-Nabati.[15]

Other scholars insist on the historical existence of Jabir. What is not disputed, however, is the contribution that the Jabirian corpus made to European thought, particularly the Sulphur/Mercury theory.

THE SULPHUR/MERCURY THEORY

The medieval alchemist's laboratory may seem a very long way from the pagodas of China but the Jabirian Sulphur/Mercury theory is, to use a favourite alchemical phrase, the 'secret key', that unlocks the mystery of Geomancy's origins and thereby its possible historical link with the Yijing.

The Jabirian theory held that all metals were composed of a combination of Sulphur and Mercury in various proportions. Sulphur was hot, fiery, dry and gaseous whilst Mercury was moist, cool and aqueous. The alchemists hoped that, by altering the proportions of these agents, they might transmute base metals into gold.

Since ancient times, alchemy veiled the creation of the Philosopher's Stone in allegory and revealed the various ingredients and stages in the process by symbols. Colour was an important symbolic language. The so-called White and Red 'Stones' were critical phases in the process. Geber, in the *Investigation of Perfection*, tells us:

> We find Modern Artists to describe us only one Stone, both for the White and for the Red; which we grant to be true: for every Elixir that is prepared, White or Red, there is no other Thing than Argentvive [Mercury] and Sulphur, of which, one cannot act, nor be, without the other...[16]

It is not now thought that the works of 'Geber' are translations of Jabir. However, Geber uses turns of phrase which appear to indicate that he could read Arabic and almost certainly had access to the Jabirian corpus. Clearly here, Geber refers the red stone to sulphur and the white 'argentvive', literally 'living silver', to mercury.

---

15 Needham, Vol. V:4 p.392
16 E. J. Holmyard: *Alchemy*. Dover, 1990, p.136

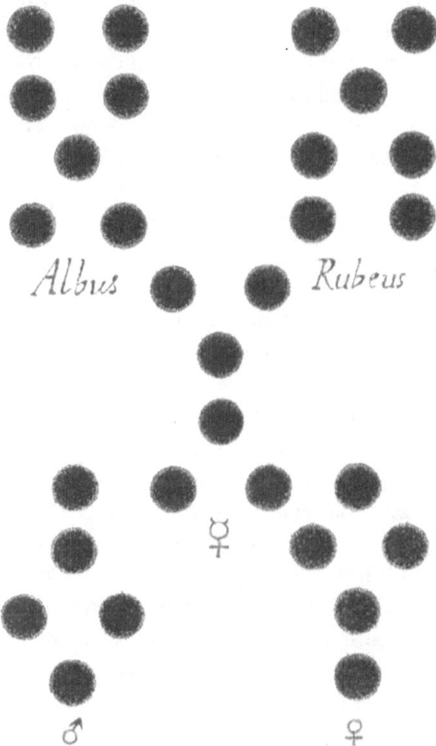

The seven points of the figure Albus *(top left) when added to those of* Conjunctio *(centre) yield the fiery figure* Rubeus *(top right). The polar opposite of* Albus *is martian* Puer *(bottom left) and that of* Rubeus, *the venereal* Puella *(bottom right).*

ALBUS & RUBEUS

Among the 16 Geomantic figures we find *Albus* and *Rubeus*. *Albus* is 'white' in Latin and *rubeus*, 'red'.

The divinatory significance of most of the Geomantic figures, like the trigrams and hexagrams of the Yijing, can be implied from their structures. The downward pointing triangles of *Acquisitio* indicate gain, and are balanced by the reverse figure, *Amissio*, whose upward pointing triangles presage loss. *Populus*, the figure with the highest number of points signifies a gathering, whilst the configuration of *Via* suggests a path or road. In other cases, the divinatory significance of the figure is apparent from its Latin name e.g., *Fortuna Major, Laetitia*, etc.

The significance of *Albus* or *Rubeus* is less easy to interpret from either their structures or names. *Albus* is the reverse of *Rubeus*. Both, of course, have traditional meanings, but these appear to derive entirely from their astrological attributions.

The fiery aspect of Mars in Scorpio lends *Rubeus* a violent and sinister nature; so much so that if it appears in the first house of Geomantic chart, the divination must be abandoned. Red is an instinctive warning colour, its association with blood undoubtedly lending it a dark reputation.

Albus is perhaps even more difficult to understand. Its subsidiary titles in both Arabic and Latin indicate dazzling whiteness, and a blank sheet of paper. Its most common attribution to the sign of Gemini gives us little to judge it by. But traditionally *Albus* is a good figure ruled by the planet Mercury and indicates wisdom, sagacity and clear thought.

Structurally, *Albus* and *Rubeus* can be related to two other figures, *Puer* and *Puella*. The latter are their respective structural opposites. By changing the double and single points of *Albus* and *Rubeus* to their opposites, we find that *Puer* and *Puella* form a set of pairs. *Puer* literally means 'boy'. Its other Latin titles include *gladius erigendus* or 'erect sword'. The configuration of the points might be construed as either a sword or, as Skinner indicates, an erect phallus.[17] Its opposite, *Puella* means 'girl' and carries the meaning of an unstained complexion and virginity.

Paired as structural opposites we see an immediate polarity between the pale *Albus* and the phallic *Puer*, and between the fiery *Rubeus* and the virgin *Puella*. This polarity would also strongly suggest that *Albus* and *Rubeus* correspond to the cool, feminine *argentvive* or Mercury and the hot, masculine Sulphur.

In the Geomantic tradition it is common to combine two figures by the addition of their points to produce a third, often resolving figure. The combination of *Rubeus* and *Albus* results in the figure *Conjunctio*. Graphically, *Conjunctio* appears to be two triangles apex to apex. *Conjunctio* is attributed to the planet Mercury and its generally divinatory meaning is to meet or to assemble but has the deeper significance of a union of opposites. Perhaps even more interestingly, in alchemy 'Conjunctio' is a critical phase in the 'Great Work'; the mystical union of the male and female elements of the Philosopher's Stone. The constellation of *Albus*, *Rubeus* and *Conjunctio* may represent the 'chemical wedding' of philosophical mercury and sulphur.

THE YIJING & CHINESE ALCHEMY

The similarities between the polarity of *Albus* and *Rubeus* and that of Yin and Yang in Chinese cosmology are striking. Originally, *yang* simply meant the sunny side of a hill whilst *yin* meant the shadowy side of a valley. By the fourth century B.C.E. Yin and Yang had acquired a deeper, philosophical significance and, by the first century B.C.E. had become fundamental principles of Chinese cosmology and its applied arts; divination, *fengshui*, medicine and alchemy.

In the Yijing, Yang is represented as an unbroken line made with a single stroke of the brush and Yin as a divided or 'broken' line made with two strokes of the brush. The majority of Chinese alchemical texts use the symbols of the Yijing, its trigrams and hexagrams, to describe alchemical processes.

In Chinese alchemy, or more specifically Daoist alchemy, the quest was not for a Philosopher's Stone that would transmute lead into gold, but the compounding of an elixir of immortality. Daoism is almost unique among the world's religious traditions

---

17 Skinner, p.245

in that it is not concerned with eternal life in the next world but the prolongation of life in this one. That quest began as early as the second century B.C.E. and included the search for mineral compounds that could confer physical immortality, breathing exercises to circulate vital energy within the subtle body, meditation practices aimed at creating a spiritualised body and the ingestion of medicinal herbs that were thought to extend life indefinitely.

The mandarin Ge Hong (283-343 C.E.) was one of China's foremost alchemists. The so-called 'Inner Chapters' of his *Baopuzi*, 'The Master Who Embraces Simplicity', became one of the most influential texts in the corpus of Chinese alchemical literature.

Ge Hong studied the esoteric arts under the renowned scholar Zheng Yin who was himself a disciple of Ge's great-uncle Ge Xuan (164-244 C.E.). Interestingly, Crowley claimed to be a reincarnation of Ge Xuan and adopted this persona to write his 'translations' of Laozi's classic the *Daodejing* ('The Way & Its Virtue'), Ge Xuan's own work the *Qingjingjing* ('The Classic of Purity') and, of course, his own paraphrase of the Yijing.

As a keen natural scientist, Ge Hong engaged in the great cosmological debate of his period, skilfully deploying quotations from the Yijing and using Yijing hexagrams to support the theory that the earth was suspended like a yoke in the centre of a cosmic egg. This debate was of considerable importance for the manufacture of accurate astronomical instruments; not for the purposes of calendrical science but to establish correct timings for the compounding of the elixir.

Ge's work stood in a long alchemical tradition of using Yijing trigrams and hexagrams to demonstrate cycles of time, much which was also incorporated into *fengshui* practices. As early as the second century C.E., the inventor of gunpowder, Wei Boyang, in his commentary on the Yijing, the *Can Dong Qi* ('Three Ways Unified'), aligned the trigrams with the phases of the moon.

It is difficult to find direct parallels with *Albus* and *Rubeus* among the eight trigrams of the Yijing. The trigram *Zhen* ('The Arousing'), which Crowley attributes to the element Fire and the planet Mars, has the bold, often rash nature of *Puer*. And the trigram *Dui* ('The Joyous'), which Crowley attributes to Water and Venus, has the pleasant but sometimes fickle character of *Puella*. However, neither the violence of *Rubeus* nor the wisdom of *Albus* are characteristics of any single trigram.

At least one pairing of Yijing hexagrams, No.s 63 & 64, have a similarly opposite structure and alchemical connotations as *Albus/Rubeus*.

Hexagram 63, Jiji, After Completion

Hexagram 63, *Jiji* ('After Completion') comprises the trigram *Li* beneath its structural opposite, *Kan*. Traditionally, *Li* is a solar trigram attributed to the Chinese element Fire whilst *Kan* is lunar and attributed to the element Water.

The lower trigram *Li* is said to be rising whilst the upper trigram *Kan* is descending.

But rather than dousing the flames, in this hexagram Fire and Water are not seen as being in opposition but in equilibrium.

Trigrams *Li* and *Kan* are used as primary symbols of yang and yin in Chinese alchemy. Their configuration in Hexagram 63 represents the process of heating or refining the elixir in the equivalent vessel to the Western alembic, the *Dantian*.

Hexagram 63 is the only one in the Yijing in which all six lines are in 'correct' positions. Single, unbroken yang lines occupy the odd-numbered positions 1, 3 & 5 whilst divided or 'broken' yin lines occupy the even-numbered positions 2, 4 & 6.

But this perfect equilibrium is a delicate and difficult balance to maintain. Changing the yang lines to yin and vice-versa, effectively reversing the entire hexagram, results in the discordant Hexagram 64, *Wei Ji* ('Before Completion'). The union or equilibrium is broken; *Li* now rises to separate from *Kan* as it sinks down.

There are clearly philosophical parallels between the alchemical symbolism of Yijing Hexagrams 63 & 64 and the constellation of the Geomantic figures *Albus, Rubeus & Conjunctio* that extend beyond the obvious dichotomies of the sulphur/mercury and yang and yin theories.

CULTURAL INFLUENCE

The sulphur/mercury theory and the apparent alchemical symbolism of the *Albus, Rubeus & Conjunctio* 'constellation' provide us with another link between Ja'far, the Isma'ili tradition and the origin of Islamic Geomancy. If indeed *Rubeus* and *Albus* represent the red/white, sulphur/mercury dichotomy then Geomancy, in its developed form, must post-date, or at least be contemporary with, the Jabirian sulphur-mercury theory. This gives us not only a time-frame for possible Chinese influence on Geomancy's development but also an area of common interest; alchemy.

If there was any historical connection between the Chinese and Arab binary divination systems, we might start to look to the ninth century and to the Isma'ili, particularly Jabir, for evidence of that influence. However, before we do so, we must first consider whether such an influence was even possible at that date.

We very often consider Chinese culture in isolation. In fact, the extent of contact between the Near-East and China, particularly during the ninth century, was considerable, affording opportunities for both people and ideas to traverse the physical and cultural gulf that separated East and West.

China under the great Tang dynasty (618-907) was truly cosmopolitan. The capital, Changan, had a population of two million, twice the size of Constantinople, and played host to an international community of 25,000 foreign diplomats, merchants and artisans. Among them were refugees fleeing political turmoil and persecution. Nestorian Christians, Sogdian Zoroastrians and Jews found tolerance and safety in China. Recent research has suggested that even the Tang imperial family itself was not ethnically Han Chinese but descended from a Turkic people originally from China's north-western frontier.[18]

---

18 Samping Chen: 'Succession struggle and the ethnic identity of the T'ang imperial house', *Journal of the Royal Asiatic Society* III (6), pp. 379-406

In the year 878 some 120,000 Muslim, Christian, Jewish and Zoroastrian traders are reported by Abu Zayd of Siraf as resident in Canton, then as now a great southern Chinese port. The Tang poet Zhangji warned a friend leaving for an official appointment in Canton of the 'babble of barbarian voices in the night market'.[19] For a brief period China became literally the centre of the civilised world.

There were two principal routes by which contact between China and the West could be made; a land route composed of a network of caravan roads across Central Asia, the so-called 'Silk Road' and a sea route, the 'Cinnamon Road', to eastern Africa via Vietnam, Indonesia and Ceylon.

The fabled Silk Road across Central Asia, first opened up during the second century B.C.E., was not a single, well-trodden caravan route but a string of cities, settlements and oases linking Lanzhao in north-western China to the ports of Syria and the Black Sea. It did not achieve any cultural significance until the second century C.E. when Buddhist missionary activity established important places of pilgrimage in Central Asia. Among them were the famous cave-temples hewn from the living rock at Dunhuang in Gansu Province.

The Silk Road was, however, economically less important than the southern sea route. The large number of foreign merchants in Canton attests to the volume of trade using the warm currents to carry goods across the Indian Ocean to the ports of Arabia and Eastern Africa. It is believed that the silks worn by Queen Cleopatra during the first century B.C.E were brought to Alexandria by sea rather than land.

Culturally, however, the Silk Road was more significant and provides us with evidence that astrological and divinatory systems based on the Yijing were travelling westwards during the Tang period.

In the early years of the 20th century a library containing over 30,000 manuscripts and the earliest known printed books was discovered in the Cave of a Thousand Buddhas, revealing the extent of both the cultural achievements of the Buddhist community at Dunhuang and the cultural 'traffic' passing along the Silk Road. Some of the manuscripts discovered in this treasure house dated from as early as the fourth century and were already ancient when the library was sealed around the year 1000 C.E.

THE DUNHUANG LIBRARY

Among the manuscripts and books found at Dunhuang were fragments of calendars which carried *Luoshu* diagrams and the names of the eight trigrams of the Yijing.

The *Luoshu* or 'Writing of the Luo River' was a mysterious document or plan that, according to legend, was offered to the mythical Sage-Emperor Yu on the shell of a tortoise that emerged from the receding flood waters of the Luo River. The legend is of considerable antiquity. Even in the *Analects*, Confucius laments that 'the rivers give forth no more diagrams'. But none of the ancient sources reveal exactly what form the *Luoshu* took. By the Han period (202 BCE – 220 CE) it had become closely identified with the so-called 'magic' square of three; the planetary seal or *kamea* of Saturn in the Western occultism.

---

19 S.A.M. Adshead: *China in World History.* Macmillan, 1988, p.77

At an early stage, the *Luoshu* was also associated with a circular arrangement of the eight Yijing trigrams, the so-called Later Heaven or King Wen Arrangement. Together, the *Luoshu* in the form of the 'magic' square of three surrounded by the King Wen Arrangement of trigrams was regarded as a cosmic map and became the basis of a number of astrological and *fengshui* systems, some of which are still practiced today.

4	9	2
3	5	7
8	1	6

The Luoshu *or 'Luo River Writing'*

One of the Dunhuang calendrical fragments, dated to the year 982, shows the appropriate diagrams for that year as a whole and those of the first three months of the year. The individual 'cells' of the square are marked with the Chinese characters indicating their colours, rather than their numerical values.[20]

Perhaps more importantly, another very early printed calendar contains not only illustrations of the 12 animal signs of the Chinese zodiac but tables on which the eight trigrams of the Yijing are named. This calendar is undated but, from a reference to an intercalary moon and other observations, it very probably dates from the year 877.

These calendar fragments give us physical evidence that Yijing related material was available along the Silk Road during the ninth and tenth centuries.

Nine Star Astrology

As has been stated above, the term 'geomancy' is a very misleading one when applied to a divinatory system that was, in fact, a speculative rather than operative form of astrology. The calendrical and divinatory charts and diagrams found at Dunhuang were similarly based on a purely theoretical 'astrological' system.

The so-called 'Nine Star' astrological system is derived from the numbers of the *Luoshu* diagram and their associated Yijing trigrams. Nine Star 'astrology' reached its final form during the Tang period. In China, such purely theoretical systems were developed by the *Fangshi*, or Occult Practitioners, because the calculation of the relative position of actual stars and planets was forbidden due to its connection with calendar-making, a primary imperial prerogative.

Some form of nine house system based on the *Luoshu* and the eight trigrams was already in existence by the late Han period (first century C.E.) During the Sui period (581-618) the *Fangshi* occultist Xiao Ji synthesised the nine house system with other popular 'astrological' techniques. His work became the basis of the final form of Nine Star 'astrology' during the Tang.[21]

The importance attached to the Nine Star system during the Tang is illustrated by the elaborate imperial sacrifices to the nine deities associated with nine numerological

---

20 Derek Walters: *Chinese Astrology.* Aquarian Press, 1992, pp.240-242
21 Victor Xiong: 'Ritual Innovations & Taoism under Tang Xuanzong', *T'oung Pao*, Vol. 82, 1996, p.273

'stars' inaugurated in 744 by the Tang Emperor Xuanzong. An altar in the form of the *Luoshu* was erected in the eastern suburb of Changan and sacrifices offered in the first month of each season.[22]

The reason for Xuanxong's ritual innovations was linked to his interest in alchemy. Xuanxong was fascinated by Daoist alchemy. Even prior to his accession to the imperial throne, he was patron of the leading Daoist adepts of his day. During his reign, alchemists flocked to his court. It is even reported that he considered abdicating in later life to devote his energies to the quest for the elixir of immortality.

The then current theory was that the compounding of the elixir was heavily influenced by the cyclical movement of the nine 'stars' of the Big Dipper; the seven visible stars of Ursa Major and two more imaginary 'invisible' stars. These nine 'stars' were represented by the nine numbers of the *Luoshu*.

TIBETAN DIVINATION

Tibet offers us the clearest evidence that divination techniques related to the Yijing were in fact being exported beyond the perceived Western borders of the Chinese empire during the Tang period. Although extant Tibetan works on the subject are relatively late, the Tibetan Nine Star system of divination relied upon the *Luoshu* and the eight trigrams rather than the 64 hexagrams. This system has been practised by the Tibetans until the present day.

What is equally interesting is that the Tibetan system recognises 16 astrological houses (the 12 signs of the Sino-Tibetan zodiac plus the 4 Chinese elements of the cardinal points, Wood, Fire, Metal & Water). This corresponds even more closely to the Islamic system of 16 houses (12 signs of the zodiac plus 4 Greek elements, Air, Fire, Water & Earth) than does the Chinese Nine Star system based purely on the *Luoshu*.

The evidence that this system was first introduced into Tibet during the Tang is found in the Tibetan alphabetic transliterations of the trigrams' Chinese names. These preserve the Tang pronunciation.[23]

The Tibetans themselves credited the introduction of Chinese divinatory practices into Tibet, along with Buddhism, to Kong-jo, a Tang Princess, rather than the monastic community at Dunhuang. Kong-jo is in fact the Tibetan transliteration of the Chinese *gongzhu*, the title of the daughters of the emperor, two of whom married Tibetan kings.

The Gongzhu Wencheng, a daughter of the Taizong Emperor, was married to the Tibetan King Sontsen Gampo around the year 641. Tibetan accounts say that, before her departure from China, she requested a 'striped roll of trigrams in 34 sections', though she was actually given 'a divination chart in 300 sections executed according to the Chinese divinatory sciences'.

Another Chinese princess, the Gongzhu Jincheng, was married to King Trede Tsuktsen in 710. She was the daughter of the Xuangzong Emperor and, in 730, wrote to her father asking for copies of the Confucian classics – including the Yijing.

Given the importance attached to the nine stellar gods by Xuanzong, and the evi-

---

22 *Ibid* pp. 278-279
23 Gary Dickinson & Steve Moore: 'Trigrams & Tortoises', *The Oracle*, Vol. 1, No. 5, 1997

dence provided by the *Luoshu* and the eight trigrams, Chinese divinatory systems were almost certainly introduced into Tibet during the Tang through royal marriages.

ISLAMIC CONTACT WITH THE YIJING

The cultural links between Tibet and China are well documented, if still the source of political tension today. From the foregoing discussion we can see that there were also numerous opportunities for contact between China and the Islamic world from the seventh through to the tenth centuries. But, what evidence exists that Islamic scholars had contact with Chinese arts and sciences related to the Yijing?

That some did, and scholars whose names in fact connected to the Geomantic tradition, is beyond doubt. Perhaps the most famous was the Persian philosopher, mathematician and astronomer Nasir al-Din al-Tusi (1201-75).

Known later as al-Muhaqqiq or 'the Inquisitive', two important works on Geomancy are attributed to al-Tusi: the *al-Risala al-sultaniya fi khatt al-raml* or *The Royal Epistle on Sand Divination* and the *Kitab fi 'ilm al-raml* or *Perfect Treatise on Sand Divination*. A number of other Geomancies in Persian and Arabic are also attributed to him.[24]

Born in the city of Tus in Khorassan (north-eastern Iran), the birth-place of Jabir himself, al-Tusi was kidnapped as a child by the Isma'ili governor of Quhistan and dispatched to Alamut, the stronghold of the Assassins. A sect of the Isma'ili, the Assassins derived their name from their practice of taking hashish (Assassin = *hasishim* i.e. one who takes hashish). Once again, we have a connection with both Jabir and the Isma'ili.

The Assassins' reign of terror was ended in 1256 when Alamut was surrounded by the Mongol hordes of Halagu Khan (a grandson of Genghis). On the advice of al-Tusi the Assassins surrendered peacefully. Al-Tusi himself entered the service of the Mongols. Halagu Khan appears to have fallen under al-Tusi's spell, rarely undertaking anything without al-Tusi's astrological advice.[25]

After the sack of Baghdad in 1258, Halagu commissioned al-Tusi to found a great observatory at Maraghah in modern Azerbaidjan. The observatory was equipped with the finest instruments of the day and a library said to contain over 400,000 volumes. The staff under al-Tusi included at least one Chinese astronomer, Fu Mengji, and another from far away Moorish Spain.

Crowley might have been tempted to diagnose Yahya ibn Muhammad ibn abu'l-Shukr al-Maghribi al-Andulusi as a sufferer of acute nomenclature but the Moorish scientist's work included the *Risalat al-Khita wa'il-Ighur* (On the Calendar of the Chinese and the Uighurs).[26]

Astronomy and astrology were then synonymous in both the Islamic and Chinese worlds. Al-Tusi himself was astronomer, astrologer and geomancer. And, in China, astronomical or astrological consideration of the stars and planets and calendrical science were closely bound-up with a cosmology based on the Yijing tradition. It seems highly likely, therefore, that al-Tusi would have come into contact with material relating to the Yijing.

---

24 Savage-Smith & Smith: pp.5-6
25 Skinner: p.35
26 Needham, Vol. I (1954), p.218

Al-Hamdani's Circular Arrangement of the Trigrams: The eight trigrams correlated with the stages of a fever from Rashid al-Din al-Hamdani's 14th century encyclopaedia of Chinese medicine.

Another Islamic scholar certainly did. Rahid al-Din al-Hamdani (1247-1318) also worked for the Mongol rulers of Persia. Physician and prime minister to Ghazan Mahmud Khan, in 1313 al-Hamdani commissioned an encyclopaedia of Chinese medicine, the *Tanksuq-namah-i Ilkhan dar funun-I 'ulum-I Khitai* or 'Treasures of the Ilkhan on the Sciences of Cathay'.

As with astrology, Chinese medical theory relied on the cosmology developed from the symbols of the Yijing. Al-Hamdani's encyclopaedia includes a circular diagram which displays the eight trigrams of the Yijing in the so-called King Wen Arrangement. The Persian text explains that the rise and fall of a patient's fever is related to periods of the day and night ruled over by each of the trigrams.[27]

Al-Hamdani does not himself have any Geomancies attributed to him, but it is significant that he should be one of the sources quoted by Ahmad ben 'Ali Zunbul, the 16th century Arab Geomancer.[28]

It is tempting to identify these Islamic scholars working for the Mongols as the point of historical contact between the Chinese Yijing and Arab Geomancy. Al-Tusi's observatory at Maraghah provided excellent opportunities for this cultural exchange to have happened and al-Hamdani's work demonstrates a knowledge of at least the symbols of the Yijing. But Geomancy had already been introduced into Europe from the Islamic world over a century before. We must therefore return to Jabir and alchemy for evidence of similar but earlier contacts and possible Chinese influences

27 *Ibid*, plate xii, facing p.218
28 Skinner, p. 35

prior to the date of Hugh of Santalla's translation of circa 1150.

ALCHEMY

It is now generally accepted that the emergence of alchemy in the Islamic world during the ninth century was influenced by some elements of the Chinese alchemical tradition. Needham and other eminent sinologists, as well as scholars of Western alchemy such as Holmyard, are in agreement that the corpus of works attributed to Jabir Ibn Hayyan appear to have been the most heavily influenced by Chinese alchemy.

We have already discussed Jabir's most important contribution to Western alchemy, the sulphur-mercury theory, in relation to the historical development of geomancy. And indeed it is this theory that appears to owe the greatest debt to Chinese alchemy.

Jabirian alchemy recognised seven metals corresponding to the seven 'planets' of astrology; gold, silver, lead, tin, copper, iron and *khar sini*.[29] The last of these, associated with the planet Mercury, means 'Chinese iron' in Arabic. It is thought that this refers to an alloy of copper, zinc and nickel known in China as *baitong* or 'white copper'. This white metal alloy was used in China to manufacture jewellery and mirrors, though some Islamic writers believed that it was also used by the Chinese to cast bells particularly melodic in tone. Jabirian writers, therefore, at least had access to Chinese materials.

Gold, the noblest of metals, was thought to contain the perfect equilibrium or balance of sulphur and mercury. Alchemists hoped, by altering the proportions of these agents in base metals, they might be transmuted into gold. Needham points out:

> Of all the theories which the pioneers of chemistry entertained through the ages none was more important or more widespread than the belief that all metals, or all fusible bodies, were composed of mercury and sulphur in one form or another. It is generally acknowledged that this doctrine first appears in Arabic alchemy at the beginning of the 9th century, there being no antecedent for it in the writings of the Hellenistic protochemists. But after that its ramifications continued down to the 18th century, even across the threshold, one might say, of modern chemistry.[30]

It seems significant that the chemical combination of these two agents in nature produces mercuric sulphide or cinnabar, which Needham describes as the single most important raw material used by Chinese alchemists. Its Chinese name, *tan*, was used as the word for 'elixir'. A number of Chinese alchemists and a couple of emperors poisoned themselves in their attempts to achieve immortality by ingesting cinnabar.

The sudden occurrence of the ingredients of the Chinese elixir in the Jabirian corpus at a time when there was ample opportunity for contact with Chinese alchemy, and the polarity of fiery, active sulphur and the cool, passive mercury, so strongly suggestive of yang and yin, led Needham to conclude:

---

29 Holmyard, p. 80
30 Needham, Vol. V:4, p.454

Mercury and sulphur played a much more prominent part in Chinese alchemy than any other substances, and... cinnabar itself, mercuric sulphide, far excelled all other chemicals for prominence in Chinese alchemical song and story. Moreover, the passage from Khang Ying-Ta [Kongyingda]... shows clearly that the element Metal was regarded in orthodox Chinese natural philosophy as a mixture of Yin and Yang, with the former predominating; and from there it would have been a very short step to the idea that the metals known to man were different in properties because of the varying proportions of Yin and Yang (mercury and sulphur) which they contained. So if the doctrine just stated was not actually received by any individual Arabic hakim from his Chinese chen jen, it could have sprung very easily from a knowledge of how the adepts of China conceived of elixir-making and aurification.[31]

The Jabirian corpus does not acknowledge any Chinese alchemical work or tradition as the source of the sulphur-mercury theory. But it is interesting to note that, in its naturally occurring form, the red mineral cinnabar will often have droplets of silvery-white mercury clinging to it. Perhaps this is the origin of the red and white symbolism of the sulphur-mercury theory. However, the similarities between the Jabirian corpus and Chinese alchemy do not end there.

THE BOOK OF BALANCES

The Book of Balances, an early ninth century work attributed to Jabir, attempts to quantify the proportions of sulphur and mercury in each type of metal. Such an analysis was not made chemically, but numerologically. The numerological value of the Arabic letters of the name of the metal were used to determine the relative proportions of the two constituent agents.

The numbers to which the Jabirians attached the most importance were 1, 3, 5 & 8 (totalling 17) and 28. The addition of 17 and 28 (i.e. 45) yields the key to understanding this curious sequence of numbers which recur throughout Jabirian literature. Needham summarized three decades of scholarly endeavour to explain the sequence:

Kraus was extremely puzzled about the origin of the numerological succession. He devoted to it an immensely learned disquisition, recalling (not very convincingly) the Timaeus and Pythagoras, searching for some connection with the music of the spheres, and alluding to the 17 consonants of the Greek language. But his work in the forties ended with no solution to the problem. During the fifties Stapleton found it in the simplest magic square, a mathematical achievement of ancient China, which Cammann during the sixties has set in its fullest perspective and context.[32]

---

31 *Ibid*, pp. 458-459
32 *Ibid*, p. 462

The 'magic square' is, of course, none other than the *Luoshu* itself. What Stapleton did was to divide its nine numbers into two groups as follows:

<table>
<tr><td>4</td><td>9</td><td>2</td></tr>
<tr><td>3</td><td>5</td><td>7</td></tr>
<tr><td>8</td><td>1</td><td>6</td></tr>
</table>

Stapleton's division of the Luoshu.

We can see immediately that the sequence of 1, 3, 5 & 8 are all contained in the lower, left hand division of the square, whilst the remaining numbers total 28. The division of the square itself into these two sections is curious and remains unexplained. But that the magic square of three should have been used by 'Jabir' to determine the 'balance' of sulphur and mercury is consistent with the use of the *Luoshu* in China.

The *Luoshu* represents numerologically a concept of equal importance to both the Confucian and Daoist traditions: *zhong*, the centre or equilibrium. The five at the centre of the *Luoshu* was the primary symbol of centrality. Five multiplied by three, the base number of the square, gives fifteen, the total of any column added vertically, horizontally or diagonally. Five multiplied by nine, the highest number in the square, yields 45, the sum of the numbers of the square added together. Five is also halfway between the pairs of numbers either side of it in the square. Five, therefore, represents the constant factor.

The Jabirian *Book of Balances* and its use of the 'magic square' of three to determine the harmonies of sulphur and mercury in various metals is, philosophically at least, entirely congruent with Chinese conceptions of the *Luoshu* and its numerological uses.

Schyler Cammann amply demonstrated that the Islamic world owed the 'magic square' of three to the Chinese. From all of this Needham concluded:

> When the Arab alchemists came into possession of the Luoshu magic square about the beginning of the ninth century, they were receiving a cosmic symbol loaded with a great weight of belief, eight centuries' worth in fact of numinous well thought out natural philosophy. There seems little cause for surprise that the Jabirians should have taken it as a great secret of the universe, whence they could extract those numbers which they believed would be found at the basis of the constitution of all natural substances.[33]

In Chinese sources, the numbers of the *Luoshu* are usually represented like constellations as linked dots, black for even numbers and white or red for odd numbers. This convention can only be dated back to the Song period and the works of Shaoyong (1011-77). We do not know how earlier writers expressed the *Luoshu's* numbers. The

---

33 *Ibid*, p. 468

Dunhuang calendar referred to above, for example, simply gives colour correspondences of particular configurations of the *Luoshu*.

Shao's contemporaries credit the *Luoshu* and other numerological diagrams to Chen Tuan, a tenth century *Fangshi* or occult practitioner. Shao Yong makes numerous references to Chen and acknowledged the influence of Chen's thought on his own. Chen himself wrote a now lost work entitled the *Longshu* or *Dragon Chart* and was noted for being the first adept to reveal previously secretly transmitted knowledge.[34]

CONCLUSION

It seems almost impossible that Arab alchemists coming into contact with Chinese alchemical traditions would not have seen the binary divination figures of the Yijing. The overwhelming majority of Chinese alchemical texts use Yijing trigrams, and sometimes even hexagrams, to describe alchemical theories and processes. The Chinese tradition may even suggest a reason for the development of Geomantic divination; the timing of the various phases of the 'Great Work' itself.

Islamic/European Geomancy most closely resembles the Chinese divination system based on the *Luoshu*; even the Geomantic figures look like the 'constellations' used to represent the nine number of the 'magic' square. That system was fully developed under the aegis of a Tang dynasty emperor obsessed with alchemy at a time when not only were there the greatest opportunities for cultural exchange between China and the Islamic world but when Yijing divination systems based on the *Luoshu* were spreading along the Silk Road and being introduced into Tibet.

It is also likely to have been during the same period that Geomancy was itself developed in the Islamic world into the form which was introduced into Europe. That development is closely linked to the Isma'ili authors of the Jabirian corpus by Islamic tradition and also to the sulphur/mercury theory by the presence of the red and white figures of Geomancy; *Rubeus* and *Albus*. That red/white, sulphur/mercury correspondence also links Arab alchemy to Chinese alchemical traditions of the period.

In this complex set of interrelated facts lies the answer to our question as to whether there was an historical link between the Yijing and European geomantic divination.

It is beyond dispute that such an historical link is possible. Admittedly, none of the sources of Islamic Geomancy directly credit Chinese influences – but nor does Islamic alchemy. Yet, it is generally accepted that Chinese concepts did influence Islamic alchemy. To this, I believe, we can now add Islamic Geomancy.

In my opinion, the evidence of the link between the development of Geomancy and the development of Islamic alchemy, when considered alongside the technical similarities between the two systems, is sufficient to say that an historical connection between the Yijing and Geomancy is not only possible but highly probable.

The legendary origin of Geomancy with Idris and Tumtum al-Hindi may be a lingering of memory of the Chinese ancestry of Geomancy. If Geomancy was the 'Daughter of Astrology', she was very probably also the granddaughter of the Yijing.

---

34 Anne D. Birdwhistell: *Transition to Neo-Confucianism – Shao Yung on Knowledge and Symbols of Reality*, Standford University Press, 1989, p. 208

Such a genealogical connection with the Yijing may extend the pedigree of European geomantic divination, but it doesn't support Crowley's 'grand theory' that the two systems were entirely independent observations of a single reality in Nature. However, an historical connection between Geomancy and the Yijing might suggest a new approach to another problem Crowley struggled with; the integration of the Yijing fully into the Western esoteric tradition.

Writing to Anne Macky in March 1943, Crowley claimed:

> I do not think that I am boasting unfairly when I say that my personal researches have been of the greatest value and importance to the study of the subject of Magick and Mysticism in general, especially my integration of the various thought-systems of the world, notably the identification of the system of the Yi King with that of the Qabalah.[35]

Crowley died four years later, his work on the Yijing uncompleted. Although his rhymed paraphrase of the Yijing and his Qabalistic correspondences have been published, to be of any practical value they still require an interpretative framework. Geomancy offers just such a framework in which to understand how a binary divination system behaves and functions within the Western Mystery Tradition. And, if there is an historical connection between the two binary systems, then the Yijing under the guise of Geomancy has already been part of that Tradition for much longer than we have previously thought.

By the same token, should we even be attempting to incorporate the Chinese Yijing into the Western Tradition when another form of it has functioned perfectly well within that Tradition for a thousand years? Perhaps what we can learn from the Yijing should be applied to our understanding of Geomancy. Jung's criticism of the 'western method's' purely mantic use certainly needs to be addressed philosophically in the light of its ancestral connection to the Yijing. Perhaps the first step is to free the system from the artificial restrictions placed on it by Mathers' attribution to Malkuth and to approach the subject at a higher level. Reviewing my original research some 12 years on, the use of the term 'geomancy' to describe Chinese *fengshui* practices may not be as misplaced as I had once thought. *Fengshui* is, in part, an application of the Yijing. If we view the European geomantic system as just another such application, it opens up many new possibilities for its wider use.

SELECTED FURTHER READING

—⚹— Crowley, Aleister: *A Handbook of Geomancy.* Sure Fire Press, 1989
—⚹— De Fancourt, William: *Warp & Weft, a Short History of the I Ching.* Capall Bann, 2011
—⚹— Greer, John Michael: *Earth Divination, Earth Magic: A Practical Guide to Geomancy.* Llwellyn, 1999

---

35 Aleister Crowley: *Magick Without Tears.* New Falcon Publications, 1994, pp. 1-2

—⁓— Greer: *The Art & Practice of Geomancy.* Weiser, 2009
—⁓— Pennick, Nigel: *The Oracle of Geomancy.* Capall Bann, 1995
—⁓— Regardie, Israel: *A Practical Guide to Geomantic Divination.* Aquarian Press, 1972
—⁓— Skinner, Stephen: *The Living Earth Manual of Feng Shui.* Penguin Arkana, 1989

Sigils and Extra Dimensionality

Robert Podgurski

Prolegomena

Extra dimensionality, a type of reality. The semantics are delimiting, as there are no *extras*, only immediacy in presences, especially in practical magick. Sigil magick in particular broaches desire, will, the subconscious, atavistic denizens, and *spaces between spaces* in particular, as Austin Spare's system would have it. Currently, the term sigil is most often used to connote a two-dimensional line drawing of a figure undecipherable to consciousness but pregnant with budding energy to the subconscious insofar as modern magicians are concerned. In connection with the projection of sigils I would reflect on a somewhat overlooked formula from the Golden Dawn: The Ritual of the Rose Cross.[1] Through this ritual the magician, in short, constructs an astral box sealed with crosses within circles. The symbol of the cross is traced in the air and inter-woven as one would construct a pentagram, hexagram, or an evocational sigil. Regardie stated: "When much distracted, use the Pentagram to banish and the Rose-cross to maintain peace."[2] The symbol is become sigil is become an astral structure enclosing and protecting, an insulating shield. In other words this structure forms an astral orgone accumulator – at least that is what my own experience has dictated. The analogue of the rose-cross is endowed with life, charge, and dimension creating a kinetic bridge between symbolic and astral manifestation. Through this type of structure a sigil may be understood as not only affecting space but providing a link to the multivalent and infinite spaces unlocked by a three-dimensional sigil energizing an astral frame or architecture.

The visual cue/key is a fundament to magick and in the most basic of invocational practices alters mind and body. As has been reiterated by numerous practitioners, through visualizing and invoking a god-form, the aspirant may acquire its qualities even down to physical characteristics. The connection between the physical and emotional or astral bodies becomes apparent in the act of invocation. By uniting with the Egyptian goddess Bastet, for example, magicians may find their thoughts, movements, and facial features eventually being molded by and mimicking the graceful leonine qualities of a cat. In this fashion the magician stretches the fabric of their being through an enflamed, passionate desire to unite with and embody the qualities of the divine persona.

Through projecting pentagrams, hexagrams, etc., magicians alter and manipulate the subtle charge of the astral space within and beyond the immediate precincts of their sphere. Besides banishing, such magical *emblemata* may be employed to invoke

---

1 Israel Regardie, *The Golden Dawn*, (St. Paul, Minn: Llewellyn Publications, 1978) pp. 46-50.
2 *Ibid*, p. 49.

or evoke specific energies. For example, astrally formed invoking pentagrams essentially act as a magnet for a given energy and at the same time extend it beyond the physical body. Through them the magician polarizes their surrounding space, thereby rendering it more conducive to manifesting a specific emanation operating on the assumption that like attracts like. Moreover, it has been asserted that when properly formulated, astral pentagrams, sigils, etc., can stay constant about a magician for 24 hours if need be. So to a large degree, space is the magician's plaything.

INSTAURATION

On July 17, 1981 I perceived a magical sigil tool that has induced me to rethink and re-formulate a methodology for working with sigils not just as two-dimensional tools but as multi-dimensional constructs. The Grid Sigil, as I have coined it, exhibited this form:

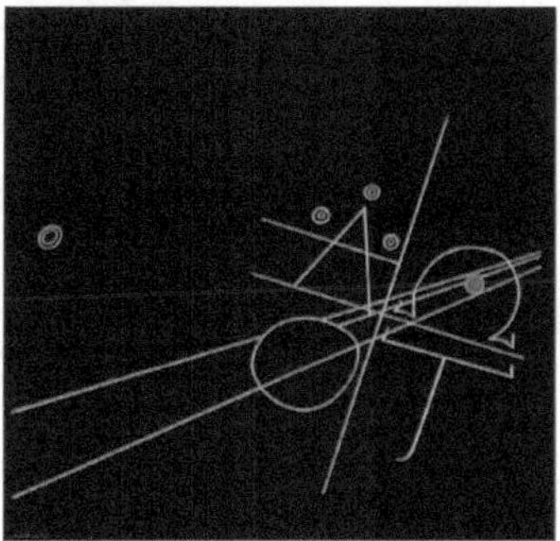

The Grid Sigil

The vision of this Grid Sigil was precipitated by rigorous and disciplined daily ritual, meditation, and explorations in lucid states of consciousness in sushupti or delta wave deep sleep.[3] Initially, I ascertained that this sigil corresponded to the first Enochian Call to spirit with the individual quadrants representing the root power of each of the four elements. Through many years of practice I have found that the Grid Sigil may be used in conjunction with the first Enochian Call or without it, often rendering similar or concomitant results. That is one of the more utilitarian aspects of this sigil: it allows the magician to work with the energies of the first Enochian call to spirit without neces-sarily having to actually intone the call. Furthermore, from using white characters on a black background I have found that it operates quite profoundly upon the optic nerve, felt and projected along those pathways. Given certain circumstantial restraints this tool can be quite advantageous allowing for some very spontaneous applications thereof.

---

3 For more details as to the operations and initiations I underwent see: *The Sacred Alignments and Dark Side of Sigils* (England: Mandrake Press Ltd) 2012, pp. 19-26.

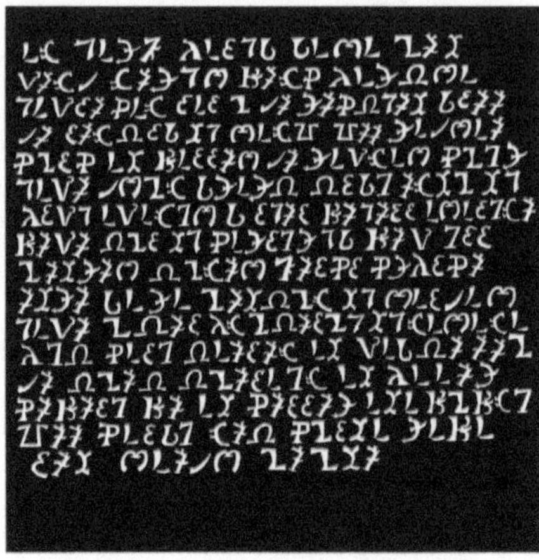

The First Enochian Call to Spirit

Initially, this sigil appears to represent another graphic interpretation of the Tetragrammaton. However, without even broaching the subtler unseen aspects of the Grid, various features of it stand out via mere visual contact. All one needs to do is to gaze at the Grid Sigil for a prolonged period to find its three-dimensional qualities elicited.

The central cross (or unifying force of spirit) seems to almost float within an ever expanding plane delineated by the diagonal lines which correspond to time and space. The omicron or air quadrant egg appears to be suspended in the expanding plane with the rays of time and space extending beyond the frame of the picture, and so on. This sigil establishes itself in its own right as an innovative form of art in contradistinction to sigils of a singular nature such as those prescribed by Austin Spare's formula that are, for the most part, a means to an end. The Grid Sigils and their various permutations as outlined in *Sacred Alignments* are indicative of their own entelechy because in and of themselves they are an end result, subconsciously awakening implements, and components of astral plane architectonics. In order to better comprehend the multivalency of the Grid Sigil we need to consider its component properties in an intuited application.

Syncretism

One particular notion led me to perceive the Grid Sigil as a primary energizing agent within the ancient pyramids. Since these pyramids were often built in congruence with certain alignments, the earth's geomagnetic grid, etc., it came to my attention that there were certain *telesmata* or sigils concealed within the structures for a specific purpose. Furthermore, I also learned that the Grid Sigil was placed within the northeast corner of certain pyramids. In this way the Grid Sigil would act as an astral energizing battery of sorts.

Much of what I have learned about this Grid Sigil has been acquired through what I like to refer to as *sigil-speak*. When I first began to catch on to Austin Spare's system of sigils and his *neither/neither* principle it seemed logical to me that using sigils that appear spontaneously to the magician may be the most powerful as they are not being fabricated from earth-bound desires and intent. I would often depict or envision a sigil and then psychometrize it and allow it to dictate what it was meant for. This is how I came to understand the import of the Grid Sigil itself.

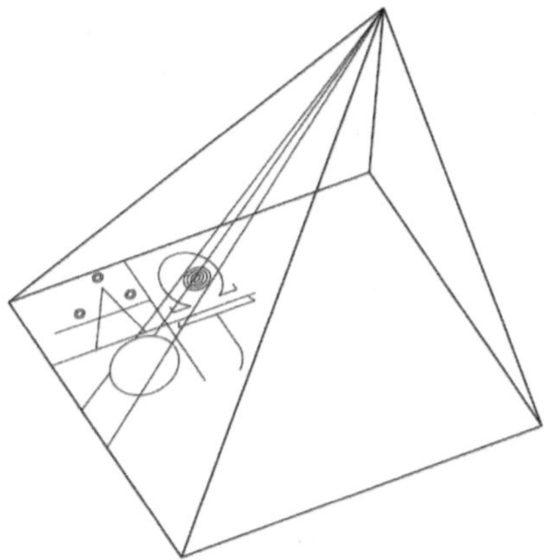

The Grid Sigil as Energizing Agent within the Pyramid.

I surmised that the Grid Sigil or ones similar to it acted as energizing agents thereby attuning a pyramid to a specific force or emanation. In fact, I encourage the intrepid practitioner to experiment by placing the Grid Sigil inscribed on parchment or engraved on metal and place it in the northeast corner of a model pyramid. Or if able, I suggest to formulate an astral pyramid much like the process prescribed in the Rose-Cross Ritual, however with the formation of each side of the pyramid intone SIRIUS or SOPDET to charge that section. The latter is quite useful as one can erect it to be any size making it the most magically versatile pyramid extant. Yet, and this is not to discount the viability and implementation of this specific utility of the Grid Sigil, I sensed that there was more to the multi-dimensional aspects of the Grid than I initially perceived. And sure enough, over time, the various other qualities of the Grid's extra dimensionality presented themselves to me as pieces of an intricate magical latticework.

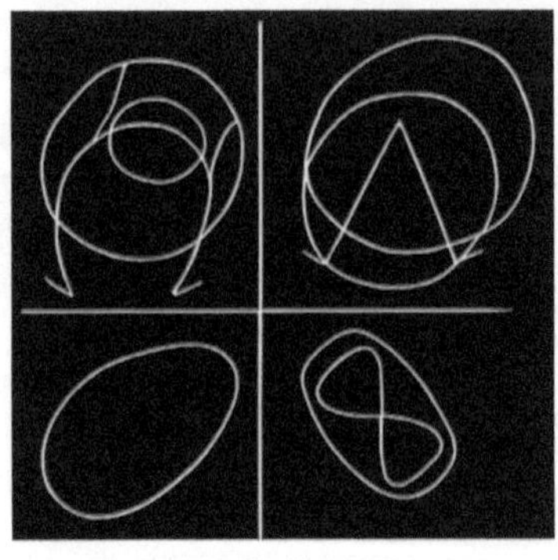

The Aeonic Grid Sigil

Grid Components interfacing with Sigil

SYNTHESIS

On March 3, 1982 I received the second piece of the sigil formula that re-opened my perspective to the vast nature of the Grid Sigil system. This second, or Aeonic Grid Sigil I understood as corresponding to the second Enochian call to spirit. This sigil mechanism is part and parcel of the three rays of the time/space continuum delineated in the Grid Sigil. Over time the picture of these two interacting sigils to form a multi-dimensional magickal machine began to materialize. And eventually I gathered that the omicron or egg shaped quadrant is co-terminal to both structures as the nexus point with the remaining three sectors of the Aeonic Grid forming a triangle about the astral pyramid.

However, as my understanding of the structure and inner workings of this sigilic mechanism began to expand I clearly came to an impasse utilizing conventional means of graphic representation. Whereas the components of the Grid Sigil are somewhat definable, the various aspects of the Aeonic or time/space sigil proved to be much more rarefied. The omega-like quadrant of the Aeonic Sigil is representative of the return point of energy and or motion as it completes its revolution to recycle. The upward pointing carrot shaped quadrant is indicative of the ignition or propulsion stage of motion. And the infinity symbol shaped quadrant is the weaving or interconnecting energy that fuses the other two quadrants. It is this infinity quadrant that best illustrates the crux of what is most salient here in depicting the extra dimensionality of these sigils: that the multiplicity of dimensions of time, space, and the aethyr may be broached through sigil-speak as opposed to mere verbal signification. For example, the plane without boundary conveyed in the rays of time and space of the Grid Sigil does not reveal itself merely through the image so much as through prolonged interaction, and gazing upon the sigil. The surface imagery provides a launching point for the seer. Here, two-dimensional imagery leads to three dimensions creating a pathway to the fourth and so on. Our modern epistemologies fall short of describing this process. Maybe the medieval notion of the *phantastica cellula*, ie the elusive region that resides somewhere between the senses and the rational mind serves more utility here in elaborating upon

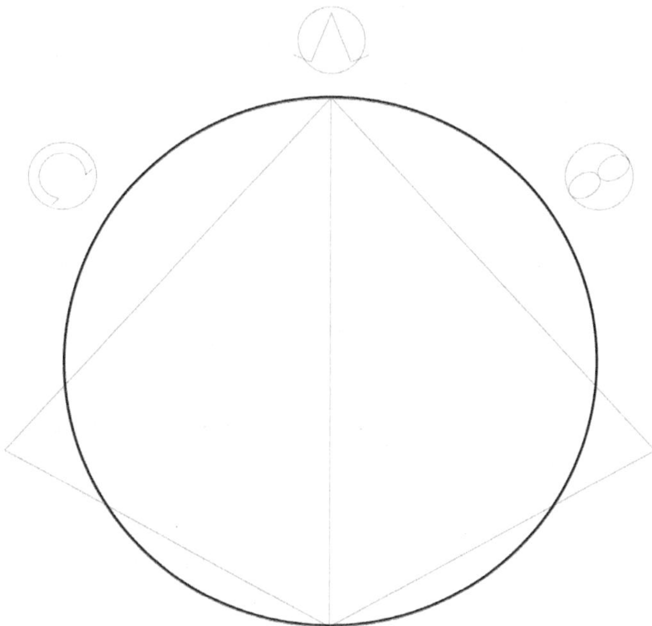

Aeonic Grid Sigil in Alignment with the Pyramid.

the manner in which such sigils operate upon us. The image of the sigil is one matter, however the phantasm that becomes animate upon the stage of the seer's imagination is another. As we make the sigil part of us, the sigil in turn transforms us; in and of itself this notion is nothing new when we consider Austin Spare's system of sigils. With the Grid and Aeonic Sigils though, this is a case where the sigilic tools are geared toward directing desire to focus and expand intent to grasp extra dimensionality itself. Here we can see what is so central to this system: that sigils derived from piercing the veils of negative existence through dream state awareness, trance, tantra, etc., are by necessity directing consciousness to multi-valent magical spaces and extra dimensional spheres of consciousness.

Clearly, I could not adequately demonstrate on paper how the infinity quadrant oscillates and spins to weave and unite the other two quadrants of the Aeonic Grid. However, as the recipient of the vision of these sigils I was induced to allow them to play upon my imagination through meditation in order to derive some rudimentary understanding of how they actually operate. It took me many years of submitting to the sigils and allowing them to work upon consciousness to get a feel for their full potential. For example, the presence of triangles as connecting junctures became prevalent. The three rays of time and space of the Aeonic Grid as they suspend the four elements and spirit in union through the Grid Sigil form a triangle. The four rings within the Omega/Root force of Fire quadrant of the Grid Sigil rise up to form a conical pyramid within the triangulated pyramid of the rays of time and space and in turn weave with one another through the infinity quadrant of the Aeonic Grid. Also, the three rings surrounding the

Alpha or Root force of water quadrant of the Grid are conduits that correspond and are related to those three rays of time and space as well. I could elaborate even further but I will concentrate on these few examples in order to illustrate how my ability to visualize such antithetical and paradoxical relationships was challenged and mutated given the loaded nature of the Grid's complexity and burgeoning potential. Moreover, this challenge, once acquiesced to, granted a new way of seeing and understanding spacial/energy-field/extra dimensional relationships freeing my mind's eye in part from the bonds forged by my physical eye and initial earth-bound perspective.

As I've come to grow and expand with the Grid Sigil my original inclination that it is a unifying tool between an array of magical systems and methods continues to be reified and compounded by the rich reservoir of magical significance it unravels. In asserting that the Grid Sigil is an extra dimensional tool I am speaking of it conceptually as well. Initially, I made the association between the sigil and the Enochian call to spirit as my primary contact with the tool had been facilitated to the best of my knowledge by the archangel Uriel. But then it became apparent that it was not limited to one application. When utilizing the Grid Sigil in a pyramid, physically or astrally formulated, I discovered that through the pyramid the Grid could be projected into the criss-crossing lines of geomagnetic energy, ie ley lines that surround the globe as a tool whereby to harness and manipulate these cords of power.[4] The Aeonic Grid was perceived via post tantric rites and so I gathered that since it had to do with time/space that it was useful as a mechanism whereby to explore and harness kalic emanations. On one hand, due to the limited breadth of this article I will not attempt to overview all of these ancillary aspects of the Grid and its component sigils. On the other, I am reticent to carefully delineate or establish a prescribed set practices and applications for the Grid Sigil as it is a potent key to the imagination. To dictate as such is to confine the multivalent within a narrow dimension and hence run counter to the entire premise of this project. It is incumbent for magicians to grapple with magical implements and create them anew in their own practices. Within this context I'm reminded of William Blake's concluding statement in *There is NO Natural Religion:* "Therefore God becomes as we are, that we may be as he is." Along similar lines the Grid Sigil provides a powerful catalyst to this same assimilative process.

---

4 See chapter 3 "Formation of the Grid Sigil and the Astral and Terrestrial Power of the Pyramid", *Sacred Alignments*, pp. 45-50.

Liber Al As-if[1]

Issues in Authenticating and Identifying Arcane Novelties,
From the Necronomicon to the Book of the Law

Frater Nigris

The distinction between grimoire and scripture may be smaller than we might at first imagine. Their superordinary origins or inspirations making possible a relationship with the transcendant or subordinate, each concludes as well as establishes the grounds for contact with unusual and potentially influential intelligences. Yet the ease of identifying their contents is at marked contrast when examined in the specific. Below two primary examples of identification (one challenging, the other simple yet refined) are considered.

Grimoires

In its most crude and popular vein, this takes the form of special pleading and manipulative rhetoric, arguing for prior contact with ancient astronauts who became our gods or demons. The fiery 'chariot' ridden through the sky is as much a product of its time as the 'landing strips' required, for some reason, to accommodate, interstellar visitation. With the advent of genuine archaeology and anthropology, however, these fantastic apologies and projections may be relegated to the realms of delusion or metaphor. Their desperate abuse of ignorance to entertain or deceive may hold no quarter in our refinements of knowledge. That their contents may overlap or in fact descend from the same sources[2] seems demonstrable, yet That which they may rationally apply to occupies a more and more restricted zone as retention and expanse of knowledge is facilitated by technology – the mark of knowledge's application, in fact.

In the questionable realm of grimoires, their origins in fiction or as a reaction to establishment religion makes an evaluation of their content challenging. Where their name ostensibly describes a pragmatic result, subjective assistance may be facilitated by placebo place-holding. Authenticity, therefore, especially in an aged or fictive grimoire, will cohere to the reputation or character previously described by occultists and archival reporters, or by creative artists fomenting a plot device. Some grimoires achieve a measure of notoriety through time and translation, especially as they ride upon the

---

1 "Al As-if": This is the name given by the mad Arab, Abdul Alhazred, to the grimoire known as the *Necronomicon*, used as an artifice in the fiction of Howard P. Lovecraft and subsequently applied to numerous books purporting to approximate this prop.

2 See *The Cult of Alien Gods: H. P. Lovecraft and Extraterrestrial Pop Culture*, by Jason Colavito, Prometheus Books 2004.

condemnation of conventional religion (the general character of 'books on magic'). These, such as those attributed to Honorius or Cyprian, or the German/Danish/Swedish 'black books', tend to have conventional scholarly descriptions and contents which one may find have been fraudulently proliferated in publication and translation. As time wears on and these books come to be commonly catalogued and reprinted, such deceptions will likely decrease in number.

Grimoires with a less confirmable content and an amusing or controversial status are those derived from fraudulent paraphrase (such as the *Book of Dzyan* by Blavatsky, an uncredited paraphrase of the Sanskrit *Rg Veda*), or those emergent from fiction that has achieved a degree of popularity[3] (e.g. the *Book of Eibon,* invented by Clark Ashton Smith and attributed to a wizard in the land of Hyperborea; *De Vermis Mysteriis,* invented by Robert Bloch, who translated its title as *Mysteries of the Worm; Nameless Cults,* invented by Robert E. Howard and attributed to the mad German, Friedrich von Junzt, also known as *The Black Book,* with its title translated by Derleth as *Unaussprechlichen Kulten;* the *Delomelanicon,* invented by Arturo Pérez-Reverte and attributed to Satan; and the *Necronomicon,* invented by Howard P. Lovecraft, the title translated in various ways, and attributed to the mad Arab, Abdul Alhazred).

Leaving the first category behind as easily evaluated by reference to that which they used in construction, the primary example of the last (the *Necronomicon*) has developed a significant set of possible authentication parameters, some of which apply to any circumstance. In the variation of published versions of the *Necronimicon,* for example, minimum criteria have been attempted (ostensibly for humorous effect, that being the construction in 1973 by George Scithers and L. Sprague de Camp, of a set of pages scrawled with faux Arabic and Syriac mimicry), but only through the course of time and breadth of knowledge have standards for what ought to be included as a *convincing* version of said tome been seriously considered and described. Details such as that moral, dualistic, or Aristotlean categories imposed upon what some, after the controversial Derleth called 'the Cthulhu Mythos' are a rational and sustainable disqualifier for any so called *Necronomicon.* More specific and cogent quotation as from the writ of Lovecraft himself in excerpt features as a desirable element to any approximation.[4]

Scripture

In contrast, one may identify and evaluate scriptures of small cults such as that of Thelema by form and content without much difficulty. Tracking them is often achieved by the cultists themselves at points and, where aggrandized, by their proponents and opponents. Contents and standards for its scripture in particular are variant, as it is described and arrives from its ostensible author and scribe (Aleister Crowley), and yet

---

3 See http://en.wikipedia.org/wiki/Category:Fictional_grimoires (accessed 12/27/11) for a list of fictional grimoires.

4 There are platforms from which derivation of *new* versions of the *Necronomicon* may be justified as either communications *from* Lovecraft or the manifestation of that which Lovecraft identified. See *Liber Grimoiris: the Parallels of East and West: Termas, Grimoires and the Necronomicon* (http://www.luckymojo.com/avidyana/ gnostik/liber-grimoiris.html accessed 12/27/11), by Frater Nigris; *The Necronomicon: Selected Stories and Essays Concerning the Blasphemous Tome of the Mad Arab,* by Robert M. Price; and *The Necronomicon Files,* by Daniel Harms. Contrast these with the usual standards for scriptures!

through time these presentations have refined and achieved a coherent standard, even in binding and paper quality.

It began as *Liber L. vel Legis* ("given from the mouth of Aiwass to the ear of The Beast"), a product of automatic writing, was presented as the outcome of spirit contact with Crowley's wife Rose, in association to their visit to the Boulaq Museum in Cairo (since renamed), where a particular exhibit (#666) was said to relate to this contact (with the gods Nuit, Hadit, and Ra-Hoor-Khuit). It was compromised by intrusions of the automatic writer or channel and in a couple of places was later amended by Rose. Subsequently it was republished as *Liber Al vel Legis* and promoted as the reception of a channelled document from Crowley's Holy Guardian Angel, Aiwass, affixed with commentaries in two passes (Old and New respectively), and then edited or annotated by various people inclusive of Crowley himself, Israel Regardie, Marcelo Motta, Kenneth Grant, Bill Heidrick, and Hymenæus Beta. These survive to the present day, with variable form and content embellishing the core documentation.

Criteria of their inclusion have been whether the work, when published, contained the following elements: the holographs of the original pages; a photographic reproduction of the Boulaq Museum's #666 stele (the Stele of Revealing) and its translation; the 'Tunisian Comment' (a brief statement ostensibly from 'The Priest of the Princes, Ankh-n-f-Khonsu' as to the authority or interpretation of the text); the Old or New commentaries from Crowley; a description of the circumstances and manner of reception and composition by Crowley; an introduction by the editor; photographs of associated locales and persons attendant to the scripture's reception (e.g. Rose); and associated holy books.

There has been one attempt to strip the intrusion of the receiver or scribe from the content (resulting in *The Booklet of the Law*[5]) and there are no known attempts to fraudulently substitute some other document for the scripture on the order of a grimoire (contention as to their publishing seem to have ceased after legal battles establishing copyright ownership subsided in the wake of the author's unsettled affairs). With the amount of attention paid to the work itself (by its adorers), it is somewhat surprising how little has been comparably provided to the commentaries by their scribe or his editors, though a website attempting to showcase the origin and development of these, as well as the commentaries on said scripture, is now in place and undergoing final revision.[6]

The amusing challenge of identifying fictive grimoires is helpfully contrasted against the ease with which scripture of particular cults may be specified. The former establishes its standards from the outside-inward, and what it ought contain through time, whereas the latter grows more specialized and strict with dedicated study by those devoted to their cause. Arcane scholars are advised to resist drawing hard and fast categories based on a 'real' and 'fake' which have as their criteria mere inherence to fictional contexts. While *The Book of the Law* is not an artifice of this type, like many others, it has been made use of for reference in fictional contexts, and at times for condemnatory purpose or without reference to its specific contents.

---

5 *Librette Al vel Legis: the Booklet of the Law* – http://www.luckymojo.com/avidyana/gnostik/librette-al-vel-legis.html (accessed 12/27/11), by Frater Nigris.
6 http://www.book-of-the-law.com (accessed 12/27/11)

The Abbey must be built

Peter Grey

We begin with dynamite, as Ivan Chtcheglov looks out from his garret window at the incessantly winking lights and plans to annihilate the Eiffel Tower, an act that ends in the reassuring buckled cuff embrace of the Asylum. There is something very appealing about planned destruction on a grand and iconic scale. Something about buildings that just asks us to tear them down.

Even mentioning the Abbey is enough for some to start reaching for the hammers and Semtex. The Masons among you will be relieved that I am not numbered among them. I will today suggest that we reach for our set squares and trowels rather than lapsing into the banality that says that as the body is a temple therefore we should shun all structures. This is not a time for millenarian levelling, however appealing that might be. Rather, I am demanding that the Abbey must be built.

Churchill said 'we shape our buildings and our buildings shape us'. But I say, so do the dreams of buildings, whether the Vault of the Adepts, mythical Sicily, or Alamut. We cannot privilege a particular form from the rejected ashlars. There need to be many Abbeys, but we must ask the demons to help us raise stone upon stone or they will remain simply dreams. Crowley was right: it is only by daring to live that we can bring a new world into being. Crowley was right: we need an Abbey.

But back to our saboteur whose contribution is not destruction, but a particular kind of building. Chtchehglov is remembered for his *Formulary for a New Urbanism*, a seemingly doomed manifesto that contains these stirring words:

> And you, forgotten, your memories ravaged by all the consternations of two hemispheres, stranded in the Red Cellars of Pali-Kao, without music and without geography, no longer setting out for the haçienda where the roots think of the child and where the wine is finished off with fables from an old almanac. That's all over. You'll never see the haçienda. It doesn't exist. The haçienda must be built.

These cryptic words are a call that has resounded in different forms from Rabelais to Fourier to Dashwood to Crowley to the Solar Lodge to Spahn Ranch to Waco. They conjure a dream of non-conformists, political dissidents, religious crazies, cult leaders, sexual outlaws, poets and dreamers. An Abbey, an Alamut, a Pleasure Dome is decreed. Having gathered here today, it is probably your dream too. Perhaps it is time that we realised it.

Chtcheglov is appalled by the banality of the modern urban condition as he promenades through the Parisian streets. He is angered by the architecture that he sees: '*... destroying the last remnants of joy. And of love, passion, freedom.*' Sentiments Crowley would recognise.

Furthermore, he argues that we are alienated from the natural world and its cycles by the industrial slavery of our Metropolis. He writes:

> Darkness and obscurity are banished by artificial lighting, and the seasons by air conditioning. Night and summer are losing their charm and dawn is disappearing. The urban population think they have escaped from cosmic reality, but there is no corresponding expansion of their dream life. The reason is clear: dreams spring from reality and are realized in it.

As I have argued in *The Red Goddess*, the world is now such a city, and not one simply forested with billboards, but one that has expanded into a digital dimension that has infested our dreams. As such we must develop new strategies against the pervasive architecture of control. A vital element of this is our reorientation to the natural cycles, something that the practitioners of *Liber Resh* experienced warming their bones in Cefalu, that the ecstasy-drenched ravers felt at sunrise, that the State fought on Salisbury plain with every Solstice. This is the essential human experience as reverenced in magic and witchcraft, but it is being lost. The Abbey of Thelema is a clear example of this, caught in the sprawl and now shadowed by the spectacle of a soccer stadium whilst its guardians have gouched out on past glories. Where has the sense of urgency gone? Why have we forgotten? The answer is that we have collectively, culturally and magically entered trance.

Chtcheglov and Guy Debord developed a technique to defeat this numbing trance of modern life, the engineering of moments that break this state which they styled as 'Situations'. Chtcheglov and the Situationists are responsible for the *dérive*, the drift through the city streets. Yet the Situationists are not simply a random swaggering into bars and colliding with back streets and the glimpsed strata of previous events. It is not a mere literary trope. The drift was an attempt to replace the spectacle of consumer capitalism with an initiatory moment.

I am proposing that Magick can offer a super-charged version of the Situation, and in doing so it can reforge the connection between symbols and meanings. This is initiation as a dynamic procedure rather than empty mummery, and one that is situated in our own immediate predicament.

Guy Debord wrote his *Society of the Spectacle* as a deliberate attack on the edifice. What we might call a curse, though he would disdain such a term.

He opens it with this statement:

> The whole life of those societies in which modern conditions of production prevails presents itself as an immense accumulation of spectacles. All that was once directly lived has become mere representation.

The critique of Debord could be applied to advertising, to talent shows, to pornography, to Facebook. The meanings have been stripped from the symbols, in a deliberate disenchantment. The infantilism of the postmodern project renders us helpless, passive consumers. We are not the surly teenagers of the Æon of Horus, we are swaddled and suckling with precious little sustenance. Advertising is not the milk of the stars, yet we are grown obese and addicted on empty calories. Our mirror neurons make us mistake watching for doing, whether football or fucking or shopping. In the same way, reading endless biographies of Crowley does not make us Crowley. This is not the visceral transformation of initiation. Magick is the answer only when it is not spectating, but when it is doing, when it dares to engage and change.

What Debord did not foresee was the sophistication of the chameleon path the modern world would take, where once the meanings had been stripped from the symbols, we would be attacked by a parasitic meme that learns and mimics us to sell us counterfeit versions of our real desires. We inhabit an archonic age that even Phillip K Dick at his most amphetamined would balk at. Our Abbey should not be a heroin clinic, it should aim to cure us of these, our more pernicious modern addictions.

Debord ends his own fatal situation with six shot revolver roulette. A bullet in the heart for having bet everything on red, only to see his generation teeter, bounce, clack and settle finally on black. The revolution never came. Just as Crowley never saw Thelema become a world religion.

But what of the Haçienda?

The lineage re-emerges in Manchester as clown svengali Tony Wilson presses into the hands of each new employee of the Haçienda nightclub a copy of Chtcheglov's manifesto. Tony Wilson presides over an ecstatic eruption of Dionysos that ends, as with any prohibition that does not achieve full-blooded revolution, in a sordid sprawl of guns and gangsters. Just as most wannabe Cefalus end in junkiedom and squalid sexual jealousy. The moral here is one we must pay careful attention to: neither the Abbey, nor the Haçienda, nor 1003 South Orange Grove Avenue are immune to outside forces. Rather they become alembics that must distil everything that exists outside through the toxic stages of poison and nigredo, which more often than not destroys the magician before the Great Work is accomplished.

The ideas of the Situationists are taken up by Hakim Bey and flower into the Temporary Autonomous Zone. Ever the Anarchist, Hakim Bey observed the horror spawned by Marxist-Leninist revolutions, and reached the conclusion that a permanent structure ended up killing creativity. He does not share Debord's disdain for 'the occult' and his calligraphic flourishes are highly suggestive to the heretically minded. He writes:

> If History IS "Time," as it claims to be, then the uprising is a moment that springs up and out of Time, violates the "law" of History. If the State IS History, as it claims to be, then the insurrection is the forbidden moment, an unforgivable denial of the dialectic – himmying up the pole and out of the smoke hole, a shaman's manoeuvre carried out at an "impossible angle" to the universe. History says the Revolution attains "permanence," or at least duration, while the uprising is "temporary." In

this sense an uprising is like a "peak experience" as opposed to the standard of "ordinary" consciousness and experience. Like festivals, uprisings cannot happen every day – otherwise they would not be "non-ordinary." But such moments of intensity give shape and meaning to the entirety of a life. The shaman returns – you can't stay up on the roof forever – but things have changed, shifts and integrations have occurred – a difference is made.

Time for a sharp intake of breath: This is an exacting critique of many approaches to magic. They do not engage in uprising. In the language of Witchcraft, they do not fly to the Sabbat.

TOPY did however embrace the TAZ in an exuberant eruption of plasma. Hymenæus Beta said as much to Genesis P-Orridge, as Jason Louv relates in *Thee Psychick Bible:*

> TOPY was truly representing and doing the work of the active current that the OTO had mined in the early half of the century, and that his current job as head of the OTO was more akin to that of a museum curator.

But I am not about to privilege TOPY over the OTO. Neither approach seems to be complete, and both can benefit from critique. We need perpetual revolution.

TAZ led to the San Francsisco based Cacophany Society whose trips into the zone created Burning Man. The idea of the TAZ is also found persisting in the Occupy movement. But is this guerrilla approach to subverting control really the right way for us to proceed as magicians?

Neither Burning Man nor the commercialised free festivals have proved to be anything other than a pressure valve. Spectacles in themselves, where the silicon glitterati slum it with the perpetual ravers and the dreadlocked trustafarians. A few days with grey dust in their teeth, some nudity and a research chemical does not confer absolution.

The second part of the TAZ thesis is that there has been a closing of the map. That we cannot escape the machinery of control and find our Tortuga, make our journey to Xtul, scrawl that we have 'gone to Croatan.' We can only hit and run. Crowley found this out to his cost, expelled from Sicily by Mussolini and his Abbey abandoned to the lizards and slinking cats.

But Time has not stood still for Hakim Bey. The manifestos, though flamboyant reading, must by necessity be revised by our generation. His Pirate Utopias have been absorbed by the society of the spectacle and détourned by Disney and Depp into bland product. We have good news though: the map is yawning open again. As Chicago School capitalism attempts to own and exploit the water, earth and air in a desperate scramble for resources, the whole edifice, which is only sustained by oil, is doomed. It is onto this battlefield that we must emerge. I am suggesting that we do so fortifed from time spent preparing in our Abbeys that we begin to build the alternative structures in parallel to the architecture of control.

Scarlet Imprint's collection *XVI* is dedicated to Chtcheglov for good reason, predicated on the idea of the destruction of the Tower, and the great hanging ghost slabs of 9/11 and Empire. As these fall, what will endure until the end?

Here we can quote the *Book of the Law* III.34:

> 34. But your holy place shall be untouched throughout the centuries: though with fire and sword it be burnt down & shattered, yet an invisible house there standeth, and shall stand until the fall of the Great Equinox; when Hrumachis shall arise and the double-wanded one assume my throne and place.

The Holy place referred to here is Boleskine. But the cultic real estate is not what I want to stress. I want to reveal the inner meaning. Behind every outer temple, there is an inner temple, and it is this inner temple which is manifested in stone. Kether in Malkuth. Those who only talk about the esoteric are simplifiers. There is no esoteric without an exoteric, they are interpenetrated; it is best expressed in a word beloved to Kenneth Grant: *perichoresis*.

This also tells us how to destroy the buildings of our enemies. We need dynamism before dynamite. We must destroy the inner in order to destroy the outer. This is the occult warfare that the warrior monks of Thelema should be engaged in. We must attach our charges to the load bearing columns of their dreaming structures. When culture collapses into its own footprint our Abbeys will then be revealed gleaming in the light. Let us describe it this way. The Temporary Autonomous Zone is the Sabbat in full festal riot. But where do witches leave their bodies when they set out on their night flights? They need a charmed and defended space: an Abbey. The Temporary Autonomous Zone can then be realised as a projection from the Abbey which appears spontaneous, wondrous and devastating. Magical. The two spaces can be alchemically wedded rather than set against each other as antagonists.

Chtcheglov writes that:

> Everyone wavers between the emotionally still-alive past and the already dead future.

Magick faces this same dilemma. The answer is to be here Now.

It may be 'all in the egg' but the egg has hatched, the Æon tremors before us, the children of the bomb, like a heat haze, like an orgasm, like an Apocalypse. So rather than regurgitate the past like a hawk feeding its chicks, vomiting up scraps of ill-digested biography, let us instead delineate the hunting grounds of our gaze and let the new generation test the strength of their own wings. Magick has spent too long in the nest picking over the bones. Though old bones need to be venerated, they make poor eating. It is time to rebuild the high towers and nourished on blood inspire this generation to soar into the void.

Magick must manifest in form. The Abbey must be rebuilt in dream, in deed, in bricks and mortar. The outer Abbey is built in the image of the inner Abbey and when the doors swing open they will miraculously lead onto the wild heath where we are naked and aflame. Thus magick is in the final analysis revealed as witchcraft. The sacred architecture and proportion of the Abbey is revealed to be the concealed secret of nature Herself and the Abbey must be built in Her image.

A Different Perspective of the Undead:
Balkan Vampire Myths and Legends

Vera Mladenovska Nikolich

Considering the almost constant presence of vampires in entertainment today, one thing seems certain: vampires may be killed off, but definitely not the myth. If there is something undead that keeps haunting contemporary humans, it is the spectre of the nocturnal, the odd one out, the devil, the loner and the possible parasite. Simply put, the archetype of the "demonized other." The perspectives have certainly changed during the past few decades though. From having been blood-thirsty scapegoats evoking little or no sympathy at all, the entertainment industry vampire has become "cool" and "hip". And thereby more profitable than ever.

Tracing this mythic figure back to its roots, we find superstitious projections stemming from rural beliefs. All cultures apparently have an inherent need of a devil figure to scare the kids with and, possibly, to keep the adults faithful. In Eastern Europe specifically, this need generated a blood-sucking, death-defying and decidedly evil figure, but also an array of techniques and rituals to help fight it.

The rich history of the Balkan region supplies us with an immense flow of folklore and creative energy, aiding the depiction and colorful imagery of myths and characters intertwined in the past and present belief systems. The majority of the stories are deeply embedded in the Slavic cultural pool, yet undergoing developments just as the world outside kept changing through time.

The Slavic origins can be traced far into the past, first to be found in the Northeastern parts of Europe. With the 6th and 7th century migrations, much of the vibrant ancestral heritage was spread southwards – reaching down to the Balkan Peninsula, and swarming the lands with the thick roots of Slavic culture and ways of life. The adaptation followed easily, as if these people were meant to live on this newly-found ground and there go on to shape history on a much larger scale than before.

There is a solid collection of evidence regarding the development of the cultural and, to a larger extent, religious characteristics of the people inhabiting the Southeastern parts of Europe. However, the aim of this text is to focus on only a small portion of the populace and on their understanding of certain natural and seemingly unnatural processes, as well as their interpretation of some of the most common subjects of all ages: death and aspects of life, interrelated.

Paganism was, and to this day is, practiced by the people who reside in the region, regardless of Christianity and the influences of such a restrictive system. A lot of the ancient customs were adopted and adapted by the imposed religion, and vice versa, which allowed for the colorful heritage to be preserved rather than eradicated.

The myth of the Vampire in the Slavic mythological pool varies across the cultural nuances of the nations. This creature of the afterlife, with magical and often demonic attributes, appears in as many shapes and forms as there are regions in Eastern Europe, and can best be observed from the viewpoint of a populace in a specific region, showing unique characteristics in an almost general myth. This demonstration of the Vampire myth is of course intimately associated with the persistent development of the large death cult Christianity, but the essential note of the myth is indisputably linked to the "pagan" understandings of the Slavic people, their deities and mythological inclinations in general, and their manifestations within the later religious practices.

My personal observation is that the myth of the Vampire became stronger and gained more popularity through the second attempt of Christianity to infiltrate these parts of the world (the first being represented by St. Paul's mission). Far more successful and permanent results were made by the Eastern Roman Empire (Byzantine), which operated under the pretext of literacy and education in general. As a death cult, Christianity imposed a bizarre fascination with all things dead, the concept of death and possible forms of resurrection, even though the general perceptions of such concepts were very contradictory in nature.

The Vampire, as seen in the Macedonian beliefs and in the spoken prose, is generally one of the least researched demonic creatures specific to the region, both from ethnological and folkloristic perspectives. Although there is a sufficient amount of collected written and spoken materials from the 19th century until present day, the materials collected in the recent years lay bare the vitality of this character. The recent studies also contribute to a more eloquent Gesamt image (the sum of the "Macedonian Vampire", so to speak) from which the beliefs of the people can be evaluated according to a specific time period and the changes pertinent to that period. In this context we can look for the basic changes that took place in the legends and the mythical stories dealing with vampires. Through these we can also perceive the similarities or the differences between the beliefs of "our people" and the people from the other Slavic regions.

Probably the first official scriptures of the region containing the Vampire as a character belong to the first Macedonian collector of spoken prose, Marko Cepenkov, most of them related to the South-western region of the country. However, these beliefs were widely spread over all parts of Macedonia. The creation of these legends and beliefs is based on the experience of the people as well as the encounters linked to vampires. Every single piece of evidence that has been collected is of extreme importance and essential to the studies dealing with Macedonian demonology. The value of the evidence increases with the addition of the masterful descriptions and the collector's analysis of the terrifying experiences of the people who've had encounters with vampires. Still, if a comparison is made between the past and the present collected works, the observer will be able to see that there is little or no difference in the stories told by the common people.

The vampire as a character is usually neglected in the scientific research of the renowned ethnologists in the region. Even so, the survival of the beliefs and the legends suggests that this character is deeply rooted in the core of the Slavic culture, interconnected with the symbols that made a huge impact on the present perceptions and the spreading of other adapted beliefs.[1]

The notion of the vampire as seen in the belief system of the Macedonians originates from ancient times. In fact, these notions are recognizable throughout many cultures and nations and are usually related to the fear of the dead leaving their graves and coming back to the living, usually to the family and the closest friends. The faith in the existence of the vampires reflects certain understandings and viewpoints of the people, connected with terms such as "soul", "death" and the "outside world".

The vampire appears as two types: as a ghost of the deceased character (this type is invisible) and as a living corpse/a corpse revived by its own spirit.[2]

THE VAMPIRE AS A GHOST

There are different legends of how a deceased person can become such a vampire. The legends vary in different parts of the country but are usually associated with improper burials, the given time period for departure of the soul (the proper time being usually six weeks or 40 days), the deceased person being jumped over by an animal (usually a cat, a fox or other small animals), etc.

THE VAMPIRE AS A LIVING CORPSE

A corpse of the deceased wandering about. The transformation in this kind of vampire is related to unsettled dues, revenge, the nostalgia for the homeland and the family (these corpse vampires were quite often men who went to make a living in another country, died there and returned as vampires in their homeland, not giving away their true nature. The living family couldn't suspect at first that their husband, father, son or brother was a vampire until strange events started to occur, mostly nighttime activities, death of the cattle, death of another member of the family, etc. (The physical characteristics would show too, but more about that later in the text). The origins of this type are again associated with the rituals of improper burial, the temper of the person while he/she was alive, and of course magical aspects that either came from a practitioner of magic associated with the person or even from higher forces acting out in favor of the events.

There are four distinct groups or divisions of the term as a basis for a study of the vampire as a demon from the afterlife in the Macedonian belief system:

1. Notions of persons who after their death were transformed into vampires,

2. Notions of the existential characteristics of the vampires,

3. Notions of the relations between the people, and

---

1 *The Vampires in the Macedonian legends and beliefs* – Leposava Spirovska, Tanas Vrazhinovski, Institute of folklore "Marko Cepenkov" – Skopje, Skopje 1998; Tanas Vrazhinovski, *Macedonian folkloristic mythology, Folkloristic Demonology of the Macedonian people.*
2 Kazimierz Moszyiiski, *Kultura ludowa Slowian, Kultura duchowa*, M, Warszawa, 1967

4. Notions of the death of the vampires, termination of their lives in the social environments in which they appear.[3]

All of these notions form a somewhat full profile of how the vampire is created, how it interacts with the environment and how the vampire's "life" gets terminated.

In the context of the first point there are two important elements that need to be regarded: means to prevent the dead from becoming vampires and, if that fails, the act through which the dead actually become vampires.

In order to prevent the deceased from becoming a vampire it is of extreme importance to keep watch over the dead man's body. There are mainly two representations of prevention: not allowing the deceased to be jumped over by an animal and not allowing for things to be passed over the dead man's body (objects, food, etc). However, if there is a suspicion of vampirism or suspicion that the mentioned preventive means were disregarded, there are a few other ways of reassurance or secondary prevention like sticking a needle into the belly button of the deceased, sticking a needle into the chest or cutting the chest of the deceased with a knife, puncturing the stomach of the deceased with a needle, etc. All of these are pre-burial prevention means. The after-burial prevention of vampirism incorporates placing large stones over the body of the deceased, creating a circle of water around the grave and doing this every day for 40 days (which according to the legend closes the grave and prevents the spirit of the deceased from rising). Basically this can be sublimated to plunging a sharp object into the body of the deceased, or acts performed on the graves that disable the deceased from getting up and out.

There are also other preventive means, like placing poppies or sickles into the coffin, placing pebbles or coins under the tongue of the deceased, tying of the fingers of the deceased to his/her shoulders, cutting the heels, cutting the muscles under the knees, cutting off the head of the deceased and placing the head on the feet, the stomach or the chest, plunging the heart or the head of the deceased with a wooden stick, piercing a nail deeply in the forehead. Some of these acts were performed if the body had swollen parts, which was considered a clear sign of future vampirism.[4]

⸺⸺ ⸺ ⸺

The act of becoming a vampire combines different incidents. The popular belief in the Balkans is that the soul remains in the body for a short period of time after death has occurred. This gives way to all kinds of possibilities in regard to the creation of a vampire. Oddly, the people in this area believed that if an animal jumps over the deceased, the animal would take the soul and switch it with its own, therefore making the deceased some kind of human-animal creature. In this case it was believed that the deceased after the actual act of vampirism can become a shapeshifter, taking on the shape of the animal that took its soul.

A person can become a vampire if the religious ritual of passage is not performed correctly. The invitation of a priest to read from the scriptures over the body is still a

3 Tanas Vrazhinovski, *The Vampires in the Macedonian legends and beliefs*, Skopje 2009
4 Tanas Vrazhinovski, *The Vampires in the Macedonian legends and beliefs*, Skopje 2009 (*The demon from the afterlife – a collection of transcribed stories*)

common practice even today. The strongest superstitions in relation to vampires are connected with the religious component, i.e. not fulfilling the religious duties before or after the burial. The "sinful" soul of the deceased is however not entirely out of the picture. The recently passed life of sin may very well lead to the creation of a vampire, a creature that would continue its practice of doing wrong to people after his/her body is departed from the world of the living.

There is also another possibility for the creation of a vampire somewhat related to the religious rituals and the "sinning", which exists through a direct link with the immediate family of the deceased. There are many stories depicting one of the spouses becoming a vampire due to the sins of the other, or the disbelief in and disrespect of the Church, or the religious rituals in general.

The eternal vampire is an interesting concept that probably inspired the spread of the legends across the world, which then kept on changing as the time passed. The vampire, as depicted in the Balkan mythology is tightly connected with death itself, and there are rarely any stories that indicate cases where a person has become a vampire by biting or any other known and popular concepts of "creation". The vampire becomes eternal if, after six weeks or 40 days after his/her death has occurred, the spirit of the roaming vampire is not in its grave when the priest comes to chant his/her way to heaven. If the spirit has failed to return to the grave after the break of dawn, and the priest has already performed the ritual over an empty grave, the vampire or the spirit of the deceased becomes eternal and therefore cannot be cast away from the material world.

In this context it is very interesting to mention that the vampire spirit of the deceased over time, through the drinking of blood from people and cattle, would gain a boneless body, which again over a long period of uninterrupted life could gain new bones and become a human-like creature difficult to discern from a regular person. The boneless vampires were able to move through the smallest passages and sneak around houses and barns, seeking more blood.

A violent death can be another motive for becoming a vampire. There are many stories depicting battlefields (the Balkan region was and still is a part of the world where war is very common) where vampires would appear making noises of pain and haunting the people that lived around the battlefields. The soldiers would return from their graves, usually determined to go back to their families.

There are beliefs that the "witches", the women who were associated with the practice of magic or pagan rituals, were the ones who most frequently became vampires due to the communication with "impure" forces. There is a rather different understanding of the term "witch" in the Balkans, and the legends tell that these women will pray to the demons to give them power to heal and do magic, which possibly made them socially unacceptable for people in general, even though the common people kept turning to them when in need. These witches are to this day called "bayatchkee" and still operate as healers of children and adults. There is another type of witch that engages solely in practice of "black magic" or harmful magic. These women were very eligible candidates for projected vampirism.

Another belief is that babies could also become vampires. It is a popular notion, somehow associated with Christianity, that babies are impure up to 40 days after their birth. If a baby died before the expiration of that initial 40 day period, then there was a great risk that the baby would become a vampire. In relation to the vampire babies, there is a belief that a baby conceived from a vampire and a living person will actually have powers to exterminate the vampires – people called "vampeerjee".

People with bad eye-sight were known to become vampires quite often. There is a widespread belief that certain people can influence the health of other people just by looking at them.

The inevitable conclusion is that every human being has the potential to become a vampire. In regard to this, we can derive two general assumptions: there are people who become vampires by the influences of their immediate surroundings and not by their own fault, and people who become vampires by their own indirect choice, meaning that they have lived sinful lives, caused misfortune to other people, etc. In either of the cases, the individuals are in direct contact with the misfortune and the evil and are influenced by those two even in the afterlife.

Still, there is a rather mixed concept of what the vampire really is, if we compare the understanding of the vampire in the Balkans with the one that is now widely accepted throughout the world. The vampires of the Balkan folklore are rarely seen as creatures that possessed the ability to turn others into vampires. This common trait developed later as the myth spread to the West and eventually hit the movie industry. Another specific trait is that the vampire in the Balkans is portrayed as a highly individual creature, except for the cases where the stories encompass events related to the deaths of a group of people. Up to a certain point, the concept of the vampire in the Balkan folklore bears a resemblance with that of the zombies appearing in other cultures. The concept of the Slavic vampire is rather broad and contains a group of elements which makes it unique and not so common.

⸻ ⸻ ⸻

The existential component in the vampire legends is usually in accordance with the belief that the existence of the vampire is somehow equal to the existence of a living person. The main difference is that the vampires operate at night until the first dawn breaks; they get out of their graves and temporarily come back among the living. This causes an imbalance in the natural cycle of things and thus causes chaos in the world of the living.

Although there is a great resemblance between the vampire and the living person, the distinctive characteristics of a vampire would be coldness of the body and the inability to cast a shadow. These were usually the most common indicators of a vampire presence, along with confusion and inexplicable behavior. Some stories tell that there were dogs that could detect the presence of a vampire. These dogs were no ordinary hounds and they usually had four eyes, placed above the temples and in different colors.

The interaction of the vampires with the humans is the basic motif in almost every story. The vampire would appear as a friendly or unfriendly creature that is keen on helping the family or causing fear and damage to the close ones. The interaction is diversified in two main groups: the deceased in the world of the living, and a living person in the world of the dead. The second category seems to appear only rarely. However, there are stories depicting a living person who has been caught in the dance of the dead, at first unaware, but when it all becomes clear the living person will face the fear and die immediately or afterwards, struck by sickness or mysterious death.

In regard to the concept where the vampire is someone who comes back from the grave, there is a colorful myriad of tales depicting the vampire as a husband and a sexual partner that in some cases was able to impregnate the wife and create offspring (the offspring was depicted as pale, cold and unable to look up, always looking at the ground), the vampire as a head of the family where he would help raise the children or help around with the chores, the vampire as a cattle slaughterer, etc…

Another common story element is the vampire-butcher. Butcher Vampires were especially common, mostly because they had easy access to blood. Some of the legends depict butchers that weren't spilling blood while processing the meat, were accidentally stabbed with knives and turned into boneless mass, etc.

In the natural cycle of things, one could say that if there are vampires, there are means or people that can banish the vampires from the world of the living. One popular method was chanting a magical formula or a part of a religious ritual which would affect the presence of the vampire. There was a notion that the vampires don't like the word "wolf", so whenever a person would encounter a vampire it was enough to say "wolf" out loud and the vampire would disappear.

However, there is another elaborate way of banishing the vampires which is related to people who specialize in doing this. These would appear with an arsenal of weapons, crosses, secret books or secret herbs that when put to use would banish or exterminate the vampire forever. This profession was passed from generation to generation, and the secret knowledge of killing vampires was kept within the family. As a common element in the stories appears that if the vampire slayer wanted to see the vampire, he would just have to put a secret herb under his tongue and the vampire would become visible for him. One basic way of luring the vampire out of its grave is by inviting it to a village wedding, a visit or a trip to a known place. Then the vampire would be led to a bridge and, once he had crossed to the other side of the river, the vampire would be unable to return. In certain situations a common person was able to kill a vampire by the simple use of firearms.

When a vampire dies, according to many stories, he/she turns into a boneless mixture of blood and vampire flesh. This mixture was then burnt or infused with boiling water, which disabled the vampire from coming back to life. According to these story elements, the body of the vampire consisted of this boneless mass and a spirit, and after its death the spirit turns into ash. The material appearance of the spirit in such tales is an interesting concept that rarely appears in other regions than the Balkan ones.

There are other colorful and elaborate means to kill or banish a vampire: placing a knife under the pillow of the boy in the family, keeping the fire in the house constantly burning (there was a widespread idea that vampires are scared of fire and light in general), baking a loaf of bread and leaving the bread in another house (the vampire would pass through the bread from one house to the other, where the one who made the bread would become free of vampires and the other would have a vampire or an infestation of vampires), placing thorns around the graves or the houses that were potential for vampire attacks, putting tar on the doors, pouring boiling water into the graves, etc.

After the vampire was finally dead – regardless of whether it was killed by a person, dog or a wolf – the evidence of its death was always the boneless blood mixture that was left behind. These remains, as mentioned, were burned and the ashes were thrown in the river.

The vampire in the Macedonian folklore is also known as a creature feeding on human blood, usually from small children.

These mentioned vampire types seem quite active on many levels, but among them the most popular is the vampire that causes damages and bothers people in various manners. One of the most common components of almost all stories is that the main consequence of vampire activity is the further spreading of fear and the causing of misfortune for the people with whom it interacts.

In the Macedonian belief system and its mythic tales exists another type of vampire, which is called the vampire-animal/beast. In this case the tales deal with the secondary transformation such as: first the vampire appears in the type of man, and through metamorphosis then appears as a dog, cat, bull or a lamb.

The activity of the vampire in relation to the humans is interpreted as either antagonistic or non-antagonistic. From our collected notes, we can observe that the antagonistic relations are prevalent. In order to discover the entire spectrum of the vampiric nature and its functions, it is necessary for another dimension of the vampire's existence to be presented, namely the threat of death. The vampire-human relations are believed to be the cause of illness or death under mysterious conditions.

In the previous mention of the vampire types is presented the means of their eradication as well. There is an entire system for defense and vampire riddance, which to some extent is connected with the type of vampire activity. These means vary from excommunication from the community to bizarre killings of (supposed) vampires. Due to the awareness of the dangers this creature may cause, it should be noted that the people have created a very complicated system aimed at defense against this magical-demonic creature from the afterlife. Included in this defense system are many religious and pagan rites. Regardless of whether we're dealing with prevention or intervention, the aim of this entire system is to eradicate the body of the deceased in reality or symbolically.

Various appearances

A ROLLING BLOB OF BLOOD: In some parts of Macedonia the people have described and seen the vampires as rolling blobs of blood that gained strength and size as they continued their feeding practices. These vampire types didn't have a human shape and their existence was shady. The same ways of extermination applied to this type as well.

A CATERPILLAR-LIKE VAMPIRE: Basically, this type is seen as a huge caterpillar, often with a human head but not necessarily, crawling and feeding on human and cattle blood. The body, as with the rolling blob of blood, is boneless and gains size through its feeding practices. It was believed that if such a type of vampire is pierced with a knife or basically any sharp object it will burst into a splash of blood.

HALF-HUMAN, HALF-VAMPIRE: This type of vampire had two levels of existence, one human and one entirely vampiric. The metamorphosis occurred daily as the human changed to vampire and vice versa. Usually the vampiric nature would manifest at night and by dawn the metamorphosis would occur again. These vampires, as seen in the stories, were hard to spot and even harder to exterminate because they were usually members of the community who performed their community and family duties. Usually they were unmasked by an unexpected event after a long period of suspicion, ambush or by a simple confession from the human-vampire. It is important to note that when the vampire cycle occurred, the person was not in control of his/her actions.

To this very day there are stories to scare little children about women who live on the edges of villages, and who transform themselves into vampires and do harm to the villagers.

—◊— —◊— —◊—

Recent decades have brought to light a renewed fascination with the concept of vampires and vampirism, especially in the media and the popular culture. The Macedonian or, in a broad context, Slavic perception of vampires does not align with the Egyptian (Nosferatu) or Romanian (Dracula) aspects of this archetype. As such, its roots are more archaic and heavily influenced by the blood and death cult of Christianity, something that resembles the Haitian native cult of Voodoo, which was later also hybridized with Christianity. The very concept of vampires involves an inherent fear of death and a morbid obsession with blood which are, from a Thelemic point of view, symbols of the old Aeon and therefore obsolete.

There aren't any suggestions of psychic vampirism and vampires are generally considered to be operating only on a physical plane of existence. A generally overlooked aspect of vampirism is the context of sexuality, which is actually strangely present in Macedonian/Slavic folklore. Nowadays though, we find that vampires are erotic, attractive, seductive and can even produce children, a concept which was also present centuries ago on the Balkan Peninsula, although the vampires were considered repulsive creatures who wrecked homes and violated their partners.

Moreover, there seems to be an overlapping of attributes between vampires and incubi/succubi. Could this perhaps be a new direction in the (research of the) evolution of this dark human archetype? One which could include sperm instead of blood as the actual medium of vampirism? We have yet to see, but maybe in the future there will be epic movies and mini-series depicting hip and fashion-conscious urban incubi and succubi, ever on the prowl for a gnostic refill.

The Great Satan

Kevin Slaughter

Part 1: Welcome to the 10 in 1.

There's an old gag common to the carnival side show. A large banner hangs among many others, all gaudily painted, but this particular one proclaims that the rube... ahem... carnival goer can witness with their very own eyes a Twenty Foot Bat. Painted on the sign itself is the most fiendish of creatures; blood dripping from a fanged maw, webbed wings spread open wide. This unnatural monster and many more delights await you... for a few pieces of silver.

Upon paid entrance into the tent, one is greeted not with some mutant Chiroptera, but with a mildly convincing and grossly oversized papier maché baseball bat, laying on the ground in some scattered sawdust, quite lifeless, and usually worn and beaten from travelling the circuit for many years. The humorless are outraged, the dull are... well, dull, and those that can appreciate the absurdities of life have a chuckle and move along to gawk at the next attraction.

This bait and switch can be a metaphor for many things, but as an introduction I'm using it in a fairly literal way. The lecture I'm to give today has been advertised as *The Great Satan: Satanism as the Most American Religion*. A fine bit of hyperbole that has successfully moved a tip into the tent.

Those rubes who want to feel cheated will, but I suspect they entered the flaps with their own agendas. Those with an appreciation for the grotesque reality of the world will hopefully have a chuckle and enjoy the gawk at the attractions.

In Charles G. Finney's Satanic masterpiece *The Circus of Dr. Lao*, the titular character, acting as barker, grinds the following:

> Oh we've spared no pains and we've spared no dough,
> And we've dug at the secrets of long ago;
> And we've risen to heaven and plunged below,
> For we wanted to make it one Hell of a show.

The mysterious Dr. Lao presented a number of wonders to the common townsfolk of the fictional Abalone, Arizona. Every aspect of the Circus played to and revealed the foibles of these folk, these salt-of-the-earth Americans.

I will certainly, by the end of my talk, have discussed both Satanism and the separation of Church and State, but between now and then there are a few mysteries, marvels, frights and delights that I'd like to present.

I want to mention my latest lecture, titled *Satanism as Weltanschauung: The Philosophy of the Church of Satan*, because this one serves as a follow-up to it. That lecture is an introduction to Satanism as a philosophy, worldview, or modern religion and it's freely available on YouTube.

I don't want to repeat the content of that lecture too much, though I will give a brief overview of Satanism because it's probably safe to assume most of you will not know what it is really about. I will use the same structure as my last lecture, giving some background and touching upon some of the basic dogma and framework of Satanism, then exploring a few subjects more in depth.

I want to proceed now with one qualification. As I told the audience of my last lecture, I will tell one intentional lie today. Any others will be merely incidental. Please hold your questions until the end. I will entertain them then.

Part 2: Damned and Defiant

I am a priest in the Church of Satan, and can speak to you in the capacity of a representative of that organization. In the lecture *Satanism as Weltanschauung* I started with a long introduction of myself, which I will not repeat. I did stress, however, that I was a graphic designer by profession, and it is only when dealing explicitly with matters relating to the Church of Satan that I use the title of Reverend.

As Anton LaVey, who was dubbed "The Black Pope" by the media, "Doctor" by his early membership, and took the mantle of "High Priest" himself, has stated: "Titles have never insured respect from others." I think I would have phrased it "should never," but the point is central to a Satanic worldview – respect is something that must be earned, and should never be assumed. It is the presumption on the part of the entitled and those that believe in those titles that leads to endless human misery. The pedophilia of the Catholic Church, the genital mutilation performed by a Mohel, or the homicidal bombing inspired by an Imam's promises of heavenly reward. The fake cures peddled by suburban shamans, oriental mysticism fetishists, or chiropractors and homeopathic doctors. None of these things would occur as often as they do without some great level of naïveté and ignorance abetted by blind acquiescence to a title.

Nietzsche, a favorite of mine, had an idea of how to handle these peddlers of piety:

> Every type of anti-nature is depraved. The most depraved type of man
> is the priest: He teaches anti-nature. Against the priest one doesn't use
> arguments, one uses the penitentiary.

Satanism is about respect to those who deserve it, who have earned it, not simply by joining a club or wearing the right kind of costume. One certainly doesn't earn my respect or trust merely because they claim to speak to god and they've managed to convince others that it's so, neither do I give even an inch to someone because they merely call themselves a Satanist.

I was asked a few years ago by an enthusiastic kid what he could do to represent Satanism. I gave him advice that Peter H. Gilmore gave out himself in his book *The*

Satanic Scriptures: Be great at something. It doesn't matter what, but excel at it. There is no "being great at Satanism," but find something real where you can cultivate a skill or talent to a level above your peers. Then, as a Satanist who is great at something, you will benefit Satanism. It should be a side-effect though, not a goal. Those who wish to jockey for rank within an organization should join any number of fraternal orders or social clubs – ass kissing is always rewarded there. An essay on the topic published in Anton LaVey's *Satan Speaks* puts it in even more brusquely and concrete terms impossible to misconstrue: Get a Life.

PART 3: STAKING THE TENT IN THE DEVIL'S SANDBOX

Satanism as a coherent worldview came into being on Walpurgisnacht of 1966 when California eccentric Anton LaVey ritually shaved his head and, in a chamber in the basement of his black Victorian, proclaimed Year One of the Age of Satan. Leading up to that point he and a close circle of occultists, bon vivants, and intellectual dissidents would gather for soirées and lectures on obscure and titillating topics. It is written that "a ship's purser might be seated next to a deep-sea diver, a dildo manufacturer next to a plastic surgeon."

It was a natural fit to the times, but it didn't exactly fit in with the popular counterculture. While the Summer of Love was to occur in 1967, wherein it advocated a blend of ego-destruction, mindless drug compulsion, and the ugliest fashions since the pilgrim hat, Anton LaVey championed a view that people should be responsible for themselves, should build their ego, and reject the status quo. Yes, the Hippies were ostensibly bucking the system as well, but they were doing it by "dropping out," taking dope, and creating a philosophy that doesn't hold up past the slogan "give peace a chance" on their bumper sticker.

LaVey worked as a calliope player in the circus, a freelance ghost hunter for the police department, a burlesque show organist, and crime scene photographer among other things. Most biographical sketches of LaVey tell the anecdote from the introduction to The Satanic Bible:

> On Saturday night, I would see men lusting after half-naked girls dancing at the carnival, and on Sunday morning when I was playing organ for tent-show evangelists at the other end of the carnival lot, I would see these same men sitting in the pews with their wives and children, asking God to forgive them and purge them of carnal desires. And the next Saturday they'd be back at the carnival or some other place of indulgence. I knew then that the Christian church thrives on hypocrisy, and that man's carnal nature will out no matter how much it is purged or scoured by any white-light religion.

A writer whose works are considered to be among the Satanic canon, Ben Hecht, in his book *Broken Necks* gives his take on the same phenomenon:

I have noted that the simpletons who squeal over the obscenity of modern literature and the simpletons who rush to the book stores to buy only obscenity are of the same lodge. They are both people whose normal stupidity is shocked by any deviation from the platitude in which their souls are buried. They are both creatures of malformed and boorish instincts which they have sugar-coated with ideals peculiar to all stupid, cowardly and dishonest natures.

Satanism is a worldview based on Epicurean atheism. While everyone else in the world is waiting for heaven or hoping to trade up on their next reincarnation, we accept that heaven or hell is to be made here on earth.

We use Satan as a metaphor because we find it to be the most useful for the story we want to tell, and for the audience who will be apt to hear it. Satanism is not for the masses. Peter H Gilmore, in the introduction to the *Satanic Bible* spells it out clearly:

> Unlike the founders of other religions who claimed 'inspiration' delivered through some supernatural entity, LaVey readily acknowledged that he used his own faculties to synthesize Satanism. He based it on both his understanding of the human animal acquired from life experience and the wisdom he'd gained from other advocates of materialism, pragmatism, and individualism.
>
> His blasphemously named 'Church of Satan' was consciously designed to be an adversary to existing 'spiritual' belief systems. It was the first organization promulgating religious philosophy championing Satan as the symbol of liberty and individualism.

It should be no surprise to anyone who pays attention to what humans do, rather than what they say, that the places you'll find the most prolific religious conversions and epiphanies are prisons, drug rehab shelters, and any gathering spot where people have hit rock bottom.

LaVey, from *The Satanic Bible:*

> If (man) hates himself, he searches out new and more complex spiritual paths of 'enlightenment' in hopes that he may split himself up again in his quest for stronger and more externalized "gods" to scourge his poor miserable shell.

How many people who you know that are happy with themselves have religious conversions? I've never met one. I have, however, had dozens of ex-junkies try to regale me with a sort of evangelistic fervor that was only matched by their former devotion to their drug of choice. Surely they have not changed, they have merely changed drugs. They are still junkies, and their behavior is just as irrational and often self-negating now as it ever has been. One day they're on a street corner fellating strangers for an out-of-body high, the next they're fellating god for heavenly reward. I see little difference, one ends up feeding money into an international criminal organization, and the other pays a drug dealer.

Some people who were raised Christians, Jews, Muslims, etc. do cease paying lip service to those faiths and embrace Satanism. This is not a conversion. Satanists are born, not made. For those that don't understand that, Mae West characterized this best when she said: "I was ashamed at the way I used to live." When asked if she'd reformed her ways, she replied, "No, I'm just no longer ashamed".

This is an adorable little news item I found yesterday, the title is "Detroit prayer event puts Muslim community on edge, Christian group plans to rally in Detroit.

In the story itself, we read:

> Leaders of The Call believe a satanic spirit is shaping all parts of U.S. society, and it must be challenged through intensive Christian prayer and fasting. Such a demonic spirit has taken hold of specific areas, Detroit among them, organizers say.

This notion that "if you really think something will be better, it will be" has made Oprah Winfrey the richest woman in the world, but only because she was selling the dream at quite a substantial mark-up. The people buying this magical thinking nostrum, well... You tell me how they're doing?

Some monasteries have supposedly held 24 hour peace vigils for centuries. In the spirit of magical thinking, our president (Barack Hussein Obama) was given the Nobel Peace Prize. Again... How's that working out?

LaVey, from *The Satanic Bible:*

> The Satanist shuns terms such as "hope" and "prayer" as they are indicative of apprehension. If we hope and pray for something to come about, we will not act in a positive way which will make it happen. The Satanist, realizing that anything he gets is of his own doing, takes command of the situation instead of praying to God for it to happen. Positive thinking and positive action add up to results.

The real audacity of hope is knowing that people are dumb enough to buy it, even if it's an empty vessel, even if they've been sold that same bill of goods time and time again. The masses are instant suckers for a good sermon or snake-oil salesman. We pay more attention to what people say they will or won't do than to what they've done in the past. We elect leaders based on their pleasant looks and enrapturing oratory.

> "You see this here fish, June?" old Britches asked me one afternoon. "This here fish is called a sucker. It's called sucker because it will swallow almost anything. There's hundreds of thousands of these suckers, June, and most of them read travel books." I never forgot the lesson that he taught me.
>
> (Corey Ford, *I Learn Something About Sex*)

I like that quote a lot, and I think it's fair to say one can easily switch out the words "travel books" with "new age books," "self-help books," or "religious books."

Detroit has a population that is 47% functionally illiterate. The School board elected as its head, with a 10-1 vote, an illiterate, and a graduate of this very institution (Wayne State University). We invested the future of their children with the notion that people should be given credit for what we want them to be, instead of what they are. They are the uplifters, the well meaning instead of the well doing. They are the wreckers of civilization.

Lao-tzu said:

> Goodie-goodies are the thieves of virtue.

In a 1899 speech by Congressman Willard Vandiver, he coined the unofficial motto of his state (Missouri) when he said:

> I come from a country that raises corn and cotton, cockleburs and Democrats, and frothy eloquence neither convinces nor satisfies me. I'm from Missouri, and you have got to show me.
>
> I won't take you on your word until you've proven it's worth more than a wooden nickel.

US Supreme court justice Louis Brandies weighed in around 1928:

> The greatest threats to liberty lurk in insidious encroachment by men of zeal – well-meaning but without understanding.

Friedrich Nietszche tackles the idea from a different angle:

> One should call the 'holy' story by the name that it deserves, as the accursed story; one should use the words 'God,' 'Saviour,' 'redeemer,' 'saint' as invectives, as criminal badges.

And after all of that, and usually much more than that, the first question that is inevitably offered is: "Why call it 'Church of Satan' when you don't actually believe in Satan?" or some variation. I think Schopenhauer put it quite nicely in his book *Studies in Pessimism:*

> A mother gave her children Aesop's fables to read, in the hope of educating and improving their minds; but they very soon brought the book back, and the eldest, wise beyond his years, delivered himself as follows: This is no book for us; it's much too childish and stupid. You can't make us believe that foxes and wolves and ravens are able to talk; we've got beyond stories of that kind! In these young hopefuls you have the enlightened Rationalists of the future.

I don't dislike the Abrahamic religions because they give moral lessons in the form of metaphor or allegory. I dislike them because the morality underneath is despicable. I loath their followers because an overwhelming majority aren't bright enough to know they're metaphor in the first place.

To bring the spotlight back to the center ring, I quote on the matter from one of the greatest and most prolific American writers, H.L. Mencken:

> I made up my mind at once that my true and natural allegiance was to the Devil's party, and it has been my firm belief ever since that all persons who devote themselves to forcing virtue on their fellow men deserve nothing better than kicks in the pants.
>
> Years later I put that belief into a proposition which I ventured to call Mencken's Law, to wit: Whenever A annoys or injures B on the pretense of saving or improving X, A is a scoundrel.

The philosophy Anton LaVey set forth in *The Satanic Bible* was a mixture of bombastic blasphemies, personal peccadilloes, and the sort of common sense that is just too damn uncommon. It's called a religion because it has a dogma that is the foundation of an ethic, though not a revelatory one, it has a ceremonial system, and it has symbols and pulls from relevant traditions of the past and created some of its own. Of the common definitions of a religion, the one thing missing is "god above," but Satanists have secularized god in the most logical way, for it is us.

Part 4: Satanism and the Satanic

When introducing a new concept, or at least a new perspective on a concept that one may have false prejudices of, it's important to define how terminology is used. There's a constant struggle between whether words are defined by the top down or bottom up. In that I mean, do words have a fixed meaning or are they defined by consensus use? The word "atheist" is believed to have started its linguistic life as a pejorative, and obviously "Satanist" has some social baggage. We use the term knowing full well the stigma, and though I may speak on the topic in order to correct misunderstandings, I don't do it from the vantage point of a victim decrying oppression.

The point is that the language used by groups of people differ in meaning, even if nuanced. Certainly Marxists and Post Modernists both have a rich and dense lexicon of neologisms for creating a sort of smokescreen of impenetrable lingo. Satanism has a few words of its own coinage, but the most obvious issue is the "S"-word itself. What we mean by the word and what others mean are different. But it's also important that I distinguish two terms from one another: "Satanism" and "Satanic". I want to elaborate on how they are used by Satanists and the Church of Satan. How other people use them, I have no control over.

What is Satanism? This is the dogma of the new religious belief codified by LaVey et al. Being a Satanist means applying these ideas to your everyday life. Satanism as a term denotes the specific philosophies and the worldview represented by the Church of Satan.

Satanism is a carnal religion, and is outlined in *The Satanic Bible*, and expounded upon in other writings by LaVey and his successor Peter H. Gilmore. Though it's not a closed system, there are specific concepts that could be considered Satanism Proper, or what I have referred to as dogma. It is explicit, and everything is above board. We are not an esoteric society where you have to pay x dollars to reach enlightenment. Scientology does that well, if you're into that, tell galactic overlord Xenu I said "Hi!"

This dogma is outlined in easy to digest bullet form in few primary documents, "The Nine Satanic Statements", "The Eleven Satanic Rules of the Earth", "The Nine Satanic Sins", and the five points of "Pentagonal Revisionism". I discussed the "Nine Satanic Statements" in my previous lecture, but so that you have a sampling of what I'm talking about, I'll relate "The Nine Satanic Sins."

While "The Nine Satanic Statements" were part of the founding of the Church in 1966, and are featured in *The Satanic Bible*, the sins were not published until 1987. As one would expect, a Satanic Sin has nothing to do with the eternal status of your soul. In pragmatic form, they are a list of what we believe are non-productive attributes and acknowledge that they should be rooted out if we find ourselves exhibiting them.

1. Stupidity – The top of the list for Satanic Sins. The Cardinal Sin of Satanism. It's too bad that stupidity isn't painful. Ignorance is one thing, but our society thrives increasingly on stupidity. It depends on people going along with whatever they are told. The media promotes a cultivated stupidity as a posture that is not only acceptable but laudable. Satanists must learn to see through the tricks and cannot afford to be stupid.

2. Pretentiousness – Empty posturing can be most irritating and isn't applying the cardinal rules of Lesser Magic. On equal footing with stupidity for what keeps the money in circulation these days. Everyone's made to feel like a big shot, whether they can come up with the goods or not.

3. Solipsism – Can be very dangerous for Satanists. Projecting your reactions, responses and sensibilities onto someone who is probably far less attuned than you are. It is the mistake of expecting people to give you the same consideration, courtesy and respect that you naturally give them. They won't. Instead, Satanists must strive to apply the dictum of "Do unto others as they do unto you." It's work for most of us and requires constant vigilance lest you slip into a comfortable illusion of everyone being like you. As has been said, certain utopias would be ideal in a nation of philosophers, but unfortunately (or perhaps fortunately, from a Machiavellian standpoint) we are far from that point.

4. Self-deceit – It's in the "Nine Satanic Statements" but deserves to be repeated here. Another cardinal sin. We must not pay homage to any of the sacred cows presented to us, including the roles we are expected to

play ourselves. The only time self-deceit should be entered into is when it's fun, and with awareness. But then, it's not self-deceit!

5. Herd Conformity – That's obvious from a Satanic stance. It's alright to conform to a person's wishes, if it ultimately benefits you. But only fools follow along with the herd, letting an impersonal entity dictate to you. The key is to choose a master wisely instead of being enslaved by the whims of the many.

6. Lack of Perspective – Again, this one can lead to a lot of pain for a Satanist. You must never lose sight of who and what you are, and what a threat you can be, by your very existence. We are making history right now, every day. Always keep the wider historical and social picture in mind. That is an important key to both Lesser and Greater Magic. See the patterns and fit things together as you want the pieces to fall into place. Do not be swayed by herd constraints – know that you are working on another level entirely from the rest of the world.

7. Forgetfulness of Past Orthodoxies – Be aware that this is one of the keys to brainwashing people into accepting something new and different, when in reality it's something that was once widely accepted but is now presented in a new package. We are expected to rave about the genius of the creator and forget the original. This makes for a disposable society.

8. Counterproductive Pride – That first word is important. Pride is great up to the point you begin to throw out the baby with the bathwater. The rule of Satanism is: if it works for you, great. When it stops working for you, when you've painted yourself into a corner and the only way out is to say, I'm sorry, I made a mistake, I wish we could compromise somehow, then do it.

9. Lack of Aesthetics – This is the physical application of the Balance Factor. Aesthetics is important in Lesser Magic and should be cultivated. It is obvious that no one can collect any money off classical standards of beauty and form most of the time so they are discouraged in a consumer society, but an eye for beauty, for balance, is an essential Satanic tool and must be applied for greatest magical effectiveness. It's not what's supposed to be pleasing – it's what is. Aesthetics is a personal thing, reflective of one's own nature, but there are universally pleasing and harmonious configurations that should not be denied.

Now that I've presented this, I will discuss the term "dogma," as most secularists have a knee jerk reaction to it. I call these sins "Dogma" because it defines what Satanism is and is not. Satanism isn't universalist, so it's not a Dogma in the sense that everyone must follow it. Satanism is elitist, and recognises that its core principals cannot be applied by most people, and so only a small number of folks will take on the label of Satanist. You are free to challenge and question Satanic dogma, as it is a human's understanding of the world, and if you find that it is not for you, then you just simply aren't a Satanist.

Of course, the term Satanism is used to mean any number of things by many people. Many Catholics still believe Jews are Satanists, many Protestants still think Catholics are Satanists. Some people believe the United Nations and President George W. Bush are Satanists. I am not the language police, but when I or a member of the Church of Satan use the term, we're not talking about goth chicks on meth playing cutting games in their parents' basement or some fantasy where a deluded sorcerer begs a demon for magic powers.

I will say, however, due to my adversarial and prankish nature, I'm often conflicted when it comes to debunking claims of International Satanic Conspiracies. I mean, when some nutjob implicates that I am a spokesperson for a secret world government that is run by a cabal of sinister puppeteers, why not let them run with this delusion? Certainly someone that dumb will not be reasoned out of his position.

Federalist founding father Fisher Ames (try saying that ten times quickly) is quoted saying two rather incisive things regarding this:

> I have heard it remarked that men are not to be reasoned out of an opinion they have not reasoned themselves into.

> Falsehood proceeds from Maine to Georgia, while truth is pulling on his boots.

So I have been asked here to talk about Satanism and I will just do it in a straightforward manner, but, again, I admit I do feel that tension and temptation. I suppose if I were Jewish, I would feel the same about debunking the *Protocols of the Learned Elders of Zion*. I mean, let's be honest, it's a great goddamn plan. But one doesn't want to be persecuted for things they don't actually believe, and I think the reality of Satanism is probably much more dangerous to the prevailing religious orthodoxy than any conspiracy.

At the very least, if I were Jewish, I'd occasionally wear a t-shirt with the words *Christ Killer* on it. I don't think I'd be able to overcome that temptation.

What is Satanic? This is an interesting concept that can be difficult for the slow folks to grapple with, but one can easily view the world through a Satanic lens without considering one's self a Satanist or referring directly to it. Something can be Satanic without necessarily being explicitly about Satanism. This may seem paradoxical, but I will explain.

We can discuss the Satanic from multiple angles, but I only have time to discuss one. What is Satanic is not a mere reversal of Christianity. For example, the Lord's Prayer being said backwards is still the Lord's Prayer. The Lord's Prayer is a supplication to a divinity, it is a beggar's bowl to a supernatural creature clamoring for intercession in personal security, the provision of food and a pleading that the Lord God steer the supplicant away from bad things. It is a total rejection of personal responsibility for the most fundamental of human needs. An explicit Satanic equivalent may be Baudelaire's *The Litanies of Satan*, where he takes the Lord's Prayer and blasphemes it up, exchanging Mary's name for Satan. Something a little more inspiring might be Carducci's *Hymn to Satan*. I've truncated to a few lines in English:

> *To you my daring*
> *verses are unleashed,*
> *you I invoke, O Satan*
> *monarch of the feast.*
>
> *Put aside your sprinkler,*
> *priest, and your litanies!*
> *No, priest, Satan*
> *does not retreat!*
>
> ...
>
> *You breathe, O Satan*
> *in my verses,*
> *when from my heart explodes*
> *a challenge to the god*
>
> *Of wicked pontiffs,*
> *bloody kings;*
> *and like lightning you*
> *shock men's minds.*
> *Sculpture, painting*
> *and poetry*
> *first lived for you, Ahriman,*
> *Adonis and Astarte,*
>
> *When Venus*
> *Anadyomene*
> *blessed the*
> *clear Ionian skies*
>
> ...
>
> *As Martin Luther*
> *threw off his monkish robes,*
> *so throw off your shackles,*
> *O mind of man,*
> *And crowned with flame,*
> *shoot lightning and thunder;*

Matter, arise;
Satan has won.

...

Hail, O Satan
O rebellion,
O you avenging force
of human reason!

All the hallmarks of Satanic worldview are there: indulgence, the beauty and wonder of the material world, a rejection of the oppressive faiths, a championing of human exceptionalism, and finally the triumph of reason. Personally, my preference would be no mocking prayer or long form poem, however fun or inspiring they may be. I like poetry well enough, but If one was in the company of friends and family, a more implicitly Satanic equivalent of a prayer could be a simple toast:

> Here's to cheating, stealing, fighting, and drinking.
> If you cheat, may you cheat death,
> If you steal, may you steal a woman's heart,
> If you fight, may you fight for a brother,
> And if you drink, may you drink with me.

These simple five lines are nothing but a series of Satanic themes. The first line is bombastic, but what follows is a carnal celebration of living in the here and now. You can keep heaven, I'll be down here with the lord of this earth.

Film noir is Satanic, Al Jolson and Richard Strauss are Satanic, Sex Dolls and Homosexuality is Satanic. Rejecting the world is the trademark of all the world's major religions. Those who hate life pray for the blessing of it to end, those who love life toast to its joys. Living for the here and now, reveling in the world as it is; tragic, flawed, beautiful, and indulgent, is Satanic.

To my wife, with whom I just celebrated five years of marriage.

To my dear friends Peter and Peggy, who just celebrated their 30th.

> Salut!
> L'Chaim!
> Cin Cin!
> Skål!

PART 5: GOOD FOR ME, NOT FOR THEE

Satanism is not evangelical. I can't say that enough. I'm not here to convince you to sell your soul to Satan. I don't believe we have souls, and if we did, they'd be a dime-a-dozen.

'I am up to my neck in souls.' said Lucifer.

So wrote Robert Nathan in his novel *The Innocent Eve.*

There are seven billion of us bugs scampering across the face of this blue orb. What makes you think you'd be so appealing? Considering Old Scratch has the likes of Jayne Mansfield to oogle, Friedrich Nietzsche to parry, and Charles Darwin categorizing the imps. Franz Liszt certainly plays piano in Hell's dive bar, with arrangements by Irving Berlin and accompaniment by every goddamn Jazz musician there was. There must be cognitive dissonance of the most egregious nature. Americans know Satan as a charming, rugged anti-hero, though most don't seem to know they know. I will explain.

Dashiell Hammett begins his aviary themed novel, *The Maltese Falcon:*

> Samuel Spade's jaw was long and bony, his chin a jutting V under the more flexible V of his mouth. His nostrils curved back to make another, smaller, V. His yellow-grey eyes were horizontal. The V motif was picked up again by thickish brows rising outward from twin creases above a hooked nose, and his pale brown hair grew down-from high flat temples-in a point on his forehead. He looked rather pleasantly like a blond Satan.

Sam Spade doesn't go about killing cats and touching kids in the wrong places, which is still the same tired scare tactics used by Christians to ward off any interest in Satanism. We know intuitively that this diabolical caricature of him tells us that he's a man to be reckoned with, strong-minded, tough, fiercely independent, and dangerously intelligent. He is all those things. If someone was described as angelic, we would understand they were soft, probably a bit of a stick in the mud, beautiful but sexless, and in most cases boorishly naïve.

As a side note, I find it incredibly ironic that child molestation and animal mutilation are still proposed as standard Satanic activity. I'm sure Freud would have something to say about it, and for all I know he might have, but one needs to look no further than the evening news to see who it is that is molesting the children. And one merely needs to remember history to know that it was Pope Gregory the ninth, in his infinite superstitious stupidity that wrote the Papal Bull *Vox in Rama* in which he is condemning supposed devil worship. In it, he proclaimed that cats were the instruments of Satan. This triggered such a wave of felinicide that the population of cats dwindled to the point that allowed the rats to take control of Europe. And the rodents were the carriers of the Black Death that ultimately killed up to 60% of the entire population. It took 150 years to recover from this imbecility, and guess who got the blame for all of it? It wasn't the man responsible, no, it was the eternal scapegoat. You tell me, if cats had a religion, you think it would be that of his Holiness?

De facto Satanist Mark Twain typified the Satanic outlook on the human condition in his posthumously published work *Letters from the Earth.* Satan, being banished from heaven, decides to check out this out-of-the-way planet which hosts one of God's small experiments; humans. He writes a series of letters to his fellow archangels, and this is the first:

> This is a strange place, and extraordinary place, and interesting. There is nothing resembling it at home. The people are all insane, the other animals are all insane, the earth is insane, Nature itself is insane. Man is a marvelous curiosity. When he is at his very very best he is a sort of low grade nickel-plated angel; at is worst he is unspeakable, unimaginable; and first and last and all the time he is a sarcasm. Yet he blandly and in all sincerity calls himself the "noblest work of God." This is the truth I am telling you. And this is not a new idea with him, he has talked it through all the ages, and believed it. Believed it, and found nobody among all his race to laugh at it.
>
> Moreover – if I may put another strain upon you – he thinks he is the Creator's pet. He believes the Creator is proud of him; he even believes the Creator loves him; has a passion for him; sits up nights to admire him; yes, and watch over him and keep him out of trouble. He prays to Him, and thinks He listens. Isn't it a quaint idea? Fills his prayers with crude and bald and florid flatteries of Him, and thinks He sits and purrs over these extravagancies and enjoys them. He prays for help, and favor, and protection, every day; and does it with hopefulness and confidence, too, although no prayer of his has ever been answered. The daily affront, the daily defeat, do not discourage him, he goes on praying just the same. There is something almost fine about this perseverance. I must put one more strain upon you: he thinks he is going to heaven!

Satan's third letter begins as follows:

> You have noticed that the human being is a curiosity. In times past he has had (and worn out and flung away) hundreds and hundreds of religions; today he has hundreds and hundreds of religions, and launches not fewer than three new ones every year. I could enlarge that number and still be within the facts.
>
> One of his principle religions is called the Christian. A sketch of it will interest you. It sets forth in detail in a book containing two million words, called the Old and New Testaments. Also it has another name – The Word of God. For the Christian thinks every word of it was dictated by God – the one I have been speaking of.
>
> It is full of interest. It has noble poetry in it; and some clever fables;

and some blood-drenched history; and some good morals; and a wealth of obscenity; and upwards of a thousand lies.

PART 6: ATHEIST, MATERIALIST, EPICUREAN

I do not believe in any god. As the saying goes, popular among atheists, my faith in gods is the same as the Christian, except with just one god less. I don't care to spend too much time on the subject explicitly because everything I say is premised on the notion that no gods exist, but I will tell you how utterly frustrated I am in the inevitability that some believer thinks they've invented Pascal's Wager. What's the harm, they say! But Pascal's Wager only makes sense to a Christian who believes there can only BE one god. To an atheist who doesn't believe in any of the millions of gods that have existed, it's a joke.

But Satanism is not atheism. Atheism is a statement of negation. It merely states "I don't accept the proposition of god." It's also true that some Satanists believe in things that cannot be explained by science, as all humans do. Scratch at the surface of many atheists and you'll find something that just doesn't fit with the science. Satanism is the same thing to atheism as Humanism or Objectivism is. Humans cannot function in the world without prejudices, and worldviews provide a system of prejudices that allows people to make intellectual shortcuts. I suppose I'm not going to win many accolades with that, but I think it's an honest statement: we see the effects of bias and prejudice everywhere, and certainly even in the sciences.

PART 7: ON HUMANISM

Now, once we've cleared up the whole Satan as metaphor angle, and those first learning about Satanism come to terms with the idea that we are indeed godless, many still unable to grasp the idea of Satanism say "Why don't you call yourselves humanists or something less confrontational?" So let's look into that. The International Humanist and Ethical Union states:

> Humanism is a democratic and ethical life stance, which affirms that human beings have the right and responsibility to give meaning and shape to their own lives. It stands for the building of a more humane society through an ethic based on human and other natural values in the spirit of reason and free inquiry through human capabilities. It is not theistic, and it does not accept supernatural views of reality.

I agree that human beings have the responsibility to give meaning and shape to their own lives, but this is not necessarily a feature of democracy. Democracy is a way to restrict individual liberties, not enhance them. It may be the least restrictive form of governing, but all organizational principals set limits. Democracies have voted in dictatorships, democracies are at the whims of majorities.

One can look at it like recycling... Sure, it's not the best analogy, but it'll serve its purpose. Recycling is not a positive environmental activity. It does not create something new, it just uses energy to reuse part of what would be waste. At best, it takes less energy and uses fewer resources to recycle something that exists into another thing than to create it out of new materials. It's not making things better, just a stalling tactic so things don't get worse as quickly. In reality, it is generally a wasteful exercise in making people feel good about themselves and creating tax-subsidized jobs.

Come to think about it, it's not such a bad analogy after all.

But the question must be pressed, are "human and natural values" really ones that build a more humane society? By humane, I assume they mean something along the lines of:

> Characterized by tenderness, compassion, and sympathy for people and animals, especially for the suffering or distressed.

A number of the "New Atheists" have stated that the quickest way to produce an atheist is to have someone read the Bible. Penn Jillette comes to mind as someone who's said it. This is obviously not axiomatically true, for many sincere and intelligent believers actually have read the book, though obviously many believers haven't.

My quip would be that the quickest way to produce a misanthrope is to make them live among humanity unvarnished.

Giacomo Leopardi said this before me:

> Real misanthropes are not found in solitude, but in the world; since it is experience of life, and not philosophy, which produces real hatred of mankind.

This is obviously as true (and therefore as false) as the Bible premise, but if you've ever heard those who work with the poor and with criminals, at least when they believe they can speak honestly and candidly without either some sort of moral reproach (or something more dangerous to their self-interest, a cut in funding) you will certainly get an earful about what unappreciative shits these damn poor folks often are. You'll hear about how little real hope they have in making a difference, even if their manpower was multiplied a hundred-fold and they were given a blank check and unlimited resources to aide their humanitarian efforts. They recognize, privately, that some people are just rotten. Not all of them, but plenty, and too many.

The seventh of "The Nine Satanic Statements", a founding bit of dogma in Satanism states:

> Satan represents man as just another animal, sometimes better, more often worse than those that walk on all-fours, who, because of his "divine spiritual and intellectual development," has become the most vicious animal of all! Elevating the human species as somehow innately superior to other animals is blatant self-deceit. Humanity is driven by the same natural urges that other animals experience. While our intellect

has allowed us to accomplish truly great things (which should be appreciated), it can also be credited with incredible and wanton acts of cruelty throughout history.

I credit LaVey with introducing me to the notion, but we can look all the way back to Roman playwright Titus Maccius Plautus in his *Asinaria* where he wrote "lupus est homo homini" roughly, "man is man's wolf."

Robert Burns, in his poem *Man was Made to Mourn*, illustrates the idea beautifully in verse:

> Many and sharp the num'rous ills
> Inwoven with our frame!
> More pointed still we make ourselves,
> Regret, remorse, and shame!
> And man, whose heav'n-erected face
> The smiles of love adorn, –
> Man's inhumanity to man
> Makes countless thousands mourn!

Burns' poetic Bard notes quite clearly that even though man may worship the heavens, he still decimates his fellow man.

PART 8: THE BLOW-OFF

Normally, in a good ten in one, if you're really lucky, there's what's known as a blow-off. One of my favorite writers, Jim Tully, a hobo turned Hollywood muckraker and tough as nails novelist, writes about it in his book *Circus Parade*. In a girly show, the barker walks on stage and appeals to the gathered tip :

> Lefita, the favorite dancer of the Sultan, who escaped the horrors of a Turkish harem and was brought to this country by the generous owners of this circus to present for you the secret dances of Egypt. She knows the lure of the dances of the world. She it was who danced for the kings of impotent glory.: E-v-e-r-y mu-s-cl-e-e-v-e-ry-fib-er in this little la-dees ana-tom-ee quiver-s and shakes like an aspen leaf in a gale of wind—or like a bowl of jell-ee, gentlemen—on a cold and frost-ee morning. She makes the old feel young and the young feel gay, the blind to see and cripples to throw their crutches away.

Once inside, the show began:

> The drum throbbed. The clarinet shrieked. Lefita shivered languidly.
> The music became more violent and Lefita's body kept in tune. It moved like something boneless but sensuous.

The movement ended in a gyration that seemed to leave her exhausted. It was a short dance. The onlookers stood curious and expectant. The spieler then called them closer and said blandly, "I recognize some real sports amongst you, gentlemen, with good red blood coursing through your corpuscles. But would you like it, gentlemen, if this little lady would put on a special show for you? She just told me inside that she had never seen so many handsome men – and the young lady sees a great many."

"Of course, gentlemen, there will be an extra charge for this – just a thin silver dollar apiece – and of course all that we collect will go to the little lady herself. The little girl will be glad to give the special engagement for you. Move closer boys, move closer." He made a motion with his hand. "Listen, if you boys ever had that funny feeling – you know – she'll give it to you as you've never had it before. You know the Sultan of Turkey and the King of England's each got a lot of wives and seeing women is of course no preponderant mystery to them, but they got a rise out of Lefita…"

An audience member who is really in cahoots with the carny speaks up:

"I say, Professor, I wonder if she'll give that doniker dance she put on over in Emoryville the other night."

Between the man on stage, the shills in the audience and the natural lust of the men in the audience, the price of this extra dance keeps going up as more and more is promised:

"What do you say, gentlemen, if we all chip in another half dollar and give it to the lady. Two little silver dollars ain't much and look what a show we'll see. We may as well be real sports. We don't see things like this every day, and I'm for helpin' the little girl. We've all got sisters and mothers and they've got to git along. And if we gentlemen don't help them, who will?" Two other shillabers cried, "Here's my two dollars."

And it builds, and the professor moves the tip into a special room off to the side…

"Say, Professor," spoke up a shillaber when the music ceased, "now that we're in here you be a good sport. What's the matter with having the little lady do the dance – without – you know!"

The spieler looked concerned and cautious at the same time. He held up a long smooth hand. "Why, boys, I can't ask her to do that. Gracious, gentlemen, this is too much. You should have told me before I let you in here that you wanted the whole show. Why she got five dollars apiece from the Elks last week for putting that on. Sometimes the Shriners give her even ten dollars apiece." He looked about, then spoke softly. "But wait, I'll ask her."

"Yes, gentlemen, I'll be fair. One dollar more each and I'll see that she gives the whole show the Egyptian dance, the doniker dance, and the wonderful dance without. Think of it, gentlemen, the soul-stirring – the voluptuous – the sensuous – the wonderful – the maddening dance without." They all rushed forward with another dollar.

"Thank you, thank you, thank you, gentlemen," said the spieler as Lefita came through a side wall and climbed upon the platform. She danced indifferently, her body moving slowly. In a short time she disappeared.

"That was just the introduction, gentlemen, merely a warming up of her lovely body. In a few minutes she will do the dance without." He held his long smooth hand up again. "Will all you gentlemen please remove your hats'?" he said.

They did as they were told.

Lefita appeared and danced again in the same apparel. A shillaber sneered as Lefita bowed. "Without what?" he yelled gruffly.

"Without your hats on," came the bland voice of the spieler.

Suddenly the side-walls dropped and the astonished spectators found themselves standing in the open air.

They looked at each other sheepishly and melted into the crowd.

This is the blow-off. It's worked time and again from city slickers to country bumpkins. It relies on humans to be predictable and easily led by their natures. People are greedy, selfish, and stupid. If they weren't, we wouldn't have the troubles we do. If humans could easily change, those troubles wouldn't be the same damn ones we've had for ages. As I quoted LaVey at the top of this very lecture, "Man's nature will out!"

Now, since I'm actually planning on entertaining some questions later, I will not be performing such a stunt. For future lectures though, I may just have to write two endings... one to top off my speech, and one to clear the room.

Here, at last, I will come to discuss head-on the proposition of the hyperbolic side-show style title of my lecture.

Part 9: The Great Satan

America, as an idea, and largely in practice, has been utterly Satanic. New York journalist and author, Benjamin De Casseres wrote in the literary journal *The American Mercury* a piece entitled "Hymn to Satan":

The grandeur of America today is satanic, materialistic, irreligious, unethical... The settlement of America was the birth of a New Reality. It began the dethronement of the mystical God and the rejuvination of the Prince of This World – prince of this world not in the Old World theological sense, but as the spirit of the Will to Material Power.

As proof of this idea of America as a new Satanic empire, he states:

> Read the preamble. There is not an ounce of imagination, religion, meta-
> physics or poetry in it... the Constitution came into this world like a
> prolonged cynicism in the mouth of an atheistic lawyer... The Constitu-
> tion is the cold sun of Reason.

Thomas Paine said:

> I do not believe in the creed professed by the Jewish church, by the
> Roman church, by the Greek church, by the Turkish church, by the
> Protestant church, nor by any church that I know of. My own mind is
> my own church.

Later, it was William Taft who said he did not believe in the literal truth of the Bible. Can you imagine a modern presidential candidate admitting to not being a Christian? He said:

> If a man can be a Christian only when he believes in the literal truth of
> the creed as it is recited in the orthodox evangelical churches, then we
> Unitarians are not Christians.

But really, we can pull quotes from the founding fathers and former presidents all day and it means very little. This old man said so and so in his private correspondences, that one expressed this frustration in his diary, etc. ad nauseam. So, I will finish with one last quote. And I can't think of a more persuasive argument than it, on the validity of the separation of church and state:

> Congress shall make no law respecting an establishment of religion, or
> prohibiting the free exercise thereof; or abridging the freedom of speech,
> or of the press, or the right of the people peaceably to assemble, and to
> petition the Government for a redress of grievances.

Thank you. I'll take questions now.

(audience member) "What is the one lie that you told?"

Ah, a fine specimen of skeptical inquiry. I'm glad I asked you to ask me that. The lie I told was "... as I told the audience of my last lecture, I will tell one intentional lie today."

I had all sorts of stuff written about the Liar's paradox and misdirection, but I've spoken too long as it is. This is what I lied about... I lied about telling my previous audience I was going to lie to them. It's a silly prankish way to use psychology to overtly prime you to think critically about my talk. If I told you anything could be a lie, you will listen as if everything is potentially one, and hopefully if there's something you agree with that you'll have to consider it more because of that.

The Art of Evil
The Satan Game revisited

Lionel Snell

The Fenris Wolf 2, 1990, published an article by me entitled: *The Satan Game – reflections on recent hysteria amongst fundamentalist Christians*. As the subtitle suggests, the article was one of a series I wrote in the context of a then-current media campaign attacking occultists and magicians and rolling out the usual clichés, such as:

—⁓— All magic leads to, or is, "black magic".

—⁓— Black magic is magic deliberately practiced for evil purposes.

—⁓— A worldwide conspiracy is promoting black magic, and has recruited millions of clandestine followers that already infiltrate every level of society.

In the article I argued that it was absurd to believe that a large proportion of the population were deliberately practicing magic for evil ends—indeed, most evil acts are the result of a distorted idea of what is good, rather than intentional evil. Taking Nazism as the classic exemplar of evil: its attraction was that it set out to create a "better" Germany, rather than selling itself as a party offering wonderful opportunities for people to express their evil natures. Greedy bankers do not set out deliberately to trash the economy, instead they mostly achieve that by insisting that they are stimulating economic growth, or by believing in a "trickle-down effect", or even that "greed is good".

My argument at the time was this: one defining quality of magic is that it is generally practiced in order to achieve some outer or inner purpose or result; so it would be ridiculous to do magic for a result that is purely bad, with no redeeming feature. OK, people do do ridiculous things, so I am not saying that no one has ever used magic for totally evil purposes, but that to do so would be an anomaly rather than a universal world problem – as was being proposed in the media at that time.

So I was not suggesting that no one in the wide world had ever taken up the maxim "evil be thou my good", but rather that it had little to do with mainstream magical practice – and so was not relevant to my then current writing.

It does, however, remain an interesting issue, and one that features heavily in novels and movies. Fantasy literature would be sorely depleted if we took away all those "Princes of Darkness", mad geniuses, Count Draculas, black magicians, insane scientists and other embodiments of absolute evil.

The popular notion is that such people really do exist, and fingers will be pointed at promising candidates – such as Aleister Crowley, Adolf Hitler, Charles Manson or Osama bin Laden. A mass of evidence will be presented to "prove" the case but, in my experience, anyone who sets out to write a serious biography of such people will end up revealing a human being – albeit just a deluded or unbalanced human being – behind that mask of darkness. At worst they uncover a psychopath – the chilling discovery of an amoral and therefore incomplete soul, but not a human being with a conscience, one who knows both good and evil, but has deliberately chosen the latter.

It would, however, be ridiculous to suggest that no-one could ever choose a path of ultimate evil. The scope of human invention is so great that any such claim would be one good reason to attempt that very choice. So, in this article I want to explore reasons and circumstances that could lead someone to dedicate themselves wholeheartedly to absolute evil.

ATTITUDES TO THE DEMONIC

A few years ago I ran an Arcanorium course on personal demons. As in my *The Little Book of Demons*, the course extended the notion of demon to embrace all sorts of ongoing problems. Auric Goldfinger had a wonderful saying: "the first time is happenstance, the second time is coincidence, but the third time, Mister Bond, it is enemy action". In a similar manner I suggested that one unhappy love affair, or work failure, was bad luck; but when it happened again and again as a pattern, then you could call it a demon and work with it accordingly.

At one point in the course I drew a comparison between the ways different cultures approach and deal with demons. I illustrated this by using my SSOTBME[1] model that extended CP Snow's two cultures, art and science, to four cultures – art, religion, magic and science.

The "art" culture is broadly understood as centering on "art", i.e. the subjects one would study at art college, but extending to a whole range of activities including music, drama, art appreciation, even journalism and anything (such as motorcycle maintenance) that can be described as "as much art as science". The "science" culture obviously centers on laboratory science but also embraces theoretical science, applied mathematics and a whole swathe of popular "scientism" – as when someone says "I'll believe that when I see it!" My version of religious culture centers on organised religion as practiced in temples and churches, but extends to all ideas that bind people together, as the Latin word "religare" suggests – so the culture embraces politics, being a sports fan or member of a professional body or any cult that excludes and includes members. Finally, my view of a "magical" culture clearly centers on ritual and initiatory magic, but also extends way beyond them to include divination, most alternative healing and applied psychology, as well as activities such as marketing and advertising.

What I suggested was that these four cultures had four quite distinct approaches to the demonic. In any "religious" culture there is no place for the demonic. Demons must simply be banished or destroyed: so we have religious exorcisms, political purging, banishment of dissidents, a war on terror, or simply blackballing unpopular club members.

---

1 *SSOTBME – An Essay on Magic*, Nigel Grey-Turner, London, 1979.

"Scientific" cultures do not approve of the term "demon", but similarly see such recurring issues as problems to be solved, cured, eliminated – or even proven not to exist.

Magical cultures, however, often recognise the demonic as an energy or resource that may have a purpose and may be bargained with for useful effect, as in traditional demonic pacts. For example, susceptibility to colds and flu can really get you down, but it can also be a handy way to get off work and have time to read books. An inferiority complex can turn a nice person into a pain in the ass, but it can also spur one to amazing achievements. New Age men's workshops advocate working with one's woundedness, and trendy business handbooks insist that: "what others call problems, we see as opportunities". Note that this is never a question of surrendering to the demon, but rather of forming a new, more useful relationship with it.

So far so good – but I then went on to make a rather radical suggestion that an arts culture might actually celebrate evil. I did not attempt to suggest that this was a defining characteristic of art, but simply that an arts culture fosters an attitude towards evil that is utterly different from the religious, scientific, or magical approaches.

The Evil in Art

I will illustrate this with some examples. The first has already been mentioned, namely the popularity of figures of evil in film and literature: the many versions of Dracula, Frankenstein monsters, evil scientists, fiends from outer space and characters in cartoons and movies, like the Joker and Freddy Krueger. These are not just popular with the public – actors queue up for the role of a really wicked villain.

Moving a little further up the art market, consider how critics rate the better television detective series. In the 1950s there was a British TV series called *Dixon of Dock Green*, featuring a lovable old "bobby" doing a fine community job keeping the peace in Dock Green, London. In the 1960s the series gave way to a new cop drama called *Z Cars*, which was championed by the critics for its "realism" because it replaced the old style bobby on a bicycle with tough young policemen in cars doing realistic things like swearing.

Since then, the rule of thumb for judging the quality of a police drama is that the worse the detectives' personal problems, the better, or more "classy" the drama. Among the most highly rated TV detective series in the 1980s was *Prime Suspect*, in which Helen Mirren played a woman detective with severe personal problems including alcohol, smoking, relationships and an abortion. Since then it seems that no fictional detective can be taken seriously unless they have at least a drink problem. This has become such a cliché, that I find myself yearning for a tough gritty detective series in which the tough gritty detective is a vegan, teetotal health freak, growling things like: "geez, what a god awful day! I'd kill for a carrot juice."

Moving closer to the core of the arts culture, may I suggest the following thought experiment?

Walking through town one night, you pause by the lighted window of an art gallery. There you see a painting depicting a single orchid abandoned on a flight of stone steps. There is something very moving about the contrast between the fresh beauty of the flower and the unforgiving hardness of the stairs. A drop of moisture on the white petals emphasises the freshness of the bloom, but also suggests a tear: why is this beautiful flower lost in this way? Did it fall out of someone's buttonhole? Why were they in such a hurry?

You walk home haunted by this image and decide that you must find out about the artist and what this painting meant to its creator. At this point, I offer two experimental outcomes:

1) You discover the artist was a young man who achieved fame prematurely, was lionized by the establishment and became an overnight sensation. But he was so disgusted by the commercialism and hypocrisy in the fine art world, that he turned his back on it and lived a life of gutter poverty, painting pictures in return for food, lodging and, above all, gin. His health deteriorated and he succumbed to drink and drugs. As a final dying act he sold every last thing he possessed to purchase paint and canvas for one final painting – The Orchid on the Steps – encapsulating the tragedy of a beautiful young soul cast out in a grey, uncaring world.

2) You discover that the artist is alive and living in a Hollywood mansion where he sells his paintings and portraits at exorbitant prices to stars and celebrities. Paintings like "The Orchid on the Steps" cost hundreds of thousands of dollars for those lucky and exclusive enough to get their hands on them.

My question is this: after each of these two possibilities how would you now feel about the painting?

My guess is that in the first case the artist's misery, rejection and suffering would add value to the painting. It begins to look like a masterpiece. In the second case, however, the very same painting begins to look somewhat kitsch – one would feel a little embarrassed giving wall space to anything like that.

Now I may have overdone it with this example, with its blatant artistic snobbery, but it does convey something true: that the many evils of suffering, rejection, exploitation and poverty can add significant value in an artistic culture. Contrast that example with the purchase of some everyday object – an iPad or a pair of jeans. If, after the purchase, you discover that the object was manufactured in a far Eastern sweatshop where orphaned children was starved and exploited for cheap labour, in this case the suffering would not add value to the object, instead most people would feel rather bad about having purchased it.

What these examples point towards is a suggestion that an arts culture can embrace and celebrate evil in a manner very different from that of religious, scientific or even magical cultures. In a scientific culture the demons of poverty and pain must be eliminated; in a religious culture these demons must either be banished or else transmuted – so that poverty no longer implies starvation, but rather a monk-like simplicity of soul, and that pain becomes sanctified as a pathway to transcendence. In magical culture too, one does not seek out poverty or pain, but one might form some sort of working relationship with them in order to achieve some specific purpose.

By contrast, evil seems positively welcome in an arts culture – it plays a very important role. But what is that role?

BEING EVIL

If what I am suggesting is true, then the person who consciously chooses evil, who says "evil, be thou my good", is not doing anything either magical or religious so much as making an artistic statement.

It's the sort of statement that can transform a fairly average heavy metal band into a significant cultural phenomenon. This fact seems to be widely recognised, to judge by the amount of Satanic imagery adopted by more extreme metal groups. But, looking back at my series of articles from the 90s, it is clear that I was writing from a magical rather than an artistic viewpoint. I did not focus on Satanism as a dramatic artistic statement, but as a purposeful choice.

Those essays broadly addressed two types of Satanism. The first was an intention to explore deeply atavistic forces such as power, pride, lust and animal appetites, and that Satan was chosen as a chthonic deity to be one's guide in these regions. There is nothing inherently evil in this type of Satanism, it is simply a form of research to gain knowledge or understanding – comparable to a scientist studying bacteria in order to find out their properties, but with no intention of developing biological weapons. Nor is it necessarily a foolish thing to do: the fact that this earthy Satan has a strong trickster streak is certainly reason to be careful, just as a careful researcher needs to take precautionary measures when dealing with highly infectious organisms.

The second type of Satanism I considered was a bit more radical: where Satan is chosen as a "devil" or polar opposite of some positive power. An example of this is St Secaire's alleged black mass held in the crypt of his Christian church in order to purge that institution of its sin. The political equivalent would be a Prime Minister having secret negotiations with the leader of the opposition in order to resolve a crisis. In this case Satan is addressed not as a positive natural phenomenon, but rather in his role as a negation or denial of some positive power. Again there is nothing inherently evil about this type of Satanism, though it can seem very shocking to devotees of the opposite pole.

But what I did not address in those essays was Satanism as pure devotion to absolute evil, as opposed to an attempt to form a relationship with animal or antinomian powers. As explained, this type of Satanism now makes more sense to me when considered as an artistic statement. As stated: I believe that purpose is fundamental to magic and, in those terms, devotion to absolute evil makes little sense. If, for example, a rock group decides to adopt Satanic imagery in order to sell more records – even going so far as to claim that they are worshipping Satan – then their purpose is to sell more records, and that in itself is not inherently evil. So Satanism, in that case, becomes simply a specific means to achieve what every other rock group is trying to do, and so not outstandingly evil.

What then about devotion to absolute evil as a religious act? Again, I find this hard to accept. For the nature of religious culture is to devote oneself what one considers to be absolute good, even though it might seem very evil to others. One would have to have a very high opinion of evil to want to devote oneself to it in a religious sense, and that is in itself paradoxical. Offering something as positive as devotion to something as negative as absolute evil implies a sort of confusion of soul. In fact the very idea of absolute evil is paradoxical. What would be an absolutely evil act? Nowadays most people would consider the act of killing an innocent infant as absolutely evil and yet, in so doing, you are also destroying the child's own potential for evil – might he not be tomorrow's serial killer? Killing the child is certainly an evil act, but it would take a lot of hindsight to be sure that it was *absolutely* evil.

Of my four cultures, the one where paradox is most at home is the artistic culture. The sort of problems I've been describing when one devotes oneself to evil for magical or religious purposes vanish when one considers such devotion as a work of art. Raising one's fists to heaven and screaming "evil, be thou my good" as a pure expression of life's rage and frustration is an act that goes beyond any purpose or meaning. Whereas the wearing of an inverted crucifix in order to sell more records, or to stir up media outrage, is a simple piece of magic, a truly artistic form of Satanism may be the agonised howl of a soul trying to break free from the limitations of its chosen medium of expression.

In my first attempt at writing a novel, my character Angerford felt that he had achieved nothing until he had stirred his audience to acts of mass suicide whenever his music played. It was not what he really wished to achieve, but rather a claustrophobic soul's scream for "more!" in a world hedged in by moral, social and physical laws and prohibitions.

But what does evil do to the practitioner?

Nothing that any real human does can be truly absolute, not even a dedication to absolute evil. One might feel the full intensity of rage and frustration that I have just described, and it might drive one to adopt a defiant mask of evil or devotion to Satan as described above – but what might happen in actual practice?

I am reminded of one of Gerald Suster's early slasher novels, *The Offering*. It described a young couple moving to a house that had been occupied by a notorious punk musician named Kevin Street. The book slowly builds up a picture of Street as the wild rock star turned evil, who came to an untimely end and now haunts the house they live in. As things turned more and more nasty, one character sets out to find the awful truth about Kevin Street, and tracks down an old friend who says that: "Kevin Street was one of the nicest, sweetest, most creative men I've ever met." It's a very dramatic moment, a bursting of the bubble of evil that the novel had created. But it does ring true.

Although I do not fully subscribe to the notion that we are all born equal, I am aware of a sort of moral balance about a point of equilibrium – typically between the inner and the outer. It can take many forms: the preacher of morality who harbours private vices; the man with a deep sense of inferiority, who compensates by behaving as a bully; the comedian who makes the world rock with laughter but suffers from lonely depression, and so on. So, on reflection, the idea of a rock star who plays the role of ultimate evil, and yet in his private life reveals a tender core, is not so surprising.

Oscar Wilde's novel *The Picture of Dorian Gray* provides an inverse metaphor for this: a man who remains young and beautiful while the portrait that hangs in his basement grows old and ugly, reflecting the debauchery of his outer life.

Why would anyone want to devote himself to absolute evil? A few paragraphs earlier I invoked the idea of an artistic statement, an expression of outrage and frustration. But I suspect that it takes a truly sensitive soul to really feel that level of outrage.

A brutal person can be very evil, but the level of evil is limited to the capacity of their brutal soul – like a jug merely filled with poison. The ability and the inclination to reach out and invoke infinite evil require something more: the creativity and imagination of an artist. Again, we see this in fiction: beyond the mere murderous thug, we find the master criminal, James Bond's arch enemy, Sherlock Holmes's Moriarty, the man who wishes to elevate crime to fine art and in the penultimate act says: "Alas, what a pity that I have to kill you now, the only man in the world with sufficient intellect and refinement to truly appreciate my art".

In my own experience, just as the path to hell is said to be paved with good intentions, so have those who tread the left-hand path and explore the sinister byways of thought, turned out to be among the most warm and sensitive people that I have met. So, in answer to the question at the beginning of this section "what might happen in actual practice?" I would suggest that in actual practice those who devote themselves to absolute evil will turn out to be sheep in wolves' clothing – even if buried very deeply within that wolf skin.

But does it have to be so? The nature of art is to be unbounded and unrestrained. Put any limits on it, and in no time there will be artists exceeding those limits. Lay down any boundary such as Expressionism versus Impressionism, or classical versus jazz, and there will soon be artists creating works that bridge that boundary. Invent some label to describe an art movement, and promptly there will be artists rejecting that very label. So, the very fact that I have suggested that one needs a soft centre to aspire to absolute evil, is reason enough for someone to try to prove otherwise. But I still don't think it would be easy.

I remember a time when I wished to create a movie of ultra-violence – two hours of non-stop, unmitigated gore and splatter. It was not that I liked the sight of blood, or would have watched such a movie myself, but rather an act of defiance against the increasing violence portrayed in the media. You would hear people saying "I was disgusted by that film, it was nothing but blood and butchery", even though, if you analysed the film frame by frame, it might only contain a surprisingly small percentage of actual scenes of bloodshed. What was happening was that year on year films were coming out each a little more violent than those of the year before. This is what people meant when they complained about a film been nothing but violence: they were really saying that the film contained more violence then they had so far become accustomed to. So my impulse was to attack this creeping hypocrisy by creating a film of such total bloody destruction that anything that came after it would have to be tame by comparison, if it left any room for plot or dialogue.

My favourite pornographer in the 1970s was Mary Whitehouse, the advocate of decency who took a stand against the permissive society. She had a wonderful way of describing erotic books and movies in words that made them so much more sexy than the originals. Like the hellfire preacher ranting against bestiality and filth, natural functions became imbued with intoxicating, supernatural power. I didn't need to buy the pornography, I just had to hear the phrases she used to describe it to get an erection.

INFINITE, BUT BOUNDED

So I suspect that any attempt to invoke or devote oneself to absolute evil would be just too paradoxical for a real, rounded human being to achieve. It would demand an incompleteness that would in itself set limits. Instead, like the movie industry, those who aspire to evil must content themselves with being just that much more evil than those who went before. Characters in novels will struggle for the evil Gold medal, while real, non-fiction humans will be limited to attempts to break the record for the number of serial killer victims – and they will probably fail to do it with any great style.

I've already quoted Gerald Suster, so now let's turn to Gerald Yorke, the highly respected ex-disciple of Aleister Crowley. One day when the gardens of his house in Gloucestershire were open to the public, a visiting lady commented on some shrivelled buds, saying: "isn't it sad to see what the drought have done to these beautiful bushes!" Gerald Yorke replied: "yes, but isn't there something rather nice about the way these sad things happen from time to time?"

I think there is something rather nice about the way real people struggle, and yet fail, to be utterly evil.

And yet, what would I feel if I really got to know one of my favourite *bêtes noirs* – say, Rupert Murdoch or Margaret Thatcher – and found that, as a person, I quite liked them? The thought is so horrific, that it makes me want to tear up this essay and lock myself in the lavatory.

So maybe we really need our demons, and should be grateful for those artists – and I include journalists – who paint those evil pictures that hang in our basements?

Ars longa, vita brevis.

The Quintessence of Daimonic Ipseity

Phenex Apollonius

Summoning demons is frequently and erroneously associated with practices of moralistic compulsion due to the influence of the medieval goetia on the western magical tradition. This error tends to occur through disregard, or ignorance, of the original context of the concept of the *daimon* as well as the goetic magical tradition of sorcery as it existed in the Hellenistic world prior to the onset of Christianity.

The vilification of the "demons," that is, the *daimone*, through the work of early Christian dogmatists has ultimately given us the concept of 'demonization.' The transformation of the *daimone* into mythological beings signifying opposition is now linguistically archetypal of the transmogrification of neutral or even benevolent magical powers into enemies of religion – and ultimately into enemies of the state. Such a condition necessitates an approach to the summoning arts that takes this condition of mythic opposition into account: that which was once seen to be beneficial is now regarded by the predominant social reality as inimical. Hence, a magician who chooses to treat them as friends has the benefit of a historical context surpassing that of the temporally and aeonically ignorant, and the detriment of having set hirself against prevailing trends.

Originally, the *daimone* were terrestrial spirits associated with particular manifest phenomena; that is, a given person had its 'patron *daimon*,' and so did a place, or a political structure. The "deities" were considered to be a specific class of *daimone* which were not confined to the terrestrial sphere – they were general rather than particular. In as much as the modern mind makes "God" a particular, it treats a particular *daimon* as a deity and thereby perpetuates imbalance. The primary mistake of the religious is always to assume that the magician thinks in terms of absolute dependence on one particular mythology (as superstitionist religions imply) rather than cultivating a choice of beliefs. As such, the assumption that the demonic magician somehow practices an 'infernal religion' is almost a given to the monotheist mind – thereby revealing the flaws and limitations of such a perspective. Hence, this essay is written according to an ethos of *quid pro quo* rather than an ethos of ideological addiction frequently called "faith". "Faith" to the demoniast is, much like the term "demon," a concept derived from a more traditional linguistic stratum and referencing the expectation of reliability in one's patrons – and supporters.

However, a condition of *quid pro quo* presupposes that the summoner has something of value to offer in exchange for the assistance of the *daimone* in question. This is again in contrast to the medieval methodology of binding and compelling the magically useful *daimone* by means of the monomaniacal tyranny of the religious obsessions then current. Hence the most important condition for the successful summoning of "demons" is having something worthwhile and interesting to offer them. Wealth, art, attention, and pleasure are all familiar forms of commodity relevant to the demonic paradigm and stand in stark contrast to the authoritarian paranoia characteristic of the monotheist "goetia." Which, indeed, is something of a misnomer anyway, since the original "goetia" referred to the works of the *goes*, the sorcerer, whose name derived from a Greek word associated with howling and "barbaric speech" generally. The only aspect of the original tradition that survives into the medieval grimoires claiming its provenance is the confused names of the 'demons' that appear therein.

The most desirable commodities to the *daimone* are forms of direct sensory access to the flesh, and access to the world of meanings and ideas offered by communion with the human mind and will. That is, they desire alignment with those characteristics of humanity generally understood as the 'body' and the 'ego,' both of which are not surprisingly condemned by transcendentalist religious systems such as monotheism, the primary aim of which is to ensure the total possession of the human body-mind by one *daimonic* power which sets itself against the rest through the aforementioned process of "demonization." As such, the first concern of the would-be demoniast is to establish both a precise relation between hir body and hir ego as well as the capacity to transgress them at will, allowing the *daimone* access to hir senses in exchange for greater knowledge and power of the arcane alignments governing their manifestation into the flesh. Only a magician capable of full self-modification and self-creation remains sufficiently flexible whilst simultaneously sufficiently durable to handle congress with the minds of the *daimone* which are at once alien to the human flesh yet depend upon it for their continued continuity and power.

Thus, the deliberate cultivation of an ego capable of persisting in conditions of sensory magical ecstasy is the path of *ipseity*, being the state of self-referential awareness reified in flesh, and the power of identification of the consciousness with the self or the other. Even without demonic congress, such an awareness affords significant insight and power as consciousness naturally attracts to itself a *bodily form* suitable to its perceptual alignment. Thus the whole totality of the magician's sensory experience acts as a magical "circle of art" wherein the primal arcana of hir hidden *daimonic* nature becomes physical reality, its alignments revealing the contours of the magician's ecstasy as outward signs of an inward power. The psycho-physical effects of "confidence" on self and others offer a mundane analogy for the visceral influence the ipseic magician can exercise upon those ensorceled by hir art, and ultimately upon the material world under the shadow of hir senses.

It is the transmutation of this power of *ipseity* betwixt its self-referential and obsessional forms that allows the magician to ride the surging currents of power embodied by the *daimone*, as these beings cannot necessarily be said to have "egos" of their own but do have the tendency to inspire the generation of such by their manifest presence – how the magician chooses to align hir own ipseic awareness with the legionary consciousness of the *daimone* provides the context for hir practice of the summoning art, and indicates hir trajectory along the five-fold path of Ipseity. This *daimonic* consciousness self-identifies as Legion, *"for we are Many,"* and in communion with the sole ego of the magician (whether such is regarded as a factor of empty centrality or an acentric/eccentric force of opposition and self-revolution) it becomes the union of the singular and multiple, the general and particular, and thus expresses in living flesh the *quintessence of daimonic ipseity:* undying, continuous, ecstatic identification of the self with the other.

In hir quest for self-overcoming, the daimonic magician will utilize the ipseic power not to sacrifice or transcend hir carnality but rather to cultivate it as a source and commodity of power. This act of "self-conjuration" becomes the primal magical act wherein the ipseic quintessence is rendered itself *daimonic;* this process of "self-deification" often referred to in left-hand path magical traditions does not depend on any particular context of the ego itself, but rather upon the ego's precise alignment and relation with the flesh in such manner that it is, with respect to the rest of the carnal world, equivalent to a *daimon* itself. Thus, although the manifold transformations of ipseity will lead the magician across ways both crooked and serpentine into a labyrinthe of self, the ultimate act of *daimonic* sorcery is a "self-demonization" – the Self made Other has become both the First and the Last: the ultimate circumferential boundary of the void-circle of art which is always just beyond the carnal reach whilst including within itself the body entire.

In practice the magical extension of this is indeed the "conjuration" of desires through purely ipseic consciousness, whether the magician has associated with a self-defined *daimon* or has simply opened hir ego as it is, to the totality of the Legion. The two alternatives to this state of self-union form the horned points of the ipseic pentagram which is itself the entire *daimonic* quintessesnce expressed as the Hand of the Demon, with its unblinking eye – the Void – open as an emptiness in its central palm. These phases of dual opposition are association and disassocation. The primal state of ipseity could be considered "associative" only if there is understood to be something *else*, an otherness, for it to associate *with*. But in as much as Total Ipseity *is* self-otherness, and the Ego of the magician the Self, (as the Legion might be considered to be the Total Self in its unitary phase and Total Otherness as the Many), so is the state of 'association' – when Total – the possession of the magician's flesh by a consciousness of sole Otherness, being the *daimon* as an independent magical reality. This is the consciousness generally referred to as "invocation," whilst its opposite, disassociation, is the abstraction of the self from all otherness to such extent that it is association with nothing other than itself – which being empty of any qualities, could just as well be considered non-self. This is the ipseic phase most useful for oracular insight as derived from the consciousness of the 'watcher within,' which if aligned to the ego is only such when the ego is *dis-associated* from everything else – including its own otherness. In mythic terms, the "watchers" are forms of the *daimone* particularly concerned about congress with humanity and the teaching of the magical arts, as chronicled in the *Book of Enoch* and other such apocryphal texts. Indeed, those entities most frequently recognized as 'demons' in Judaeo-Christian lore are often directly identified with these "fallen watchers" who sought marriage to the daughters of men and whose progeny were routinely associated with acts of magic, power, and defiance of the divine order. It may be that access to the total disassociation of the magical Seer is one of the gifts of the Watchers in exchange for flesh – they who desire the flesh, and lack it, grant the ability to step beyond it, to those who are of their kin, or ken. Whereas the invocation of the *daimon* is indeed to grant it both body *and* ego, often in exchange for the knowledge derived from ecstatic union with the absolutely other, or power that can only be released into the carnal realm by the intrusion of a power subtler than the magician hirself.

The remaining arts of transvocation and evocation relate to invocation and disassociation much as conjuration does to those latter two. From the total otherness of the full invocation, the magician either conjoins this otherness once more with the self-referential ipseity to become totally egocentric, resuming the conjuration as a self-daimonized power, or separates the ego from the *daimon* allowing both to align to one flesh yet remain distinct. Such is the phase of transvocation and it has the advantages (and detriments) of retaining the magician's habitual ego whilst simultaneously infusing the flesh with the power of the daimonic ipseity. Evocation, then, is the association of the disassociated self-consciousness with the otherness, but in such manner that there is no reassociation of the otherness to the flesh: that is, the *daimon* is exteriorized 'outside' the summoner, with the summoner's ego acting as a channel of attention, or even devotion (in the case of "religious" evocations) to the entity outside of hir bodily consciousness. This pattern of representing the five-fold ipseity also makes it clear that from a state of transvocation, the magician will find it easy to shift either to invocation (total interiorization in ego and flesh) or evocation (total exteriorization of the *daimon*) as the situation requires. Similarly, the evoking magician, once the other has been exteriorized, choose also to disassociate the ego from the flesh, or invite the *daimon* that has just been called forth to share the sensations of the carnal form. These various 'gestures' of the Hand of Ipseity, in all their possible combinations, can ultimately be evolved by the magician into a somatic and sensory language of demonic desire that renders the fluctuations of hir sense of self into living signs of arcane power.

This is not to say that these channels of 'magical power' fully contextualize the range of ipseic transmutations. Another pattern of power can be perceived even within the confines of the suggested model; this pattern being the circumambulation of the magician around the circle of ipseic art in either the sinistral or dextral direction. Both might be seen as paths of 'mysticism,' the dextral path of *daimonic* mysticism seeking self-daimonization through the use of daimonic transvocation as a means to disassociation of the ego followed by full possession, ultimately allowing the daimon to evoke itself into the world of flesh surrounding the summoner who is thus rendered daimonic hirself; the sinistral path also seeking self-daimonization, but by means of evoking the daimon with the intent of making the 'pact of possession' *and then* freeing the ego of its mortal confines so that it rides the *daimon* from within in an act of final transvocation of self-otherness. While both paths lead to self-daimonization, the 'right-hand path' as a form of mysticism is frequently associated with eventual ego-loss and submission to the totality of otherness: the frequent use of this method by "right-hand path" religions to control their adherents does not necessarily reflect on its worth as a mystical methodology. Similarly, the association of the sinistral methods of the left-hand path with forms of antinomian magic does not necessarily rule them out as successful forms of mysticism, since the illuminations offered by daimonic congress pertain as well to the cultivation of insight as they do to power.

The circle of magical art is often depicted as the serpent eating its own tail; this seems to be a fitting symbol for the state of self-union implied by either path of mysticism. The imagery suggests, as well, that ultimately the ego – and even the *daimone*, when they are manifest – are generally bound within the circumference of this draconian power. To transgress the habitual boundaries of self so far into Otherness Entire as to associate with the full Dragon of Ipseity is to gain the power to uncouple its head from its tail and, either becoming or riding the dragon, strike out into the absolute void hidden within the carnal form as the omnipresent point – and revealed as the boundless space beyond the body of the Oroborous. As the Hand of Ipseity is the magician's organ of sensory perception and manipulation, so the five-pointed figure of the Human may be regarded as the Hand of the Opposer expressing its will to self-overcome through interaction with, and incarnation within, the sensory world. Experientially realizing this occult daimonic correspondence betwixt the magical microcosm and the draconian macrocosm of perpetually transmogrifying nature, the magician discerns the secret alignments and esoteric arcana and executes those antinomian gestures which grant hir total liberation from the confines of *body, ego,* and *otherness* and thereby attains to the *Ipseity of the Void:* the self-beholding Eye of the Opposer. This act of total will-perception culminates – and initiates – the draconian quest for limitless understanding and power which characterizes the daimonic manifestation. That which sustains the magician on this quest is the quintessence of ipseity.

Infernal Diabolism in Theory and Practice

Phanes Apollonius

The Devil's Prayer

Infernal Opposer,
Who art below the Hell-realms,
Legion are Thy Names.

Thou art the Sovereign of Selfhood, whose Will to Power
reigns from beneath the worlds and within them,

As We partake of the body and blood of enemies slain unto You,
We trespass against weakness and avenge ourselves against those
who would undermine Us.

Lead us forever through Temptation, that we might know
Good and Evil.
For Ours are Mastery, Splendour, and Victory:
Now,
but Hidden.

The Diabolical Decision

The opposite of the symbolic is the diabolic. Rather than joining things together, the Diabolist throws them apart. This sinister way of Separation disjoins the individual from the cosmos and sets it against the mass. This makes Diabolism the proper contrary of Symbolism and distinguishes its practice from the prevailing occult and esoteric trends of relying on symbolic correspondences for meaning and power. Arcana, alphabets of desire, qabalahs, and similarly structured magical systems generally operate, or purport to operate, by making a given sign meaningfully equivalent to a string of associations all of which ostensibly refer to the real concept indicated. Most such systems ultimately collapse to a unity and therein partake of the classical process of successive, mediated emanation from the One. The Diabolist also uses correspondence structures for sorcerous praxis, but the basic conception of the Diabolical Arcana is opposed: it presents not a primary "symbol" for unity, but a primary "diabol" – the Devil – for duality; a horned mask placed over the void, a cunning lie told by the forked tongue of the serpent, the two-faced draconian mask. The rest of the Arcana is based on this primary "diabol," and the concepts of that Diabolical Arcana do not reflect pure forms of noumenal number into phenomenal reality; instead they obscure it behind further veils of illusion crafted by the personal and idiosyncratic intentions of their creator – for the Diabolical Arcana is a deliberate imposition of the subjective perspective of the Diabolist into the otherwise "symbolic" cosmic order, a willful perversion of the unity of the divine cosmos to the precise aims and will of the operator. While many traditional Arcana are received in states of somnolescent trance, half-consciousness, or automatism, the Diabolical Arcana is only intuited, penetrated, pronounced in a condition of wakeful consciousness capable of knowing – discriminating, Separating – Good from Evil.

Diabolism is the ultimate expression of the act of personal choice and perpetuates the distinction between the subjective awareness of the practitioner and the apparently objective reality which ceaselessly attempts to impose itself into it through the senses. The Diabolist resists this relentless effort to re-unite consciousness with cosmos. As with the ultimate role model for defiant, independent, individually self-aware consciousness, this effort strengthens will and perception, refining and honing them against the totality.

The work of the Diabolist depends in part on emulation of the Devil itself in its function as Opposer. This is not confined to the Devil's significance as a cosmological contrary in monotheist systems, since the Diabolist rejects morality and the moral deity, setting himself against those who believe in it. The Diabolist maintains that such beliefs originate in an inability to accept and comprehend the natural duality of the cosmos by vilifying one pole and trying to identify with, or even unite with, the other. Diabolism relies on a contrary approach. Identity as, and identification with, the principle of opposition and duality itself automatically renders moralistic bias impossible for the Diabolist, who is also empowered by the tension created by resisting it within and without. Not only does the Diabolist seek out extremes, he balances each by seeking out its complementary but opposing contrary. Diabolism is not so much an exercise in pursuing or embodying "ultimate evil" as it is an attempt to consciously extend the boundaries of awareness to eventually include all possible polarities, however divergent. This is why the Diabolist will inevitably have – like the Devil itself – an ethos which has the effect of promoting the establishment and development of such a precision of consciousness in the self and in others (rejecting a moral preference for either the "self" or the "other"), and therefore has, and must have, enemies. No matter how suitable the setting, environment, or arena for Diabolical practice, the dynamic tension created by such an attempt to exalt and extend consciousness will frequently bring the Diabolist into personal conflict – with both the self and with others. This conflict is empowering, and even being defeated ultimately strengthens the practitioner who can learn from each failure. The first differences one would notice if transported to a world populated only by Diabolists would be the absences of hypocrisy, willful ignorance, and self-deceit. Deception and misdirection would nevertheless remain commonplace. The Devil should not be understood so much as the "Enemy of God" but rather as the God of Enemies.

This understanding elaborates the adage that the gods of one's enemies often seem as Devils, yet leads to an inversion of the kind of formerly tribal monotheism which often emerges from the moralization of mythology. Instead of the projection of the local deity onto a world scale, the concept of the "world-Devil" is injected into all local deities, expressing its function in their opposition. In this way, even the moral gods are included in the Diabolical pantheon (the *Diabolon*) in their particular function as the Devil's enemies. (Obviously the God of Enemies has to have its own enemies in the same way that a God of Love has lovers, but the identification of these enemies and their self-understanding, or lack thereof, generates a more complex scenario.) For the Diabolist, it is not that these abstract powers actually function as personal enemies but rather that those who embody or represent these powers on a human scale will tend to become "impersonal" enemies. As such, in addition to whatever personal rivals or adversaries the individual Diabolist may cultivate, Diabolists will find that moralists and monotheists are enemies on this subtler level.

That "subtler level" could be understood as "Diabolical aeonics." In order to function effectively in its context, the Diabolist should not only be able to oppose moralistic adversaries, but also be aware of, and therefore able to obstruct or redirect, historical and socio-cultural inertia. By understanding the trends of history as they manifest through the unreflective reactivity of the masses, the Diabolist can exempt the self from slavery to these processes and ultimately gain a measure of control and influence over them. An ability to operate with a long-term perspective is an indispensable component of the Diabolical methodology of extending consciousness to extremes beyond an ordinary human lifespan. The Diabolist should therefore be concerned to know the phases of development of a civilization, how to recognize them, and what factors govern transition from one such phase or "aeon" to another. This allows for conscious choices regarding which movements or currents, if any, with which the Diabolist will align (or appear to align) the self, probably only temporarily and for a specific purpose.

In the wider context of antinomian modes of magical practice, Diabolism would be a type of immoralism, in that the Devil deliberately opposes and transgresses moral law. This is in contrast to the amoralism characterizing demonic magic generally, which despite having antinomian connotations that derive from the general association of the "demonic" with rejected and repressed figures, does not generally propose a deliberate or methodical violation of morality in particular. Some demoniasts not only reject the relevance of morality personally, but consider the whole concept (and therefore its "immoral" opposite) to be inapplicable outside of the contingent paradigms that accept it. Both "demons" and "Devils" are present in the genre of "Infernal" magic, also often antinomian due to its chthonic, pre-moral approach. As pre-moral cosmologies frequently hold the "lower" powers in particular awe, respect, fear, or even veneration, without making any assertion that they are evil, "Infernalism" predates the later diversification of systems into cosmologically oriented moral and ethical approaches, but also includes a wide variety of beings among its Legions. A particularly diabolical Infernalism would be one that opposes a pre-moral structure against moralism, taking the moralistic propositions into account within its cosmology, but rejecting their basic premises. An exclusively demonic Infernalism, by contrast, rejects both moralism and immoralism.

Diabolism distinguishes itself among immoralisms generally in being specifically focused on the emulation of the being or principle generally known as "the Devil." This can be understood simultaneously as an entity and as an abstract form, both of which can provide a model for effective practice.

These definitions would at first seem to make "Infernal Diabolism" a contradiction, if Infernalism depends on pre-moral belief structures and Diabolism, on personal immoralism. Contrary to its counterpart, "Diabolical Infernalism," which presents pre-moral belief itself as facilitating antinomian transgression of the moral norms of others, Infernal Diabolism identifies the pre-moral and the immoral. It is thus a reactionary response to the moralist proposition. In contrast to the "Nietzschean" understanding of immoralism as a further transvaluation of values once morality has exhausted its own function, Infernal Diabolism not only rejects moral values but actively repudiates them, considering the concept of morality to represent an irredeemable degeneration of consciousness. Beyond being a mere "militant pre-moralism," Infernal Diabolism understands immoralism as having a function equivalent to that which the moralist ascribes to "natural morality," a conscious understanding of the inherent order of nature: for the Infernal Diabolist, the practice of immoralism encourages total separation of, and discrimination of consciousness from, that "natural order," which is entirely pre-moral and cannot be regarded as having any kind of inherent purpose or significance, let alone value or goodness. Given that those who assert a natural morality are in fact attempting to abstract subjective values out of the observable, objective universe, they are proposing a transcendental reality which somehow emerges from, improving on, the "lower." The Infernal Diabolist proposes the opposite: subjective consciousness already immanent in, and enhanced by "inscending" deeper into, that which is more primal, more basic, more fundamental. The practice of Infernal Diabolism, then, involves reversion to the original "fundamentalism" of conscious existence pursuing itself for its own sake.

The "infernal" can also be understood as one component of a trinity shared with the terrestrial and empyreal. While the empyreal is always transcendental, the terrestrial differs from the infernal in being not only immediate and present but also lacking in a directional concept of either essence or of consciousness: the reality of the terrestrial is not "within," "beneath," or "below," but simply there, all-around, everywhere. The infernal can be found both "within" and also "beneath" or "below;" the infernalism of the internal is "inscendent," a pre-moral consciousness or existence inherent in the self, while the infernalism of the "lower" and "deeper" is "descendent," and seeks to manifest the immanent in the forms of existence and of consciousness.

INFERNALISM, DIABOLISM AND THE LEFT-HAND PATH

As a consequence of the moralism present in the Theosophical occult revival, the term "Left-Hand Path" has come to signify the opposite methodology of the "Right-Hand Path" of union with the divine. To follow the way of the Left is to be sinister, to be separate and distinct from identification with any being, self, God, or power other than the individuated consciousness itself. This requires the fullest possible discrimination of the practitioner, first identifying and distinguishing his own individuated conscious awareness, then separating it from anything that attempts to impose another identity upon it. Ultimately, the sinister magician becomes able to maintain this state of separation indefinitely, avoiding subjection to the inertia which constantly threatens to overcome it.

The concept of the two paths should not be confused with the difference between religion, characterizing belief structures which attempt to collectivize objective concepts of truth, and magic, characterizing paradigms useful in the imposition into reality of the individual, subjective will and consciousness of the practitioner. Diabolism is always a magical, never a religious, mode of thought; its proper religious corollary is diabolatry. The Diabolist does not worship the Devil, but instead emulates it. If practiced as a Right-Hand Path methodology, Diabolism literally unites the consciousness of the Diabolist with the existence of the Devil. This supreme masochism and self-abnegation would seem to be useful either as a means of liberation from an unfit self, or as an apotropeic offering to the Devil: consciousness in exchange for power, a pact with the Lord of This World. The Left-Hand Path of Diabolism takes the Devil as an archetype of supreme defiance and ultimate separation from the natural order, and emulates it.

The context of Infernalism is more varied, in that any of the beings numbered among the Infernal Host could be venerated in a religious context, and so could the whole Legion. As a religion, Infernalism proposes that the primal, pre-moral powers of the deep underlie all other cosmologies and later religious views; congress with these "old ones" reveals them as the true gods of this world. On the Right-Hand Path, the practitioner seeks to become an "Infernal Host" unto him- or herself, ultimately achieving either permanent demonic or diabolical possession, or total multiplicity of self, becoming as Legion. Left-Hand Path ("sinister") Infernalism, as a religion, proposes an opposite apotropeism to Right-Hand Path Diabolism: the Infernalist consigns his or her existence to the Legion as a priest and servitor, in exchange for greater freedom of personal will and enhanced consciousness. As a magical paradigm, Infernalism need not assert cosmological propositions, but only hold that personal alignment to the pre-moral, as described, helps empower the practitioner and liberate consciousness from constraint, either to "descend" along the Right-Hand Path to union with the chthonic realms or powers (or "inscend" on the Right-Hand Path to union with the "true self," the "daimon" within, or so forth), or follow the path of Sinister Descent (or Inscent) to discern personal consciousness as immanent in the flesh (or the personal, subjective existence). While these two sinister paths share an orientation toward the quest for self-immortalization and continuity of consciousness, they differ in the extent to which they rely on – and utilize – the carnal form.

Thus, Infernal Diabolism when practiced as a Right-Hand Path magical system is an offering of one's own consciousness to the Devil as the Infernal Sovereign of Hell in exchange for various gifts and endowments useful to the aims of the personal will (and to the aims of the personal Devil), probably being the closest magical paradigm to the lurid fantasies of the "soul-pact" elaborated by the Inquisition. As a method of sinister sorcery, however, Infernal Diabolism increases the extent to which the practitioner has immediate access to the immanent consciousness of the Infernal Host while presently in the flesh, becoming a "personal Host" to his own Legion of Diabolical Selves, each another formulation of the Absolute Otherness which characterizes the subjective, pre-moral consciousness, manifesting it in defiant acts of antinomian immoralism.

THE SINISTER EGO

None of this means that the Infernal Diabolist is an "individual-ist" in the common sense of the term. He or she is not an "undivided" unity in a world populated by similar undivided unities, all embodying an abstract principle of oneness. Rather, being a hypostasis of the principle of duality, opposition, and division, the Infernal Diabolist is divided within and amongst the apparent unity of self into the "Legion of Selves," each of which manifests as pure, distinct Personality, but which in the case of the Infernal Diabolist are ruled by the Dual Sovereigns which are the One-as-Many and the Many-as-One. The "Devil Itself" as a Being with an Ego can then be regarded as the "Supreme Personality," but the Infernal Diabolist aspires to become likewise, thus participating in the Dual Sovereignty directly.

That the Legion can manifest as personal is not to say that the sinister practitioner necessarily recognizes Personality in all apparent individuals, as most members of the mass quantity of humanity are barely even that, let alone fully developed and self-expressed people. The "individual-ism" that reduces the whole person to a unitive Ego in a perverse, post-Freudian ultra-materialist reflex is wholly contrary to the aeonic aims of the sinister in that it mires consciousness so deeply in association to the flesh that it can never distinguish itself again. The only means of "self-control" remaining once that has occurred are social constructs replacing the divine "Super-ego" of an already dead God. The Infernal Diabolist instead seeks control and power over the Ego, but from a posture of individuated, rather than "individual," consciousness, which has distinguished itself within the Legion of Selves *as* a Personal Self, having become the Master of the Crossroads of Identity. The more personal the Infernal Diabolist's consciousness, the more personal the Ego can become, but the two are bound in relation as are all the other Selves of the Diabolic Legion. This relation provides an internal, microcosmic analogy to the aeonic relation of selves and personalities in the mesocosm and the abstract relationship of Selves within the Macrocosmic Diabolon.

DIABOLICAL PRACTICE

SACRIFICE: While this is the stereotypical technique of the diabolical magician, its significance seems to be frequently misunderstood. Deriving from the traditional concept of making something sacred by distinguishing it – separating it – as dedicated to the divine, sacrifice is iconic of Diabolism specifically because it is an act of total discrimination. By selecting something as more valuable to the Devil than it is to the Diabolist's own self, the Diabolist participates in the "Legionary Economy." These acts of exchange enhance and develop not only the personal ego of the Diabolist, which has made an irrevocable decision concerning something's value, but also strengthen the magical personalities and selves, which impose a new value onto what is being sacrificed by dedicating it to the Diabolical Personality. This activity, when transgressive of habitual tastes and preferences, can be iconic of the "transvaluation of values" characterizing the practice of immoralism as the deliberate contrary to moral dualism which extends and further evolves consciousness. The means of performing the sacrifice and disposing of its remains influences its magical function. When the object of sacrifice is destroyed, it is analogous to evocation in that it feeds a theoretically external and abstracted "Devil." The offering might be propitiatory, with the aim of seeking some particular boon from the Devil, or apotropeic, with the intention of averting some possible misfortune or malice. When the offering is abandoned, it entices the Devil into manifestation in the world, perhaps in a particular location, or in a particular form. The offering can also be given away; this evokes the Devil into the recipient, which might be a person as well an organization, association, or order. A related method would be to give the sacrifice away to a representative of a class or category on or through which the Diabolist wants to have some aeonic effect. In some cases, the Devil may have already been evoked into the recipient in a magical ritual, or the recipient is already typical of the Devil in a particular form due to filling an archetypal role. The offering can also be consumed or utilized by the Diabolist personally, or collectively with colleagues. The former is invocatory, and likely to result in Diabolical inspiration if the offering is consumed after the sacrificial rite, and outright Diabolical possession if used during such a ritual. The latter is "transvocatory," and will produce a "Legionary Communion" such that the ritual operators simultaneously participate in the Diabolical Feast of the Legion of Selves. In such a rite, the personality of the Devil transvoked aligns with the consciousness of the ritualists in such a way that this personality achieves the manifest multiplicity of self usually characterizing only the Legion as a whole. Aside from its illuminatory relevance, this phenomenon has magical utility in allowing Diabolists to act in unusual concert with collective precision. These methods of sacrifice also seem to be effective when abstractly performed, offering possibilities for internal self-modification and illumination, as well as the use of inhibitory techniques of deprivation, austerity, and ordeal generally considered stereotypical or iconic of either the Right-Hand Path or of mystical transcendentalism. This infernal, diabolical subversion of transcendentalist modes such as chastity, fasting, self-harm, and so forth may provide a means by which that whole corpus of mystical and religious appropriations of magic may be re-appropriated for specifically sinister use.

CULLING: Distinct from sacrifice in being the removal (separation from the "herd") of that which the Devil holds to be without value, sorcerous culling is an indispensable weapon in the aeonic arsenal of the Diabolist. It combines the momentum of the Diabolist's will to oppose and destroy enemies, adversaries, and obstacles with the power of the Devil's own will-to-power and will-to-consciousness. It also serves the aeonic cultural function of offering common opponents both to Diabolists and to the civilizations they found, promote, and further evolve, mirroring the Devil's own ability to reflect itself and its influence in scenarios of conflict and opposition. While each aeonic situation will have its own preferred targets for culling, and each Diabolist a favorite type of Opfer or series of such, certain commonalities remain: moralists, monotheists, hypocrites, the chronically dysfunctional, the "worst" of humanity in the sense of offering no useful contribution either to the species as a whole or a given society or civilization in particular, and those who themselves deliberately obstruct the Devil and its agents seem to be generically appropriate.

The whole methodology of culling, and the theory of its effectiveness, is distinct from that of sacrifice. Both have in common that they can be used for both propitiatory and apotropeic purposes and might be offered prior to or subsequent to receiving the favor of the Devil, according to the nature and structure of the Pact. They differ in that the object of sacrifice itself fuels a spell, while in the case of culling it might be that the spell accomplishes the culling. In that case, the culling does not "fuel itself," and so it is the case that a sacrifice, or series of such, might actually be used to accomplish a culling. Similarly, a culling could be performed as a sacrifice, but in that case the favor of the Devil cannot effectively be used to accomplish it; the Diabolist must destroy the Opfer without assistance, otherwise the whole purpose will be voided.

Considering the effectiveness of abstract sacrifice, abstract culling is a rewarding aeonic practice, often undervalued. Thus, rather than merely targeting individuals, the Diabolist could target groups, institutions, spirits, ideas, and even deities which the Devil negatively values. In an aeonic context, devious applications of what at first may sound like a straightforward strategy of destruction emerge. Given agendas can be furthered through the selective undoing of enemies even when these agendas appear overtly opposed to those of the Devil. Contrarily, some currents of belief are empowered by the martyrdom of their adherents. The introduction of the practice of culling into a paradigm which previously lacked it can also help to "Diabolize" the paradigm, regardless of its original intention. Thus, moralists who themselves selectively practice evil to further that which they believe to be good are actually opening themselves to the influence of the Devil in its role as Grand Inquisitor or Witchfinder General.

These observations suggest that culling might be qualified along three categorical axes: "cryptic" or "overt"; "allopathic" or "homeopathic"; and "immunizational" or "infectious". The strategy of cryptic culling is based on the premise that the destruction of the target itself accomplishes some aim, and that therefore the less potential targets know about the aims of the Devil, the better. In these cases, the culling should seem to be a completely natural, or at least accidental, event. In the "overt" category, the culling still appears mundane or profane, but somehow blatantly connected with the reason for the culling of the Opfer, fulfilling a secondary role of either instilling fear and terror in particular categories of target or blaming a third category of target for the action and thereby scapegoating it. Another "overt" style would be associating the culling with factors in the personal life of the Opfer. These options have the advantage of either making the Opfer appear to be an innocent victim, which can increase the adversarial disposition and opposition of outrage of its supporters, embarrass the victim by making such person appear weak or defenseless if power and invincibility were part of his or her glamour, or perhaps humiliate and destroy reputation should it come to light that this event occurred due to some sordid involvements on the part of the Opfer. Finally, there may be instances in which overtly Diabolical, "Satanic," or occult-seeming scenarios may serve a useful purpose, particularly if the Diabolist has some reason to wish to promote a "Satanic panic," a wave of anti-occult persecution or hysteria, or make the Opfer appear to have had some kind of occult involvements or connections themselves.

Returning to the proposed categories, "allopathic" culling is the straightforward removal of a given target or category of target, with the theoretical, strategic intent to either weaken a given aeonic influence or remove it entirely. By contrast, "homeopathic" culling strengthens a given population by removing its worst, most unfit members. The final pair inverts the relationship of the previous two: "Immunizational" culling provokes an "immune response" in a given population through the selective destruction of particular targets the significance of which inspires massive reactions or organized reprisal, while "infectious" culling is performed in such a way that the target population's attempt to defend itself results in harm to its own members. These methods can be variously combined in order to induce "aeonic allergies" in target groups, inspiring them to turn against themselves, or some sub-group within themselves, or cause the target group itself to cause allergic reactions in others groups. This is how various political, religious, and racial hatreds and persecutions can appear organic despite being originally established on purpose or promoted deliberately by an enterprising Diabolical aeonist.

This introduces the subject of "para-culling," analogous practices applying similar theories but with sub-lethal intent. Ideological persecutions, social condemnations, ostracism, segregation, and iconoclasm are examples of means of abusing given targets or categories of target which follow strategic rules similar to those of culling itself. The socio-magical and aeonic use of diabolical satire and black humor is also related. Ancient bardic and poetic traditions occasionally combine the two motifs by describing satires so vicious as to sicken or kill their victims. Such methods can also be used on an abstract level by making certain views or positions seem too ridiculous to be taken seriously. Slander and the destruction of reputation can be a very effective means of "social culling" as well.

Much as is the case in the microbial world, both allopathic and homeopathic techniques are a useful means of destroying infection, but when they fail, they strengthen it. This phenomenon allows culling to be used for creative and supportive as well as destructive purposes.

MIMESIS: Being one of the fundamental techniques of aeonic magic, applicable to restoring, maintaining, and transmuting the manifestation of pre-existent, cyclical patterns of manifestation (although not so useful for creating novel causal forms), mimesis has significant Diabolical application on the personal scale as well as the aeonic. Emulation of the Devil has already been discussed, but the Diabolist can vary and refine this technique by the deliberate and selective mimesis and imitation of both particular cosmological and mythological instances of the Devil, and enemy figures and persons. These practices reinforce the separation of the Diabolist from anything selectively mirrored in this way, reducing it to an image, objectifying it. The analogous technique of sorcery (and strategy) is that of mirroring an enemy and then consciously introducing some sudden change. The same technique works in seduction, ranging from postural matching to reflection of the victim's own ideas or ideals. It works in negotiation and argument with deliberate escalation and de-escalation via mirroring hostility levels.

Since deception and disguise are characteristic attributes of the Devil in most cosmologies, the ability to appear as the agent of completely different and opposed aeonic agendas is an indispensable element of Diabolical strategy.

SADISM, MASOCHISM, AND SADOMASOCHISM: Since this is not a psychological treatise (although research into the human psyche is clearly a necessity for the practicing Diabolist), the important aspect of sadism to consider is the underlying theory of pleasure, which is that the sadist gains, enjoys, and exercises power by objectifying others and using them as means rather than as ends. Not only de Sade himself, but also Stirner in a different context, propose that the "Other" beyond the self be understood as a form of property to be used and disposed of. For both, it is the "Unique Being" (Sade) or the "Sole and Unique One" (Stirner) which is able to live in such a way, having emancipated itself from all moral ideas, guilt complexes, and confusion of identity. The Sole and Unique One knows that it is not its own body, instincts, impulses, thoughts, or ideas, much less anyone else's. It is not even its self, since the self or selves is also a form of property. "Property" can also be understood to mean an attribute or quality. Since the Diabolical sorcerer aims to achieve the reign of quality over the undifferentiated mass quantity, the Diabolist needs as much "property" – and as many distinct, unique "properties" – as possible, such as "selves." The distinction of self-consciousness from self makes masochism another route to power for the Diabolist, since that which the self "suffers" or "endures" then also becomes a source of power as it exhausts the momentum and inertia of any "other" which sets itself up in a temporary condition of dominance. The act of self-objectification can liberate the Diabolist's consciousness from its own identity and "individuality," dividing it into novel forms and selves. These twin poles of sadism and masochism combine in the sadomasochistic continuum of extremes wherein both domination and submission become viable avenues of Diabolical power, particularly when combined with various techniques of sexual sorcery.

THE THEORY OF INFERNAL DIABOLISM

When consciousness is capable of discriminating between itself and all others, any forgetfulness of this distinction necessarily weakens not only its identity, but the identities of the self and the other, both of which are maintained by the preservation of the condition of difference and the tension it creates. As such, the Sinister Ethos seeks to maintain the distinct separateness of consciousness from all of its properties and constituent selves – from its "Legions" – in perpetuity. Hence, every thought, word, and deed can be evaluated according to whether it promotes or undermines this conscious awareness. Instead of morality and its irreconcilable opposition of "good" and "evil," the diabolist exalts the conscious pursuit of excellence, of "quality," which overcomes the weak, flawed, and defective. The inertia of the cosmos opposes the maintenance and exaltation of consciousness to the position of Supreme Personality, but this inertia can be turned against the cosmos in the practice of Diabolical sorcery, which feeds the consciousness of the Diabolist at the same time as it liberates the consciousness of the Other from being bound up in the inertial mass. By means of the same operation, the Devil Itself awakens immanent consciousness in the sleeping mind of Nature and defies constraint, transgressing and so reinforcing the confines and boundaries of identity to achieve and impose the ultimately Personal Will to power by means of its properties.

In the Name of the Legion, as the Personality of the Infernal Host, I dedicate this Sacrifice to the Sovereign Authority of the World, Power in the Flesh, and the Glory of the Devil.

Falling With Love:
Embracing the Infernal Host

Anonymous[1]

The Inferno

The Infernal gnosis is one of *abandon*: the wild abandon of the libertine; the abandonment of cherished values and outworn forms; the abandonment of the fixed ideas and boundaries of the self, the identity, *and* the other. It is the abandonment of restraint; it is loss and sacrifice. It is the abandonment of whatever is given, offered, or sold to Hell. Most of all, it is the abandonment of *hope*, for hope is the final nail driven into the divine martyr and into the coffin of the profane, the last and worst of the divine curses levied upon the world, for it blinds the plight of the present, binds belief into the ever-coming future, and feeds parasitically on faith.

So whomever would enter into the black gnosis of Hell is enjoined to abandon all *hope*, and in the emptiness where hope and other obstructions used to reside, the black flame is enkindled, and the black light shines. The more that is abandoned to Hell, the more room for its wealth to pour in. It falls up from Hell as ripened fruit of knowledge; it uncovers itself as veins of rich but hidden ore laid open in the body of the sacrifice; it yields itself like a bursting harvest fed with rivers of blood; and its black rains pour as the infernal wealth of dead dragons, the liquid treasure hoard of prehistoric aeons. Hell abandons its riches and glory to those who are open to them, and those who know not abandon are fettered to it by their hopes and dreams, desires and fantasies, frustrations and despairs: and thus they are among its riches, unwillingly proclaiming its glory.

Its way of magic is polar but includes its own oppositions within itself. Commencing as chthonic descent, it penetrates below the terrestrial realms, plunging through diverse and boundless abysses and hells. Yet, it is not unidirectional, for it also concerns itself with the carnal ascent, the falling *up* from Hell, the release of the Titans, the raising of the Dragon, the exaltation of vanquished, exiled, forgotten, repressed, and incarcerated powers from their bondage. The infernal knowledge makes of everything a prison – even the starry heavens, as the antinomian Gnostics discerned – but also offers liberation. Its polarity attracts to its Legions the immoral as well as the amoral and pre-moral, embracing and encompassing all demons and devils, even and especially those fallen from empyreal and celestial heights. Yet, those pre-moral powers who dwell at the deepest centre of the Inferno comprise only those eldest things which shun ascent to the terrestrial world, feeding on what drains from it, coiling under the roots of the world-

---

1 Also the author of *Liber Niger Legionis: The Grimoire of Pharaon*

239

tree, lurking in the lowest of caverns beneath the peaks. Like the depths of a black singularity into which one can fall continuously and forever, the centre of the earth becomes the gateway into the inferno, but although it is the nearest gravitational point and therefore the lowest possible descent into the physical plane, it is merely the surface extrusion of lower realms far vaster, reaching into and past the substrate of reality, voids yawning not only between atoms but between the smallest and most phantasmal of particles. These sub-material layers offer access to obscure manifestations of direct magical power and open the way *beneath* the physical, to realms grosser than the flesh, and more inertial even than carnality. These are not to be confused with the para-physical (and para-psychological) manifestations of psionics or the modern and contemporary occult sciences, nor are they related to various pseudo-scientific misapprehensions of dark matter and dark energy (as useful as those models might be in certain forms of pseudo-scientific occultism, or pseudo-occult science); similarly, this concept of the *inferno* as sub-material reality denser than the physical realm to which the incarnate are generally accustomed, should not be confused with ideas of the otherworld or the netherworld, nor with the shadow-realities of doppelgangers, ghosts, and the ether. The comparison is exactly akin to the more familiar analogy in which the celestial and heavenly realms are not to be confused with the astral or mental worlds, nor the *mundus imaginalis*. Rather, the highest heavens seem to be characterized not by refinement of matter, nor even by spiritual bodies, but rather by transcendent immateriality and variously subtle states of bliss and freedom from contingency and constraint. The infernos are exactly the reverse. In the same way that the supernal reality encompasses not only the heavens but also the fullness of the celestial and empyreal worlds, while excluding the mental and imaginal, barely touching upon the most abstract and conceptual regions of the world of form, so the *infernal* reality encompasses not only the hells, but also the totality of sub-material and sub-physical planes, as well as the *underworlds* of various mythologies and traditions. It is these underworlds and the lore surrounding them that offer the best possibilities for access to, and understanding of, the infernal realities.

In the mythology of contemporary scientific cosmology, the sub-quantum obscurities and paradoxes offer a fitting *analogy* for the infernal. Where matter unravels into the emptiness of pure probability and possibility devoid of particular quality, the gates of hell begin to open, and the underworld is partially unveiled. The magical powers offered by access to this realm are therefore unlike the quasi-physical effects of "subtle energy" and other occult constructs. At their most extreme, they are the counterpart of miraculous divine descents in which the apparent laws of reality are overridden by an intrusion not bound by their dimensional contingencies. Like most magical manifestations, they remain characterized by synchronicity, although only in their most restrained are they confined to manipulations of probability and chance. In their full glory, they are black miracles erupting from hell, as chaotic, diverse, and diffuse as the interventions of heaven are precise, specific, and confined. They are not responses to prayer, adjusting the world as much as is necessary for it to remain in accord with some overarching plan or pattern, realigning the consciousness of those "privileged" to witness them with a surgical strike of numinous awe, that particularization of wonder and terror generally considered divine – and yet, they are numinous. They are numinous upsurges of unrestrained, or barely restrained, *horror*. The black miracle is the stretching, cracking, sundering, and breaking of bonds of ordinary causality and time by the desperation and despair of consciousness tormented by its limitations. It opposes by contrast not *only* the divine plan that sets the worlds in order from the highest heavens above the celestial spheres to the lowest hells of materialization, which are so pure that no defining feature or quality remains save the distinction of their tormented consciousness from pure chaos. It does oppose this plan, of course, striking up and out against the tyranny of the supernals, and the confinement of consciousness into hierarchies of body, mind, and will. But it also opposes the dualism distinguishing essence from substance, real from unreal, body from mind, and consciousness from chaos, as a whole. Yet, its anti-cosmism is not as simple as a rejection of cosmos, a plunge into nihilism and the chaotic worship of the void. The infernal consciousness offers its own inversion of the cosmic order, including it on reservations of stability, exilic islands of isolated consciousness, and vast mines and fields of material and psychic resource. But it is also free, and includes infinitely vaster realms of liberty, indulgence, uncertainty, paradox, and *doubt*. For the black miracle is a faithless miracle. It is the retaliation of joyous, unrestrained sentience against any and all limitations. In this, "poltergeist" phenomena have more in common with infernal miracles than they do with the various psychisms with which they are often confused: for what haunts the home infected with a poltergeist is most frequently the repressed, tormented desire of an adolescent female, yet to release the infernal effluvia along the accepted (yet restricted) channels of menses. The black miracle would indeed be the mere product of dualised prayer to the infernal powers, were it marked by the same submission and trust as prayer to those above. But it is not. Rather, it embodies the fully numinous and yet *horrific* power of the conscious psyche which has found the gods in itself. And this – is horrible.

Horrible that such bliss and power should be degraded and shamed by the limitations of contingency and carnality – but also horrible that the pleasures offered by these are often denied to those within them. Horrible that spirits above and beyond the flesh repress and scorn its worth, while they feed upon it and those trapped therein like parasites, but also horrible that equally numberless spirits are trapped *beneath* it, unable even to touch the sensations and indulge the experiences which drew them to incarnation in the flesh in the first place. Horrible that every choice excludes its contraries, so every decision made and pleasure embraced is the destruction of infinite others. Horrible to have every desire fulfilled, rendering boredom; horrible to have any desire denied, bringing torment. Horrible to be divine in such a world; horrible to be at the mercy of the divine, in any world. The infernal gnosis is not a reversal of the divine gnosis; it is certainly not a rejection of it. Rather, it is an inverse *consumption*, an invasive inclusion of all the divinity, possibility, and numinosity that can be actualized within the apprehension of horror. Like the infinite descent into the inferno, what is horrible becomes more so through contemplation, not less. The paradoxes of hell are not there to be resolved, but to be worsened, spread out, diffused, and ultimately pervade the cosmos until every mode of consciousness therein has turned itself inside out and embraced the whole paradox of duality and polarity within itself, defying the contingencies and constraints of reality, ultimately becoming *through the displacement of that horror* something more than a god incarnate, something simultaneously diabolical, demonic, *and* divine.

The black miracle is Carrie at the prom – dancing and happy; Regan writhing in her bed – in ecstasy; Damien in triumph holding his successor and his consort by the hand – and smiling back at God. But that is because Carrie is dancing like Shiva and Kali over the corpses of everyone dead at the prom; because Regan's guardians look on with greater horror than the audience of the Exorcist as she so clearly *enjoys* what she is doing with that crucifix; and because Damien has already consigned the religious fanatics who oppose his reign to just one of many death camps distributed across his empire. And yet, even to the infernalist, suffering, torture, and death – are horrible. Otherwise, the infernal gnosis would not be infernal, nor would it be gnosis; it would merely be a shadow of the ignorance of divinity, the blindness seared into those who have been smitten by the numinosity of the celestial heavens. The infernalist is *not* the counterpart of the celestial magician, nor a blasphemous reverser of divine ceremonies; the infernalist is tunneling a way *out* of imprisonment in duality – through the very centre of the most extreme polarities.

As such, the infernalist becomes a gravitational point toward which extremes are attracted, acquiring the most reviled of roles and embodying the most derided of stigmas, but not necessarily openly. Rather, the infernalist finds ways of sublimating and redirecting vilification for power: the subversion of martyrdom. In this, the infernalist has something in common with those who are demonized due to fear or diabolized due to moral outrage, and those who are shunned and labeled as outcasts and social "witches," but more particularly re-appropriates the power bound into disgust, revulsion, and ultimately horror. Nevertheless, all possible antagonist projections are within the domain of the infernalist's legion of personae, and all the demons and devils as well as rejected, forgotten, feared, and hated gods are numbered among and included in the "infernal host."

The Infernal Host

As the complete signifier of the identity of the one with the many, and the many with the one, the whole body – any body considered as a whole – is both inhabited by and composed of an endless multiplicity of identities, personalities, and possibilities. It not only has *a* demon, but a vast Legion of them, with which it both identifies and is identified; it is possessed, but also possesses their totality within itself. Infernalism is in summary a symbiotic, mutualistic spiritual ecology of the flesh with its roots and origins in the hells and the deep. It would be easy to mistake the members of the Infernal host with forgotten or pre-human *atavisms*, but these are terrestrial: though temporally displaced, they are present in and as the earthly flesh, their continuity manifest in their descendents. This is not to say that the Infernal Host excludes the human and animal, but its beasts are thoroughly extinct; dead ends of evolution. Its humanity includes the lost and exiled, the repressed and forgotten, the fallen and condemned. The Infernal ancestors are not those who are venerated, or who are present watching over their cultures and societies. They are the ancestors no one remembers or wants to remember – except the Infernalist.

The Infernal dead, by contrast, seem a generic and a commonplace – but because it is so easy for shades to fall below. Only a select, or elect, few seem to escape this, and so despite its seeming specificity, infernal necromancy is a broad and wide path indeed, though it leads not to destruction (except when directed against the enemies of the infernal necromancer) but rather to *recollection*. When given coherence and power by an infernal necromancer, the otherwise depersonalized shades of the generalized dead regain a semblance of identity: they become whole again through the Many, like faceless unpersons who become citizens through service in the Legions. Hence the attraction of such shades and larvae to mediums, who also can grant them flesh, albeit without direction, and substance, although half-formed. In addition to the classic means of utilizing the earthbound shades of recently deceased infants or children, executed criminals, suicides, and assorted confused or untimely dead, the infernal necromancer may be concerned with the identities of fallen and condemned dead vaguely remembered, whilst demonic and diabolical necromancies effectively draw upon those who have been culturally or morally vilified. All have in common the methods of selectively recalling the identities of *what was once human* into a coherent Legion of Selves, acting through that which singularly offers itself as Host and collectively functions as *one Host* comprising the full range of Infernal personality.

This infernal range extends through all magical arts, each having their infernal recension, and thus their own Legions among the Infernal Host, yet all are accessible to each: the goetia making their appearance at the Infernal Sabbat as well as in the circle of ceremonial art or at the crossroads of the cemetery; the sorcerer's shade descending into Hell and dancing with witches at the triple crossroads of waking, dream, and sleep; the witch descending bodily to Hell or rapt in ecstatic congress with demons, devils, or the Infernal Host itself. The less stereotypical intersections may be even more potent for their rarity: the infernal healer who restores and rejuvenates through the incubating descent into Hell; the depth psychologist who mends the fragmented soul and recovers lost ones; the exorcist who by the demons casts out the demons.

All have in common various magical personalities and identities which go among the Legions and also represent them as eidolons of the Infernal Host: the sorcerer's shade and Body of Shade (but also the Luciferian "Body of Light"); the witch's familiar or *famulus*; the shadow-form and shadow-selves of the shaman; the Demonic Self of the Satanist; the *daimone* of the *goes* and the *daimon* of the *magus*. The full Infernalist has the whole Host: a complete Legion of Selves.

THE LEGION

A whole Infernalist has the full Host: a diverse and populous Legion of Selves. Infernalism is about completeness *and* distinction; co-operation *and* divisiveness. It sets the complete – *against* the distinct and the incomplete alike; hosts co-operating *against* each other. Through the competition and conflict even amongst the Legions, the fires of Hell refine its metals, which forged into weapons, sharpen themselves against each other while also striking down the enemies of Hell. From the Infernal perspective, these "enemies" too are amongst the Legions – without realizing it themselves.

The structure, arrangement, and organization of the Legion varies from Infernalist to Infernalist; from Host to Host. The governments of Hell are infinitely diverse; their terrestrial counterparts a minimal sampling of the infinite possible arrangements of power and control, domination and submission, co-operation and collaboration, conspiracy and revolution, Hobbsean Leviathans manifest through the endless diversity of the Legions. These Legions are what they have in common: for Hell is perpetually at war. Thus all governments in Hell are *military* governments, however benignly or malignly cast – just as all divine and celestial governments are by definition theocracies. In terrestrial politics and aeonics, then, the agencies of Hell favor warfare, strife, and violence complimentarily contrasted with bureaucracy, legalism, and military order and precision. The infernal governments, legions, and states will tend to manifest as reflections of whatever terrestrial hypocrisies mark a given society or aeon. The medieval goetia appear to be organized as a feudal kingdom, but function more like an aristocracy of peers, an echo of the archaic Indo-European origins of the *daimone*. Imperial ages will project into hell visions of democratic mob rule: but the agents of Hell will rather be individualist, anarchist conspirators. Terrestrial democracies will envision their corresponding Evil Empires, but these evil imperialists enjoy a parity among themselves; socialists will see tyrants and capitalists in Hell, enslaving the workers with their Invisible Hand, but fail to notice that the workers in Hell are very well paid; anarchists will see Hell in the State, and the State in Hell, but for fascists, Hell is stateless. Anarcho-fascists and other paradoxes are beloved of Hell the way an alluring and loyal thrall is beloved of her master; while egoists are appreciated and ignored as private Hells. But the infernal glory of Hell resounds in every military coup, every armed rebellion, every violent revolution, every conspiracy of assassins – and in those secular executions which are in fact human sacrifices to unknown and forgotten infernal gods.

Within the Infernalist's own Legion then, the private Host, the infernal Bodyguard, the Infernalist might devise whatever arrangement suits his or her own disposition and tastes – so long as it is efficient and strategic – but might also wish to consider factors such as: the aeon; local culture, civilization, and history; government and politics; ancestry and heritage. Similarly, the membership of the Legion to which the Infernalist is sworn might also be determined by these factors; or perhaps the Infernalist who has a tendency to monolatric devotion might wish to be a Host *amongst* the Legion of a demon, devil, or god: or be Host in the flesh to that power. Tattooing, branding, and other signifiers of permanence are a viable means of establishing an enduring identification with a given patron; but many will have their own special mutilations and decorations.

Inevitably when a concept such as the "Infernal" is presented so directly, some will seek to find its "essence," but they will locate nothing. It is as empty, ephemeral, and immediate as their own shifting persona, as immanent as the flesh and its impending death. The search for infernal gnosis, be it of the selves, the daimone, the devils, or the infernal gods themselves, requires descent.

THE INFERNAL DESCENT

As befits the multiplicity and perpetual incompleteness of the Legions, the ways into

Hell are infinitely many. Every opposition opens at least three: two undue extremes and their mutual contradiction, and then propagates more in their complementary negation. The moral and ethical implications of this for those disposed toward the antinomian are obvious, but remain based in pre-moral polarities. Descent is a deliberate *fall*. Those deeds and experience which unbalance, destabilize, and disorient, accidentally proceeding from vertiginous stumbling to outright collapse, might also be sought out with deliberation and purpose, even elegance and grace. Thus the Infernalist learns to *abandon the self* to the gravity of experience. Instead of seeking to ascend above or beyond sensation and entanglement, or transcend either into inclusive identification with a greater whole or into a depersonalized disassociation, the Infernalist descends *further into experience.* Those who cannot endure this process, retaining their momentum and wits in spite of "losing themselves," will be absorbed and consumed; but those who Fall with precision and style will find continuity and consciousness even in overwhelming experiences of loss and ecstasy. Those who have experience with entheogens will probably be familiar with this nuanced distinction (and also find that those entheogens physically precipitating a sense of falling down or inward quite useful for pursuing an infernal descent), but other apt analogies include "falling" asleep (perhaps retaining conscious awareness in the liminal or hypnogogic state, into the lucid dream, or even into dreamless sleep), the "subspace" into which a skilled dominus or dominatrix can send his or her submissive, the "freefall" of jumping from a high place which combined heightened consciousness with anxiety and release, or the proper attitude toward thrill-rides, haunted houses, and places of horror. *Any* extreme can be used in this way, and becomes oriented toward the infernal when it risks the sense of self in a manner that does not necessarily obliterate the consciousness; this applies both to seemingly dissolving, expansive, and destructively liberating experiences (like falling through space), and crushing, constrictive, stifling experiences (like being locked into a coffin, a straightjacket, or the fettering bonds of a dominant embrace).

The descent is not restricted to the personal experience of the Infernalist. By means of seduction, temptation, and the propagation of violence and horror, the Infernalist can share the black gnosis. This is nothing like promoting religious conversion, although the Infernalist might find it useful to induce others to venerate the lower powers. Rather, the Infernalist opens the gates of Hell on Earth by sowing doubt, uncertainty, and confusion; by inspiring others to abandon faith, and abandon hope. This does not necessarily imply the purposeful exacerbation of suffering, dread, or any stereotypically evil or antinomian behavior (although it might) or require anything noticeably immoral (although it will be, at least, amoral).

In the social context, the Infernalist will flourish in circumstances of strife, mistrust, and paranoia, but also in environments of bureaucracy, legalism, competition, and dispute. In summary, Infernalism thrives on subtle conflict, its strategies depend on misdirection, and its aesthetic is either horrific or hypocritical by turns. It is not for nothing that Hell has been called "Perdition": *Loss* of innocence, *loss* of face, and *loss* of identity are all potential moments of Infernal *gnosis; sharing* of knowledge, *gaining* of status, and *formation* of identity are all potential expressions of Infernal *power.*

Should the Infernalist wish to advance the terrestrial extension of Hell more broadly, he or she would do well to study (and promote) the aesthetics of horror, the psychology of trauma and disassociation, the politics of violence, the strategies and tactics of war, the sociology of crime, the history of conspiracism and revolution, the geology of the subterranean, the biology of the hive and the swarm, and the theoretical physics of quantum gravity.

When any body can become host to any identity, when selves propagate beyond the limits and confines of the flesh, and when consciousness can apprehend itself within and beyond all of them, so that even the laws of terrestrial nature bend and break under the straining weight of its singular intent, the doors of the prison will be thrown open, those who have fallen will arise again, and those who have been exiled will return, and there will be Hell on Earth.

For now, it is apprehended dimly in the human response to the most extreme conditions. Inhospitable wastelands and desolate, lonely spaces; ruins where terrible devastations have occurred; sites where terrible atrocities have been committed; chambers of torture; houses of great suffering, anguish, and pain; forgotten temples; lost cities; battlefields; disused prisons; sanctuaries subject to sacrilege; places of execution; dens of extreme, depraved, or decadent vice, iniquity, and indulgence; the habitations of great and renowned exiles or the refuges of vast hordes of the dispossessed; the birth-places of great generals and mass murderers; and the dwellings of Infernalists – all these are the Gates of Hell.

THE INFERNAL ASCENT

When they are opened, in whole or in part, something may Ascend from Hell. For its spirits, incarnation is transcendence and the flesh is ecstasy. For them, definition and distinction are liberty and release.

To elicit such an Ascent, the Infernalist must offer a medium of manifestation which the refugee from Hell might inhabit, temporarily or semi-permanently. These may be of almost any nature, but the nature will condition the manifestation. The ideal offering is a vital, healthy, intelligent, attractive, and willing being to serve as Host. But lacking any other offering, the attention of the Infernalist may serve. The more potent the Infernalist, the more easily the conscious will might break down the barriers between the flesh and Hell. All aesthetics are situational, incidental, cultural, or personal; a study of them is rewarding in itself and rewards the Infernalist with power. Sufficient knowledge of the underlying patterns and currents of consciousness allows access to Infernal power in almost any circumstance; but previously established channels and currents, or previously conjured Legions, are even more accessible – hence the popularity and utility of the grimoire. By naming and calling up the powers of Hell, they are brought into conscious and definite being, and ultimately given access to the flesh. Those that desire this offer their power, devotion, and dedicated assistance as humans to the gods: and thus, they may aid the Infernalist to *become like a god*. Others desire company in descent, and will rise up to gain it, as humans would seek to call down avatars and incarnate their heroes anew. But others will wait in Hell, mystics of the Inferno, praying for the descent of the whole world, the occasional black miracle erupting into the flesh as they direct their baleful wills upward from the deep.

The retaking of Heaven by the Fallen is also an Infernal ascent, as is the Faustian quest of humanity for the stars, the physical conquest of the celestial realm above.

From the perspective of the most abstract and refined divinity, the whole material cosmos, including these starry heavens, is confining, and even the celestial realms of bliss a materializing descent. For the most transcendent Gnostic, the whole cosmos is Hell, and all otherworldly wandering merely navigation through the underworld. This too can be understood as an "Infernal" Gnosis – the descent of the mystic back into the prison of the flesh, the womb as tomb, or the tomb as womb of rebirth as undead or unliving.

The Underworld

For most Infernalists, however – those less mystically and gnostically inclined – the "Underworld" will signify the totality of the Infernal regions "beneath" the terrestrial existence, as well as those aspects of it which remain obscured to the conscious world. Thus, the realms of the subconscious and unconscious, the ancestral and atavistic realities, but also the "lower" dimensions. These latter, excluding the human unconscious, and the terrestrial underworlds, comprise the Inferno. Their regions have been mythically mapped by cultures the world over, with expected variation. These differences will be of interest to the individual Infernalist depending on background, society, location, aims, and predilection – but the commonalities are of interest to the Infernal Host, as a whole.

The most obvious commonplace of the Underworld is that it is "underneath" us. However, the contemporary Infernalist will find the "journey to the center of the earth" to be either implausible even when figurative, or merely preliminary to the Infernal work. Its role in shamanism and alchemy remains prominent and significant, but the Infernalist must find a way to penetrate *through* the terrestrial entirely, or bring the Infernal into the terrestrial underworld by some means. The techniques of shamanic descent and incubation, with or without entheogens, and the self-intoxicating effects of alchemical elixirs, erotic kalas, and so forth, may all be applied by the Infernalist in the quest of descent. It is the combination of these techniques with the appropriate intentions, aesthetics, and circumstances which seems to lead most directly to the Infernal gnosis – so engaging these practices in suitable locations and situations is one way to facilitate the experience. Another appropriate angle would be approaching the "underworld" through antinomian scenarios of cultural tension, hence the application of that concept to whole sectors of society who might exist in its "underbelly." As such, aeonically inclined and antinomian Infernalists might approach the underworld through the tensions implied in criminality, subversion, and the generally illicit.

Although the personal and collective unconscious hardly approach the Inferno, there are paths through the gates of dream and beyond the "wall of Sleep." The ability to retain lucidity at the "triple crossroads" where waking, dream, and sleep all meet seems to be a prerequisite for gaining access to the Infernal realms while simultaneously retaining consciousness in the flesh; alternatively, the ability to "wake up" in deep sleep while the body remains comatose opens the Gates of Hell from the realms of Hypnos. To achieve the Infernal from the dreaming realms of Morpheus requires the ability to retain consciousness as deep sleep approaches, or even plunge toward these depths deliberately through a dream. One avenue toward this seems to be the induction of horrific nightmares which induce acute consciousness as the dream instinctively attempts to awaken – but with the previous intent to instead flee in the other direction, into the deeper realms of slumber. This often involves either worsening the nightmare, or at least abandoning oneself to its self-propagating horrors. Even without the use of nightmares, the apprehension of the fathomless voids of sleep from the perspective of a dream – even a lucid one – can be horrific in itself. The mind seems given to producing subtle and dreadful transmutations difficult to describe, apparently in response to the ineffability of the yawning void. This is to be encouraged – as the seemingly empty, dreamless sleep – for the Infernalist – opens the tunnel *into Hell*, rather than signifying some final nothingness appropriate to inverse transcendentalism. As such, the horrific transformations and permutations of consciousness must be followed through and encouraged to blossom in and pervade the mind of the Infernalist in order to apprehend the eternal and infinite glory of the Infernal labyrinth within.

Similar experiences, from the waking state, can characterize the deliberately induced "bad trip," generally regarded as baneful by psychonauts, and at best endured as a Gnostic or mystical learning experience. For the Infernalist, deliberately induced bad trips are routes not only to knowledge, but power; the externalization of horror which they can afford occasionally producing the "black miracles" earlier considered. Almost any entheogenic or even generically mind-altering substance can be useful for this purpose. Purposeful overconsumption, skirting the boundaries of overdose, is a significant element in this practice – but so is indulgence under seemingly inappropriate, stressful, or generally horrible conditions. The applications of this type of practice go beyond chemognosis toward the magical use of "bad experiences" generally, and a skilled Infernalist can thereby convert even seeming disasters and failures into successes and bids for power. Similarly, temporary set-backs, incarcerations, tortures, losses, and injuries may thereby be used as episodes of black mysticism, and either expended more swiftly, endured more efficaciously, or even internalized as initiations or converted into blessings.

While the various cultural underworlds are too diverse and particular to be enumerated or explored here without inadvertent preferential bias as well as verbosity, *realms* of the underworld will be briefly considered. These include realms of the dead, realms of lower beings or dark beings (dark elves, dwarves, various fae), atavistic realms, fallen places of lore or fiction which appear in various mythic cycles (like Atlantis or R'lyeh), and liminal zones which have "fallen" into the underworld through disuse, abundant Infernal practices, or some manner of devastation. The vastest category, however, is *Hell*.

Hell

As with any subterranean strata, in the Underworld, deeper is older. As such, the deepest, oldest, most primal Hell is that original Infernal realm which bears the name.

Initially, it had only one L, and signified both the lowest of the Nine Worlds of the ancient Teutonic cosmology, and its personification in the medieval Norse Eddas as a half-dark goddess ruling the "straw dead" whose life ends in bed, of age or illness. The Edda presents her as sister of the Fenris wolf, their father the enigmatic trickster Loki, but it would seem that her realm must pre-exist her. The name of Hel originates in Proto-Germanic "khalija," the "coverer" or "hider," in turn deriving from the Proto-Indo-European root "kel," also related to "cell," "hall," and "hole," and probably also to the Indian dark goddess Kali. An archaic, but not Indo-European, cognate would be Ereshkigal, but she seems to have a personality more distinct from her realm. Ereshkigal's underworld was a far gloomier, hungrier, and thirstier realm than Hel, however, whose halls were generally of comfort and sustenance. Like the Greek Hades, Hel had a specific realm of punishment and torment: Nastraand, the corpse-isle of the dishonored dead. Perhaps such realms are all of Hel that the monotheists could perceive, but in later aeons, Hel became Hell, absorbing the whole heritage of infernal realms populated by the demonic and diabolical, as well as the damned and dead. Already said to be the Ruler of Nine Worlds, perhaps an infinite regress of nines within her realm, the Ninth, Hel has swollen into Hell, to include all the lower infernalities within, and most of the old gods with them. In her own myths, the bright god Balder falls to her when slain, like some descending Apollo, recalling the latter's origins in the incubation of shamanic descent among an archaic Anatolian cult. But in later aeons, when Odin himself is diabolized, Valhalla itself falls into Hell, one hall among Many, its einherjar among the Legions. And yet beneath all the novelties of younger aeons and younger gods, the first strata of Hel remains: a restful and sustaining grave, a tomb that may even be a womb, for those whose descendents find means of recalling them into the flesh. It is this attribute of benign protection and wholeness which distinguishes Hell from other realms of death and the dead, and certainly from the netherworlds of ghosts and shades. Despite its later association only with the worst afterlives, Hell is mainly the welcoming home of the numberless Legions of the Infernal Host. Like Perillos consigned to the burning belly of the brazen bull of his own torturous devising, the vast hosts of the One, faithful but enmeshed by their own doctrines of sin and guilt, may be surprised to find themselves sampling the extensions to Hell's more punitive realms which they have so lovingly and thoroughly designed and envisioned. This is not necessarily to suggest a literal post-mortem continuity of consciousness except for a select few. Even among those few, most are more likely to find themselves in the Hadean wastes than in the Halls of Hell, which are regarded as rather difficult to access (except for the appropriate dead). Even riding Odin's eight-legged horse Sleipnir, it takes Hermod, Balder's brother, nine days and nine nights to reach it on his mission to rescue his brother – during which he, having found the Road to Hel in the North, rode through valleys so deep and dark he saw nothing. This could imply shamanic descent trances of extreme duration and sensory deprivation.

A more clearly shamanic tradition in the North is *seidhr*, which can be used in shamanic descents and seership, particularly by seeresses called *volvas*. One of them is compelled by Odin from her mound outside the Gates of Hel to prophesy about the final doom of the gods. *Seidhr* had unfortunate associations in ancient Teutonic culture, making it highly antinomian (especially for men) and therefore of great interest to the Infernalist, especially given its Hellish nature. It literally means "seething" or "boiling," and suggest a seizure-like trance. It was also associated with states of weakness, passivity, and effeminacy. Odin was taught *seidhr* by his divine lover Freya and wore women's clothes while learning; the shamanic references to gender-bending and liminality are obvious; Hel's father Loki, by comparison, had shapeshifted into a mare on one occasion and become the *mother* of Sleipnir as well as the father of monsters. Generally among men, however, *seidhr* was among the practices (along with passive male homosexuality) that could lead to accusations of *argr*, a condition of unmanliness so humiliating that the ascription of the word was automatically a killing insult – a challenge which required the insulted man to attempt to slay the accuser to prove his innocence of the charge. *Seidhr* was also associated with witchcraft, malicious sorcery, and the (usually malevolent) use of the power of *ginnung*, which seems to have been a sort of dark chaos-ether from the primal gap. Thus, the most coherent traditional and historical referent to the "black miracles" earlier described seems to have been the use of *ginnung* for sorcery while in a seidh-trance – however, in this sense the use of *ginnung* was the original "chaos" magic and never seemed to rely on the agency of spirits or entities; so more properly, the "black miracle" is an Infernal intervention likely to have been mediated by the Legions of Hell, or inflicted by an Infernalist in a conscious state of self-daimonization.

However, in Hell itself, it is difficult to retain consciousness, even for the Infernalist. In that sense, the journey "to Hell" is restorative (assuming one does not become ensnared or misdirected by realms of torment), but still dangerous; aside from specific realms particularly hospitable to different sorts of magical consciousness, the risk of Hell is that it is too inertial, too restful, and *too* heavy – such that even the Infernalist might not *want* to return. Unlike the equivalent risk of transcendental mysticism, or dissolution of the will into the celestial empyrean, this happens not due to the Infernalist becoming enamored of some other greater pattern or power, but rather due to being overcome by the downward weight of his *own*, responding to the "gravity" of Hell. Ultimately, the risk in both "directions" is the same – loss of consciousness – comparable to death being the ultimate consequence of too much heat or too much cold. The Infernalist will probably *not* find celestial domination blissful, however (the will-withering nature of such an experience being obvious) but must always be wary of each "journey to Hell," since its deepest recesses leave nothing else to oppose except the Self.

The path to these depths varies from journey to journey, Infernalist to Infernalist, and setting to setting. Over the aeons, Hell has outgrown its cultural and mythic origins and attracted into itself such a vast diversity of possibilities that it can best be mapped and explored by each practitioner for himself.

The Abyss

The Abyss, by contrast, can be explored by the Infernalist, but not mapped. Its origins are in complementary opposition to those of Hell. Its proximate origin is the *abyssos* in Greek, the bottomless depths, but probably a borrowing from Mesopotamian *abzu*, the masculine, fresh-water aspect of the primal sea. Presumably, since the *abzu* also referred to the house of the fish-goat god of wisdom, Enki, and to vessels of temple water, it was taken in transmission to be an original and impersonal term (in contrast to the obviously personified and monstrous Tiamat). Just as Hel expanded to become "Hell," so the *abzu* deepened to become the Abyss; in terms of personalization, the process was reversed: Hel acquired a personality and became a goddess; Abzu gradually lost his personality and became a place. Thus, Hell seems to have an emergent consciousness and sentience throughout; the Abyss has a self-forgetful, slumbering sentience that can periodically be recalled.

At first, the Abyss might be thought to be equivalent to the *ginnungagap*, but that primal "gap" is more properly the primordial chaos in-between, and as such no more infernal than celestial. Rather, the role of the Abyss seems analogically similar to that of Niflhel, which has an ambiguous status in the Teutonic myths, seemingly conflating Niflheim (the misty realm of primordial cold which derived from the "north" of the *ginnungagap*) and Hel. Complicating matters further, the evil are assigned to Niflhel after death in some sources, rather than Nastraand, and Niflhel is said to be "in the Ninth World." One solution seems to be ascribing Nine "Hells" *to the Ninth World*, which is *Hel*, each equivalent to one of the *Nine Worlds*; Niflhel would be the Hellish equivalent of Niflheim, and the deepest, coldest, darkest, and perhaps most primordial part of Hel, while Nastraand would be the "Hell" of "Hel." Oath-breakers, murderers, and the seducers of others' wives would be in Nastraand, other "evil" dead would be in Niflhel. It may be identifiable with Hvergelmir, the bubbling spring of cold in Niflheim from whence the eleven primal rivers flow. The Prose Edda describes the corpse-eating dragon devouring dead corpses there, so this may be an annihilationist implication that some of the dead are totally lost or consumed, or still identifiable with their corpses. As such, Niflhel as the coldest, deepest, and darkest of Hells may be the ultimate fate of those dead who can in no sense endure or persist (which, in annihilationist models, is almost everyone; in more moral or ethical cosmologies, only the particularly depraved are thoroughly destroyed at death; in the most punitive versions of those cosmologies, they are constantly being *devoured*, making Niflhel the worst of all possibilities, an endless death that never quite finishes, similar to falling into a singularity – so Niflhel would be comparable to a "black hole"). In this sense, Niflhel could be regarded as the opening to the infinite depths of the *abyss* – especially given Hvergelmir's status as a primordial, cold, *fresh-water* spring, despite that the Greeks clearly received the *abzu* as pertaining to *oceanic* depths.

Just as Hell has fully expanded beyond its Northern cultural origins, so the Abyss has deepened to include all primordial depths, not merely the watery, and so is the proper Infernal referent for the bottomless primordial deep beneath Hell, but also accessible as the bottomless depths of the Underworld itself, and similarly accessible by sinking into their lowest depths. In Hell, this would seem to be achieved by sinking toward not just inertial rest but toward non-existence, annihilation, or a "second death," suggesting practices of nihilistic mysticism, outright self-destruction or self-undoing, *or* abandonment to the unconscious inertias and compulsions of the self, to reactivity and repetition. The requisite states of consciousness (approaching unconsciousness), when achieved in an already Infernal trance, seem to approach the depths of the Abyss, but these are also useless to the Infernalist without the ability to wake up *within* the obliterating annihilation and resume consciousness. It would seem that the primary attraction to such an effort would be the certain knowledge that one's consciousness has achieved sufficient continuity to survive even annihilation of all its qualities and attributes, the Abyssal *gnosis* as an enhancement to the Infernal, for the magical knowledge of negation that can thereby be gained, and for the magical power to inflict annihilation and oblivion by drawing on the power of the Abyss. There are also traditions that the depths of the Abyss (or the black holes of "singularities") act as gateways between worlds or universes; even if taken only metaphorically, this would seem to suggest that routes to cosmological restructuring are available through the states of infernal non-being. These states should also not be confused with void-concepts typical of Eastern mysticism, or even with "the primordial void," all of which are entirely non-local and have as much and as little to do with the Infernal as with anything else. Similarly, while the "meon" of some contemporary Gnostic traditions is accessible through these means, it is also accessible in a variety of other ways, and not particularly Infernal in nature.

The Abyss has also been applied to the endless gap between the phenomenal and noumenal world in Qabalistically-influenced traditions which posit the Supernals as ontologically in-accessible to the worlds below them, save by crossing the "abyss" of Knowledge. This seems to suggest some Gnostic influence, as this would technically make the planetary spheres below the supposed firmament "infernal," and create a cosmology in which the terrestrial itself is *below* the limits of the infernal, or within it. In some of these Qabalistic models, the truly "infernal" realms would be the "shells" of the primordial creation which are in the roots of the cosmic Tree of Life, in positions similar to the "Hells," in other interpretations, the Tree is itself inverted (but the relational positions of the shells and the spheres would be equivalent), and still others have the Shells (Qlippoth) as the "back" of the Tree (or bark of the tree), *outer* husks rather than inner or deeper worlds, or on an entirely separate Tree of Death (Tree of "Knowledge"). These models are further complicated by the location of the Abyss *not* within the Firmament or between the Firmament and the planets, but between Saturn and Jupiter; some contemporary sinister Infernal Hermetic traditions have located *that* Abyss at the asteroid belt between Mars and Jupiter, but other sinister traditions (Hermetic and otherwise) have placed the Abyss as accessible between Mars and Sol. Clearly the Knowledge of the Abyss is surrounded by confusion, although these various cosmological models generally seem at least consistent among themselves. The suggestions offered here are conjectures that may be useful to practitioners taking an Infernal perspective *in pursuing their own Gnostic experience*, the only final arbiter where the Infernal is concerned.

From the Infernal perspective, the Qabalistic cosmologies only make sense if their purported terrestrial sphere is already regarded as either describing reality from an otherworldly vantage or as indicative of some kind of cosmological dislocation. That makes these maps potentially deceptive and dangerous, but it would still be useful for the Infernalist to know how to apply them. What the Qabalah generally describes as the seemingly terrestrial world, "The Kingdom," should be understood by the Infernalist as an aeonically specific recension of the human world, the social cosmos. Its "qlippothic" reflex is equivalent to the Underworld as described; no Qabalistic model refers to what an Infernalist would understand as terrestrial reality, or "the flesh." Thus, in the Qabalistic model of "lower Qlippoth," these are all lower realms in the Underworld. Coherently, in such a model, the Abyss is indeed located beneath them, but they propose even lower Shells which might be taken to correspond to the meontic depths earlier described.

But what about variations wherein it is also possible to *ascend* through the Shells? These would seem to suggest an Infernal Qabalistic Gnosticism wherein the planetary spheres are seen from an Infernal perspective, but depending on whether the Infernalist sought power within the prison, or freedom from it, either the "front" or the "back" of the Tree might seem more Infernal or celestial. For those Infernalists wishing to engage the infernal aspects of the planetary spheres, it would make sense to apply the Qlippothic model to them; for those Infernalists engaging in an oppositional ascent, an assault upon Heaven, they might interpret the Qabalistic spheres as akin to Gnostic archons exercising celestial dominion from above. (Especially given that the lowest Supernal is often associated with the planet Saturn and therefore has an accessible Infernal counterpart.) A further interpretation of the "higher" Qlippoth is that they can signify the "shells" – the material realities – of various celestial forms (that is, they are the forms of "the planets"), as well as the infernal realities *within* them. This would make the "planetary spheres" their spiritual counterparts. If the Infernalist needs to engage with a model proposing two *separate trees*, it is probably wisest if they are complementary, nested opposites like yin and yang: one is the Tree *within the Infernalist*, the other the *Tree of worlds*. Both contain spheres and Shells, and both can be regarded as of Life or of Knowledge/Death, but the relationship between sphere and Shell is in each case reversed, such that the *shells* of the Tree within give Life, and the *spheres*, knowledge, whilst outwardly it is the Shells which offer up Gnosis, and the spheres – when consumed – their Life. If the Shells, then, have Infernal aspects, the other Infernal realms can be accessed from any of them – and therefore, so can the Abyss. This is the easiest and simplest resolution to the multiply located Qabalistic and sinister Abyss which seems to insinuate its way all the way toward the Supernals.

It is not, however, the most precise or specific. To fully appreciate the dislocation of the Abyss into the heavens, the Infernalist must be familiar with the myths of the fallen Watchers of Middle-Eastern lore, angels set over humanity who became enamored of human women and shared the secrets of sorcery and science with them, as well as their seed. In the Enochian traditions (of the Hebrews, not yet of John Dee), these Watchers when condemned were consigned to a *celestial* place of torment, and this seems to have fallen into the Hells in later aeons – much as the Qabalah has the Kingdom "fall" from its place on the Tree, leaving the Abyss as the gap. This seems to be the Qabalistic version of the "fall" of the world, or of man – along with various versions of the Fall of the Angels. This could be an interpretation of the "fall" of consciousness into matter – or a variation on the theme of deliberate imprisonment of consciousness within the cosmos by malevolent divinities. As such, in a Qabalah of Infernal ascent, the standard Qabalistic Abyss located between the sphere of Jupiter and the sphere of Saturn not only defends the Supernals from Infernal assault, it also somehow traps the Watchers;

but from an Infernal perspective, it is also a means of transition between the worlds of the shells and the spheres, and so perhaps a way of directly offering access between the *Infernal* and *Terrestrial* worlds, projected into the heavens. Some of the sinister traditions propose a "nexion," or infernal gateway, located in space between Jupiter and Saturn, and this may correlate with the peculiar location of the Abyss in standard Qabalah. These sinister traditions, however, locate the Abyss between Sol and Mars, but as they lack any opposition between shells and spheres, entirely rejecting constructions of the supernal in favor of a mirrored balance between infernal and celestial directions within a terrestrial cosmos, their Abyss refers to the transition between moving toward and away from the Sun – in this sense, to pass out of its orbit is to approach the "abyss of space" – which is ultimately found to *include* the Sun and all that seems to be in its power. The sinister Hermetic traditions which locate an Abyss at the asteroid belt seem to do so because, rather than rejecting the Supernal constructions entirely, they identify them with the further, outer planets, and continue beyond them toward the 'outermost' to parallel the 'uttermost' descent of the Infernalist, whose own access to the Abysses *below* and *within* offers a journey as endless as that into outer space.

Given its Enochian origins and Qabalistic transmission, the "celestial Abyss" has developed great significance in modern and contemporary occultism thanks to the influence of Thelema, which makes its crossing a primary initiatory ordeal and demonic confrontation. Considering that the Abyss and its patron Coronzon have been demonized and diabolized so thoroughly that even much of chaos magic and various Left-Hand Path traditions have continued the trend, this otherwise obscure subject might be of great interest to the Infernalist. Given the Infernalist's concern with primal origins, it is significant that the first reference to Coronzon seems to have been in an anonymous Agrippan-style rite appearing in Reginald Scot's *Discoverie of Witchcraft* in 1665, which it must therefore predate. The rite summons the Dionysian satyr-like spirit Balkin, apparently classified in whatever system originated the rite as a "Northern" spirit. The magician wears bearskin and writes various angelic (here said to be "Olympick") names in a circle – but one of these names is Coronzon. It is repeated again after "per flammam ignis" in "per vitam Coronzon" just before Amen, perhaps suggesting some identity as a divine name related to vital spirit. He is mentioned again as a "mighty prince" after the usual invocations of Hebrew divine names, angels, archangels, and various holy persons such as Abel, Seth, and Noah. The whole conjuration is clearly Christian as it concludes with the Father, Son, and Holy Ghost, and it is alleged to follow the rules of "Vaganostus the Norwegian." Correlating the angels named in the ritual with the *Heptameron*, they appear to be Martial, which said angels are in that text also ascribed to the North. As the same appendix to Scot also references Edward Kelly's necromantic activities which were depicted in a period engraving as utilizing the same type of circle, it appears that Kelly may have been familiar with Coronzon *prior* to his receiving angelic revelations with the magus, Dr. John Dee, who was apparently attempting to recover knowledge from the original Enochian tradition.

What Kelly seems to have received from the angels is, rather than the contents of the lost Books of Enoch, an aeonically updated form of monotheism which seems to be based on a literal counter-Gnosticism in which Ialtabaoth (Iad Baltah) is worshipped as God. The Gnostic redeemer, a serpent from beyond, is diabolized in the name of Coronzon and identified with Satan (which would have been very familiar to the Church fathers who diabolized Gnosticism as a many-headed hydra of heresy, making it interesting that the "many-headed dragon" appears attacking the divine spheres in the design on the floor of the Golden Dawn's "Vault of the Adepts"; Mathers, its founder, was fascinated by Dee's Enochiana). Aside from modifications to the monotheist doctrines and a cosmology of thirty aethyrs which seem to surround and interpenetrate the terrestrial world, Dee's cosmology offers nothing new other than the detailed "elemental watchtowers" and the angelic language. The first of the aethyrs is the subtlest, and the tenth seems to be identifiable with the Abyss, but seemingly exactly in the sense that there was once a place of punishment and restriction for the Watchers in Heaven, such that the tenth might be the aethyr in which the Devil is *trapped*. This accords with the idea of the Devil as the "prince of the powers of the air," as fallen from heaven, and as having access to the terrestrial world to go to and fro upon it, as well as presiding over Hell. (But these are matters of diabolism more than Infernalism proper; the reader can refer to the section on Infernal Diabolism for a Gnostic interaction of these concepts). Coronzon, then, is unambiguously "the Devil" in Enochian, and perhaps has the rare distinction of being the only Devil to be *further demonized* in the course of aeons, being identified in modern ceremonial magic also as the *demon of the Abyss*, acquiring the traits of the Dweller on the Threshold and the Evil Genius as well. It is unclear what Coronzon may have been to begin with; the name is unattested outside the ritual described earlier, and it seems extraordinarily out of place within it. Yet, it seems likely that the ritual predates Enochian. If Vaganostus was really "a Norwegian," it is possible that the name could owe something to Scandinavian magic (making it a greatly unexpected irony of aeonics that the triple triangle which has come to be associated with Coronzon thanks to Crowley's re-spelling of its name as Choronzon to make it equal 333 in Hebrew, looks much like an Odinic *valknot*); it is possible that Coronzon was to be interpreted as a Prince of Mars; and it is possible that it has some obscure Gnostic significance, as it is mentioned in the conjuration along with great respect to Seth. An Infernal interpretation of Coronzon (without Crowley's intervention) would most plausibly presume it had an independent Northern magical significance and that its potentially demonic/diabolic (but certainly Infernal) character was readily identified by the Enochian angels even if not by Kelly, who then diabolized it. Had Crowley not adopted and adapted Enochian magic from the Golden Dawn, Coronzon would probably now be yet another name for the Devil and little more, or even just "the Enochian devil" without further comment. Crowley's association of Coronzon with the personal ego says more about his diabolization of the ego than it does about Coronzon, but thanks to his attribution of its number 333, its identification with the Ordeal of the Abyss, and its pervasive demonization in modern occultism, Coronzon has become a figure of some significance. Since Goethe has already established Mephistopheles as a diabolical bi-name of Wotan, Coronzon (symbolized as he is by a near-valknot) might as well be regarded as his 333rd, which fits contemporary Left-Hand Path sub-culture rather well, given the persistent association between Odinic and Left-Hand Path traditions. (It also fits the ritual in Scot's text, since the only original ritual extant involving Coronzon apparently involves going bear-shirted – that is, *ber-serk*, all of whom were sacred to Wotan.) The contemporary Left-Hand Path association seems especially appropriate, considering the enthusiastic re-appropriation of the identity of the Black Brother by magi Michael Aquino and Edred Thorsson, it seems fitting that the "god-devil" of the Black Brothers should turn out to be that original Lord of the Left-Hand Path himself, Thorsson's "Gothic God of Darkness". As both he and Enki are gods of wisdom, the parallel between Hel/Hell and Abzu/Abyss seems to remain structurally intact in our Infernal cosmology, despite the unexpected excursion into the history of esoteric and occult transmission through the aeons. This is, perhaps, a rather academic demonstration of a technique of Infernal cosmology and practice – the deliberate pursuit of a downward or "backward," averse way into the primal, primary, and primordial origins of those beings and concepts which populate the Inferno and which later traverse the aeons as demons, Devils, and Gods.

Opening the Abyss

In the event that the Infernalist wishes to access the Abyss directly, rather than through the Infernal descent as previously described, or by approaching it through one of the mapped cosmologies already presented, the following techniques might be useful, especially in combination:

─⌇─ Methods of the mysticisms of the Negative Way, stripped of all moral and cosmological content.

─⌇─ Suspension while in darkness, perhaps combined with sensory deprivation.

─⌇─ Performance of conjurations that juxtapose the content of various systems in which the Abyss in-between becomes the only coherent commonality, particularly during in-between states or threshold times, such as just at the end of evening twilight, between waking and sleep. (Spare's notion of the "in-betweenness" concepts suggests the possibility of a whole 'abyssal arcana').

─⌇─ Deliberately inducing states of cognitive dissonance, paradox, cognitive overload.

─⌇─ The consumption of disassociative agents.

─⌇─ Antinomian actions producing a sense of self-revulsion or self-loathing.

─⌇─ The mantra "Zazas Zazas Nasatanada Zazas".

Entering the Abyss

The above, combined with attempts to unleash significant "free belief" in the Sparian sense, especially all simultaneously, can thrust the Infernalist into the Abyss, as can similar but more spontaneous dislocations of association: thus, disillusionment, shattering loss, crises of faith – but also discovery of totally novel perspectives, radical shifts of paradigm or world-view (deep, not superficial cosmetic or aesthetic modifications); the consumption of totally absorbing hallucinogens (note this should *not* be presumed to lead to Abyssal experiences unless it is combined with the rest of these methods); the deliberate violation of cherished beliefs, self-images, values, taboos, etc.

The famous Thelemic "Oath of the Abyss" is sometimes regarded as automatically provoking Abyssal ordeals, related to Crowley's cynical comment that any aspirant who wanted to claim the grade of Master of the Temple (signifying successful Abyssal crossing) had the right to do so. At first glance, this seems to be a sarcastic joke that anyone who wanted to say they were a Magister when they *hadn't* yet confronted Choronzon was welcome to their madness, but other interpretations of the context suggest that Crowley did think the ordeal could be provoked in this way. That does not mean he was recommending it, as also remarked that entering into the Abyss unprepared resulted in slavery to Coronzon. From an Infernal perspective, there is no reason to presume particular moral hostility on Coronzon's part, however, and even within the context of Thelema, Crowley's student C. F. Russell, instrumental in Chicago's "Choronzon Club" also promoted (through work with the G∴B∴G∴ – Great Brotherhood of God) a Thelemic "Short Path" which (like short path Vajrayana) aimed at sudden enlightenment. Part of this method did involve the pre-emptive use of the Abyssal oath to interpret every phenomenon as a particular dealing of God with one's own soul. (The intention here is not, particularly, to perpetuate the misunderstanding that this is the totality of Crowley's oath of the Magister Templi – but, like many subsequent interpreters, the G∴B∴G∴ seems to have taken this clause as the focus.) Given the Infernal rejection of monotheism and of the unitary soul, this would *not* seem to be a very effective abyssal oath (which God? An Infernal God? The God of the Abyss?), so an Infernalist attempting this technique would probably want to compose an original one. By inversionist example, however, we can suggest variations like "I will interpret every phenomenon as a particular communication between the Legion and the Infernal Host." Use of the *daimon* or the *genius* here is not especially recommended, as that would more properly re-appropriate the Thelemic "Holy Guardian Angel" for Infernal purposes.

A Diabolist, however, might wish to use the Devil and the Self; an antinomian Thelemite might actually wish to swear to Coronzon itself.

THE INFERNAL PACT

Obviously such an operation would be one instance of the Pact, a primary technique of Infernalism. Like all forms of exchange, pacts range from the formal to the informal, the grand to the commonplace, the temporary to the permanent. The art of making pacts is in knowing what to offer, how much, when, and to whom. The words of the High One, advice from that aforementioned god of at least 333 bi-names, are "Better not to ask than to overpledge, for a gift demands a gift." *Quid pro quo* is the Infernal axiom. Any magical system that involves dealing with spirits *respectfully* has some advice and knowledge to offer the Infernalist.

Pacts are also the antithesis of spirit compulsion. An Infernalist is advised *never* to attempt to compel any being except for those which are cosmologically inimical (the angels of the Tetragrammaton, for instance). Should the aspiring Infernalist ever have previously used methods of compulsion, he should first make a preliminary Pact to cease doing so, and then attempt to compensate any spirits (particularly any Infernal spirits) compelled in this way. It would also be wise for the new Infernalist to blaspheme and repudiate any tradition previously misused, so a Christian who compelled the Goetia in the name of the Trinity would be advised to renounce his baptism, or a Jew who followed "Solomon"'s tradition of enslaving demons should reject the Covenant with YHVH and commence ritual antinomian violations of the prohibitions in the Torah, whilst a Muslim who had used the names of Allah against the Jinn might share with them a huge feast of pork. A Thelemite who had attempted to bind or compel Coronzon might be advised to burn the Book of the Law – except that Thelema has to this degree provided for its own antinomianism, so he might proceed to further distort the Law by placing Love over Will, or purposely acting according to conscious whim, or banishing the Holy Guardian Angel in preference to the Evil Genius (or, if he had previously "strengthened the lower link," he should instead practice further self-overcoming by seeking out the shining *daimon* within, the augoeides). A would-be Infernalist originating within a paradigm misused by misjudgment rather than by design (such as an Odinist unfamiliar with the *galdrabok* traditions who presumed the *daimone* to be equivalent to *jotnar* and *thursar* and assaulted them) is a more complex position. Some contemporary antinomian anticosmic traditions like the 218 current attempt to identify with demonized figures in, for example, the Teutonic tradition; this would be one means of reconciliation – as long as no reverse demonization is practiced (the 218 current is routinely guilty of this). Another solution would be immediate pacts with the correctly identified Infernal figures corresponding to the misused tradition (so the Odinist in our example would make his pact with Mephistopheles or Coronzon, as previously considered). A third solution would be the purposeful banishment of the *original* non-Infernal adversary figures (the *thursar* of Teutonic tradition are not, in fact, particularly Infernal) by means of the Infernal figures they were misidentified with. While this sort of scenario is obscure enough to differ greatly depending on the personal situation, it is likely that the solution of re-appropriation is most appropriate when the slandered *daimone* have been diabolized; the solution of correct identification most appropriate when the misused tradition has been highly dualized or moralized; and the solution of banishment when the primary mistake is demonic misidentification.

Once the Infernalist is assured that he is not on bad terms with the Legions of Hell, he can proceed to use the method of pacts for basically any purpose. The core technique is so simple that were it excerpted from this article and properly applied by one semi-competent magician, the entirety of Infernalism could be restored, were every Infernalist in the world to find themselves exiled to Hell. "Any purpose" can be roughly divided into categories of *gnosis* and power. As long as the appropriate entity is chosen and properly paid, the only obstacles to the success of a Pact are: divine interference, terrestrial inertia, and miscommunication. The first can be resolved through greater antinomianism and ultimately through aeonics; the second overcome through enhancement of and improvement of the Infernalist and his or her material circumstances; and the third, through precision, study of arcana, cosmology, mythology, and philology.

As a general rule, most Infernal powers want variations on the same themes: access to the terrestrial world and access to the flesh.

The Great Pact

Here is an Infernalized example of a method that seems to appear in similar forms in various traditions, the core of which offers access to the aforementioned Short Path. Attempts at proper execution of this method which fail, especially due to inconstancy, are likely to result in being "damned to Hell," in some sense.

The Infernalist should choose a primary Patron who seems to be the best example of the singular unity of the Legion as the totality of the Infernal Host, based on current location and personal background and heritage. As a celebration of his or her birthday, the Infernalist (or would-be Infernalist, in the case of an operator bold enough to attempt this method with no prior experience) prepared a formal conjuration of this entity based on the best possible traditional research and personal and contemporary aesthetics. At the exact time of birth, the Infernalist completes the conjuration and recites a previously prepared Pact which offers to the Patron everything the Infernalist can imagine that it might want, for the rest of the Infernalist's life; in exchange, the Infernalists asks for the fulfillment of all present and potential future desires. For the rest of the year, the Infernalist performs a variation of this ritual as compressed as possible, at the same time – the birth-time – each day, with the intention that on the *next* birthday, the Patron will fully manifest with an omen of the acceptance of the Pact, which the Infernalist will then sign. This means that the Infernalist also has a year to revise the Pact, although the *full ritual* should be repeated for each revision.

Once the Pact is signed, the Infernalist must commence payment immediately upon the first indication that the Patron has fulfilled any part of it, and continue payment indefinitely – assuring continuity of consciousness – and fulfillment of desires – even in Hell.

The Infernal Path

Whether short or gradual, sudden or incremental, spontaneous or considered, the Infernal path is an antinomian one. Even a pre-moral culture has its norms and customs: the Infernalist violates them, liberating belief from previous fetters and refashioning it into his own. To achieve the ultimate gnosis of the Absolute, this process must be complete and thorough, ranging from the Infernalist's own personal aesthetics, compunctions, obsessions, and fetishes, to the most seemingly universal pre-moral norms of human behavior. By entirely disrupting instinctive, terrestrial reactivity and compulsion, the Infernalist makes space for something *other:* Consciousness.

How to Become an Infernalist

Collapse. Fall down. Get lost. Lose yourself. Go to Hell.

Sympathy with the Devil: Faust's Infernal Formula
A Thelemic Interpretation of the Demonic Magus

Lana Krieg

Beyond Good and Evil
The Necessity of an Esoteric Reading of Goethe's Faust

For nearly 300 years, Goethe's *Faust* has been recognized as a masterpiece of Western literature.[1] Its cultural and moral relevance have been consistently recognized by those critics who sense the work's insight, and yet the significance of its darker motifs systematically eludes reconciliation with popular interpretations. Broadly, both ancient and modern aesthetes seem to agree that certain pieces of art endure through time because they are essentially connected to, explanatory of, or promote certain relationships of the human to his reality.[2] In other words, the interaction with reality facilitated by truly sublime art is one which appeals to the spiritual adaptivity of man.

Faust unquestioningly has become one of the most revealing works on the spiritual dilemmas of modern man, and yet traditional critiques of the play which focus on its value as an exemplar of the Romantic spirit or a modernized Christian morality play seem to ignore or fail to capture the very elements of *Faust* which have ensured its prominence in the canon of Western Literature; otherwise, its Mysteries.

In general, interpretations of Goethe's masterwork focus on only the most superficial components of the spiritual instruction which the play contains, and thereby ignore the source of its force and resonance. In *Faust*, Goethe creates a protagonist representative of the spiritual dilemma which he observed – a protagonist with whom it is easy for the reader of a certain disposition to identify. For just such a reader, Goethe's play may require that identification in order for the nature of the play's resonance to be comprehensible. It seems likely that, like the secret powers after which the protagonist himself searches, the play may give up its secrets only to a reader who himself stands in the position of Faust – Frustrated with knowledge gathered vicariously and superficially, and ready to exhume the real secrets of nature and power.

The need for an esoteric reading of *Faust*, one discovered by and meant for the Magician, seems indicated and intended by the play's author. Goethe himself would likely have rejected most of the canonical readings of his play. One only needs to look to

---

1 For an example of the traditional critique of *Faust* and a discussion of its place in the Western Canon, see Gillies, A. (1957).

2 Both ancient philosophers and contemporary post-modern aesthetes seem to see something of the spiritual in art. Post-modern authors like Eli Siegel and Jean Lyotard insist that the human tendency for meaning-making created a reciprocal relationship between reality and aesthetics which account for what previous aesthetes like Kant or even Aristotle might have though of an experience of the "sublime" vs. merely the beautiful. In other words, Art may be instructive of a spiritual reality – or even create one.

Goethe's life and his own philosophical stances and interests for the evidence. Johannes Wolfgang von Goethe was in his own day, and is still considered to be, simultaneously one of the most influential poets of the German Romantic period and one of the founders of humanistic neo-classicism. His *Sorrows of Young Werther* (1774) was one of the hallmarks of the Sturm und Drang Romantic movement (and remained Goethe's most popular and influential work throughout his life). However, Goethe renounced both *Werther* and the Romantic movement in general, in the harshest of terms. One of Goethe's most famous quotations is "What is Classical is healthy; what is Romantic is everything that is sick".[3] To the end of his life, Goethe regretted the mindset which led to his creation of *Werther* and tried in vain to distance himself from that work and the Romantic movement in general.

Faust, Part I was published over 30 years after *The Sorrows of Young Werther*, and has puzzled literary critics in light of Goethe's complete renunciation of Sturm und Drang in the interim. In many ways, *Faust* could be read as a true Romantic masterpiece: Romanticism as a movement stressed strong emotion, imagination, freedom from classical correctness in art forms, rebellion against social conventions and the rationalization of nature by the Enlightenment. These themes can easily be read in *Faust* – from the main character's frustration with the world of intellectual discourse, to his "redemption" through the love of a woman.[4]

However, the spirituality of *Faust* is not a Romantic Spirituality, and an evaluation of this theme reveals Goethe's frustration with and contempt of Romantic period German Protestantism and its reduction and dismissal of ancient mysteries. Nevertheless, there is no denying *Faust's* "Romantic" form. Partially, the play's Romantic sensibility comes from its hermeneutic Medieval lineage. Romanticism was one of the first artistic movements to reappraise "low culture" – previously maligned medieval romances and national folktales started to influence literary fiction. The Romantics' fascination with Medieval themes and tales is one of the hallmarks of the movement, and *Faust's* foundation is solidly Medieval. The Faust legend is actually one of the most durable in western folklore and literature, and there is considerable evidence that the character Faust was based on one or more actual historical persons who lived in the mid-1500's. Contemporary inquiries reveal that at least one of the persons amalgamated into the Faust legend may have been an actual Doctor who was very well traveled throughout Europe and fairly well-known. This person was said to have boasted of his allegiance with the Devil, and although he reportedly performed feats of astrology and medicine, his reputation in general was an evil one. Though most Enlightenment scholars scoffed at the historical reality or the validity of Magical feats performed by such a person, this character was taken quite seriously by Reformation personalities such as Martin Luther and Philippe Melanchthon who held him up as an example of the perversity, reality and danger of sorcery.

The real or fictional Faust was, in fact, preserved alongside the likes of Agrippa, Nostradamus, and Paracelsus, as an example of a prominent Magus in Medieval lore. Although by Goethe's time Medieval texts themselves were not heavily referenced,

---

3 Lynn (1971). See this piece for a discussion on Goethe's rejection of the Romantic movement and his move toward Classicism.

4 For a discussion of *Faust* as an exemplar of Romantic literature see Bates (1906).

the Romantic artists were fascinated with Medieval aesthetics, characters and settings, which seemed to evoke the essence of European cultures. The proliferation of Romantic art based upon the Arthurian legends is evidence of this tendency. It is particularly interesting that Goethe would choose Faust for what seems at first glance to be a revivalist piece. A resurrection of the Faust legend, a staple of medieval "low-culture" infused throughout with derision for Enlightenment and Modernist sentiments would be perfectly in character for a true Romantic poet. Goethe's disdain for Romanticism in this period makes this an odd choice however, and demands a closer look into his motives.

The Renaissance through the Romantic period saw the rise of the Hermetic mystery tradition of magic that often used legendary Magi as literary placeholders for the forebears of Hermetic knowledge and the lineage of esoteric secrets. While these literati rarely included the writings or original tales of these Masters in their works, they subtly betray familiarity with source texts to varying degrees. It should be noted that the type of ritual Magic discussed in Medieval Grimoires was not similar to the naturalistic or scientifically oriented practices of the Renaissance and later Hermetics. Rather, Goethe breaks from the Romantic tradition by using the characters and Magics of the previous Faust myths in his seemingly revivalist piece. Instead, he distills a forgotten, or never fully developed, Magical instruction which is not akin to the practices of the esotericism of his day.

That esotericism was as flattering of harmony and nature as Romanticism. In defiance of extant aesthetic, religious, and intellectual cultures, Goethe describes a darker, more destructive, and more antique Magical path. To consummate this defiance, he unearths a Medieval story repugnant to the popular sentiments. Goethe chose to partake in, and perhaps be the capstone of, a Faustian mythological lineage which had promulgated a subversive and dark tradition for 300 years before him. It could be said, that rather than reviving Faust as a reconstruction placing the world-views of his own time onto the mysteries of times past, as was the tendency of the Romantics, Goethe restored the Faustian tradition of hiding antagonistic esoteric knowledge in plain sight.

The historical or imagined Medieval character of Faust was first ensured his immortality primarily through a literary oddity known as the *Faustbuch,* of anonymous authorship. This work (which spawned its own genre) first appeared around 1550 and recounted common tales of many famous Magi including Merlin, Albertus Magnus, and Roger Bacon – but attributed all of these men's feats to "Faust", the Doctor of previous legends. Although tales of the occult and even Magical Grimoires and manuals were not uncommon in this period, the *Faustbuch* was unique even among these. The tales in the *Faustbuch* were often humorous, and featured Faust as a sort of evil trickster character who duped the unwary with the help of a capering demon, Mephistopheles. However, the book also evoked a distinct spirit of horror in its vivid descriptions of Hell and the fullness and realism of character portrayed in the "savage, embittered, yet remorseful fiend Mephistopheles".[5] From the beginning, the Faustian tradition has presented both Faust and the demon as sympathetic characters, with which readers could identify, and whose power and import they might come to come to understand.

The tale and its anti-hero spread quickly in popularity inspiring an entire folk genre

---

5 Butler (1952) is an excellent source on the implications of *Faust* in the history of Magic.

of stories and plays involving the evil Faust and his pact with the devil. The *Faustbuch* was speedily translated and read throughout Europe, and the bones of the story remained popular subjects of folk art, drama, and literature for two centuries. An English prose translation of the *Faustbuch* in 1592 inspired the play *The Tragical History of Dr. Faustus* by Christopher Marlowe, which became one of the playwright's most popular and enduring works. Goethe's play effectively congeals the Faust legend, both encompassing and surpassing the content and spirit of these earlier works – creating in essence a Faustian gospel which remains the most relevant and sublime instance of the legend to date.

Faust may be not a revival of Goethe's Romantic roots, but an artfully delivered *coup de grâce* to a failing German Romanticism. Rather than a revival of a popular medieval subject, Goethe may have been attempting a thrust at the very heart of what he perceived as the Romantic "sickness". Despite drawing heavily from the earlier lineage, Faust does not revive the earlier myths with an 18th Century moral frame. The most defining contrast is found in the conclusion. In the Medieval stories and even in Marlowe's more dramatic version the fate of the "hero" is never in doubt. Faust is doomed and damned for consorting with the Devil, and is ultimately dragged to Hell. Goethe's Faust, despite or due to his arrogant, destructive, and villainous deeds, is "saved" and ascends to heaven.

Some critics have argued that this makes Goethe's work a mere reinterpretation of the familiar legend designed to succinctly highlight Christian redemption's ability to save even the worst sort of character. But Goethe does not seem to be making such a moral argument, and his detailing of Faust's salvation does not resonate well with the aesthetics of his contemporaries who attempted the same. In fact, Goethe was not the first to try his hand at the legend of Faust as a shot against Romanticism. Gotthold Lessing, another prominent Enlightenment dramatist, philosopher, and aesthete attempted a version of a Faust drama in which the character is also redeemed. Lessing, an Enlightenment rationalist, saw Faust's pursuit of knowledge as noble and arranged for the hero's reconciliation with God. Lessing, however, might be said to be truly a product of the sensibilities of his time. In his most famous works, he revived characters from the crusades such as Saladin, and the Templars, and utilized them for his promotion of religious universalism.[6] Lessing attempted to use the Faust character in the same fashion. Lessing was a major proponent of Christian Rationalism during the Enlightenment and a central promoter of religious universalism. He seemed to use the redemption of Faust as an illustration of his own idea that divine revelation was irrelevant next to the development of human understanding through rational dialectic. Lessing's Faust was saved because he approached the divine through his intellectual faculty. Lessing himself would have used the Faust myth, not unlike Marlowe and his predecessors, as a morality parable to promote a popular religious philosophy. One reading is that Goethe's version is merely an attempt at the same sort of revision of a popular medieval/Romantic trope.[7] But, while most Romantics utilized familiar characters from previous eras entirely outside their own context in order to illustrate a principle of enlightenment philosophy,

---

6 See Nathan the Wise.
7 See Hunt (2001) for a contextualization of Goethe as a Romantic revivalist.

Goethe uses the Faust legend in an entirely different fashion.

To date, none of the readings of *Faust*, either as an exemplar of the Romantic spirit, or as the thought experiment of a budding rationalist, seem entirely complete or even consistent. The majority of scholarly controversies have focused upon moral issues. Does Faust deserve to go to heaven? If so, is it because his striving accords with God's notion of human existence as described in the play's prologue, his seeming regret at some of his deeds, or his larger plans at the end of the second part for the greater good of humanity? If he does not deserve to go to heaven, then the question becomes whether it is God's grace or Gretchen's intervention that enables his ascension. Other discussions have highlighted the legal and contractual issues as the central puzzle of the play's conclusion. Who really wins the bet that Faust has with the Devil? Has he managed to trick the trickster of the ages by a clever use of a grammatical ruse? Has the Devil really won, but heaven has subverted justice and broken the most sacred aspect of civil society, the contract?[8] All of these lines of questioning assume Goethe's moral rectitude in Christian terms and attempt to discover the arresting essence of *Faust* within that framework. In most critiques for the last 300 years, *Faust* has been taken only as a variation on the "Pact with the Devil" genre. "Pact with the Devil" myths are so common in European Folklore that it has become a classification in the field of literary analysis. These are no more than parables – morality lessons in which the protagonist approaches the Lender of Last Resort in order to fulfill some materialistic desire and eventually comes undone, having lost not only the object of his desire, but his very soul – unless some merciful God or holy figure intervenes. At first glance, Goethe's *Faust* is the very prototype of this genre, and even modern critics continue to treat it as such.

In the medieval period, throughout the reformation, and into the modern era, the legend of Faust has been co-opted by Christian culture as a cautionary tale against the practice of ritual Magic. Elizabeth Butler argues this point beautifully in her *Fortunes of Faust*, the final installment of her *Myth of the Magus* Trilogy. In this volume she traces the Faust legend as a parallel to the fall of the "Magus-Priest" from a position of authority in pre-Christian Europe to the marginalized "evil sorcerer" – doomed to meet a bad end due to bucking the Christian world-order through ritual Magic. The origins of the Faust legend came at a time when medieval Grimoires were beginning to be interpreted in light of the Catholic Church's idea that Magicians were servants of Satan. The implied "Pact" in such Grimoires of ritual Magic was interpreted through this lens, and taken as a trade with the Devil – the results of the operation in exchange for the Magician's immortal soul. Butler points out that the Faust legend uses this metaphysics, perhaps in order to maintain its circulation, and that Faust does not become a publicly redeemable figure until late into the 18th Century. She argues that it is no coincidence that the possibility of Faust's "salvation" is only introduced during a time period which

---

8 It is noteworthy that one strand of quasi-heterodox Jewish lore the development of which both presaged a and paralleled the Qabalah involved clever attempts to utilize legalistic loopholes in interpretation of Torah and Talmud even against the "heavenly court." The earliest Midrashim are replete with such rhetorical trickery, continuing into later early-modern Jewish traditions of such contractual manipulations. Later examples often deal with justifying the use of magic then employed by the rising rabbinic caste of the Bisht/Tzaddik, and it was this genre of magicians taking God to court that became especially prominent, and translated into German, during the time of Goethe. The tradition has lasted even into contemporary times, such as the Holocaust incident dramatized by Elie Wiesel in which Jewish prisoners put God on trial.

also saw a revival of interest in the occult sciences and the rise of secret societies devoted to the Hermetic Arts (Butler, 1952). In one sense the Romanticism of Goethe's day rebuked prevailing Christian metaphysics through its appreciation of neo-Hermeticism's Magic, alchemy and the like, yet both Goethe's contemporaries and those critics who followed continued to use *Faust* as the ground for Christian philosophical debates.

It was not uncommon in Protestant Europe for the Church of Rome's concerns, as well as magic, esotericism, and the occult sciences, to be stripped of their intimidating air by being utilized as caricatures in Protestant moral discourse. Alternatively, as magic was fit into the frame of science and philosophy by the Neo-Hermeticists, Christianity would ignore its more occult elements and consider it in a purely moral discourse. The central focus of Christian debate in this time was a concern with salvation vs. damnation, guilt vs. innocence and the direct relationship of human action and sin to God's purity.

Today's literary critics seem to have difficulty with the idea that Faust's rash, self-serving, and often destructive actions can merit "salvation". At the very best, in these critics' views, Faust is spared perdition by the chastity and love of Gretchen who is enshrined as a Christian ideal – glorified in her complexity as a "saved sinner" or a "pure whore". However, this story arose in the midst of early modern German Protestantism in which the maximum sin was seen as the most attractive to God's grace.[9] Once again, Goethe may seem like only a product of his time, creating a work which plays to the popular religious philosophy.

Gillies demonstrates this attitude when he insists that Gretchen's ascension is based on her embodiment of the Christian ideal of self-sacrifice: "She has withstood the temptations of evil... and gained redemption. How she wishes that Faust could share her rapture and her victory over the devil!... Her fate thus partakes of the nature of self-sacrifice." Bates, a prominent Faustian commentator, also partakes in this theory of Gretchen as an embodiment of virtue: "The charm of innocence clings to Gretchen in the midst of her guilt, and herein the poet shows his wonderful skill; for he does not try to veil or excuse her offense, and instead he fills us with that love of the heroine which purity alone can inspire". In this reading, it is only the purity of Gretchen, seen as an embodiment of traditional Christian Germany which redeems Faust. It is also worthy of note that he claims that only "purity" can inspire love for a heroine. This critique still does not expose the depths of the metaphysics of *Faust*. Goethe, even in the play itself, denounces such a reading of Gretchen's character. Like the character "Valentine" in this very play, Bates is denying the value of Gretchen's womanhood in favor of an idealistic notion of her "purity". Valentine is an overbearing character whose demise is framed to be enjoyed by readers. Even in the superficially heinous act of killing his lover's own brother, Faust comes across as the hero because of Valentine's foolish, pompous, and narrow attitude toward femininity. Bates-like arguments are skewered by Goethe's own presentation of such as thoroughly as Valentine is impaled upon Faust's sword. It is obvious at least that Goethe did not write a traditionally Protestant play. Indeed it

---

9 The requirement of the Antithesis for the existence of Thesis in Hegelian Dialectic, or Marx's explanation that the more tyrannical systems of the Middle Ages were necessary for human development, arise out of a culture in which sin was believed to be necessary for redemption. This justification was often cited by Theological scholars as a rationale for Free Will and the ability to "choose sin".

does not seem like a coincidence that Goethe's "redemption" of Faust occurred during a period which saw the revival of the occult sciences on a grand scale. There is an alternate history of the character Faust which would not place him as simply a Christian scapegoat or illustration of the ills of self indulgence in a series of cautionary parables.

Goethe's version of this story may be an unveiling of Faust, not as a tragic anti-hero, or a villain saved by the forgiveness of Gretchen, but as a hero proper – a protagonist representative of the esoteric heroes of an ancient tradition of European Magi, revived by Goethe. Within *Faust* are rejections of both the decadence of Romanticism and the hollow faith of Rationalism in purely intellectual discourse.[10] Instead, Goethe presents an alternative to either a Christian world-view that denies the potency of the individual or the humanistic philosophies of his contemporaries which seem to uplift knowledge (any and all) for its own sake. Goethe may actually be taking Faust back to his roots and exposing a very real method for Magical attainment which has never been the province of literary criticism.

In order to understand a more esoteric reading of *Faust*, it is necessary to look to the origins of the legend, with which Goethe was undoubtedly familiar. As previously mentioned, the original *Faustbuch* was a German re-telling of the legends of prominent pre- and post-Christian Magi. The anonymous author attributed the stories of Merlin, Albertus Magnus, Paracelsus, Roger Bacon and other prominent Magi and "sorcerers" all to the character of Faust.[11] This character became the stand-in for all the great legendary (and historical) esotericists of European history. It is no coincidence that this character spawned a genre of Christian morality plays, the injunction of which would have been to renounce sorcerers like any of these characters. Nor is it surprising that this book also spawned a parallel set of popular works – Grimoires and Magical manuals which instructed the reader on the art of making (and escaping or sidestepping) "Pacts with the Devil". A whole series of such manuals emerged during the era of the Faust legend's greatest popularity in the Medieval Period and several of these focused on the topic of how to avoid a bilateral or detrimental compact with a Devil, or how to break such a pact. Although these Grimoires were billed as cautionary tales about the dangers of black Magic and the forces of Satan, they were also very detailed manuals which gave enough instruction and theory to perform the very rituals they cautioned against. The most famous of these, the *Magia Naturalis et Innaturalis*, was in the Grand-Ducal library in Weimar, Germany, and was certainly known to J.W. von Goethe. It may be that Goethe's play follows more closely in the footsteps of this particular Faustian genre, the Grimoire, than that of the subsequent morality plays, or the Medieval revivals of Goethe's time. Yet, while the style of these grimoires consistently displays a fairly linear development of the premise of compelling demonic or diabolical spirits by the power of the Christian deity, with a few possible variations including cautious offerings to the

---

10 All this may be consonant with Goethe's attraction to the Illuminati, who combined an esoteric and occult aesthetic with a condemnation of obscurantism and their contemporary adversaries, the neo-Rosicrucians. It is unclear how familiar Goethe would have been with their thorough secularism, but their rejection of Romanticism in combination with the promotion of Enlightenment ideals in a subversive context forms a parallel to the argument presented here about the style and aesthetics of Goethe's *Faust*.

11 It is interesting that many of these characters: Merlin, Paracelsus, Roger Bacon, etc. are also among Aleister Crowley's Gnostic Saints. A reading in which Faust is taken as truly the embodiment of such men, and the play as an instructive grimoire, explains Goethe's placement among the roster.

demons or pacts easily escaped, Goethe presents a complex re-interpretation. Faust's pact with Mephistopheles is as binding as the *literary* Faustian tradition implies, and yet it is described in a manner more suggestive of the worldview of the grimoire more than that of the pulpit. Its conclusion, like the implied conclusion of these grimoires, is that redemption is possible for the magician, yet its magical formula is as subtle and obscure as the grimoires' is blatant and simplistic.

Unlike these Grimoires, *Faust* attempts to impart a particular sort of Magical knowledge while couching this knowledge in a format and in terms which might be overlooked by those who would take issue with its purpose. Evidence of the success of this operation is provided by its common interpretation as an exemplar of traditional Christian principles. A closer reading of *Faust* quickly reveals its underlying themes. Goethe's *Faust* is not only a characterization of the dilemma of Western man as he emerges from a period in which the Church was the primary authority, into an era supposedly driven by the light of reason within himself. Rather, Goethe revives and recreates a fascinating allegory of initiation in the modern age, and may even reveal specific practical formulae of illumination available to a modern mind.

This work, still so evocative and puzzling, is undoubtedly one of the masterworks of Western literature, possessing a cultural and philosophical heritage that remains relevant to those who may seek an illumination beyond Christian morality and modern intellectualism. It seems as critical that this heritage and formula be revealed in this day and age, when the active spirit of the individual has been all but swallowed by the consumptive impulse of post-modernism, as it was in Goethe's day when the dangers of modern decadence were first becoming apparent.

This essay will attempt to shed light on a reading of *Faust* outside the common literary discourse in order to illustrate the potency and relevance Goethe discovered in this durable legend. In the lines of *Faust*, Goethe describes not a Christian parable, nor a rationalist tract, but a formula perhaps known by the Magi of previous eras whom the character Faust represents. It is high time that this discovery and heritage, perhaps recognized by Crowley in Goethe's work, be investigated by contemporary occultists in order to ensure that it is neither lost nor reduced through erosion in the literary discourse. Such an interpretation is not only owed to Goethe, whose philosophy was not limited to the narrow Protestant views of his contemporaries, but is also vital to the modern Magician, who may find it not only of intellectual interest, but practical relevance.

This method of practical and esoteric interpretation is not useful to all. In order to apprehend the Faustian initiation, it is perhaps necessary to approach the text from the mindset of Faust himself. In the play, Mephistopheles, Faust's demonic instructor offers up his secrets and elixirs only to the mind which is "like unto himself". Faust as a character is quite sympathetic for the Magician whose disposition leads to frustration with the sorts of purported illumination offered by his culture – who craves a more liberated, dangerous, and potentially destructive path. It may be that *Faust* offers up its secrets only to the mind which is like that of its protagonist.

After clarifying some of the theoretical background, this essay will review Magical instructions offered in Goethe's Grimoire. However, a certain level of occult knowledge and a cursory familiarity with the text supports the reading of such an exposition. This is not an example of literary criticism, but rather is intended for an audience of Magicians who wish to delve into this text and dig for its secrets.

After understanding the symbols and aesthetics of Goethe's *Faust*, this essay will explore the initiatory Magical formulae revealed in Part I of the play. The two parts of *Faust* are truly separate though complimentary works, written over 20 years apart, and it is in the first portion of the work that the formula is revealed and set into motion in order that it may culminate in the "redemption" of Part II. This essay focuses primarily on *Faust*, Part I in which the completeness of Faust's formulae are detailed – these seem to be culminated rather than introduced in Part II.

Part I of *Faust* begins with a Prologue in Heaven in which God argues with the demon Mephistopheles about the nature of man's divinity. God claims that man's greatest asset is his reason, while Mephistopheles insists that this is the source of all of man's torment. They decide to take Faust as an example of this, and God gives Mephistopheles leave to hound Faust and attempt to tempt him to the devil's cause. Faust enters the narrative in his study, where he rebukes the rewards of science and intellectual pursuits. He feels that he has mastered all of academic knowledge but has only realized that this cannot give him what he truly desires – real power and experience. Faust desires to be like God – not only to know but to be able to affect and experience all of human existence. He also strongly desires a return to primal nature, liberated from the torments of his own ruminations and redundant studies. Faust becomes so frustrated that he makes a suicidal gesture, nearly quaffing fatal poisons, but settles on a more traditional remedy for holiday blues and spends his Easter Day drunk, ambulating around town, where he inevitably encounters Mephistopheles in the form of a black dog. The dog follows Faust back to his study where Faust has been practicing ritual magic, exploring old Grimoires in the hope that nigrimancy and necromancy will give him the sort of real experience which his academic books have not. As Faust conjures, Mephisto appears, and they seem to make a classic Devil's Pact: Mephisto will attempt to entertain Faust, to give him whatever he impulsively desires, but, if Faust should find a moment of true happiness and contentment, Mephisto will take Faust's soul. Sealing this compact in blood they depart on an adventure. Mephisto takes Faust first to a bar of students arguing about the nature of love. He tricks them with false wine, presumably for Faust's amusement, but when Faust becomes frustrated they move to a witch's cave where Mephisto induces the witch to make a love potion for Faust. This induces great desire in him and he sees a vision of beautiful female legendary figures culminating in a vision of a young German village maiden. Mephisto takes him to the village where she lives and Faust meets Margarete/Gretchen. He demands that Mephistopheles help him woo her, and he proceeds to court and seduce her with the demon's help. Seducing her away from her family and her church, Faust copulates with Gretchen and she becomes pregnant. Faust seemingly abandons her as she gives birth and is rejected by her village. While Mephistopheles spirits him away to a demonic Walpurgisnacht celebration, Gretchen goes mad and murders her baby in the church. Convicted of murder, she is sentenced to death, and Faust and Mephistopheles return only in time to see her on the eve of her execution. Faust attempts to rescue her, but she refuses to go, ostensibly because of her remorse, and she is burned at the stake. Faust lets Mephisto save him from the same fate, and Part I ends with Gretchen's death and Faust fleeing the scene.

It is easy to read this play in the same fashion which has been characteristic of criticism to date. This essay will attempt a walk-through of the Magical symbolism which offers an entirely different reading of the play, based primarily on the broad context of Western esotericism. While a few specific citations will be provided from particular texts, readers unfamiliar with the field as a whole would be advised to consult general references on the subject.[12] While nearly every episode of the play's action contributes to the symbolism of the play, those most relevant to the exposition of the Magical formulae of interest will receive the majority of focus.

FAUST'S DILEMMA – THE MIND AND ITS DEMONS

The Prologue in Heaven introduces the play, and it has been the source of most literary debate on the nature of Faust's pact, and why Goethe can "justify" Faust's ostensible redemption. While previous critics may have focused on various elements of this interchange, it seems universally accepted that the Prologue introduces the central dilemma of the play, and foreshadows its conclusion.

The play opens with the Lord being attended upon by the Archangels who introduce themselves in turn with descriptions of their spheres of influence, the Heavens, the Earth, and the Physical Laws which govern these. Mephistopheles, the demon, enters upon this scene and begins to goad the Lord about the nature and purpose of mankind. This prompts the Lord to offer Mephistopheles a wager over whether Doctor Faustus will end by serving God's interests (and Faust's own nature) or not.

This scene, in which the celestial spirits wait court upon the heavenly throne, is reminiscent of the *Book of Job* in which the celestial hierarchy was also assembled to witness a wager between God and the Devil. In *Job*, however, the Devil's wager was that Job, a devout man, served only for earthly rewards and if he was stripped of these he would despair. Job's redemption and virtue was his continued and steadfast faith. Most later versions of man's encounters with Satan from the Middle Ages through the Renaissance, like the folk tales of the Pact with the Devil, bear out this same formula of redemption. Only through faith or vicarious redemption is man spared the consequences of his temptation and folly.

Faust's dilemma and redemption are, in many ways, exactly the opposite of Job and the protagonists of similar parables. In the beginning of Job's story, Job is living a happy, complete, and contented life. Faust by contrast is deeply discontent and feels that after many years of labor and alleged attainment he is left with nothing which he values. Faust is on a continuous, unsuccessful quest for truth. His despair does not need to be created by God or the Devil – it is palpable from the beginning. Ultimately, his

---

12 Useful secondary sources include Antoine Faivre, *Access to Western Esotericism*, Nicholas Goodrick-Clarke, *The Western Esoteric Traditions*, and the Brill *Dictionary of Gnosis and Western Esotericism*, edited by Wouter Hanegraaff. The primary source materials most relevant to the perspective on esotericism and occultism applied here are not only the Faustian corpus as a whole, but also the works of Aleister Crowley, and antecedents including Paracelsus, Robert Fludd, and various Christian Qabalists such as Agrippa. Familiarity with the archaic heritage of Gnosticism is helpful in understanding the ancient religious background of these esoteric traditions, but an introduction to that field is beyond the scope of this article. A good compendium of Gnostic texts is *The Gnostic Scriptures*, edited and translated by Bentley Layton.

redeemer will be neither his steadfastness nor his virtue, but the very path of temptation which seemed so spiritually dangerous in previous eras. Rather than being an antagonist, in this tale, the Devil catalyzes Faust's transmutation and, in the process, is transformed himself.

The first allusion to reciprocal redemption is in the Prologue. First, the nature of Mephistopheles and his place in the divine hierarchy are characterized. The first to speak are the Archangels Raphael, Gabriel, and Michael. The speech of each characterizes his specific celestial domain, the stars and heavens, the earth, and the elemental forces respectively. Such conceptualizations of the heavenly hierarchies, with Archangels ruling over specific astronomical principles parallel Angelic Hierarchies outlined by Renaissance occultists such as Trithemius. The use of such correspondences in the opening of the play betrays Goethe's knowledge of esoteric correspondences and pronounces that this work will be operating such a framework. In the very Prologue of the play Goethe sets up the work as belonging to the esoteric genre which is not only occult but subversive in nature.

Faust's ultimate redemption by the agency of Mephistopheles subverts the orthodox Christian understanding of the divine and demonic hierarchy in a fashion reminiscent of, but not identical to, the Gnostic assimilation of diabolized figures like the serpent to the role of savior.[13] Goethe goes even farther in his inversion. Rather than embodying, as in the Gnostic case, a savior emanated by the Light beyond, Mephistopheles embodies a dark adversary, a Satanic antagonist toward the cosmos. While Goethe was clearly not anti-cosmic enough to have been generating a Germanic Gnosticism, he does provide an esoteric method of revaluing the adversary. He also aligns this adversary with the nature of humankind, also slightly reminiscent of Gnosticism. While Mephistopheles[14] is presented as one of the primordial powers of the cosmos, like the archangels, he still manifests within the ordered cosmos, and as such affiliates more toward seemingly subordinate elements such as the human will and psyche than toward the ordered precision of nature.

This by no means makes Mephistopheles a "humanist" or humanitarian: Rather his own capacity for chaos finds sympathy with an element of human nature. His salvific potential is not necessarily by his own design, and while he ultimately contributes to Faust's redemption, his diabolical malice wouldn't bother to spare those who are utilized for this purpose, such as Faust's understudy, the bar-going lovestruck students, or even Gretchen. Goethe also places Mephistopheles within the celestial hierarchy – as a necessary and perhaps desirable adversary for both man and God. Mephisto's speech, antagonistic as it is, characterizes the domain of his concern just like those of the archangels: He mirrors the speeches of the other Angels but is ironically concerned only with "how human beings torment themselves" (l.280). It is ironic that Mephisto is introduced

---

13 Goethe could have had no direct access to Gnostic texts, as the *Nag Hammadi* corpus was not unearthed until 1945, but he would have likely been familiar with the demonization of Gnostic doctrines by "heresy" hunters like St. Irenaeus. As a "Gnosis," Goethe's interpretation is far more diabolical than that of any Gnostic cult except the possibly confabulated "Cainites," the only Gnostic cult to alleged to actually honor the antagonist figures of the Torah.

14 For a detailed examination of Shaitanic currents in Sufism, see Annemarie Schimmel, *Mystical Dimensions of Islam* (University of North Carolina Press, 1978).

as the adversary to man, but quickly displays his sympathy. It is the very nature of his domain which also places him as the antagonist to the rest of the divine system. This Romanticizing of the antagonist very much mirrors the Sufi placement of Iblis[15], and implies that Faust, elite in his own culture, may be able to take advantage of Mephisto's nature to expose Faust's own divinity.

While the workings of the heavens, the orbit of the earth, and the laws of the elements governed by Michael, Raphael, and Gabriel may be straightforward, orderly, and predictable things – the consciousness or reason of humankind is understood as chaotic and torturous from the vantage of divine agents, be they divinities or the moral public. "Somewhat [Man's] life would be in better plight / if you had not given him the shine of Heaven's light", declares Mephisto to the Lord, "He calls it reason / and uses it to be more bestial than any beast" (ll.283-6). Mephisto's concern is the human psyche, a strange and disordered thing, and his behavior is in some ways a mirror for it – he is analogous to man's mind as the other Archangels are analogous to their domains. For example, the Lord accuses Mephisto: "Do you have nothing else to say to me? / And never come but finding fault always? /Never a thing on earth gives you content?" (ll.293-5).

Mephisto's fault-finding is very much like Faust's restless and disillusioned cynicism. This is a feature of Mankind's superiority to the Archangels that passively indulge "heaven's light". The force which Mephisto represents is not mere resentment, but a force witnessed as active discontent, one that inspires rebellion, revolution, and transformation. Mephisto's discontent is in some ways much like Faust's. He seems to share in the plight of mankind's reason – he has seen and been a part of "heaven's light", but is now separated from it. Faust begins the play longing for the heavenly crown and to apprehend all that is on the earth or in the heavens, discontent with his own realm of study.

Faust is unable to see the divine light within him, and Mephisto is similarly incapable of apprehending this "light" within man. The disdain the Devil initially felt, and maintains, towards man caused his separation from God and the rest of the celestial hierarchy. He is not only concerned with the plight of mankind, but in a way, may be particularly sympathetic to it. Conversely, Faust's discontent is a passive and enervating force. It is Mephisto who wakes Faust to action, transforming Faust's natural dissatisfaction into a revolutionary power. In *The Book of the Law*, Crowley discusses the light within man as well, in his descriptions of Hadit, as the force which moves, the knowledge of life and death, and the destroyer of sorrow.[16] Elsewhere Crowley speaks of this "Light" as Lucifer – and the descriptions given to Hadit in many ways easily fit Goethe's Mephisto as well. Hadit says "I am alone: there is no God where I am" – a decent description of the initial plight of Faust and the very nature of Mephisto. At the very least, Mephisto spurs Faust and awakens him to his own further mastery.[17] The Prologue

---

15 One might compare this motif to the veneration of Iblis in Shaitanically-inclined currents of Sufism; Iblis is regarded as an ideal model of ultimate devotion to the divine in an iconoclastic, anti-human and elitist fashion. However, Iblis is certainly not considered to be a friend of mankind, a race of clay to which the proud Son of Fire refuses to prostrate himself despite its creation in the image of Allah.

16 *Liber Al vel Legis*, Ch. II, v. 6-9, 19, & 23.

17 Though alluded to many times throughout this piece, the reader should note the complex relationship

strongly suggests even Mephisto, in his agitation and discontent, serves a purpose.

The very source of Faust's torment – his restless mind – may be the faculty which leads him to actualization, and as his mental faculty is rectified so is the nature of Mephisto, previously the antagonist. Mephisto, in his separate speeches, treats reason as the source of all mankind's pain but also as the thing which gives man power over him, the devil. Both are true, and Mephisto's efforts to lead Faust "astray" are the actual mechanism by which Faust is freed from his contract. This seems like the inverse of a Romantic tragedy. Rather than the protagonist's nobler qualities leading to a defeat, his seemingly inferior qualities lead to his triumph.

Mephisto may even understand that he is an instrument of initiation and a spur to purposeful action for Faust to some degree. When he at last introduces himself to the Doctor, Mephisto states that he is "A part of the power who / wills evil always but always works the good" (ll.1336-7). Although it is never his intention to help Faust, the demon seems to have an understanding of his own part in the Divine scheme. The Lord argues that although Faust labors "in confusion", he is serving the Lord even through his mental restlessness and spiritual agitation. In fact, the Lord asserts that He will soon "lead [Faust] into clarity" (l.309). Mephisto's immediate response to this is to ask if he might "lead" Faust for a while – the same word-choice which the Lord has just utilized. The Lord's response seems to particularly foreshadow the means of Faust's redemption: "So long / as human beings strive they will go wrong" (ll.316-17). This is an odd statement since it is with this in mind that the Lord agrees to Mephisto's wager. It seems that he thinks Faust's agitation inevitable, and yet he participates in promoting that striving through which Faust will "go wrong". This is an early hint that to "go wrong" is exactly what Faust needs in order to achieve the "heavenly light" he desires.

The Lord concedes to Mephisto's wager and allies himself with the Devil's methodology by endorsing the induction of a demonic conflict for Faust. The Lord emphasizes that he does not see Mephisto as an enemy "Because Man's energies flag all too easily / and peace and quiet are soon his sole ambition / I like to make the devil his companion / to prick and work and be a mover willy-nilly" (ll.340-3). Even though "striving" causes man to "go wrong", the Lord willingly initiated strife. If this Devil is somehow consonant with or derivative of man's consciousness or reason, then it is the Lord's idea that this tormentor will cause a restlessness which will lead man to motion, presumably for the ultimate purpose of "clarity" – or the rectification of that same restless mind. The use of the phrase "willy-nilly" is interesting as it means literally with or against the will.[18]

---

between the addressee in *The Book of the Law*, Chapter 2, and the speaker, Hadit, who Crowley later came to equate to Satan – the "flame that burns in every heart of man, and in the core of every star." Hadit also declares that while Nuit shall be known, "[he] never," and that he is "the Magician and the Exorcist... 'Come unto me' is a foolish word, for it is I that go." Also: "I see thee hate the hand & the pen; but I am stronger. Because of me in Thee which thou knewest not. for why? Because thou wast the knower, and me." The veneration of Hadit, the core of being, or Satan, is regarded as erroneous inasmuch as he is "the worshipper," so whatsoever can be worshiped is something other than he. All this concordance between the Devil and the Magician becomes interesting in light of Mephisto and Faust's seeming antagonism that lends itself to their 'salvation'. Such redemption is neither reciprocal nor coincidental, for these imply two agents undergoing a transformation, but rather their redemptions are one in the same, and the errands of Faust can be seen as a historical comment on the Devil's initiation as an elaboration on Faust's will.

18 In one sense it does not matter that Faust's will has turned entirely to self-destructiveness. Although Faust has a Will only toward nothing at this point, Mephistopheles may be the power which moves him "with or

In this usage the devil of consciousness is neither for nor against the will but is meant to cause friction or catalyze motion.[19] The introduction of Mephisto alludes to the first portion of Faust's formula – Faust's problem is that his rational mind cannot rise above itself. He longs for an apprehension and command over the universe which is beyond him: "From heaven he wants the fairest star / and from the earth every highest pleasure / And all things near and all things far". It is his rational mind, or his consciousness, which allows him to long for these things, and yet his discontent is also the source of his torment.

Mephisto, a spirit sympathetic to this condition, seems to be attracted to Faust's plight, not in order to alleviate it, but in order to aggravate it. He is a demon which is very much akin to Faust's conscious mind – discontent, an agitator, an antagonist, and for Faust, an enabler. And he represents a paradox: Even as the Lord grants the source of man's divinity and the source of his "most bestial" nature within the same package – the mind – so too he allows Mephisto, the tormentor, to be introduced in order to "lead" man to "go wrong" which seems identical with "leading" him into "clarity". His source of torment is the agitated mind that cannot achieve what it desires, and this is also the catalyst to set the rest of the process into motion.

This abstract subject helps understand the reciprocal and self-catalyzing formula presented in *Faust*. The mind creates (or attracts) something which will in turn goad it to transform, correct, and rise above. The question of how this is to be done continues to be exposed throughout Part I. Mephisto is the demon whose domain is not some celestial law or the order of the planets, but the strange and troubled consciousness of man. He is to be both tormentor and initiator, quite literally. His own alienation from the heavenly throne is not unlike Faust's sense of alienation, also derived from the dilemma of his own consciousness and struggle. But this torment itself is necessary to ignite the engine of his active transformation. The idea of thought as the initial source of catalyzing restlessness is corroborated in Faust's first scene.

Part II: Reason to Be Troubled – From Thought to Word

Our introduction to the protagonist illustrates perfectly the nature of his dilemma of thought and his state of readiness for the sub-textual initiation which is to take place. Faust is reading in his dark study at the academy, lamenting the contents of his life and all his years of study. As implied in the introduction, Faust has a profound yearning for knowledge and experience, but feels that his pursuits in the world of academia and learning have not in any way satisfied this, but only made him jaded and wasted his time. Despite being a "Master and Doctor" of a variety of sciences, Faust calls himself a "poor fool" (1.359). He is distressed by the idea that after all his study he has only

---

against" the will and is able to transform this will to nothing into a will toward action. Although the term "willy-nilly" seems to have been first used in philosophy by Schopenhauer in his discussions on the nature of will, Nietzsche describes the concept that the Will toward Nothing as exhibited in Nihilism is at least a Will of some sort and may foreshadow or even instigate the Will to Power. (*Geneaology of Morals*, Nietzsche, 1887). This seems akin to what Mephisto helps Faust to accomplish.

19 *Liber AL vel Legis*, 1:42 – "Let it be that state of manyhood bound and loathing. So with thy all, thou hast no right but to do thy will."

discovered that "what we can know is: naught" (l.364). He is disillusioned and although his knowledge leads him to have no fear of "Hell and the Devil", he blames his study for bereaving him of joy and practical accomplishment as well. He condemns both thought and word as recursive and detached from naturalistic experience and pleasure. Faust claims to disdain knowledge and the study of "words", and wishes to have what he believes are real experiences of the forces which drive the world. (ll.380-390). Faust desires an active knowledge, something other than the conglomeration of nominal forces. The value and worth of experience seems to be that they are in accord with the Will itself and that the self-referential nature of purely intellectual pursuits only mirrors the entanglement of consciousness void of a directive force.

Faust's dilemma foreshadows Nietzsche's struggles with Romanticism. In one comparison of Goethe's thinking to that of Nietzsche it is pointed out that Nietzsche believed philology to be a good destructive tool but to lack the strength to build anew. He saw the Romantic tendency as one of avoidance – the soothing of struggle through tranquility rather than creativity and true engagement with nature. Nietzsche describes the Romantic's fascination with nature as like a "vestment" of ready-made value into which snugly hide rather than venture a real relation of nature and cultural phenomena back to the human body.[20] The way in which Nietzsche proposes a disdain for Romanticism yet espouses a view of nature which might be called "Romantic" is similar to the way in which he insists that language is metaphor and illusion and yet continues to use manipulation of language to support this. Goethe does the very same, and illustrates this through Faust's interaction with words and philology.

In *Genealogy of Morals*, Nietzsche seems to propose that philology and the construction of words is the root of the problem – but that its utilization is also necessary for "the cure". This cure is also necessary for Faust. He despairs of his wordy natural sciences which may be only the hollowed out shells of meaning removed from object – but he searches within these very shells for agency in life which might justify his existence. He, like Nietzsche, is searching for creative agency which might be redeemed or distilled from the corrosive influence of philology. The hollow and dead nature of these sciences to Faust is further illustrated by the fact that Faust immediately turns to Grimoires of Necromancy in order to find what he has been looking for. In despair of being able to apprehend truth through natural science, Faust claims he has turned to Necromancy and Sorcery in order to discover the underlying nature of things that he may "never again...speak of things I do not know" (ll.380-381). He claims to want to understand "power" and not "the wordy trade" (l.385).

It is during his deriding of academia, science, and philosophy – the veneration of the words of others, removed from experience, dead words – that Faust begins to speak to the moon. This is a fascinating scene as it invokes a magical *Leitmotif* into the drama. The moon, a glyph of the imagination and the subconscious, the natural forces which underlie the workings of the daytime world, gives a first hint that Faust's story will take place in an underworld. The play is begun at night, and Faust's journey into this strange initiation will be by moonlight. This suggests that whatever formula will be played out, it will be a dark one. Faust's initiation will not be a an airy climb to the divine throne,

---

20 See Blondel, E., 1991; Del Caro, A, 1989.

but rather a descent into the world of witches and demons, an inversion of his previous straining toward the heights of knowledge. The wild world of witchcraft, presided over by the moon, seems like the perfect opposite of the sanctimonious and predictable academy which has driven Faust to despair.

Faust describes the properties of the moon in sharp contrast to the dry, unmoving, and un-natural aspects of the academy. He prays to the moon for death or release into a free and wild state: "O full moonlight, would that this were / Your last sight of my torment here!... chained to / print and script... / Could I but walk in the mountains, high / In your beloved light, could I / Hover at mountain caves with ghosts, / Weave in the meadows of your mists, / Slough off the dross of knowing and in / Your dew bathe myself well again!" (ll.386-96). This speech is reminiscent of the longing of the werewolf.[21] Faust's longing for the primitive and savage natural world is not the longing of a Romantic poet for a demure and orderly sort of nature. Faust longs with a great passion to retreat into the world of the moon in order to be free of the "dross of knowing" which he feels "chains" and imprisons his true nature. The sub-luminal nighttime world lit only by the strange moon – the province of "ghosts" and "mists" is the perfect contrast to Faust's orderly study which seems now like a trap. Faust goes on to describe his study as a "dungeon" and a "cursed hole-in-the-wall / Where even the lovely daylight shines /Muddily through the painted panes" (ll.400-401).

The final line of this speech to the moon "in / Your dew bathe myself well again" (l.396) describes a baptism in the moonlight. Faust wishes to dedicate himself to a new sort of path – down and out of the ivory towers away from the sun, into an opposite and inverse world of bestial and infernal darkness – a moonlit night. The moon might also be thought to celestially correspond to Mephistopheles. While the other Archangels rule over the planetary and celestial realms, the moon as representative of the illusions of the mind might also be representative of the mind's phantasms. Faust's pleas to the moon certainly foreshadow his demonic descent, and his evocation of Mephistopheles seems to be initiated by this speech. This lycanthropic sort of desire is also revealing of Faust's nature and the drives which set him apart. The Faust character has been taken as a voice of the spirit of Goethe's Germany and its dilemmas. Faust's longing for a return to nature could be thought to imitate either the Romantic's praise and desire for nature, or the Modernist's love for the uncomplicated pastoral countryside. However, Faust's desire is neither of these.

In his essay *Man Into Wolf* Robert Eisler describes the evolutionary distance between those men who experienced the world's Ice Age and those, in the tropical belt, who presumably did not. He paints this difference as a transformative one, from people who generally survived off their intellect and the bounty of the land, to hunters struggling for survival, killing for food and fighting for mates. He insists that the instincts necessary for such survival bred components into man designed to experience blood-lust as well as the ability to endure pain. He argues that this process is what originated the myth of the werewolf – the transformation of peaceful man into a hunter and killer, more like a wolf, and likens this archetype to a rougher more savage

---

21 See, Eisler, R. *Man Into Wolf; An Anthropological Interpretation of Sadism, Masochism and Lycanthropy*, 1948.

kind of man girt with weaponry and wearing animal skins.

He also insists that these instincts are responsible for the phenomena of Sadism and Masochism, which desires to exercise those parts of man designed to do harm or to endure pain. These instincts confined and suppressed by "civilized" society are destined to erupt, Eisler argues, in some violent fashion – so that extant society is actually endangered by these wolf-men unless this nature finds an alternate outlet. The culture and nature of the German people could be thought to be lycanthropic in Eisler's definition of the term, and if Faust is representative of the dilemma of his people, then his own confinement by Christianity and rationalism could be a goad for the eruption of his wolf-like and antagonistic nature.

This reading of Faust's desire is supported further by his Sadistic and Masochistic tendencies. He seems to wish to experience intensity of any kind – pleasurable, painful, or otherwise, much as Eisler describes. When Mephisto asks Faust about his desires he says he would gladly "take the wildering whirl, / enjoyment's keenest pain, /Enamored hate, exhilarant disdain. / My bosom, of its thirst for knowledge sated, / Shall not, henceforth, from any pang be wrested / And all of life for all mankind created, /Shall be within mine inmost being tested / The highest, lowest forms my soul shall borrow, / Shall heap upon itself their bliss and sorrow, / And thus, my own sole self to all their selves expanded, / I too, at last, shall with them all be stranded."

He wishes not for pleasure, but for the extremes of human experience whatever they may be. This fits perfectly with Eisler's view that the components of man which respond to such stimuli are sated through their exercise, and that there is a sort of curve of experience (only a portion of it pleasurable) which man desires to explore fully. In order to discover the range and capability of his nature, Faust must venture outside of the realms defined for him by his academic society and the Christian faith of his upbringing. What he longs for is indeed a return to his German roots, and to a wild and desirable Nature – but not the idyllic and controlled "nature" of the Romantics and Modernists – instead Faust descends further and more deeply into a vastly more primitive, violent, and powerful heritage.

Goethe, in making Faust a wild and destructive sort of character, restless and motile, nearly seems to prophesy not only the Lycanthropy described by Eisler more than a century later, but the phenomenon of pagan revival and Teutonic ferocity seen shortly after the first World War and described by C.G. Jung. In an essay on the revival of the German worship of Wotan, the ancient god, and the subsequent mass obsession and possession of the German people by his ecstatic power, Jung states: "What is more than curious – indeed, piquant to a degree – is that an ancient God of storm and frenzy, the long quiescent Wotan, should awake, like an extinct volcano, to new activity, in a civilized country that had long been supposed to have outgrown the Middle Ages." Goethe also revives the Faust character of eras past in a Germany "long thought to have outgrown the Middle Ages", but after a different model than the scapegoat of Christian morality tales. Instead, Faust embodies the esoteric heroes of ages past and seems imbued with the wild and warlike spirit of a darker pre-Christian German folk. The Christian mythos could never truly subsume the hunter-like masculinity of earlier Northern traditions. The Abrahamic tradition would have originated with "tropical" and not "lycanthropic" man, and Faust, like Germany, finds himself chafing at the bonds of Christian society on his destructive and sexual nature.

This parallel seems an accurate characterization of the spirit in which *Faust*, Eisler's essay, and Jung's *Wotan* were intended. For example, Goethe's Mephisto (and to a degree the Faust character throughout the centuries) matches perfectly Jung's description of Wotan himself: "Wotan is a restless wanderer who creates unrest and stirs up strife, now here, now there, and works Magic. He was soon changed by Christianity into the devil" (Jung, 1936). This is nearly like the transformation of Faust, the Magus, into an evil sorcerer, and his companion spirit who "stirs up strife" or is "made to prick and be a mover", as a Devil. Mephistopheles is even recognized as Wotan by a witch in *Faust*, who questions the whereabouts of his two ravens, surprised by his transformation of aesthetic in a new era. Wotan probably had as much similarity, mythologically speaking, to the Greek Dionysus, or even Christ himself than a demonic figure (Jung, 1936), though Wotan is more complex than either of these deities, or any demon, and includes within his archetypal complex hundreds of bi-names and numerous hypostases, some of which are openly baleful, and others of which appear entirely benign. Unlike Dionysus and Christ, Wotan is always depicted as either slayer or self-slayer, never as the victim or sacrifice of another. Mephisto, throughout the play, goads Faust to embrace his own Dionysian and Wotanic impulses, as will be illustrated, and it is in his moments of Wotanic-Dionysian, inspired destructiveness that Faust seems to make his greatest strides toward his own nature and desire. Considering the Wotanic cult's aristocratic rise to prominence in the Viking Age, it is plausible that his depiction as hanged inverted from the World-Tree in his self-sacrifice to himself was consciously, simultaneously compared and contrasted with the Christ image, making a diabolical manifestation of Wotan like Mephistopheles within a Christianized cosmology mythologically plausible.

The first hints of Faust's primeval nature are invoked in his speech to the moon. It seems to be with the expression of his longing for a lycanthropian baptism in its "dew" that his restlessness first attracts his demonic counterpart, and his transformation is begun. It is in this speech that he first admits not only his restlessness, discontent, and depression with his current state, but his vision for a preferable one. Faust finds the means for such a lycanthropian baptism soon enough. Looking about at his study, the world of his thought, knowledge, and reason, Faust sees a dead man's tomb. He makes his study into a coffin – "the dust shrouds and the worms eat at it"(l.404), and "Round you in reek and moulder are / Beast's skeletons and the bones of the dead" (ll.418-19). This seems like an allusion to Shakespeare's similar speech for Hamlet, in which death or dreaming sleep are contemplated as the only potential alternatives to the hollowness of a meaningless life. After his long speech deriding books, knowledge, and study, in the vein of self-referential rhetoric, Faust turns to a manual of a different sort. Disgusted with "knowledge" based on rhetoric and argumentation rather than experiment and experience, Faust decides to try his hand at last at a book of "necromantic" spells. It is with this action that his discourse in a new sphere – not an academic but a truly natural one – a discourse of spirits, begins.

This is Faust's first experiment in manipulating both the mind and the natural world through his words. At first he tries the "sign of the Macrocosm" attempting to apprehend everything at once, and for a moment feels like "a god" (l.439). But this experience is not human or interactive enough, and he declares it only "theater" (l.454). He longs for the whole of nature as for a mother or a woman, but he cannot reach it through the "Sign of the Macrocosm" saying, "Where can I grasp you, never-ending nature? / Breasts where? You founts of all life / that earth and heaven hang with love / and where the parched soul craves to be, / You flow, you give to drink, but not to me" (ll.455-459). This experience with "God" or the "macrocosm" in fact only makes him feel more disconnected. It is very clear here that going "up" to the more general and the higher will not work for Faust. The "Sign of the Macrocosm" might be a reference to the Hexagram, which Paracelsus describes as two interlocking triangles.[22] But Faust's result from the use of this sign is alienating to him, and he only becomes frustrated. The perfection of "Never ending nature" perhaps reflected in the dual-trinities of the Hexagram, are unfathomable to Faust.

Goethe would have been familiar with Paracelsus' Macrocosmic sign, and purposely set this up as a contrast to the pentagram which Faust uses to summon Mephisto. The demonic nature is more akin to that of Faust, and the pentagram is the sign more akin to the nature of man. The renowned occultist Eliphas Levi describes the use of the pentagram for Conjuration, an idea which Paracelsus describes as black magic. Paracelsus notes that the pentagram, being in the shape of man (head, arms, legs) can, like man, be "inverted", while the hexagram, perfectly proportioned, cannot. But Faust is on a downward path where everything must be inverted. The evocation of the perfect macrocosm avails him nothing. Goethe seems aware of the importance of directionality of the pentagram. Levi notes that the pentagram with the point of "spirit" upright admits benevolent spirits, while the averse pentagram admits malevolent spirits. Old Magicians might pay attention to the directionality of the pentagram protecting their doorway. Goethe seems to make reference to this when later, Faust's "mistakenly drawn" pentagram allows Mephisto to enter his home, but not to leave. Further, Levi identifies the pentagram with the directional manifestation of will as it is transformed into action. For Faust to break his stagnancy he requires a signifier of direction rather than wholesomeness, and that direction is down.

Faust is progressively moved toward the selection of the correct, demonic, operation as he experiments with the Grimoire. This is not a random fumbling, however, but a necessary progression. He tries again by summoning the spirit of Earth, here signifying the microcosm, the material world, the space in which Faust wishes to operate. At first, summoning the Earth spirit, Faust feels himself to be like a god in relation to it. At first the interaction with the Earth spirit seems as fruitless as the conjuration of the Macrocosm, as Faust is rebuked. However, the interaction with the Earth spirit might be a precursor to Faust's first meeting of Mephistopheles. Jung describes, from his dream work, a Dwarf as the guardian of the unconscious and a sort of keeper of the doorway to the power of the collective unconscious. The dwarf is his helper in destroying the hero archetype and opening the lower worlds like the land of the dead, the caverns of the earth, or other downward going realms. The Earth Spirit might act in this way for Faust, opening the way for him to encounter the demon Mephisto.

---

22 Paracelsus, *Of the Supreme Mysteries of Nature.*

Before the summoning, Faust believes that these Magical experiments will give him the relationship with nature which he has craved, and yet, when the spirit appears he greets it with shrinking anxiety: Turning away from the spirit of the earth he states "You fill my eyes with fear" (l.483). As Faust turns away from the spirit of nature in fear the spirit taunts him "I have appeared. And now what piteous / terror Übermensch![23] ... Where is the heart that made a world and held / and harbored it within and swelled / On shocks of joy to be with us, the spirits, equal?" (ll.490-3). Faust's initial passion upon attempting the spell is enough to compel the spirit of the elements to appear and engage him. The compulsion, almost like a neurosis in Faust which inspired the conjuration, is too much for his rational mind to bear. In the moment of his conjuring, Faust leaves off his rumination and gives himself over to experience, but when the spirit appears he is afraid. Although a moment ago his heart held and shaped a world in godlike fashion, he is unable to maintain this action of joy, the "shocks" of which move him to compel the spirit of nature. His impulse carried him more quickly than his mind was ready to follow. Here the joy itself (the same word Faust uses to describe his only goal and desire) is what gives him godlike power. This is the experience of joy (of active command or creation) which he craved but he cannot maintain it, perhaps through a lack of understanding of his own nature. It is clear that a real transformation, test and initiation will be required of Faust before he can command the Earth in the fashion he desires. But this is an inverted sort of journey. Faust will not be climbing toward the Throne of God. Rather, he goes downward, embracing his most animalistic desires. They key to the formula of *Faust* is how this most animalistic (or "bestial", as Mephisto said the Prologue in Heaven) element of Man can be the key to his divine power.

The answer to Faust's dilemma is near at hand. These early experiments with ritual Magic are driving Faust toward the lycanthropian baptism and necessary descentfore-shadowed in his speech to the moon. When Faust asserts his likeness to the spirit of the elements, the spirit denies this saying "You are like the spirit you can comprehend / Not me" (ll.512-3). This can be taken in many ways. Either there is a specific spirit to which the Earth Spirit is referring (most likely Mephisto whom has already been shown to be sympathetic with Faust's nature), or the Earth Spirit is advising that Faust is like unto whatever spirit he is able to comprehend – to become sympathetic with or obtain command over. This may be a challenge to Faust. What spirit, in the end, will he be able to capture and comprehend within himself? That of God? That of the Devil? For the present, Faust is left confounded by the response – it will be his task to discover the

---

23 There is some evidence that Goethe helped to inspire Nietzsche, and the character of Faust is, perhaps an early example of the archetype Nietzsche refers to in describing the Übermensch. Some authors, like Bertram & Norton, draw a direct link between Nietzsche's concept of the Übermensch and Goethe's *Faust* (See: *Nietzsche: Attempt at a Mythology*. Bertram, E. Norton, R. Ed., 2009). In *Thus Spake Zarathustra*, Nietzsche states: "All beings so far have created something beyond themselves; and do you want to be the ebb of this great flood and even go back to the beasts rather than overcome man? What is the ape to man? A laughingstock or a painful embarrassment. And man shall be just that for the overman: a laughingstock or a painful embarrassment. You have made your way from worm to man, and much in you is still worm. Once you were apes, and even now, too, man is more ape than any ape." The idea of becoming more than oneself, transcending the system, is a major theme in *Faust*, and it seems plausible that this character is the prototype for the Übermensch, and the first use of the term. Nietzsche himself wrote on this very subject to Rhodes: "There was, after Luther and Goethe, a third step still to take," he writes to Rhodes about the language of Zarathustra.

spirit he can comprehend – his own spirit. Faust responds to the spirit distressed: "Who then? / After God's likeness and yet / Not even you?"

Wagner enters immediately as if in answer to the question. Wagner, like Faust, is a scholar, but is perfectly content in his academic role. Wagner seems to be an embodiment of everything Faust detests. He embraces scholarship, the pursuit of "knowledge for its own sake" and the mundane life of the academic with simplistic good cheer. Wagner is Faust's manservant and student within the university system, and like the Student character shortly introduced is meant to mirror one aspect of Faust. In this case, Wagner represents the role of the completely emasculated academic which Faust wishes to avoid becoming. Faust's spite for Wagner is evident from the beginning, and their arguments and discourse represent Faust's argument with rationalism as a whole.

Wagner, the famulus[24], is described by Faust as a "creeper in the dust", a potential reference to the serpent having been cast out of Eden. Or perhaps he is likening Wagner to the worms which would be appropriate denizens of the graveyard which the academic world has become to him. Faust may see Wagner as a liar or hypocrite in his role as a wholly content academic who endorses the intellectualism which Faust rails against. Wagner's entrance is timely in response to Faust's question about the spirit which is like him. Indeed Faust has felt himself to be like Wagner, but this is not the whole answer to the question. Rather, this is Faust's final breaking away from his previous life and definition. As he argues with and denounces Wagner, he makes a final break from attempting to find himself through science and experiments of thought.

The interaction with Wagner is a foreshadowing of the true answer to the Earth Spirit's riddle of the "spirit [Faust] can comprehend" – it is of course, Mephistopheles. Faust's arguments with Wagner seem to represent his struggle against the kind of intellectual "games of words" which have led him to knowledge of "naught", and his turning toward the possibility of a different kind of knowing which he will seek through Mephisto. His need is for joy and refreshment, but he denies that Wagner's scholarship can offer anything of the kind. "Is parchment then the holy well," he scolds Wagner, "that drinking from you never thirst again? / It's not refreshment you have won / Unless it springs from your own soul" (ll.566-9). Once again Goethe strikes at not only academic rationalism, but also the Church. This line refers to the parable of the Woman at the Well where "parchment" substituting for the well itself may symbolize the Bible being substituted for a genuine experience of inspiration. Neither scholarship nor the religion of the Book will be enough to save Faust.

Instead he claims that the refreshment he seeks must come from himself – most importantly through the finding of the soul, perhaps equated with his nature. In the same breath as denying "parchment" he denounces that this may be accomplished through though the working of the mind which leads only recursively back into his own psyche "What you call a mind of the times / at bottom that mind is yours and it reveals / only its reflection... and verily that is a dismal sight / ... A lumber room, a rubbish bin" (ll.577-581). The exercises of the mind, Faust claims, can only reveal the mind itself and not the truths of the natural world which he truly desires.

---

24 A famulus is a close attendant, but this term particularly denotes a servant or someone who is servile. Wagner is Faust's student, but the choice of this term, which mirrors the German, seems to denote that he is also Faust's inferior.

Faust's love of nature is not the love of the Romantics for what they perceived as nature. The ordered, benign nature of the Neo-Hermeticists did not fit with Goethe's seeming fascination with a more tangible science. Goethe recognizes man's bestial nature but instead of separating what makes man distinct and human he recognizes that it arises out of his animal heritage. The nature which Faust craves is the bestial impulse which will unleash his elite nature as a hunter or destroyer.

This is the key to his divine light, and not the more civilized science of the university – the natural science of the Enlightenment.

In pronouncing a final distinction between himself and Wagner, Faust outlines a new course for himself. When Wagner asks how a man absorbed in study and isolated from the world should "guide it through oratory" (l.532) Faust gives a fine answer: "What you don't feel you'll never get by chasing / Unless it presses from the soul / and with a primal deed of zestful pleasing… heart to heart you'll never move / unless your starting place is there" (ll.534-43). He recognizes that the only meaningful word is born out of the soul and the nature – through action and desire, and suggests that the motion of this word originates in the heart[25] – like love, or the sating of desire, or perhaps like blood which also originates in the heart. In this line, he also seems to endorse nature and inherent temperament over acquired knowledge. The blood is also a symbol of heritage or the inherent nature of a person. Faust seems to be telling Wagner that one either has the inherent ability to achieve mastery through desire or one does not, or similarly that one's existential possibilities are limited and defined by one's nature. Faust presumably is capable of this sort of attainment, while Wagner would chase after knowledge without any hope for consummation. "A primal deed of zestful pleasing" is a strikingly sexual phrase – the combination of desire and action is where Faust must look for his "soul". Faust is struggling to find a new formula, a new way to exist, but the question in this scene is how the Word may be part of the equation. Faust has dismissed "thought", reason, and knowledge as somewhat irredeemable though necessary to his nature. He recognizes the consciousness as recursive and unable to rise above itself or move outside of itself. He needs a new element in order to break through this Gordian knot.[26] This element is introduced only through Faust's ultimate decision that he must find a way out. Seeing none in his present state, he eventually returns to his contemplation of sleep/death as the only way out of his hollow existence. This contemplation leads not to an end, but to the decisive action which is the necessary impetus for his conversion.

As Wagner departs, leaving Faust entirely convinced that the world of intellectualism leaves nothing for him, Faust is left again to mull over his frustrations of the evening. He creates his own answer to the spirits riddle of whom he is like. He longs to be able to be a shaper of the "splendors" his spirit conceives" (l.635) "I am not like the gods… I am like the worm that works the dust / and living in dust, and by dust fed / Is crushed and buried by the walker's head" (ll.652-56). This is reminiscent of Faust's comparison of Wagner to the serpent – He now claims he himself is like the adversary

---

25 See *Liber Al vel Legis*, Ch. 1, v. 6: Hadit, the mover, is addressed as both heart & tongue. A close relationship between the heart, the word, and the ability to go is implied by Goethe.

26 In *The Book of Lies, L. 333*, Crowley discusses the Fool's Knot in relation to the formula of IAO. IAO is also an important formula for Faust, for by this method he liberates himself from the self-perpetuating pursuit of Nothing, the "Naught-y knot".

– or like one being crushed by him. In one reading, Faust is comparing himself to the serpent, in *Genesis* (3:15), doomed to be crushed beneath the heel of the son of woman. Or he may be alluding to the *Book of Job* (1:7) in which Satan himself is described as the "walker" who goes to and fro on the earth. He simultaneously likens himself to the devil and to one trodden upon by him – it may be for Faust to comprehend which will ultimately be the case – and he vows to escape from the "high walls" closing in.

Nature is described like a cold woman who "will not permit the removing of her veil". He chooses a journey down and out, into the underworld, and contemplates suicide and death by poison. What Faust longs for is refreshment and action, and he consummates this wish by reaching for the draught of death. Here there is a strange sleight of hand: Faust first reaches for a vial of poison praising it as the "vessel like none other" (l.690) which will take him to a new realm where he can indeed be like the gods. His praise of the poison exposes the role which poison will play in this story.

Faust speaks of it as a thing of liberation as well as destruction – and his path to godhood. This could be dismissed as the longings of the suicidal tendency, but the poison actually does place him along his path to both destruction and ascension. Faust salutes Easter morning – not only a day of resurrection, but the morning after his first descent into the lycanthropic realms of the full moon[27] with a drink (potentially a drink of death). "This drink, this last, my making, my own choosing" (l.733) he says – a line which strongly states the intent of suicide, and Faust indeed raises the vessel to his lips. This is Faust's declared willful act, and it is a destructive one. Poison will be a vehicle of the destructive and invigorating impulse throughout the play. Faust's consumption of the drink is the first action that sets him in motion, causing him to leave the confines of his study which has worn out its usefulness. The poison/alcohol puts him in motion for the first time, foreshadowing the further poison with which Mephisto will awaken his desire. The suicidal impulse then, the Thanatos, seems related to Faust's lycanthropic/hunter impulse which is the essence of his ability to move and to be a mover.

This draught of poison is as vitalizing as it is destructive, in a complex fashion. This poison draught which Faust has kept in his study might be a remnant of the very same "toxic medicine" which he later remembers to Wagner. Faust recalls that his father, a famous doctor, created a medicine to cure the plague and took it to infected households – but the medicine was not curative, it was a poison which killed everyone it was administered to. This is ironic – Faust laments that the inheritance of his father, supposedly the scientific and alchemical arts designed to promote healing and even im-mortality, was in the end an inheritance of poison. His own disgust with academia and his "sciences" in general is also an inheritance from his father. Interestingly, the poison, although not "curative", did liberate sufferers from the plague through death. This same poison may liberate Faust from his own plague of discontent and stagnation. Although the inheritance of his father was in itself impotent, Faust may make something new of his inheritance of "medicine" – turning the poison into the alchemical draught of im-mortality which his father's science failed to produce. This medicine may necessitate the exploration of the formula VITRIOL which in one meaning stands for "Visita Interiora

---

27 Since the first council of Nicaea, Easter Sunday has always been the morning after the full moon in April, indicating the beginning of a waning moon for the coming month.

Terrae Rectificando Invenies Occultum Lapidem".[28] This reading is supported by the other poisons/potions in this story, and also foreshadows Faust's downward descent. His descent into the lower realms, or the center of the earth, is not only according to his impulse, and the only option available to him, and it is also the necessary and correct path for fulfilling his desire for godhead.

It is ambiguous as to whether or not Faust actually downs the poison, and this may be a purposive literary device. He puts the vial down again after hearing the Easter choir, and there is no mention of toxic death. This feat parallels other initiatory myths, such as the Mystery surrounding death in the Akedah, the Binding of Isaac. In this story, Abraham binds Isaac on top of Mt. Moriah to sacrifice him at God's command. However, God seems to stop Abraham and a goat is sacrificed instead. This verbiage employed gives an insightful reader pause, for it seems like this mystical ironic ambiguity is deliberate. After the incident Isaac eludes further mention, but three years later he surprisingly returns, but from where? When he returns he has prophetic powers and is said to have been "received back from death."[29] His absence, like that of Moses, was an initiatory retreat, not onto the mountain top but into heaven or perhaps into the world of death. The earliest Qabalists poured through this and other biblical mysteries, providing numerous explanations for the paradox of a divine grammar-error, but one of vital importance. Was Isaac killed? It seems no, as a Ram (initiation animal) was offered by an angel in his stead as Abraham's falling knife was deftly stayed. Also, God forbade human sacrifice, so commanding such would invite disorder into his Law and Cult. However, Isaac did disappear and had visited the world of the dead. Isaac may have been symbolically linked to or actually have been the ram that Abraham slaughtered in his place.

Several allusions in *Faust* suggest that this is a deliberate point of reference. Although Faust seemingly switched the poison for another drink, whatever it was that he did drink had deathlike effects. The scenes following the quaffing of the potion capture the mystical death. The very significance of Easter morning places Faust in the position of other dead men, such as the story of the sacrifice of Isaac, a traditional reading offered on Easter Sunday. In both of these tales (Christ and Isaac) the one who was to die is simultaneously spared and sacrificed – transformed into one who is apart, like the dead, with strange powers. When Isaac returns from his ordeal he is said to walk "upside-down" like the dead, and to have the powers of a priest.[30] Yet, like Wotan, who hanged himself *inverted* from the world-tree after tearing out his own eye in order to behold the mysteries, Faust's death-experience is *self-inflicted*.

This upside-down-ness sets him apart from living, and Faust's inversion parallels this separation. Jesus, upon his return also seems to be in a state between life and death – he exhibits many extraordinary powers and performs more miracles in three days than in the rest of his life. He walks among the apostles, but is obviously somehow even more

---

28 "Visit the interior of the earth and there by rectification find the hidden stone". The "hidden stone" refers to the philosopher's stone, the secret medicine which grants immortality and the "perfection" or rectification of the self. This fits well with the theme of the rectification of Faust's discontent through the downward journey and averse initiation.
29 *Hebrews* 11:19
30 *Genesis:* 24

superhuman than before. Faust is also set apart from the villagers who are celebrating Easter Sunday as he goes out among them – he is almost like a dead man. As he first enters outside, the village women sing a song about wrapping and embalming Christ and it is not difficult to imagine that it is Faust who is "risen" either from death or into the world of the dead. Christ also, in half-living state – appeared to the women on Easter Sunday, and went about interacting with friends, followers, and others. Faust seems especially akin to a "risen" Christ as he is accosted by villagers who wish to praise and thank him as a teacher who helped to "cure" the plague.

As he travels in the town on this strange Easter morning, Faust is reminded of his "boyhood" in the village and wanders through the past places of his youth – reminiscing about his life almost as if he were dead to it. He does not, largely, interact with the villagers whom he obviously considers to be truly apart from himself. He calls them "soft humans: with sound among them" (1.764), emphasizing his almost ghostly nature in this scene. He only interacts with them to take a drink offered in thanks for his "knowledge" and for the legacy of his father's medicine. This offer of drink is not unlike an offering to the dead, and Faust, although he becomes drunk, only feels further alienated from the villagers and his previous life. He notes that they all are able to go outside of the city to bask in the sun escaping from their "closed cells" indoors, but he does not feel able to escape himself in this fashion. The first time Faust leaves his study-cell in the play is after drinking the poison.

His freedom comes through a kind of death, but Faust does not yet seem to comprehend the trajectory which his impulse has placed him upon. Rather than enjoying the abandon of the Easter Revelry, Faust reflects on how his father's legacy of alchemy and medicine seems hypocritical. Faust, like his father, was unable to save lives during the plague – he possessed no power over nature and failed to fulfill his father's bequest, even with all his knowledge of alchemy. He admits that the medicine he mixed at his father's instruction was actually poison that killed the patients so that he himself was like the plague.[31] Faust's inheritance is one of death – his estate, inherited from his father and built on the proceeds of this macabre "cure". Now the role of doctor and patient are reversed as Faust praises the drink offered to him by the countryman in alchemical terms as if this country alcohol is the true medicine – and it is a medicine for Faust who finds a portion of his goal in the drunkenness and celebration of the townspeople: He crosses the river, an action also necessary to a dead man,[32] and finds himself in a much rowdier place outside the city where far more primitive celebrations are taking place. The drink offered to him seems to have been his pass to a more Dionysian sort of festival, and it is here where Faust first comes into contact with a Spirit whose nature he can comprehend. Faust sees how wildly and drunkenly the townspeople are reveling.

---

31 An alternative interpretation might suggest that the destruction of the sick *was* curative – for the body of the people.

32 In Greek mythology, the dead cross the Styx. In ancient Egypt, the dead were ferried from the city of Hermopolis to the delta Necropolis. The predominant psychopomp throughout most of Egyptian myth was Anubis, the dog-headed son of Isis and Osiris, although some traditions imply him as the son of Set's successful, rather than attempted, rape of Isis. In Hellenistic Egypt, the Greek Typhon became associated with Set, diabolized in his role as slayer of Osiris. This is interesting in that Graeco-Egyptian goetic traditions implied jackals and dogs, particularly black dogs, as Typhonian creatures. Mephistopheles will shortly appear as a black dog himself.

Although Wagner is afraid, Faust claims that this is the real paradise of the people, and he wants to be a part of this vibrant Dionysian vivacity. Wagner claims "They rampage as if ridden by the Devil" (l.947), while Faust lauds the villagers' "unholy row", saying "The true heaven of the people is here and now" (ll.937-939). Faust has already identified himself with the unholy when he claimed to be like the Devil before his suicide attempt — now he identifies this state with true humanity and the wild union with nature which he has been craving.

It is here, as Faust turns into the night amid the drunken feast, that Mephistopheles first appears to him. As dusk falls, Faust longs for the company of the woodland spirits — and who should appear but a black dog, Mephisto in disguise. Faust finally understands his need to be united with his own nature, and having left the academy of knowledge behind and the idea of heaven, Faust is prepared for his infernal journey. Intoxicated by his putrefactive tincture, Faust crosses the river and is met by a traditional welcomer of the dead and the one who will promote his descent. Faust sees the black dog observing his revels and addresses it. To his delight, the dog follows him home — an emissary of the Dionysian wilderness — now an interloper into his coffin-like tower at the university. Upon returning to his study, Faust is inspired to look more into his spell book, longing to interact with the spirits once more — but this time he gets more than he expected. Before Faust actually summons Mephisto for the first time, however, he arrives at the required formula almost by accident.

Faust, still exhilarated by his drunken exploration, considers the relationship of thought, word, and deed. Reading from the German Bible he recites "In the beginning was the word" (from the *Book of John*), but finds this distasteful, and interprets "the word" as among the hollow products of intellectualism which he decries. He tries to move backward, asking "what precedes Word" and postulating "thought" and "power" as potential antecedents. These still do not satisfy, and, inspired by "the spirit", he decides that "In the beginning was The Deed" (l.1237). By this formula, Action precedes thought which precedes "the word". With this conclusion, Faust is determined to act, and is called once more to the book of spells. This particular evocation seems to unite thought, word, and deed, in a ritual. Considering previously analysis of Goethe's reception of the Faustian tradition, it is also interesting that Faust precedes his evocation of Mephistopheles not with recitations from the Christian Bible as was apparently standard for medieval ceremonial magicians, but with a deliberate, personal heresy of the same. The formula which Faust uses to entice Mephisto into being is an elemental one, a physical one — illustrating Mephisto's own alliance with Nature also indicated in his form of the Dog. His is not the "nature" of the Earth spirit, but is instead more akin to Faust's own. As Mephisto begins to appear Faust only becomes more decisive — not shrinking away as he did when summoning the Earth Spirit. This is indicative of the greater sympathy between Faust and Mephisto. Perhaps Faust is emboldened after his death-like excursion, or perhaps he intuitively understands that this is the spirit whose nature is like his own — the fulfillment of the averse pentagram. Faust himself is an averse pentagram, having entered the world of the dead he may be thought to be inverted.[33] This essential preparation being accomplished, he seamlessly evokes.

---

33 The Egyptian world of the Dead and sometimes the Greek was thought to be at the center of the earth,

In this conjuration Faust again places his deed before thought. Both will soon be sealed in the Word. Mephisto appears – a manifestation of thought following upon action – as a wandering scholar. In fact, the entirety of Faust's journey since he took the action of lifting the poison to his lips might be considered a single active phase which initiates his attraction and summoning of Mephisto. In *Liber ABA*, Aleister Crowley illustrates the essence of the Oath, saying that the ritual process should reverberate, like the unending ringing of a bell, into the world beyond the time and place of the ritual. For that moment the temple becomes all time and space, and the mechanism by which the ritual's consequences are carried forward. Faust's speech to the moon sealed with his consumption of the poison was the cry that resonated through the universe and initiated the momentum of the ritual. Faust went out among the villagers and thought through his identity and history as if an accountant preparing to be audited; otherwise, this is the part of the Oath where the Magician declares what has led them to that moment of the operation. The Oath extends intentions beyond expectations and likewise Faust out of the confines of his tower. As Faust's declarative momentum carries him through the evocation, Mephistopheles appears more easily than the other spirits, for his coming was the inevitable result of the momentum of all Faust's being.

Mephisto is once again a mirror of the mind of Faust as he appeared to be in the Prologue.[34] He first appears as a traveling scholar, an academic like Faust, but one with the ability to travel – to go – he is not confined as Faust has felt himself to be. He appears as the unfettered intellect, like Mercury, the traveler. Like the Mephistopheles of the original *Faustbuch*, Goethe's Mephisto is to be a companion to Faust, and he will imbue Faust with his mercurial power; the ability to move and steal away. This imagery enhances his imitation of Faust in his scholarly dress, and his nature which is so sympathetic to that of Faust evokes Crowley's lines in *Liber Tzaddi*, Verses 33-35:

> I reveal unto you a great mystery. Ye stand between the abyss of height and the abyss of depth. In either awaits you a Companion; and that Companion is Yourself. Ye can have no other Companion.

By summoning an infernal companion with whom he found a subtle yet essential sympathy, Faust has reconciled himself to the "abyss of depth". Mephisto will play both the villain and the Psychopomp for Faust during Part I of the play, leading him through this underworld. Mephisto's nature as a source of debate and insight into his origins may reveal a bit about his relationship to Faust. In the simplest reading, he is just a stand-in for Satan, but the name Mephistopheles does not appear in any religious or mythological text outside of the Faust legends. Its first known use appears in the original *Faustbuch*, and the intended etymology is unclear. In 1904, Julius Goebel attempted an etymology of the name, theorizing that "Mephistopheles" could be dissected etymologically

---

and to be upside down or inverted. Faust seems to have visited this and is now encountering a sympathetic Friend of the Dead emerging from his black dog.

34 Mephisto seems like a projection of Faust's own nature – like Faust's Shadow. The ambivalent role of the Devil as both the Prince of Darkness and the Light-Bearer is implied in Faust's relationship to Mephistopheles; if Mephistopheles is understood as Faust's Shadow, Faust becomes a Luciferian figure, pursuing self-deification through his antinomian deeds.

as either "Destroyer and liar" from the Hebrew "Mephiz"[35] and "tophel", or Goethe's idea of a hybrid name implying a "love of destruction" from "mephiz" and the Greek "philus". Mephisto is an enabler, both encouraging Faust's more destructive impulses and helping him execute his errands. A fully Greek origin for the name might be "non-light-lover" (me-phos-to-philes), which in its negativity focuses not on Mephisto's antagonistic, destructive aspects, but rather on his rejection from and separation from the divine light, as earlier discussed in this essay. Another etymology has been suggested which would make Mephistopheles a shortened version of the Graeco-Latin phrase "Me Fausto Filos" – the friend of Faust. This interpretation emphasizes Mephisto as the friend, sympathizer, and mirror of Faust's own nature. Before the demon can lead Faust away on his journey, the problem of recursive consciousness must at last be put to rest.

Although Faust has derided learning, knowledge, and the arts of the mind, his mind has a natural propensity that allows him to keep an edge on Mephisto, such as was revealed during their discussion as to whether Mephisto could leave Faust's home. It is by an accident in drawing the pentagram, some unconscious slip of the mind or hand, that the Devil is caught in Faust's house. It is Faust's impulsive action united with his thought which gives him the upper hand over the Devil. But, when Mephisto asks the spirits to sing Faust a song about all the mighty deeds he will perform, he falls asleep. The spirits weave him a dream of fantastical deeds and lull Faust to sleep, thereby also subduing his mental advantage over Mephisto. When Faust is acting out what he is driven to by his own restless nature he tends to have the upper hand, but when he allows himself to only imagine action, he loses that control. There is a distance created: rather than the unification of thought and deed (or deed preceding thought), thought is misspent representing false actions. Later, Mephisto explains that the spirits counsel Faust "to enjoy and to do" (l. 1630). Mephisto is like the restless thoughts which turned Faust to black magic and away from science. He always prods Faust toward action and away from rumination and stagnation. To make Mephisto the best tool for Faust's transformation a final element is required. They must dislodge themselves from the confines of self-referential (and inconsequential) thought and into the world of deed. The process of the Oath which began with Faust ingesting the poison and subsequent separation from the living world must now be sealed with the contract proper. Faust first began to transform himself with the drought of poison/liquor. Now he proceeds to transform Mephistopheles, who will in turn make possible the final transformation for Faust. At first, Faust scorned "wordy knowledge" in his distaste for intellectualism. But, just as thought is rectified through its restlessness and the summoning of Mephisto, the Word is now to be rectified through its application to the Oath.

Upon Mephistopheles' appearance, Faust makes his demands. Faust's desire is to be like God. He wants all the joy and sorrow of mankind, to experience everything, and

---

35 Modern non-Jewish Qabalists (such as Goethe and Crowley) have been more interested in the Gematria or numeric correspondences of such words than simply their Hebrew meaning. In this case Mephiz may enumerate to 137 which also corresponds to the Hebrew words for "the Belly" and "the Wheel". This is interesting as the Wheel of Fortune comes to mind with Mephistopheles as the inevitable fulfillment of Faust's nature. Faust sets Mephisto in motion, and Mephisto in turn sets him in motion, bringing to him power over the elements as well as the ability of free movement, both associated with the rotating Wheel. The Belly is also an important concept in the alchemy of the "secret medicine" which is such a central concept in *Faust*, and association of the Belly *with* the Wheel suggests the impulsion or compulsion of self-maintaining Desire.

claims that life is useless if he cannot "get the crown of the human race / After which all senses chase" (ll.1804-5), but Mephisto answers him that he cannot be truly like God and experience the joy and sorrow of others – only his own. "You are in the end... the thing you are" (l.1806). It is implied that Mephisto will indeed help Faust to discover "the thing he is", but Faust's formula will not be Christ-like in embracing humanity or society. Rather it will be a formula of alienation consonant with Faust's destructive and adversarial nature. The companion he has summoned is not a wholesome Jesus, but the Adversary himself – Faust's own antagonistic reflection. As Faust queries Mephisto about what the demon could possibly offer him, he remains frustrated and confounded. He does not know how to remove himself from the inconsequential world of his own mind. He knows that his desires are beyond his capacity but does not believe that they can ever be fulfilled – he is desperate. Faust is frustrated that although he has studied every science, "No force in [him] that's new can be divined" (l.1814). Mephistopheles suggests that supreme knowledge probably is beyond Faust, but assures him that he can help Faust find contentment within his own experience. Faust agrees to try giving up on all-encompassing knowledge and settle for his own experience, but despairs that not even Mephisto can show him anything new, which he does not already know, but it is here at last that he discovers the utility of "the word". Just before Mephisto makes the pact with Faust there is a strange interlude with a "Student" during which the special significance of the Word to Mephisto is discussed. In the middle of his discourse with Mephisto about contentment and what he can and cannot have, Faust is interrupted by a knock on his study door – a new student seeking Faust's advice. Mephisto, dressed as Faust, takes the call and debates with the student, giving him a dose of the same philosophy he uses to drive Faust – a foretaste of what Mephisto has to offer. Mephisto proclaims his philosophy on "the word" in order to confound the student. "There must be some meaning in the word" (l.1903) asserts the student. The devil replies, "No doubt. But don't torment yourself too hard / For where a meaning's wanting there precisely / Up pops, on cue, a word /...With words a system can be elevated / Words are eminently believable, Not one jot of a word can be abated" (ll.1994-2000). Then, "playing the devil in earnest" (l.2010), Mephisto counsels the student away from all his studies and insists that he should have sex with as many women as possible in order to understand the "Sovereign Medicine". Although this speech is meant to undermine the student, Mephisto speaks the truth: "Where meaning's wanting there precisely / Up pops... a word". Faust himself has been "wanting meaning". In order to resolve this want, he offers up his word, his oath on Mephistopheles' pact. Mephistopheles also points out "with words a system can be elevated" but it is unclear at first how this is the case. Kurt Godel famously proved that the mathematical system, like any such formal system cannot contain itself, nor alter itself to the point of a new level of analysis (Godel, 1931; Lipscomb, 2010). When walking with Wagner, he insists that what knowledge he could use, he does not possess, and that all the knowledge he has is useless to him. In other words the system – the consciousness – which contains knowledge, and the desire for knowledge, cannot elevate itself to a level which could untangle its own recursive nature. Faust can begin to break out of this system – through a word. After Mephisto exposes the nature of the word to the Student, an agreement is set that if Mephisto can bring Faust real satisfaction, so that Faust himself can rest (and is no longer restless), then Faust agrees to be his slave. It is interesting to note that the word which begins Faust on the path of his rectification could be thought to be a lie. Although in the end the devil wins the wager by giving Faust a taste of contentment, he does not receive Faust's servitude in return. Whether intentionally a lie or no, it is this very word and pact which makes Faust's redemption possible and removes him from Mephisto's clutches. The Word allows Faust to transcend the system of his own consciousness in this scene, but the Word also sets into motion events that allow Faust to transcend the system of the Pact at the end of the play. Faust's Word, put into action is both the catalyst of Mephisto's efficacy and his undoing. This is proof that the word is transcendent – it elevates the very system which necessitated it. In order to receive "pleasure" or contentment from consciousness it is necessary for Faust to transcend it, and so the means of his liberation from the contract is written into it from the beginning.

As at their first interaction, the Word gives Faust command over Mephisto – when first summoned he asks the demon for his name. Mephisto responds that he is "A part of the power who / Wills evil always but always works the good... the spirit of saying no... Destruction, if brief / evil – is the element [he is] at home in" (ll.1335-1344). Mephisto himself is the "spirit of saying no", a liar like Faust's own word. He matches Faust's own destructive impulses and is undone in the end by Faust's lie (he is now made unnecessary when Faust fulfills his own formula). Faust, in his study, feels confined in his current life, and cut off from his creative nature, but with his thought and word he summons a spirit of destruction. Mephisto described how he would like to destroy all creation, but instead starts only with a single man – the "gateway" to all the rest. This is immediately followed with a discussion of how Mephisto cannot exit the house except by the way he came in – a way now blocked by a mistake in Faust's pentagram. By an unconscious slip Faust has trapped the Devil inside, and he can only leave with Faust's permission. Similarly Mephisto is bound to Faust, who is as much the Demon's "gateway" to his true desire as he is the gateway to Faust's.

Mephistopheles' insistence upon a written agreement signed in blood is also of interest. Faust is surprised and annoyed that his "word" is not acceptable and that Mephisto wants a physical document. He asks if the talisman must be made of gold or some precious material – but Mephisto replies that "Any scrap of paper will do" – whatever is on hand. This may seem to be a trivial exchange, but this is also pointed out as a necessary component of Mephisto's operation. In order for the pact to be put into action, the word must be materialized – etched in matter. The assurance that whatever is at hand will do for a contract/talisman suggests that this enaction or materialization of the word should be executed in whatever present circumstances, context, or environment exist. Faust is to put down his word immediately and with the materials on hand, as he will soon do in the world.

Mephisto further requires that this pact be sealed with a drop of blood which he calls "a quite particular juice" (l.1740). The blood might be thought of as itself a part of Faust's nature, or even as a representation of that active and creative word *Logos*, which Faust referenced when denying the validity of *The Gospel of John*. *The Gospel of John* identifies the *Logos*, through which all things are made, as divine and further identifies Jesus as the incarnation of the *Logos*. Interestingly, it is Faust who is set up as the word made flesh in this story. Faust's initial pact with Mephistopheles leads him to seek fulfillment in "sensuality" and action in the world. The catalyst for his creativity (or destructiveness) is his word, sealed in blood. Faust vows that "in the deep of sensuality / I'll quench my passion's heat" (ll.1750-1). This act of creating the Word and giving it "flesh" through blood – setting Mephisto into motion, is a godlike act on Faust's part. Like God with Christ, Faust imbues Mephisto with a genetic link to himself (perhaps a better Latin etymology for Mephistopheles would be "[Me] Fausto Filius", the Son of Faust"). From this point onward, Mephisto acts not as a tempter of Faust, in general, but to carry out Faust's wishes and desires. He has become an infernal Christ to Faust's destructive God. This analogy is borne out nicely in the first scene of their journey together in which Mephisto makes false wine out of water for the cynical students.

Before beginning his journey, Faust had to discover a single function of his mind – to engender the restlessness which brings him to Mephisto.[36] It is this mind which gives him his initial dominion over the demon. Now he has also discovered the utility of his Word – to be able to make the devil's pact. The Word allows him to overcome his ruminations and doubts, and set out on his journey into the world of action and deed. Faust's word gives direction and structure to his restlessness much as he himself gives focus to Mephisto's efforts. Mephisto's power comes from his ability to provoke (and perturb) thought whereas Faust's power here comes from his word. It is upon Faust offering his oath that the action of the play is set into motion – the journey outside the study begins. The word therefore sets the thought into action, and the interaction between thought and word catalyzes motion through the final component of Faust's transformative formula.

The Word Made Flesh

The Pact with the Devil being made firm upon the completion of the oath, Faust's wish for a moonlit outing is granted by his new best friend, the demon Mephistopheles. Mephisto takes him down and out of the college tower into several settings which very much resemble the ghostly cave Faust longed for. His infernal descent and initiation truly begins. The first destination is a tavern which is literally underground – a first stop on the downward journey. This tavern is the very real Auerbach's Keller, a more than 500-year old "cellar" tavern where Goethe himself passed many hours in Leipzig where he wrote *Faust*, Part I. The legend of the Tavern – which Goethe may have heard on his own visits – is that the original Doctor Faustus visited the tavern in 1525. This location was not only an inspiration for Goethe's tale, but is the first underground destination on Faust's downward journey to the center of the Earth.

Here Mephisto shows Faust an example of the results of the academy – three stu-

---

36 It is extremely unlikely that Goethe, or any other proponents of the Faust myth, could have known this, but the literal translation of the name of the first diabolical figure attested in history, a being of complete darkness and shadow who "does not love the light," is *Angra mainyu*, meaning in Avestan, the language of the Zarathushtrian Gathas, "the angstful mind." Like Mephistopheles, Angra Mainyu willed only evil, but he set in motion through his assault on the Light, the creation of the world and humankind. Angra Mainyu evolves in later Zoroastrianism into Ahriman, ultimately rendered as an archontic being by Manichaeans, and a materialistic devil by the founder of Anthroposophy, Rudolf Steiner, who was a great enthusiast of the work of Goethe and frequently sought to discern esoteric and occult meaning therein.

dents in different years speaking of the nature of love over their drinks. The Freshman pines for love while the others exhort him upon its dangers and pitfalls. Their conversation is crude, and each more advanced student is increasingly jaded. Mephisto interrupts and offers them a "miracle of nature" if they will only "believe it." He then creates false wine out of their imaginations and desires, but when he departs leaves them empty-handed. "It seemed to me I was drinking wine", declares the freshman, referring to the ecstasy of drink, "And the bunches of grapes, how about those?", asks the sophmoric brander who has understood as far as thought allowed. The upperclassman, Altmayer, declares "There are no miracles nowadays!", showing the cynicism of learning as a removal from the initial experience (ll.2333-6). Mephisto plays with the students as a lesson for Faust. The students are all content to sit in the pub and only talk about love.

Unlike the wine which Jesus created in the parable of the wedding at Canaan, Mephistopheles' wine is not for the disillusioned students, but instead, he has a potion only for Faust. This potion is not for the society of the pub, but will bring about an alienation in Faust between himself and other men which is necessary for the satiation of his own desire. The drunken students, representing in a sense the Germanic Modernists and Romantics talking about love and nature and never indulging in it, are incapable of consuming the draught Mephisto intends for Faust. Mephisto always intends for Faust to act on and quench his pleasure in sensuality as he intended in his oath. The false wine is for the students who sit idle in the bowels of the academy singing songs of that with which they have no experience. For Faust, who gave his word, Mephisto finds a stronger drink. As Faust set Mephisto in motion with the elixir of his own blood on the contract, Mephisto brings Faust deeper into the earth to find a potion analogous and opposite to Faust's toxic medicine.

Instead of imaginary wine, Mephisto promises Faust a witch's brew which he claims will make Faust immortal. This has been interpreted as a lie or joke on Mephisto's part by some literary analysts (Gillies, 1957), however it is this potion which leads Faust to attain his desires, and promises to truly be the key to his immortality. This potion is the necessary component which eventually leads to both Faust's seeming destruction and eventual redemption. In this regard, it could be paralleled to the fruit of the Tree of Knowledge, which the serpent claims will lead to life.

To obtain the witch's potion, the two need to descend to a new and lower level under the earth to a witch's hut. From the earthiest possible environment (a cave in the ground where beasts tend the witch's cauldron) Mephisto obtains the draught which will cure Faust of his ineffectuality and indirection. The witch herself is taught by Mephisto to create this potion. It seems like no coincidence that the devil of the human mind has invented a potion which induces desire. The troubled consciousness of Faust is what led to his original desires to unite with nature. As much as Mephisto prodded Faust to action, the devil is also the one who taught the witch to create this potion since he cannot make it himself. There is something about her odd and feminine art which is necessary for its creation. The witch is a very primal creature; living in a hole in the ground, surrounded by animals. This is a representation of the dangerous and untamed nature which Faust longed for in his lycanthropic speech to the moon. When Faust complains about the witch's strange and superstitious methods Mephisto insists that all of this is necessary. It may be necessary to penetrate the weird and wild essence of the crude earth in order to discover the pure divine feminine to which Faust will be led by this potion. This also evokes the formula V.I.T.R.I.O.L. like the poison in Faust's study. Faust has gone further toward the center of the earth and is closer to the Philosopher's Stone.

The witch and her potion may represent a distillation of nature – her science is not of Faust's academy, but is a raw, emotional, and unstructured thing which Faust calls "nonsense". It is Faust's first genuine encounter with natural desire and the powers within it. The witch dishes out this potion of nature from which she insists a man may die if he is "not prepared." The potion is a poison. It is very reminiscent of the potion which Faust nearly drank when contemplating suicide which started this entire drama. This time Faust is immune against the poisonous effects as the potion aids him on his initiatory descent. This poison is poignantly invigorating. The two draughts are analogous, but this one is a potent toxin with greater vivifying affects. It is a stronger arousing aphrodisiac than the Dionysian liquor which Faust consumed on Easter. Mephisto asserts that a friend of the devil will only benefit from the drink and not be harmed. If Mephisto is a spirit who insists upon action before reason, then he implies that the one who can act on them will benefit from his natural desires whereas the one who cannot may die from them.[37] The "poison" strips Faust of the last of his pretenses and ineffectuality causing a self-destruction of one kind, and an unveiling of a more instinctive self. The "suicidal" element is necessary for Faust to kill off the last of his ruminating and inactive professorship and to unleash the more animal nature he so longed to unite with in his speech beneath the moon. This is accomplished through making the sexual desire a primary driving force. Mephisto describes the effect of the potion: "In flesh the paragon of all woman / will stand before your very eyes / With that drink in you, you will see Helen / Soon enough in every woman" (ll.2603-4). This implies a drunken desire, but also that Faust will be able to see the perfection in the female – her archetype within the example. In fact, upon drinking the potion, Faust not only has a vision of Helen (foreshadowing the second Part of the play in which the mythical Helen becomes his lover), but also of Margerete/Gretchen. [38]

Margarete/Gretchen is the representation of Faust's ability to love and his desire for life and nature, but may also be a representation of pure human nature, untouched by rationalism, but held in the grip of traditional society and the church. She is constantly described as "pure" and "fresh," young and beautiful, the perfect image of a German

---

37 This implication is among the subtle Gnostic themes in *Faust*, more of which will be referenced later. In the Gnostic *Gospel of Thomas*, the savior advises "If you bring forth what is within you, what is within you will save you, but if you do not bring forth what is within you, what is within you will destroy you."

38 Gretchen is like Helen of Troy to Faust. As he has followed his destructive impulse downward to claim this potion, he will dare destruction to claim Magarete/Gretchen. She is paralleled by Helen in *Part II* of the play, but in this portion she represents Helen. It seems interesting that Helen is known as the Torch, while Lucifer is sometimes symbolized in a Promethean role as the Torch Bearer. Mephistopheles leads Faust to Gretchen who is like Sophia for Faust. The strong link between the Gnostic Sophia and Helen (like the Helen of Simon Magus) and the link between Helen of Troy and Gretchen strengthen the argument of Gretchen as Sophia. It also strengthens the argument of Faust himself as a Gnostic figure in the Simonian mold; one of the titles of Simon Magus was "Faustus," the fortunate or lucky one; there was also a renowned Manichaean called Faustus, attacked by Augustin for his extreme anti-Judaism and his rejection of the Gospels themselves as Judaized, along with the doctrine of the incarnation of Jesus.

maiden, but she is controlled by her Mother, her brother Valentine, and the Church. Faust's desire for her is the first truly unbridled action of his nature in which he fully indulges. Mephistopheles encourages Faust's lust for Gretchen, ostensibly believing that he can manipulate Faust into a self-destructive situation. However, here Mephisto is planting the seeds of Faust's own undoing (or perhaps of his own redemption). Faust's destructive/creative impulse, awoken to life with the help of Mephisto, is the very faculty which places him above the Demon, and will eventually liberate Faust from his pact. In the meantime, however, Faust attempts to win Gretchen, in order to quench his passion in sensuality. Gretchen does, in fact, make a fine symbol of the female nature and the "world" in which Faust wishes to act and to consummate his desire. She is pure, not only in the sense of being untouched, but in her honest and uncalculating responses to Faust's overtures. Faust seems to recognize the archetypal nature of Gretchen when he honors her with a noble title on their first meeting although she is a commoner. The emptiness or purity of Gretchen (from the taint of society, perhaps, or of pretense) is what makes her the perfect parchment on which Faust can etch his word in the world.

When he enters her home for the first time he compares her in his allusions to all the ancient heroines who inspire love (and the downfall of men). "Sweet evening radiance in this sanctum", he declares, perhaps evoking Eve, the first lover of man who led him into a fall "... Fasten on my heart sweet pains of love," recalling Cleopatra's demise and her contrivance of the same fate for Antony. He continues, "That on the dew of hope thirstily live." This is reminiscent not only of his first longings to be baptized in the "dew" of the moon, but also of his lament of Nature herself as a cold woman who would not allow him to suckle at her teat. "Breathe and the feel of stillness round me, / Of order and contentedness, / What abundance in this poverty / And in this prison such a blessedness!" (ll.2687-93) Faust treats Gretchen as the embodiment of the sacred woman, and in this speech Faust confesses he has found a place of rest and stillness where he would not be idle and restless – potentially the fulfillment of Mephisto's end of the bargain and the undoing of Faust. The perfect woman for whom Faust would risk his own destruction for contentedness (by losing his bet with Mephistopheles) also makes her like Helen of Troy. Faust proves himself willing enough to destroy her world and perhaps his own in order to have her. Faust recognizes Gretchen's "sanctum" as a holy place, because it belongs to her – and perhaps Mephisto does not count on the sanctity, even in its destructiveness, of Faust's desire for Gretchen. Gretchen in her sanctum is the final center of the earth on Faust's downward descent. Even more secret than the witch's cavern, Faust finds in Gretchen's sanctum the core of his world and the fire (of desire) in which his own immortality was ensured. The discovery of the untouched and perfect woman at the end of the descent invites an alchemical motif of critical importance, one that may have been known to Goethe through *The Chemical Wedding of Christian Rosenkreutz*, an allegorical recipe for the secret medicine. The protagonist discovers that Venus lies in a type of stasis in deepest cellar of the magical castle. Even as the formula Rosenkreutz seeks is exposed, he asks the meaning and is told: "Here lies buried Lady Venus, that beauty which hath undone many a great man, both in fortune, honor, blessing and prosperity."[39] The connections Faust draws between Gretchen and

---

39 *The Chemical Wedding of Christian Rosenkreutz*, Fifth Day.

all the seductresses who tempt men to their doom in history makes her seem like this very Venus "which hath undone many a great man". Gretchen is the key to Faust's formula which is the key to the final fulfillment of his nature.

The love of Faust and Gretchen, often depicted as a doomed romance by literary critics,[40] does in fact evolve quite naturally. Gretchen, perhaps playing out her nature as a woman more like Eve, Cleopatra, or Helen, than the shrinking Virgin Mary most critics would paint her as, does not at any point seem averse to Faust's overtures. Although Mephisto says she is pure and innocent, she appreciates Faust's bawdy song and his gifts for her. Gretchen's purity is of a different sort than the Christian ideal of demure chastity. Her naturalistic and organic response to Faust is actually part of what makes her a representation of the "pure" feminine. She is pure not in the sense of being sexually uninterested, but in that she is untainted by the inhibition of real femininity which is pervasive in the other characters of her village. But it quickly becomes clear that although Gretchen is uncorrupted by either the ills of modern and decadent society (as represented by her greedy and careless mother), or the bonds of tradition and the Romanticism of the previous era (as represented by her brother Valentine), she is held captive by both. When Faust sends gifts to her, they are stolen by her mother and donated to the Church. The Church plays a very interesting role for Gretchen. She is entirely dedicated to the holiness of the Church, and her faith seems to be a part of her purity. The chastity of Gretchen is in line with the concept of chastity as a singularity of devotion as outlined in discussions of Catholic priesthood, or the concept of "chastity in marriage" in which devotion to the husband is a proxy for physical virginity (Catechism of the Catholic Church, 1999). This concept places "chastity" in opposition to "lust," not due to lack of desire but in its desire toward one object – in a sense lust toward a single object rather and dispersive lusts, is potentially a sort of chastity. This concept seems contrary to the sort of chastity Valentine and Gretchen's mother would envision for her – in which she is entirely removed as a subject of desire and isolated from creative and reproductive potential. It seems significant that Gretchen's love for the Church is immediately replaced with a singularity of devotion toward Faust. In one sense her relationship with Faust could be said to cement or culminate her chastity and purity making this into an active rather and a passive quality.

Indeed, it is not Faust *per se* who brings about Gretchen's destruction. Instead, the impositions of the Church and her society eventually lead to her undoing. That the gifts Faust sends her would be donated to the Church might be a representation of how the corruption of society stands in opposition to Faust's instinctive desire taking its natural course. It is somewhat ironic that in Goethe's time the protestant faiths had essentially dismantled the Church itself but maintained the ecclesiastical hierarchy. Gretchen as the pure and sacred woman may represent the true Church itself, the seat of sanctuary, while the "church" comprised of the pastor who takes her gifts and jewelry is only the representative of a hollowed-out institution in which sanctity no longer resides. Faust's attempts to honor the true church of Gretchen herself are thwarted by a society which hands his gifts to the corrupt ecclesia: The society (in the form of Gretchen's mother) steals what should rightfully be the property of the sacred feminine and hands it over to

---

40 See Gillies, 1957, Butler, 1952.

a sinister and patriarchal establishment which has outlived its use for the likes of Faust. Mephisto chides the corruption of the ecclesiastical hierarchy as it poses as an intercessor for the divine feminine: "That jewelry – who'd have believed it? / Got for Gretchen, a Priest has thieved it!" (ll.2813-14). Gretchen's mother, he claims, insisted that the jewelry be offered up to "the Mother of God", but naturally the priest ends up with the jewelry. This is reminiscent of Jung's essay Wotan discussed earlier. The organic Germanic impulses have here been constrained by Abrahamic religion – altered into a sort of bondage which will eventually inspire revolt. Faust, in his bucking of Christianity and tradition is a sort of revolutionary of impulse in this section of the play. Faust's tumultuous and confusing difficulties in uniting with Gretchen, along with the resultant destruction, is Goethe's commentary on the primal German spirit fettered and sterilized by alien morality.

The Church and the moralistic society are not the only things standing in the way of Faust's necessary consummation. Valentine also attempts to thwart Faust's desire. Valentine represents himself as traditional, but because one's class delimits their historical breadth he instead reflects more Romanticism and the vain restoration of chivalry. He puts Gretchen on a pedestal while blaspheming her true nature as a woman. The obligation which tradition places on the individual to put family and church before desire is shown as destructive rather than virtuous. When Valentine is out drinking with his friends, he praises Gretchen's beauty and purity in the highest terms, at points becoming lewd and potentially incestuous. However, when he hears Faust attempting to seduce her himself, and hears that someone has actually slept with his sister, he becomes indignant and assaults Faust.

Mephisto aids Faust in killing Valentine – in removing the last interference of chivalric/Romantic morality with the true nature of woman. Although Gretchen is aggrieved by Valentine's destruction, she does not reject Faust either for her brother's death or for any of the destruction visited on her. It seems unintuitive to argue that Faust is actually enacting a sort of redemption for himself, for Mephisto, and even for Gretchen by unleashing his destructive and animalistic desire. The traditional reading of the storyline of Gretchen is that her pure love for Faust saves him despite himself, even though he is a selfish and undeserving person who truly deserved to be enslaved by the Devil. This seems like too simple a reading for such a subtle play which has so far presented us with a much more useful formula.

The downfall and undoing of Gretchen is the key point in Part I of the play and initiates an evolution of Faust's character. The strength of Faust's desire for Gretchen is transformed into a returned chastity. Faust again employs his word, but now as an oath to her. Faust swears to love Gretchen, and this oath is in direct contrast to the outcome of his pact with Mephisto. Her death is necessary for his future liberation from the consequences of the pact with Mephisto, and it is through his uninhibited desire that her necessary destruction and elevation to the Throne of Heaven is accomplished. It might be easy to believe that Faust destroys Gretchen through defilement, removing her from the safety of her faith and relationship with "mother church." But, essentially, Faust and Gretchen are performing an act of desecration, an abomination which turns her into a whore when they copulate and create a child outside of wedlock. Her abomination is further sealed when she kills her own child inside the church. Despite the rampant sacrilege, Gretchen ascends to heaven and is made into a component of the Holy Mother.[41] It is this ascension which allows her to intercede of Faust's behalf. She becomes not only a whore but a Divine Whore, the Mother of Abominations. Like Helen of Troy, whose symbolical relevance to the story is so great that she became a character in Part II, Gretchen's sacrifice initiated an Apocalypse, that being a violent transition between worlds and the establishment of a new formula.

Faust's defilement of Gretchen fits an ancient archetype of sexual violation such as was captured in the better-known kidnapping of Persephone by Hades. These mythological "rapes" created a new world order in which infernal initiation was possible – a separation between the perpetual Eden of pre-history and the era of human agency. Like these myths, the kidnapping of Helen was a destruction of a previous era in favor of a heroic one – an era inaugurated with war. Faust's destruction of her implements the apocalypse of the Germany of the Romantic/Modern period with its failing Christian morality. As Faust satiates his desire for Gretchen, he removes her from her previous society and plants the seeds of its destruction along with hers. This is not simply an ill-fated act of impulse, but indeed an act of war in which culminates in his process of alienation and creates the foundation of his eventual ascent. Goethe has essentially given a myth of the divine rape or alternately the divine whore to the Christian world – a myth which might be considered at its most benign to be Gnostic and at its most esoteric dangerously Heretical. Gretchen herself, far from being the tragic figure most readings of Faust would make her into, is a willful co-conspirator in her own "destruction." She seems to recognize her role in Faust's formula as a part of her purpose and nature and complies with each necessary component. When she first falls in love with Faust she tells him about how she cared for her little sister as a baby, but the child died. Her desire is to have a child, and when she falls in love at last with Faust, she is complicit in the plot to help him enter her bedchamber. The madness which follows her pregnancy comes not from Faust's absence, but from the malice of Gretchen's corrupt community. She does not begin to lament her child or pregnancy until another woman gossips with her about a girl who is pregnant and talks about destroying her reputation. Previously, Gretchen had sought her only comfort and placed all her faith in the Church. She fears Mephisto when he is with Faust, potentially because Mephisto causes the same self-questioning in her that he does in Faust. Still, when Faust gives her a child outside the boundaries of social norms, rather than nurturing it, she kills the child. This too is necessary. Faust's desire and intent is not to be fulfilled in the form of a living child – rather his union with Gretchen is fulfilled in the saving of his own life and liberty at the end of Act II. The sacrifice of the child seals the destruction of Gretchen herself, which she accepts as her duty.

The events of Faust's Walpurgisnacht experience are beyond the scope of this essay – this is one of the few direct ties between the first and second parts of the play. But his experience in the mystical other-world parallels Gretchen's own mystical experience

---

41 In Gnostic terms, perhaps *not* destroying the child would have been the sacrilege, and it would be unsurprising to find a Simonian Helen restored to her role as Divine Sophia after denying further offspring to be victimized by the corrupt, fallen world of the Demiurge and his archons, although in this case, it is not the material world itself, but the social *cosmos* of Christianized Europe.

of her place in the world. She enters the church to which she had formerly so securely clung, and realizes her own removal from this institution. It is interesting that on Walpurgisnacht – traditionally a holiday for the consummation of desires and the conception of children – Gretchen is driven to kill her own child. This makes sense only if the sacrifice itself is the consummation of the desire of Faust and Gretchen. In this sacrifice, Gretchen sets out to fulfill her true purpose and goes willingly to her execution. Although she is driven "mad" by the judgment of the society, Gretchen's "insane" ravings are not unlike the Magical revelations which Faust was experiencing at Walpurgisnacht. For example, upon entering the prison Faust hears her sing "My mother, the whore, / she murdered me / my father, the rogue, he supped on me" (ll.4411-4414). She refers perhaps to mother Church (the whore), who is now responsible for her execution (the punishment which, ironically, will place her in the seat of the true divine feminine as the Holy Mother as revealed at the end of the play). The "father" is a Saturnine figure "supping" on his child – perhaps the moralistic and patriarchal society which has driven her to kill her own child.

And yet, when Gretchen is offered the chance to escape with Faust she refuses. Instead, she goes willingly to her death. She claims that the morning of her death "should have been her wedding day". In one sense it is – as the result of Faust's formula is finally enacted. She insists to Faust that instead of saving her he go and "save his child." Although the child of their union is dead, Faust still has plenty of work to do – to save his own spirit – in Part II of the play. She seems content that her execution is her fate. In fact, she seems to become a part of Faust, and a part of his continuing drama even in her death. A Simonian Gnostic reading of Gretchen's character makes a great deal of sense. Mephisto, the demon of thought, causes Faust to act as *Logos* to Gretchen as Nature. Rather than being a destructive influence for her, Faust actually fulfills Gretchen's only desire. While Gretchen aids Faust in at last breaking his remaining ties to traditional morality, in consummating this supposed defilement, Faust actually fulfills Gretchen's true nature in a way that her mother/society, the Romantics/Valentine, and the Church cannot. Gretchen reveals her nature and her relationship to Faust when she is first introduced, in the allegorical song she sings about the King of Thule before finding Faust's first gift.

The King of Thule, she says, had a golden "drinking cup" (l.2760) given to him by his dying sweetheart. He loses all his other worldly possessions, and keeps it even at his own death. Upon dying, he flings the golden cup, which is his most prized possession, into the sea. This poem has many implications for the character of Gretchen. The poem does not appear to correlate with any historical or traditional myth of a King in Thule. Goethe wrote this poem around the same time as he was working on *Faust* Part I and simply inserted it for the Gretchen character. However, the idea of the Kingdom of Thule may have been an important one for Goethe. Thule or "Ultima Thule" is a mythological kingdom which may or may not have related to a real historical place in Northern Europe. It has been used as a proxy for the concept of a place beyond the northern boundaries of the world and is associated with legendary origins of the Germanic peoples often imagined during the modern period. Thule here may represent the lost primal Germanic roots to which Goethe has alluded throughout the play. This implies a very special importance for Gretchen which is in line with other readings of her character. Gretchen herself may be the "mistress" in this poem for whom the dying king pines, or alternately, she may be the golden cup itself. Gretchen is the grail of Germanic nature and sexuality. Although the mistress is dead, the gift through which she is recalled (the golden cup) remains. It seems important that as the king feels his own death approaching he throws the golden cup into the sea (returning it to an even greater, more primal, and more archetypal manifestation of the feminine). Gretchen herself is Faust's golden cup. She is the grail of his nature through which he realizes his own desire and re-creates the link between his own will and his world. She is also the means by which Faust evades damnation, achieving eternity while living. Symbolically, Faust does this through all of Germany. The wolf-man has let his true nature out, and now he recalls the mysteries of sexuality through his shameless ravishing of the chaste German maiden. But, like the King of Thule, Faust's destruction is also imminent. His pact with Mephisto is meant to be a fatal one, and now he must concern himself with resentful villagers. He "throws his golden cup into the ocean" in that he is forced to allow Gretchen to be sacrificed in order that she be consigned to the greater amalgam of the divine feminine who pardons him in Part II. The destruction of the cup and of Gretchen are neither careless nor idle, these are necessary acts to complete the formula. In the Gnostic myth, Sophia, impregnated by the Son, ascends to the throne of the Divine Mother. Faust employs this formula, but the indiscretion of the profane age imposes hardships and malice. Gretchen understands her role early on during her romance with Faust and nonetheless accepts this dark fate. She senses the danger for her in Faust when he catches her playing "he loves me-he loves me not." "Do you know what it means that he loves you" (l.3185), asks Faust and she replies "My blood runs cold" (l.1386). And yet at the end of this exchange she admits that although she should be angry and ashamed by Faust's behavior, "I stand here blushing and answer 'yes' to everything!" (ll.3213-14). Gretchen in her true purity does not suppress her natural response to Faust, even sensing his destructive nature. The sacrifice of Gretchen is purposeful on both their parts – and especially her own. Mephisto aids in this, following through the course of action initiated by Faust's oath, and Faust is complicit despite his regret at losing Gretchen. Even the killing of the child – the union of pure German Nature with the rebellious wolf-man – is made necessary by nature of the society which gave rise to Faust's abomination. Gretchen herself goes willingly to the fire.

Graeco-Egyptian Hermetism posited a Magical formula interpreted by modern Neo-Hermetic magicians as signifying the mystery of resurrection: the formula of IAO. This formula might be summarized in several ways. In *Book 4*, Crowley states that IAO stands for Isis/Nature, ruined by Apophis/the Destroyer, and restored to life by Osiris/ the Redeemer. This explanation might parallel the story of Gretchen – she represents Nature (I) "ruined" by Faust under the influence of Mephisto (A) and then ascended and redeemed after death (O). There is a more complex relationship which can be found in this formula however. The entire interaction between Faust and Gretchen might be said to complete the formula of IAO. This has also been described as the destruction which is necessary in any endeavor for the novice to be destroyed and replaced by the adept. Crowley describes this as the initial passion or interest, which inevitably becomes effort, agony, and destruction, which at last creates a new kind of transcendent state similar to but greater than the first. By this description, Faust and Gretchen's initially playful and passionate interaction must meet pain that their more perfect love may survive Gretchen's death.

In the final scene of Act I, Gretchen is burned to death. She refuses Faust's intent to save her, a willful act which might stand in her own part for the initial "I" of intent. Mephisto forces Faust to save himself rather than Gretchen, thus acting as the Destroyer in this scene. But this destruction, "A," has an effect that even Mephisto does not seem to anticipate. As she dies Mephisto declares "she is judged" (l.4611), but the "voice from above" contradicts him – "[she] Is Saved" – or redeemed, completing the "O" portion of this formula (l.4612). The complementary and inverted form of this formula is also present in the plot of Gretchen and Faust. Crowley makes clear in *Liber Stellae Rubae* that OAI is central to his conceptualization of Magic, and this is also evident in *Faust*. In truth, this inversion compliments the Neo-Hermetic IAO embodied by Gretchen. OAI may indeed be the essence of the formula which catapults Faust into the Second Part of the Play and completes his triumph over Mephisto. Crowley likens the OAI formula to the sacrifice of a child. Rather than the birth-like formula of resurrection in which the destruction of the initial impulse is necessary for resurrection and fruition, OAI seems to be exactly the opposite: The orgasmic ecstasy is transformed into agony through the destruction of the offspring (and perhaps of the mother, O, through the offspring) – and yet this destruction yields a new intent and a new momentum. This "child sacrifice" is the very essence of the infernal pact and completes Faust's infernal initiation. While Faust and Gretchen are separated in the dream-like/death-like underworld of Walpurgisnacht she initiates this formula (even as Faust initiated IAO in his courtship of her) and kills their child. It is this which leads to her execution – that destruction which is so central to Faust's ability to break Mephisto's pact. The moment Gretchen kills the child, the initial desire of Faust's original oath is guaranteed to be fulfilled (and this is the only way it can be fulfilled). This may be the only fashion in which Gretchen can truly elevate Faust in the fashion described by the Hermetic interpretation of IHVH, the exaltation of the Son to divinity through the elevation of the Daughter to the throne of the Mother, and identification with her. When Faust first encounters Mephisto he declares that he wants to be like god, and understand all things from an omniscient perspective. Mephisto, the demon of consciousness, dissuades him because Mephisto cannot deliver. Where Mephisto fails, Faust and Gretchen succeed. In the end of Part II, Gretchen is able to receive and elevate Faust to the Throne because of the momentum of the formula which had already been put into motion and completed in Part I. The debate over whether Faust tricked Mephistopheles, or whether the pact was invalid, or God nullified it, or Grace saved Faust becomes irrelevant in light of this formula – Faust becomes like God, and so he can do whatever he wants with the pact. He is free from Mephisto because he has sublimated Mephisto's very nature into his Will.

The final voice is that of Gretchen, but it is said to come "from within" – calling Faust's own first name "Heinrich, Heinrich" (ll.4615). Faust's desire is no longer simply an animal and lustful desire. In one sense it could be said that he has transformed the parts of his soul. His animal desire, "Nephesh" in the Qabalistic tradition, has been elevated through his love of the woman, the eternal Neshamah aspect of the soul. She now speaks to him through his inner voice, which might be said to correspond to Chiah, or the second-highest part of his soul, the life force or energetic dynamism which propels him through the second part of the play. This Chiah is now inexorably connected to Gretchen, Neshamah who has become permanent and eternal – now in the position of the Holy Mother. It is this connection – Faust's desire consummated in Gretchen, his "passion quenched in sensuality" now elevated to a divine position which gives him ultimate power over Mephisto. Mephisto, in the beginning of the play might have acted as Faust's Ruach – or intellectual portion of the soul. It is the creation of link to Neshamah which allows Faust the ability to liberate himself from the consequences of his initial infernal pact. This also supports the formula of OAI proposed previously. The animal desire quenched in Gretchen (O) is able to reverse Faust's descent through destruction (A) and a new directional momentum, through a link to the higher (I).

After Gretchen's death Faust is no longer descending. His consummation of desire, far from ensuring his fall to Mephistopheles, might be thought of as his final act of descent into the center of the world, his final suicidal act. Risking his destruction, he commingles his desire with Gretchen's, creating the secret medicine of immortality in their very lovemaking. The sacrifice of the child and Gretchen's own ascent assure Faust's ultimate triumph. From her Golden Cup, Faust takes his final elixir, and his downward path is reversed – he rises above the earth.[42]

The Faustian Formula

The action of Part II is not a new formula, but rather a fulfillment of what has been set in motion in Part I. In this separate portion of the work, written decades later, the actions which Faust began in Part I are played out on a higher level – above the earth, in the world of Archetypes. The play opens with Faust reclining in a field surrounded by the spirits of the Air, now clearly above the earth. He makes a sort of ascent through the empyreal worlds. He is able to conjure the spirit of Helen because of a Magic he obtains from the Eternal Mothers who live in the center of the world. They favor Faust, perhaps because he has already fulfilled the descent into the center of the earth with Gretchen. It seems that both the Mothers below in the Earth, and those Above the Heavens favor Faust because of Gretchen's intercession. Faust performs Magic for the Sun Emperor, perhaps a reference to the Sun, the gateway to the higher worlds. He conjures the spirits of the dead with the power of the Mothers, but upon seeing Helen's spirit he is determined to have her as he did Gretchen. In order to capture Helen of Troy, the Archetype to whom Gretchen was compared when Faust first saw her, Faust requires the instruction of a Centaur who was the teacher of Aesclepius, the god of medicine. The alchemical references in Part II are more blatant than Part I, and they reveal Goethe's

---

42 Not only the Neo-Hermetic formulae of Aleister Crowley, but also the work of Axis esotericists such as Traditionalist Julius Evola, and esoteric Hitlerist Miguel Serrano, are consonant with this interpretation. Evola writes about the redemptive destruction, immolation, and assimilation of the female in Left-Hand Path Indian Tantra and in more orthodox Indian traditions such as *suttee*, and Miguel Serrano's Gnostic parable *EL/ELLA: A Book of Magic Love* seems to describe a Gnostic interpretation of the absorption of sacrificed female into the will and identity of a redeemed male protagonist.

alchemical knowledge and support an esoteric reading of Part I as well. For example, Wagner, the pure scientist, has managed to create a Homunculus whom he carries in a vial in Part II. This character helps drive the plot in his quest to become fully human which parallels Faust's own struggles.

For Faust, the drama of the play is similar to Part I but on another level. Faust encounters the old character of Wagner who has become a prosperous scholar, and steals Helen of Troy for himself. They live in a Paradise-like prosperity for some time, totally removed from the world in which Faust was so engaged in Part I. They have a son who accidentally kills himself falling from a cliff while exploring, presumably because he has inherited Faust's restless nature. This Second Part of the play seems to reverse and thereby complete the action of the First Part. He resides in the world of archetypes (like the mythological figures of the Sun Emperor and Helen of Troy). The death of Helen and her son is as necessary for Faust to begin his final action on the Earth as Gretchen and her child's were to elevate Faust above it. After Helen's suicide, Mephisto attempts to lure Faust off on another decadent adventure, but Faust decides that he wishes to challenge his own abilities instead. Having ascended to the world of the Higher Woman in the form of Helen and her abode by the sea, Faust descends again to earth, the kingdom, to rule his own city by the sea (reminiscent of the "King of Thule" from Gretchen's song). He organizes the people to build a great city, although it is not Helen's paradise, it is the work of Faust's own mind and hands on the Earth. Eventually he finds his "moment of happiness" in creating something tangible in the world – during a project in which he has tasked his people to dig. In this moment, Mephisto may have triumphed – but Faust's final act is a lasting and creative one. He realizes his own divine nature through accomplishing and manifesting his own designs in his kingdom. The death of Helen and her son Euphorion (perhaps the embodiment of Faust's desires) directs him back from the world of myth and archetype which he was able to achieve in Gretchen's sacrifice. He at last consummates his creativity on the Earth itself through the creation of his city. This last project seems like the completion of the pattern inaugurated through Gretchen, Faust's "golden cup", and it ultimately admits him to the Divine Throne.

At the end of Part Two, Gretchen appears as a triune aspect of the Divine Mother who now does the job of exalting Faust to the Throne of the Lord (the very Throne which he craved when he first encountered Mephisto). He escapes the past not because of some divine pardon – but because he is like God and can do whatever he wants. The full utilization of his bestial nature has resulted inexorably in the inauguration of the "Divine Light" to which it was wedded in the *Prologue in Heaven*. The death of the Child and Gretchen were made because of the friction caused by Faust engaging his nature against the degenerate social order and the constraints of his own rational mind.

Only this sacrifice of Gretchen and her child created the momentum through which Faust could complete his transformation in Part II and be truly liberated from that which erstwhile confined him. The formula by which Faust discovers himself and unleashes his creative/destructive force – becoming, as was his wish, like a God, on the earth but not of it – is revealed in Part I of the play. The use of these powers in a personal epic is the substance of Part II. Part II describes how this same formula plays out in Faust's completion and liberation; he first endures a dark night of the soul and ends in the arms of Helen. But the idealism and Golden-Age nostalgia embodied by Helen is also not sufficient to produce life, similar to the cataclysm of his procreative attempt with Gretchen. Eventually Faust is freed from his pact with Mephistopheles, which may be taken, in one sense, as the fulfillment of Mephisto's own purpose. Mephisto was tricked into engaging man and ultimately recognize man's divine creative power. The denial of God in Man is the very sin for which the Devil was supposedly cast out of heaven, according to Islam and some Eastern Christian sects which influenced it, and it is that divine nature which Mephisto mocks in the *Prologue*.

Based on the direction of the Word, the Devil introduces the potion of desire, which unleashes Faust's most primal essence. It is through the fulfillment of this desire – the desire for which the initial thought became restless – in copulation with Gretchen that Faust ensures his own immortality and freedom. Mephisto hinted that the "secret medicine" is in the sexual act – but it does not seem that he truly understood what his own argument foreshadowed. The final elixir in Part I is the combination of Faust and Gretchen's sexual fluids which results in the sacrificed child. It is through this "secret medicine" that Faust is truly guaranteed immortality. Similarly, in the destruction of Gretchen through her copulation with Faust, her own purpose is fulfilled, and she is able to ascend to the throne of the Divine Mother. Faust, since his own passion wrought this destruction and his inspiration of love created Gretchen's sacrifice, retains his link to her. She becomes his own inner voice, his animal desire elevated to the position of the perfect soul. Because of this, all of Faust's destructive actions culminate in Faust's only truly creative act in the creation of the kingdom and finally the intercession of the Holy Mother to save him from the clutches of Mephisto. He achieves the divine seat to which he aspired and which Mephisto was unable to guarantee.

The formula of the thought, word, and deed, first extolled by Faust in his reinterpretation of John's Gospel, contains within it a valuable lesson for the student of the occult. In an age where a darker disposition is alienated by the Church, rationalism, and modernism, the vicarious redemption of Christ is not an option for attainment but rather a blind, a pacifier and mechanism of control. Instead, a downward and perhaps destructive path is necessary, a suicide of the constructed self and a commingling of beast, man, and god. Faust redeems the power and potential of the Wolf-Man, simultaneously destroying the Christian morality which enslaved his sexual desire and restoring the Woman to her Divine throne. Destructive sacrifice is necessitated in that thought alone cannot transcend the confining system of consciousness, such as the rational-moralistic society which confined Gretchen. The restless thought alone was not enough. The limitation and direction of Word and the fire of Deed were necessary to achieve Faust's descent. It is not at all surprising that Crowley would have been inspired by this tale, as was Nietzsche. Both endorsed the full utilization and exploration of Man's nature, even if the core of being is a devil. As modern scholars have suggested that Faust was the prototype for Nietzsche's Overman, so his myth may remain a parable for the contemporary Magician. It is not the Christian parable of redemption through pure love which has been suggested by many critics, but rather a precise instruction manual (even more than the *Faustbuch* from whence it derives its heritage) of the Satanic Pact, and the initiation and liberation which might be derived therefrom.

Aleister Crowley undoubtedly recognized the esoteric genius and practical value of *Faust*. Crowley canonized Goethe as one of the Ecclesia Gnostica Catholica's Gnostic Saints. Crowley's motto as Magister Templi, V.V.V.V.V., has long been reported to be a reference from "Doctor Faustus" – "Vi Veri Vniversum Vivus Vici",[43] however this quotation is found nowhere in Goethe's work, nor in any previous renditions of *Faust*. This isn't unlike Crowley's offhanded allusions to deeper mysteries contained in other mythos, and certainly Crowley would not have imagined *Faust* as simply a Western fairy-tale exposing the state of German culture. In his "Initiated Interpretation of Ceremonial Magick" which introduces Mather's edition of *The Lesser Key of Solomon*, Crowley offers his thoughts on the depth of Magical instruction which can be found in religious texts and works of cultural fiction. He discusses the superficial understanding of both Magick and sacred texts by "the Philistine" and notes that secrets like the Qabalah of the *Bible* and the mystical secrets of the *Arabian Nights* are hidden from the many, but will offer up their hidden treasures to the probing of the careful student. Crowley insists that these secrets, like those of the *Key of Solomon*, are specific and scientific methodologies which may be utilized to understand our own natures, take command of own brains, and thereby master the world. He seems to disdain those who would fear the Key of Solomon as a Black Magick text, stating "the world of Magic is a mirror, wherein who sees muck is muck." Similarly the allegory of *Faust* is an instruction meant for those who would conquer their self and their world through the exploration of the destructive formula expounded therein. It is no more to be feared or to be taken as a superficial text than the old Faustian grimoires were merely novelties or parables.

Goethe's conflict with Romanticism and embrace of the ancient sciences is as relevant today as it was in his own time, and Crowley may have recognized this. Romanticism in the 18th Century was as derisive of form and exalting of unexamined "creativity" as is today's post-modernism. The Romantic neo-Hermeticists revived "ancient knowledge" but forced it into the particular worldview of their time. Further, much of their writing teemed with resent and confusion, such as Keats' "Ode to a Grecian Urn." By Goethe's day the Medieval grimoires would have been considered quaint and fanciful at best and superstition at worst, not to be confounded with the seemingly more ordered scientific approach which occult practitioners of the day favored. Goethe in *Faust* seems to advocate a more truly naturalistic science – an experiential, uncontrolled, and dangerous Black Magic, honest in its embrace of instinct and terrifying in the powers it evokes.

This particular kind of formula may be necessary for the student who shares Faust's own disposition. For Eisler's Lycanthrope, no benign tropical mysticism will suffice. The path out of the self-referential and fruitless knot of consciousness is a violent cutting. For those in whom the Thanatoic death-instinct is strong, the path to attainment may first need to be a downward one. In his *Commentary on Liber 65*, Crowley discusses that according to the nature of the student and his previous work, the Holy Guardian Angel – that indescribable Other-Self which is the guide and method of the Magician's attainment, may fail to manifest, but that instead a dark "Dweller on the Threshold"

---

43 "By the power of truth, I, a living man, have conquered the universe."

may appear. He describes this "Dweller" as the "Evil Genius" stating:

> Spirit may therefore be manifested either as the Holy Guardian Angel or as the Evil Persona, the Dweller on the Threshold…The doctrine is also frequently found in folk-lore, where man is represented as attended by both a good and an evil genius. The horror of the latter is intensified by his function as the alternative to the Holy Guardian Angel.

Crowley describes how this Dweller may potentially bring disaster to the Adept – he is in one sense identical with the chaos of consciousness embodied by Choronzon who may keep the Adept in the dispersion of the Abyss if he is not overcome. However, Crowley goes on to state that the Evil Genius is also itself "within the Sanctuary of the Temple of the Rosy Cross whose formula is 'love under will.'" He enjoins the Magician who has mistaken his Evil Genius for his Holy Guardian Angel to persist. Should this mistake occur through despair or fear: "Let him remember the words of my brother: 'If the fool would persist in his folly he would become wise.' Let him resolutely continue in iniquity, invoking the vengeance of the Gods, so that at the end the excess of his love and its transcendence of anguish may bring him back into the way of truth."

This is not to say that the formula revealed in *Faust* is only useful to one who has erred, though Mephistopheles mirrors Faust in the fashion which a Shadow or an Evil Genius might. Like the Evil Genius, he represents in one sense the dispersion of the mind and attempts Faust's destruction through Faust's own oath. However, Mephistopheles also provides the necessary impetus for Faust to overcome the reclusiveness of his intellect, and the conditions under which he can quench his desires in the center of the earth, ensuring immortality. Although the infernal pact with Mephistopheles is a black one, like the Holy Guardian Angel, Mephisto is useful for Faust to create the conditions whereby he may ascend above the earth to the higher worlds, and eventually return, complete and altered to create his Kingdom. In the end it does not matter that the path of descent was necessary for Faust – the seeming disaster or trap of his pact with Mephistopheles is avoided altogether through the fulfillment of Faust's own formula and the overriding nature of his attainment.

In the case of Faust, (and perhaps those who can identify with him), it is inherent in the personal nature to require the Devil's pact and the infernal initiation. In *Book 4*, Crowley states "In order to invoke the Devil it is only necessary to call him with your whole Will."[44] He also states that the demons and "powers of 'evil' nature are wild beasts; they must be tamed, trained to the saddle and the bride; they will bear you well." As Faust was attempting to discover the utility of his own bestial nature the evocation of the demon was necessary. Once given appropriate reign, this animalism, and death-instinct, become not destructive or dangerous forces to the Magician but his greatest assets. Although Crowley criticizes the use of pacts, and the apparent hypocrisy of trying to con one's way out of them at the last moment ("With regard to Pacts, they are rarely lawful. There should be no bargain struck. Magick is not a trade, and no hucksters need apply. Master everything, but give generously to your servants, once they have uncon-

---

44 Crowley, A. *Liber ABA*, 1913. *Of Pacts With the Devil.*

ditionally submitted."), he also asserts that the very concept of the Devil is a false one invented to ascribe unity to the disunited demonic world, and that, Man being the only God, "the whole will of every man is in reality the whole will of the Universe."

As such, for those in whom the destructive instinct runs rampant, the Faustian formula may be a required rectification. *Faust* remains a grimoire for the antagonist, and its aura and significance lie not in its excellent cultural motifs, nor in its moving and human characters, but in the sub-luminal resonance of its esoteric spiritual formula.

REFERENCES

—⁓— Andreae, J.V. (1459). *The Chemical Wedding of Christian Rosenkruetz.* Retrieved from http://www.alchemylab.com/chemical_wedding_rosenkruetz.htm, on 7/23/2011.

—⁓— Crowley, A. (1913). *Magick. Book 4: Liber ABA.* Weiser Books, MA. ed. 2000.

—⁓— Crowley, A. (1913). *The Book of Lies, Liber 333.* Weiser Books, MA. Ed. 1981.

—⁓— Crowley, A. (1926). *Liber Al vel Legis, The Book of the Law.* Red Wheel/Weiser, MA. 2004, Centennial Ed.

—⁓— Crowley, A. (1996). *Commentaries on the Holy Books and Other Papers* (Equinox). Weiser Books, MA.

—⁓— Bates, A. (1906). *The Drama: Its History, Literature and Influence on Civilization,* vol. 11. ed. London: Historical Publishing Company, pp. 41-49.

—⁓— Blondel, E. (1991). *Nietzsche: The Body as Culture: Philosophy as a Philological Genealogy,* Translator Sen Hand, London: The Athlone Press.

—⁓— Del Caro, A. (1989). *Nietzsche Contra Nietzsche: Creativity and the Anti-Romantic,* Baton Rouge: Louisiana State University.

—⁓— Butler, E.M. (1952). *The Fortunes of Faust.* Penn State Press: PA.

—⁓— Eisler, R. (1948). *Man Into Wolf* in *The Iron Youth Reader,* vol. 1. Eds. Slaughter, K. et al. Underworld Amusements: USA. 2008.

—⁓— Gillies, A. (1957). *Goethe's Faust, An Interpretation.* Colombia University Press: NY

—⁓— Goethe, J.W. (1808). *Faust, Part I.* Penguin Classics: NY.

—⁓— Hunt, L. (2001). *The Columbia Encyclopedia of Literature.* Sixth Edition. New York: Columbia University Press.

—⁓— Jung, C.G. (1946). *Wotan.* Originally published as *Vorwort to Aufstatze Zur Zeitgeschichte,* in *Essays on Contemporary Events* (London, 1947) Translator Welsh, E.

—⁓— Lynn, H (1971). *The Makings of the West: Peoples and Cultures.* Bedford/St. Martins Press.

—⁓— Pagel, L. (1858). *Doctor Faustus of the popular legend, Marlowe, the Puppet-Play, Goethe, and Lenau, treated historically and critically. — A parallel between Goethe and Schiller. — An historic outline of German Literature.* Gage & Co.: Toronto, CA.

—⁓— Paracelsus (1655). *Of the Supreme Mysteries of Nature.* Translated by Turner, R. Boork & Harson, London.

—⁓— Phillips, Mary Elizabeth (1895). *A Handbook of German Literature.* George Bell and Sons.

STATE OF THE ART
THE BIRTH-PANGS OF A MEGA-GOLEM

Carl Abrahamsson

This text was originally delivered as a lecture at the Knowledge & Delight-symposium hosted by the Ameth Lodge of Ordo Templi Orientis in London, England, on September 11th 2011.

Meetings, symposia and conferences like the present one are important, in that they help define where occult development is situated today. In a literal sense, nothing is really essentially occult anymore (as in "hidden"). Groups are fairly easy to find (in fact, the market is flooded), initiated practitioners can communicate with each other cross order-related borders, and even with people on the so-called outside. I wouldn't go so far as to say there are no secrets anymore, but it seems that a renewed openness is one of the most constructive results of this more tangible networking process that's inevitably going on.

There are many perspectives one could choose, if one wanted to look at this phenomenon closer. One could be looking from the perspective of a tradition in change: how occult traditions are not necessarily tied in with secrecy but have now rather taken the form of transparency – texts, rituals, teachings, etc are visible to a greater degree than ever before, but still need to be delved into or worked through if one is a serious student.

One could also look at it from the perspective of urgency, meaning that there are cosmic forces which are, in a sense, allowing a greater mercurial openness in the service of higher goals. This of course presupposes that there are such things as higher goals and cosmic forces. If that's the case, these goals could perhaps be summarized as "survival strategies" and could be looked at, more in detail, in various areas like holistic philosophy, quantum physics, ecology, organic cultivation, re-cycling, yoga, esoteric manifestations in art and culture, etc. Many of these things used to be regarded as philosophies of and for freaks but have been heavily integrated into a Western mind frame in just a few decades. We can at least toy with the idea that there is some sense behind this.

The quite recent boom of bibliophile aspects of occult publishing could be another angle of relevance. Publishers seem to want to make visible and preserve radical and useful ideas through tangible media – something that can be contained and left behind for the benefit of future generations.

So, that's where we are today, if we can live with these extreme simplifications I've made. We have something to say, we are willing to say it and also have the means to say it, and to preserve it. That really is quite a big step if we look back 100 years, 50 years and even 25 years. Occult philosophy, dressed in various costumes, has grown up and its voice can now be heard in many other spheres than the inter-order, literally esoteric and quite often secteristic ones. Academic interest is one newly impregnated sphere, and cultural presence another.

It is this cultural and artistic sphere that interests me here today. Not only in terms of how this has happened, but mainly in terms of where it will go. Does it have any kind of say-so beyond those already on the inside? Basically: can esoteric thought and practice reach out and touch the exoteric world in tangible ways, more than what is merely perceived from the point of view of the magician causing the possible change to occur?

One of the reasons why this is interesting to look at is that there are simply so many similarities between artistic creation and magical practice that a new grey area has popped up, with a distinct emphasis on art, I'd say. This to such an extent that perhaps much of the traditional magical terminology has become obsolete in the presence of a much more dynamic and contemporary kit or set of tools.

The esoteric field has always been attractive to the artist on more or less conscious levels, because he or she intuitively realizes that quite often it is a mere terminology that sets these fields apart. The attraction doesn't need to be thematic at all, ie dealing with magic or occultism on a content-level. In fact, very few artists are interested in that. However, on the proto-creative level, the level that deals with how ideas become translated into general form, I suspect that any artist with just some slight sensitivity will feel a resonating affinity with the shaman or ancient sorcerer. The intuitive and experimental approach in expressing inner feelings is the same.

Way back in pre-history, the creation of totemistic, fetishistic or talismanic objects was first and foremost a creative process, and secondly a magical one. The energy invested in the making of something was a vastly important part of its magical charge and efficiency. This was also the case in proto-religious, mystical or magical states of mind: These were brought forth by artistic means, such as rhythm, music, singing, optical phenomena, painting, poetry, etc.

Then followed a more distinct separation. When tribal structures turned into more complex societies, more and more ancient practices became proxy-ones. Things were distanced from the actual source(eror) in order to facilitate and plan for an integration of many more individuals. The merely practical aspects integrated the existing skills and turned them into handicraft and manufacture. The oratory and visual skills became cornerstones of teaching processes. The history awareness process (in its oral and visual aspects) turned magical preservation techniques and living myth into politics and propaganda. The former magical techniques and sciences succumbed to commodification and demands of communal efficiency, and those in the know played along until nothing of conscious substance remained.

The last sentence is not true, of course. As always, the underground nurtured and cared for ancient teachings and techniques. Non-Status Quo outsiders who realized the need for preservation, preserved. Also, new technological developments were integrated in magical creativity, which occasionally fed back (as much as was safe) to the more accepted new fields of various sanctioned sciences.

Similar developments can be found in different cultures. Then, as monotheistic dominance paved the way for the development of materialistic "progress", for good and bad, the obscure and always radical minds and ideas were deemed "heretic" and disposed of – unless they succumbed and called their work something else under the blood-soaked umbrellas of Church and State.

As time went by, the artist as an integrated role now constituted a specific profession, catering to the currently sanctioned tastes, a pre-bourgeois decorative or illustrative art containing what was accepted by the powers that ruled.

The 20th century showed, more than any previous century, how important art can be in its magical, liberating, balancing functions. The violent developments of the times were all somehow countered by artistic explosions, as if art were an organic survival counterforce needed and actually embedded in our genes – a language of the divine, if you will. For instance, 19th century romanticism developing into a poetic pre-Raphaelite dream state, countering brutally rapacious wars, imperialism and industrialism. The manifestation of visible magic (as in people, orders, books, groups) runs parallel to the artistic manifestations, quite often with overlaps.

The French and other decadents were balancing the literary naturalism that was tied to orderly bourgeois lifestyles, often weaving in tales and images of the fantastic, macabre and the occult. The occult movements and persons were becoming integrated in artistic environments and colouring works of art – and vice versa. The development of deep-reaching psychology, sexuality and myth as a counterforce to repression and post-theocratic tyranny was also important. For every tin, there was a lid being torn open. The more chaotic and violent the times, the more chaotic and violent the art movements and spiritual directions.

The main paradigm shift was the actual direction of the gaze. From having been obsessed by portraying nature (human as well as general) in a clinical, empirical way, the direction was now turned inwards. Early on, looking back to mythical times and out into a world that could be systematically conquered by imperialism, but now, in the late 1800s, looking inside. The results were, as we know, incredibly powerful: a mélange of the mind containing psychology, resurgence of mythical themes, comparative religions, intuitive exotica à la Gauguin, displaying inner worlds, occultism, spiritualism, etc.

Of course, as occultists have always known, when you look inside, you find other things than when you look outside. Documenting these inner worlds, a new kind of more suitable language appeared that was in itself irrational, sensory, emotional, sexual, dreamy, compensatory, symbolic, automatic, etc.

In many ways, it was as if the magical world made itself apparent and visible through art, simply because there was a deep-rooted need for it. Applications in art of seemingly chaotic concepts like the Dada and Surrealist "chance" and Duchamp's "readymades" that were soon revered just like consciously "real" artworks turned the bourgeois preconceptions overboard. And then later, of course, turned into new hegemonies (but that's another story).

We shouldn't forget another interesting area: technology. Artists have always been interested in being on the forefront and trying things out, as if they are indeed (as we suspect) some kind of reflective surfaces with depth. With the development of film, there were suddenly new ways of expressing inherent desires in a way that very concretely resembled inner visions. Take a film like Méliès' "A trip to the moon" from 1902 for example. What is it? It is an artwork, a film, that uses tricks and almost stage-magical gimmicks to amaze the viewer into a surprised state of mind. But, if we want to, we can of course regard it as an almost incredibly powerful talisman, that in a symbolic fashion uses an artistic sense and recent technology to pave the way for real space travel while the viewer is in a state of utter amazement. Science fiction eventually becomes science fact. The key to this process lies predominantly in two conjoined concepts: art and magic. A cross-fertlization process.

Before we leave the technological sphere and enter the art-magic realm further, it could be interesting to note that one of the world's largest public companies, Apple, has been an active protagonist and synthesizer of all of these aspects. Not only in terms of its corporate symbol, the bitten apple of knowledge from the garden of Eden. And not only because of its success either (the company presently has more money than the US government). Owner and leader Steve Jobs, now with liver problems just like the original mythical Prometheus, and his creative engineers helped pave the way for an integration of an inuition-based creative technology with immense artistic and mercurial possibilities. These have in many ways redefined modern lifestyles as well as contemporary expressions.

Radical creative ideas and their applications through new and groundbreaking technology is no longer a pipe dream but a very apparent and present fact. This area has gone from a tantalizing terminology stemming from science fiction and psychedelics to a powerful agenda-altering application of modern life. Change, it seems, is absolutely possible.

From that perspective, the strictly magical process seems a little bit stuck within its historically based terminology. Using key memes from alchemy, hermeticism and ceremonial occultism, the practitioner tries to define a refinement process – an improvement, an existential elevation – through a grid of well-known but at the same time pretty confusing and obfuscating symbols.

The human desire for change on other levels than the merely instinctual and causal is inherent in our species system on all levels. A culture is very much defined by how it relates to this human trait. Is the arcane, hermetic terminology the most suitable one in terms of actual or potential change or is it actually counter-productive, in that it draws the aspirant into a glamorous web of escapism and seemingly insurmountable structures instead?

We can't really deny it: for good and bad, empirical science has demystified many of the concepts of the ancients. Our apprehension and early definitions of space and nature were fodder for the creative imagination of the proto-philosophers in different cultures. But what happens when the planetary, elemental and chemical spheres are so out in the open, stripped bare by their scientists even, that they simply cannot contain that kind of evocative enchantment anymore? What happens when psychology becomes an everyday preoccupation for professional and amateur alike, all wanting to become healthier, more balanced and more aware as human beings? Do the fascinating demons of yesterday lose or gain in say-so?

Ritual magic is usually thought of in terms of a causality of its own. One performs a ritual to achieve something specific and, as we've speculated at least, one uses a creative process to activate this. The idea being that the mere state of mind or residue of this state of mind will then help out.

This is true of the artist's work as well, but not necessarily in that causal way. The same process is used in an overall constructive behaviour, in which creativity and the specific creation in itself are parts of a necessary emotional hygiene. The artist could perhaps, very simplified again, be summed up as "I need" and the magician as "I want". As everyone with just an inkling of psychological insight realizes, these two emotional-existential vantage points need to be merged, unified. The key is now, as always: Know thyself.

Aleister Crowley penned it thus, magically stark and ever inspiring new generations of magicians: "Do what thou wilt shall be the whole of the Law", with the almost always adjoining, "Love is the law, love under will." Jean Cocteau developed it further, in detail, from the artist's point of view: "Never do what a specialist can do better. Discover your own specialty. Do not despair if your specialty appears to be more delicate, a lesser thing. Make up in finesse what you lose in force."

The specific causality of the magician's sphere can be counter-productive if there's no overall goal or existential insight. The specific acausality of the artist's sphere, ditto. Magic without spiritual presence is mere psychonautic escapism. Art without spiritual presence is mere decoration. Marcel Duchamp summed this relationship up very distinctly, when describing his own take on the 20th century: "We have thought of other things to use as decorative. Art is taking more the form of a sign, if you wish; it's no longer reduced to a decorative role. This is the feeling that has directed me all my life."

One decisive similarity is that both fields require an openness to direct sensory input. And also a direct interpretation of that input. We are so acustomed to rational filtering and peer-based interpretation that we hardly see the distinction between our own interpretations and those of the authorities around us. Magic, being an intimate, very private sphere, almost requires a setting aside of those rational interpretations and behavioural modes, in favour of irrational and emotional ones. Anton LaVey aptly called the temple space and temple time the "intellectual decompression chamber."

In art, we are also most often alone in our direct apprehension and appreciation of the artwork in question (regardless of what medium we're talking about). Art after World War II has been filled with post-modern theories and an increase of strictly intellectual discourse, but it doesn't change the fact: art affects directly, whether experienced "live" or through reproduction. And it affects us emotionally, not intellectually. The short-circuiting of the rational and intellectual opens up for new, inner vistas of potentially divine or spiritual experiences.

There's also a suitable analogy to literature and to comprehension in general here: when something is intelligently and poetically constructed in an enchanting and captivating manner, it can allow you to read "between the lines" and thereby receive a more elevated form of message, which can even be in opposition to the visible, rational lines of letters and sentences.

Another aspect that unites is that both fields house different strains, ranging from the museal-conservative to the radically experimental. In fact, one could argue that it is this inter-dynamic between extremes that creates the overall health of the field or sphere in question. Young generations are often quick to overthrow the old by infusing new interpretations of ideas that may or may not be timeless. It may be that it's the same in science, but I don't know that area well enough to dare to speculate, except for that little bite of the Apple, previously. In the fields of art and magic however, I think we all know how disparate and desperate the overall dynamic has been, and continues to be. If we look closer, we find that the content is usually the same over time, dealing with existential worth and eternal questions of will, love and personal development. It's mainly the form that changes: the expressions, the languages, the styles and directions.

Both processes are creative in the spheres of the subconscious. In magic, at least in the meta-programmatic aspects where the human psyche is involved. This in comparison with science, for instance, where a predominant rational, creatively deductive process leads to results both anticipated/suspected and, I hope, completely surprising.

The artist resembles the magician, and vice versa, in the ability to evaluate seemingly causal processes in non-causal ways. Being aware that his or her own process of creation contains an element that is quite impossible to explain – and superstitiously refraining from wanting to explain it – the entire analysis becomes wrapped in the non-rational. Being able to explain all the whys and wherefores is likely to hamper both the art-creation and the magic-creation. The essence seems to consist of an intuition-based "flow", in which thought, ideas and associations buzz around in synergetic and synchronistic surroundings, distilling or filtering everything down to one, single expression, like a will-driven opening in time and space. There is an indefinite potential of expression in both fields, yet a singular one becomes distinct and evident as a result of trusting this intuitive filtering process. However, any of the above speculations does not automatically make every artist a magician, nor vice versa. For this, we should probably be very grateful.

The wonderful scene in Disney's *Fantasia*, in which Mickey Mouse becomes the sorceror's apprentice (or the artist's, if you will), with disastrous results, is lovingly and humourously accurate in its portrayal of unrestrained will and enthusiasm. The occult path is lined with traps of this kind: the inspiration and enthusiasm expressed in the arcane, symbolical language often becomes an ego-inflating booster. But inflated quite often just with hot air instead of with spirit and genuine self-knowledge. This is very true of the art world as well, filled as it is with so much "art for art's sake" and cunning market strategists.

As both these fields are attractive, powerful and thereby glamorous, there will always be a lot of poseurs around, building careers on attributes and associations rather than on essential work and development. Creative seed-sowers may not always reap the harvests of their own work, a sad but perhaps inevitable phenomenon that also unites the fields of art and magic.

Self-knowledge is of the utmost importance, perhaps now even more than ever before. That's the essential dilemma or challenge of our plentiful Mickey Mouse times: having access to great tools by no means creates either artist or magician. It all begins on the inside, as it always has. Only an elevated psychological awareness allows the creative individual to meta-program his or her surroundings. By that stage of elevation and maturity, the tools in themselves become increasingly redundant. Paradoxically almost, our contemporary access leads to a denial in the timeless individuation sense. Gluttony is not the same as hunger. Being encouraged to choose between the presented A and the presented B is not the same as having freedom of choice.

A relevant shift in the terminologies of our present history of occultism could – and I stress the word "could" – be in favour of that of artistic creation. Not only because of their ties in the history of culture but also because the terminology of art is very much a terminology of the present times. We are surrounded by more art than ever before, for good and bad, as well as by more fiction, also for good and bad. As these aren't only signs of the times but also very concrete languages with an inherent driving force, it is perhaps of greater benefit to the spiritually inclined creative human being to re-integrate a proto-magical, ie an artistic, attitude in the structuring of the individual life-span?

Certainly, this is a discussion of details and of abstractions. But if you think about it, and if you allow yourself to drift for a while, away from the museum of magic that, I suspect, more or less all of us have ties to, then you can see that a free, non-denominational, non-secteristic overview and integration of magic in life really is nothing else than the creation of a highly individual Gesamt artwork composed of basic human elements, like occupation, sustenance, love, sex, respect, family, friends, stimulation and, of course, the ever-present fear of death. Our lives are indeed artworks and the more we are in charge of them, the happier we are – at least from a Thelemic point of view.

As an experiment, try to leave the hermetic and arcane frames of reference alone for a while and use instead those of artistic creation and, if you feel really daring, of fiction. We are already familiar with common parables like "life is a canvas", a stage, a slab of wet clay or a even a road. Here's another example, an imperative of sorts: As an artist, use your inner and outer studio to conceptualize and sketch what would be ideal for you, based on your unique artistic skills, and then ingrain your artworks-to-be and special soul-reaching performances with a sense of genuine desire. The public, fellow artists, curators and collectors will then all be there to do your bidding and manifest your will, consciously or not.

If you're critical to this and say, "Why should I change something that's worked for so long?", the answer is, "You don't have to". The water finds its own levels and everyone needs to find their own terminology or system that resonates. But one should take into account that developments on higher levels than the merely personal one often occur in jumps, starts, shocks, accidents and eurekas as a result of thinking and acting in new ways, out of the magic box, so to speak. Also, success in ritual situations usually requires a mind set that is not safe, complacent or even comfortable. Embracing and integrating new methods is a way of learning – an active dissociation from the past.

Schematically, we could say that art is the eternally projected myth, whichever it may be, and magic is the more technical projecting process. What my thesis or premise suggests then, is that it may be favourable to exchange the terminology of the historical projecting process with that of the eternal myth itself. If we accept the intimate and perhaps even inseparable relationship between the two, then I think an individual can derive more from immersion in and integration of a totality than from a distanced approach in which one plays with separate parts, no matter how poetical they are or seem to be.

Why is it favourable? I believe that we have passed and are beyond that critical point in time and space where the whole has been thoroughly divided into individual parts. We can call this an existential fragmentation, for simplicity's sake. I believe a development of magic, in essence as well as in terminology, in which attempts to recreate and reintegrate the parts into a holistic totality, is absolutely vital. On some miniscule level for all of us assembled here today, but more importantly for the entire planet. The analytical mind may have learned a thing or two but it doesn't really seem able to put the pieces back together again.

I think that art as a mythical phenomenon has a huge responsibility in this regard. Art is not merely self-reflective, as excretions from petty cry-baby egos. It really does have the potential to meta-program a unifying spirit through an active reintegration of healthy myths, rather than merely housing a desolate acceptance of profit-driven dissection frenzies. The new methods I called for may in fact only be old, perhaps even timeless, myths, currently lost in a maze of befuddled, mental over-achieving.

Many, if not most, myths essentially deal with death and rebirth. Our own times in many ways resemble the slain Osiris and the desperate reassembling of his hidden body parts. An even more fitting image for today's topic could be that of ancient Mexico, as told by Motolinia in the 16th century. In fearing that the sun wouldn't begin another circle of life-affirming blessings, a new fire was ceremonially as well as magically lit after all fires all over Mexico had been extinguished on the eve of that new solar cycle. After the new fire had been lit, representatives could get their new fires for their local regions from that central fire. Did the sun return in the morning? I'm pretty certain it did.

What I'm getting at is that there is a sun and there is indeed a central, solar fire in all of us, ready to help us illuminate our own individual magical maze. But perhaps it is enough to just realize that and to try and find a direct connection, rather than be concerned with, as was common in Mexico, who or what needs to be sacrificed in its honour (the answer to that being: noone and nothing), or which kinds of wood is best for that initial ignition, or at what time the sun will rise. The main mythical essence is that the sun will rise, not that it will rise at 4.18 am.

Also, let's not forget that the prevalence of complicated esoteric symbols and occult languages throughout history has basically been a safeguard against A) people who lacked the capacity to understand, and B) people who were opposed to the understanding itself. This situation has undoubtedly changed to the better, and perhaps it is now possible that an apple is, after all, just an apple.

I'm not after a new hegemony, in which this becomes that in a process of superceding superstitions. But I do think it'd be interesting and exciting to raise the consciousness and awareness of these basic similarities in artists and magicians already active. I do think that some pretty interesting insights could be gained by stretching out into the literally unknown and, as I suspect, seeing that art and magic are actually just areas reflecting each other deep inside the human psyche.

One challenge in this initial phase of terminology-switching could perhaps be a joint construction of a magical entity built entirely of art: cell for cell, limb for limb. To what end? The will is ingrained in its multifaceted DNA. All that's needed is a state of intent for each part, formulated by the artist-magician responsible for that specific bit. "This sculpture is the spleen of a new entity", etc. It doesn't need to emulate a specifically mammal structure either. Five heads are fine. Two vaginas and three penises also. It could just as well be generic, like "This photograph is a part of a new entity".

We are now dealing with a Golem concept that is not merely clay infused with remnants of a human and by proxy divine spirit, traditionally described in kabbalistic allusions. It is more a question of an entitiy composed of perhaps a hundred Golems, in which the first matter isn't clay at all but the individual artworks as building blocks, each infused with all existing human sentiments and all human wills. Not as something to be exhibited in a commodified art market context, to be joined together as a simulacrum of concepts like "sculpture" and "installation". No, this Mega-Golem would be united by spirit only, and the parts could be moved about geographically and indefinitely as the artist-magician responsible for that part would see fit.

No matter what, I hereby set the Mega-Golem ball rolling and free. This lecture and this text is the right side of its brain, perhaps one of many brains. It may be enough to give it life or it may not. It is an occult experiment that is also artistic. It is an artistic experiment that is also occult. I have vaguely attempted to state here today that I don't really believe there is any major difference between these spheres. What this Mega-Golem will or can do, is no longer up to me, exclusively. I have done my bit and the rest is now up to you.

Hounded by the Dogs of Reason
A Short Essay on the Mechanics of Magic

Carl Abrahamsson

Everywhere paradox. Everywhere dualism. Everywhere contradiction.

Or, so it seems.

It has been said that "the magick of Horus requires the passionate union of opposites". This simple wisdom also applies to any other form of magic.

There is normal current, or "energy". And then there's "magical" current. The latter can be used in situations of ritual, i.e. constructed, special situations you create with one or several specific goals in mind.

But the mere creation of the situation isn't enough in itself. And the current isn't either. You have to amplify the desire in question and allow the will to be so focused that it's like a virtual laserbeam headed for manifestation. And you have to short-circuit the rational mind, in order to let the current flow through it in the said situation.

Let's repeat: You need to create a setting which amplifies the constructive and the positive. For instance, by using various symbols for the different senses, all directing the mind towards the Desired.

You have to also work with the goal. Meaning you have to visually, mentally, audibly, orally etc create an inner as well as outer, all pervading, resonance with the Desired.

And you have to break down your greatest enemy in ritual situations – the rational mind. Now, this is usually the tricky part. Because we live in a culture in which the word "trance" has almost come to mean the intaking of illicit drugs. But, as with any other term, it's the essential significance of the word that matters, not the word itself. Or its moral associations.

Consider the rational mind to be a clockwork, a mechanical surface designed to help you function well in a mechanical surrounding consisting of other, similar, surfaces. If you add dirt, soil or anything else that doesn't belong there, you'll hinder the mechanical function and create an alarm on a "deeper" level. As an example: You take a strong psychedelic drug in a ritual situation, believing you'll get to where you want – fast. You then do "transcend" the "rational" – and easily so – but suddenly find yourself entangled in an even more complex web of underlying emotions and desires that all disturb your focus.

If, instead of stopping the mechanism, you help it along in an accelerating fashion, there will be a smooth transcendence into a new level of awareness. A level where you can retain, or even sharpen, your focus.

Many cultures use trance-inducing methods for this transcendence, the most classical ones being drumming and dancing. The rhythm of a beat and the physical adjustment to this beat allows the mind to transcend the mechanical dialectical process of action-reaction. There's usually just a new and fresh awareness of increased sensory sensitivity, waiting to be taken even further.

When you are familiar with this kind of state of mind, you can create whatever it is that you want to create. For instance, you can focus your inner vision on a graphical structure, designed to contain and symbolize the achievement of the Desired. Or you can exclaim relevant sounds. Or you can mold in thin air. Or you can simply build with light and vision.

A lot of people have a hard time realizing how simple this process actually is. It's probably because we are taught that life is – and should be, according to some – hard and painful, and that nothing can ever be achieved without a related amount of suffering or loss.

Remember that sacrificial magic (where you give something to get something) is essentially reactive, beginning at the end: "That I will get by giving this". Although the karmic principle has proven to work diligently and very well in all cultures and all times as long as there's been a recorded history, it's not by any means a cosmic given. Although regarded as sacrosanct, as other human inventions like mathematics and physics, the concept of karma is a human construction rooted in morals and the safety of consensus existence.

The magic of the mind is active and starts at the beginning: "It is my will that..." A free spirit is rooted in LIFE, and LIFE, as we shall se later, is the violent spasm that comes from two opposites joining for a short or for a long while. There is no other moral in LIFE than to survive, succeed and move on to the next attraction.

What other people (often less successful than the object of scrutiny) claim regarding karma should be heartily disregarded. Because when there's a moment of doubt – the wake-up call for the rational – the creative process stops and the dogs of reason start barking.

The sacrificial aspect of magic presupposes that there are higher forces at work and in charge, granting or denying human wishes. The magic of the mind presupposes the latent – now suddenly manifest – divinity of the human mind. This simple realization is by no means a sanction for the violation of other people's integrity – not even that of the moralists. It's very seldom we see a man or woman whose genuine will it is to destroy. Those who do so, are stopped sooner or later, as their existence is counterproductive to the common good – again, consensus existence. The simple realization of the unlimited potential of the human mind is a sanction for creation, nothing else.

The karmic moralists have a tendency to confuse offenders' neuroses with proper will. It is the will of very few – if any at all – to destroy. And the acts of destruction we can see on scales larger than individual (war, terrorism, etc), are actually often quite constructive if we are open-minded enough to switch points of view for just a moment. This is a huge challenge for most people stuck in binary thinking and programmed comfort.

Beauty – and the sense of justice – lies in the beholder's eyes.

Physical exhaustion permits an elevation of the mind. The protocreative act of sex permits an elevation of the mind. Working with the rational mind to the point of exhaustion permits an elevation of the mind (for instance, by methodically repeating a mantram or by using rational and complex human constructions such as the Qabalah).

When man ceases to fully grasp what's going on in his mind, there's an immediate need to categorize or create terms. This is how religion and science were created by the human rational mind, by experiencing realizations so strong and overwhelming that the given modus operandi tilts. In order not to lose its grip of the individual (or cultural) organism in question, symbols and words of power must be created by the rational mind.

On the transcendent level, where you've just left your rational rationale, there's naturally an increased sense of, and actual, freedom. The rational mind is the organism's police force. And the rules seemingly always come from someone else!

On this level, however, we are free not only to direct our Will and our Desire towards accomplishment. We're also free to research ourselves and thereby to find out more about the inner truths of our individual existence and development.

The passionate union of opposites may sound like a dialectical concept in itself, and some would argue that this concept is a prison of sorts. Intellectualism as a lifeboat in a sea of genuine wisdom. But it actually refers to more tangible illuminations too, some of which are more than obvious in the creation of the ultimate: new human life.

For simplicty's sake, let's call the transcending phase so essential in ritual "the polar ballet". Two forces of polar charge attract and interact. When they meet and/or merge, the primal energy of life is released in a violent burst. This burst is probably the closest a human being can ever come to experiencing "God". In the burst, in God if you will, there's a transcendence from the rational plane in a protocreative void. And now's the time to sow the seeds, whichever they are, and however you choose to do it.

In my experience, there's a great and quite counter-productive danger in assuming that there are generally valid polar definitions (such as male-female, dark-light, attraction-repellation etc). Your rational mind truly is yours, and although the forces such as male and female, minus and plus etc, may seem obvious at first, that may not always be the case. Only you can know what it is that you mentally need to merge with in order to transcend in a specific situation.

A heterosexual coitus may be an obvious encounter of diametrically different charges, but if it's an habitual ritual modus operandi, it may well be that you're not uniting opposites at all, but rather just cementing accepted patterns. This is the ultimate challenge for every magician: SINCERITY. If you're lying to yourself, then how can your creations be but perverted homunculi, destined to create havoc rather than bliss?

A polar ballet, when properly performed, receives immediate ovations from the universe. Because the universe works and creates in exactly the same way. There's attraction, repellation and new attraction. In the meetings, the short – or perhaps eternal – moments of transcendence, many cosmic seeds are sown by many cosmic minds. The space and/or time between this conception and the manifestation is the development of LIFE itself. And each manifestation always immediately attracts a new counterpart, and so the process of LIFE moves onwards.

If the director of the polar ballet isn't really conscious of what he or she is doing, the result will sooner or later prove to be malfunctioning in more or less obvious and painful ways. The main agent, the most essential part, of the ritual consciousness is SINCERITY.It takes nothing at all to adapt to expected patterns. It takes everything you have to adapt to patterns of a LIFE uniquely your own. And, as you always get what you give (an assumption, an assumption!), if you're giving everything to be true to yourself in your pursuit of development and achievement, that's exactly what you'll get: Everything you ever asked for.

(To be continued...?)

February, 1999

Contributors

Fredrik Söderberg is an artist based in Stockholm, and is a co-founder of Edda Publishing. He has had several major exhibitions in Sweden and abroad, and has illustrated a number of books and record covers. www.fredriksoderberg.org

Jason Louv is the author of *Queen Valentine* and editor of *Generation Hex, Ultraculture* and *Thee Psychick Bible,* and has written about technology and transhumanism for *Esquire Online, Humanity Plus Magazine* and *Acceler8or.* www.jasonlouv.com

Patrick Lundborg is a writer based in Stockholm, currently finishing a thorough study of psychedelic culture: *Psychedelia – Ancient Culture, Modern Lifestyle.* www.lysergia.com

Gary Lachman is the author of more than a dozen books charting the meeting ground between consciousness, culture, and the western esoteric tradition, most recently *Madame Blavatsky: The Mother of Modern Spirituality* (Penguin 2012). Other titles include *Turn Off Your Mind: The Mystic Sixties and the Dark Side of the Age of Aquarius* (Disinformation 2003), *The Secret History of Consciousness* (Lindisfarne 2003), and *Politics and the Occult* (Quest 2008). His biography of Rudolf Steiner (Penguin 2007) has been translated into Norwegian, German, Spanish, and French. He is a regular contributor to *Fortean Times, Independent on Sunday, Guardian, LA Review of Books* and other journals in the UK and US. He lectures frequently in the UK and Europe and is currently researching a book about Aleister Crowley and popular culture. In a previous life, he was a founding member of the rock group Blondie, and in 2006 was inducted into the Rock and Roll Hall of Fame. www.garylachman.co.uk

Timothy O'Neill, b.1951, A.B., U.C. Berkeley, Art History 1973 B.F.A., San Francisco Academy of Art College, 1979. Has been published in *Apocalypse Culture; Secret and Suppressed; Popular Alienation; Occulture, Steamshovel Press, Leonardo,* and worked as a staff writer at *Gnosis* magazine for ten years. He is a long-time member of Yogoda Satsanga and AMORC. He is currently working in San Francisco as a Performance Artist, musician, painter and writer interested in the Gnostic tradition.

Philip H. Farber has explored the cutting edge of magick, meditation and hypnosis for nearly thirty years. He is the author of *Brain Magick: Exercises in Meta-Magick and Invocation* (Llewellyn Worldwide, 2011), *Meta-Magick: The Book of Atem: Achieving New States of Consciousness Through NLP, Neuroscience and Ritual* (Weiser Books, 2008), *The Great Purple Hoo-Ha* (Mandrake, 2010) and *Futureritual: Magick for the 21st Century* (Eschaton Productions, 1995). His articles on magick and popular culture have appeared in *Green Egg Magazine, The Journal of Hypnotism, Hypnosis Today, Mondo 2000, High Times, Paradigm Shift, Reality Sandwich* and other unique publications and web sites. He has produced several DVD packages on magical topics and teaches workshops throughout the United States, England and Europe. Phil is an instructor for Maybe Logic Academy, a Certified Hypnotist and a Licensed Trainer of Neuro-linguistic Programming, with a private practice in New York's Hudson Valley. Visit Phil at: www. meta-magick.com

AKI CEDERBERG is a filmmaker, musician and writer from Helsinki, Finland. Relating to his engagement with various esoteric traditions and realms of knowledge and culture of which he has sought first-hand experience, as well as his interest in sites of mythological or historical significance both ancient and modern, he has travelled extensively. He received an initiation by Shri Mahant Rampuri of the Juna Akhara, an ancient order of Naga Babas in India, and was given the name Adinath Puri. He has been part of various musical and artistic projects, with whom he has completed several albums, films, exhibitions and tours. Currently he is part of the band Tuhkankantajat, with whom he has released an album titled MAA: Tuhkankantajat. He has a Bachelor of Culture and Arts (directing and scriptwriting) and works in film production. E-mail: aki.cederberg@welho.com

RENATA WIECZOREK has been involved with occult studies since she can remember, though on many occasions accidentally and with no total awareness of the true meaning of events. Professionally she is a philosopher and is specializing in theory of knowledge, philosophy of language, philosophy of mathematics, and writings of Ludwig Wittgenstein. She is also interested in the philosophical side of esoteric studies and magick. Privately she is an admirer of all things and persons interesting and remarkable.

GENESIS BREYER P-ORRIDGE is multiversal, polymathic, pandrogenous artist-magician of legendary stature. www.genesisbreyerporridge.com

STEPHEN ELLIS, born in 1950, has lived thus far in several North American eastern seaboard and midwest locations, and for several years in North Arabia. He edited, with Stephen Dignazio, 26 issues of the little magazine :that: (1992-1996), and was also the editor and publisher of over 120 broadsides and fascicles for Oasis Press (1996-2005). His publications include *A Book of Currencies* (1997), *The Long and Short of It* (1999), *Interface* (1999), *White Gravity* (1999), *A Natural History of Suchness* (2001) and *Opulence* (2010). He can be reached via General Delivery, Chester, Vermont, 05143, USA or at: stepellis@hotmail.com

HIRAM CORSO is an occult writer/researcher and a television engineer. His writings appear in *Another Mirror at the End of the Road* (where the piece about Mel Lyman has previously been published). He has recently completed a series of occult documentaries on youtube – several of which focus upon Mel Lyman. (They can be viewed at: http:// www.youtube.com/user/hiramcorso) The most recent documentary is entitled *LCN,*

OTOA and the Voudon Gnostic Magical System of Michael Bertiaux (co-produced by Malachi Gammon). He can be contacted at: hiram23@verizon.net

Gary Dickinson is a Fellow of the Royal Asiatic Society. Gary is a recognised expert on the court dress, ritual and symbolism of China's last imperial dynasty, the Qing or Manchu (1644-1911), co-authoring a source work on the subject. With over twenty years experience as an art historian, Gary has lectured in museums across the world. A life-long student of the I Ching and founder of the I Ching Society, his 'Warp & Weft – a short history of the I Ching', under the pen-name William de Fancourt, has recently been republished. Over the last two years he has researched and lectured on Aleister Crowley's interest in China and his work with the I Ching.

This article was originally published as "The Yijing and the Development of Geomantic Divination" under the name William Fancourt in *The Oracle, The Journal of Yijing Studies,* Vol.2, No.9, August 1999. It has been revised and expanded by the author to incorporate his recent researches into Crowley's work with the Yijing.

ROBERT PODGURSKI has been practicing magick, various forms of yoga, qui gong, and meditation for over 30 years. Not only has he been an avid practitioner but is actively engaged in a lifelong scholarly pursuit of the history and genesis of hermeticism, magic, alchemy, the Cabala, and western esotericism within a syncretic framework. Subsequently, for the past 20 years he has been researching as well as working with the Enochian system of angelic magic as discovered and developed by John Dee and Sir Edward Kelley. During this time he found himself initiated into a revolutionary version of the Enochian system that utilizes communicated Sigils that act as catalysts to the calls of creation and the thirty aethyrs. The end result of this endeavor is his first major work, *The Sacred Alignments and Dark Side of Sigils*, Mandrake Press Ltd, UK due for release 2012. For additional information and publication release dates see: http://gridmagick.com

FRATER NIGRIS (333; nagasiva yronwode), The Black Brother of the OTO (Nigris, 333) is a Thelemic revolutionary nascent to the SF Bay area of California. Nigris is a New Aeon herald and prophet, a Magician of Life in good standing in the (c)OTO, and is not involved in the Gnostic Catholic Church (EGC) which presides as its upper echelon. See his new website at: www.book-of-the-law.com and use the address: nigris@book-of-the-law.com for email contact.

PETER GREY is the co-founder of Scarlet Imprint (www.scarletimprint.com). The author of the acclaimed devotional work for Babalon, *The Red Goddess*. He is an exponent of the antinomian and libertarian strand of the western magical tradition. His work comes out of physical praxis. His path is one of ordeal, ecstasy, and Love.

VERA MLADENOVSKA NIKOLICH – An explorer. Dedicated to unlocking the next level of evolution. Fascinated by the communication capabilities of the human mind. Queen of Wands.

KEVIN I. SLAUGHTER is a vulgarian and elitist, half son of the American South, half child of Mother England. He is a graphic designer and book publisher by vocation and intellectual dissident and misanthropologist by avocation. He has lectured at Universities on the topic of Satanism, and two different hour long presentations are available on YouTube. Ordained a priest in the Church of Satan, and a member of the Hard Case Crime Book of the Month Club. http://www.KevinISlaughter.com | http://www.UnderworldAmusements.com

Kevin Slaughter's contribution is an edited version of a lecture given at Wayne State University on November 16th, 2011.

LIONEL SNELL AKA RAMSEY DUKES. Dukes is a discarnate entity first made manifest around 1970 when it occupied the mind of a Cambridge mathematics scholar with a long standing interest in magic, alchemy, Aleister Crowley and the occult. In return it has channeled a number of books that helped define late 20th century magick – notably *SSOTBME: An Essay on Magic* and *Thundersqueak*, both seminal texts of Chaos magick, and *Words Made Flesh*, proposing the information model of magical reality. In 1977 he performed the Abramelin operation, and he has since worked with a number of ritual groups, including the OTO and IOT, as well as founding the Arcanorium College's Department of Experimental Metaphysics. His most recent book, *How to See Fairies*, is based upon his Arcanorium College course *Experimental Clairvoyance for the Non-Psychic*.

THE ANONYMOUS AUTHOR of *Liber Niger Legionis* is host to many selves of many names – infernal, demonic, diabolical, celestial, and occasionally divine. Pharaon is one.

LANA KRIEG is a student of occult and esoteric traditions with a particular interest in European traditions and their interaction with non-European indigenous systems. She is particularly interested in the dynamic interplay of art and literature with the understanding and expression of magic and religion. She holds a Bachelor of Arts Degree in English and Comparative Literature focusing on modern European literature, and a Master of Science degree in the social sciences. Currently residing in the Southwestern United States, the author can be reached at lohne.krieg@gmail.com

CARL ABRAHAMSSON is the editor of *The Fenris Wolf* and the founder of The Institute of Comparative Magico-anthropology. He likes to write and read, take an occasional photograph and at times converse with the audio structure spirits. That's about it really. www.carlabrahamsson.com, www.trapart.net

The Fenris Wolf 10 (2020)

Carl Abrahamsson – *Editor's Introduction*, Carl Abrahamsson – *Onwards to the Source!*, Ludwig Klages – *On the Essence of Ecstasy*, David Beth – *Katabasis and Erotognosis*, Henrik Dahl – *An Introduction to Eroto-Psychedelic Art*, Peter Sjöstedt-H – *Antichrist Psychonaut: Nietzsche's Psychoactive Drugs*, Carl Abrahamsson – *Lux Per Nox – The Fenris Wolf As Libidinal Liberator*, Jesse Bransford & Max Razdow – *Revisiting the Veil of Dreams*, Christopher Webster – *Beyond the North Wind*, Kendell Geers – *A Long Boundless Systematized...*, Kadmus – *Seeking the Three-Headed Saint*, Billie Steigerwald – *The Chthonic Seed: Reflections of an Ancient Death Gnosis*, Fred Andersson – *The Gospel According to the Tomb Man*, Zaheer Gulamhusein – *Sunflower*, Charlotte Rodgers – *The Riderless Horse...*, Craig Slee – *The Occult Nature of Cripkult*, Damien Patrick Williams – *Daoism, Buddhism and Machine Consciousness*, Philip H. Farber – *Thoughts on the Creation of Memetic Entities*, Thomas Bey William Bailey – *Memetic Magick*, Mitch Horowitz – *Is Your Mind a Technology for Utopia?*, Ramsey Dukes – *I'm Gonna Blow Your Mind*, Carl Abrahamsson – *Grasping Reality with Gary Lachman*, Anders Lundgren – *Mike Mignola and the Lovecraft Circle*, Peggy Nadramia – *So It Was Written*, Peggy Nadramia – *Addendum to So It Was Written*, Nina Antonia – *Maya*, Jack Stevenson – *Häxan/Witchcraft Through the Ages*, Andrea Kundry – *The Demonic Cultural Legacy of Antonin Artaud*, Joan Pope – *The Birth of Ideas*, Genesis Breyer P-Orridge – *Idiosyncratic Use Ov Language...*, Vanessa Sinclair – *Try To Altar Everything*, Claire-Madeline Corso – *Cutting Up a New Conversation*

The Fenris Wolf 9 (2017)

Vanessa Sinclair & Carl Abrahamsson – *Editors' Introduction: Looking back at the crossroads*, Katelan Foisy – *Invocation: Homage to the spirits of the land/London*, Sharron Kraus – *Art as Alchemy*, Demetrius Lacroix – *The Seven Layers of the Vodou Soul*, Graham Duff – *Sublime Fragments: The Art of John Balance*, Ken Henson – *The American Occult Revival In My Work*, Gary Lachman – *Was Freud Afraid of the Occult?*, Peter Grey – *Fly the Light*, Val Denham – *Proclaim Present Time Over*, Katelan Foisy & Vanessa Sinclair – *The Cut In Creation*, Claire-Madeline Culkin – *Beds, Bodies and Other Books of Common Prayer – A Reading of the, Photography of Nan Goldin*, Steven Reisner – *On the Dance of the Occult and Unconscious in Freud*, Katy Bohinc – *The 12th House: Art and the Unconscious*, Olga Cox Cameron – *When Shall We 3 Meet Again? Psychoanalysis, Art and the Occult: A Clandestine Convergence*, Ingo Lambrecht – *Wairua: Following shamanic contours in psychoanalytic therapy at a Māori Mental Health Service in New Zealand*, Elliott Edge – *An Occult Reading of PAO! Imagining in the Dark with Our Vestigial Shamanism in a Shade, Shadow, Wide*, Charlotte Rodgers – *Stripped to the Core: Animistic Art Action and Magickal Revelation*, Alkistis Dimech – *Dynamics of the Occulted Body*, Fred Yee – *Cut-Up As Egregore, Oracle and Flirtation Device*, Robert Ansell – *Androgyny, Biology and Latent Memory in the Work of Austin Osman Spare*,

Ray O Neill – *Double, Double, Toil and Trouble: Psychoanalysis Burn and Surrealism Bubble*, Derek M Elmore – *Dreams and the Neither-Neither*, Julio Mendes Rodrigo – *Rebis, the Double Being*, Eve Watson – *Bowie's Non-Human Effect: Alien/Alienation in The Man Who Fell to Earth (1976) and The Hunger (1983)*, Carl Abrahamsson – *Formulating the Desired: Some similarities between ritual magic and the psychoanalytic process*

The Fenris Wolf 8 (2016)

Carl Abrahamsson – *Editor's Introduction*, Vanessa Sinclair – *Polymorphous Perversity and Pandrogeny*, Charles Stansfield Jones (Frater Achad) – *Alchymia*, Tim O'Neill: *Black Lodge/White Lodge*, Nina Antonia – *Bosie & The Beast*, Aki Cederberg – *Festivals of Spring*, Michael Moynihan – *Friedrich Hielscher's Vision of the Real Powers*, Friedrich Hielscher – *The Real Powers*, Orryelle Defenestrate Bascule – *Ear Horn: Shamanic Perspectives and Multi-Sensory Inversion*, Zbigniew Lagos – *The Figure of the Polish Magician: Czesław Czynski (1858-1932)*, Gary Lachman – *Rejected Knowledge: A Look At Our Other Way of Knowing*, Carl Abrahamsson – *Intuition as a State of Grace*, Bishop T Omphalos – *The Golden Thread: Soteriological Aspects of the Gnostic Catholicism in E.G.C.*, Kendell Geers – *iMagus*, Johan Nilsson – *Defending Paper Gods: Aleister Crowley and the Reception of Daoism in Early 20th Century Esotericism*, Gordan Djurdjevic – *The Birth of the New Aeon: Magick and Mysticism of Thelema from the Perspective of Postmodern A/Theology*, Tim O'Neill – *The Derleth Error*, Antti P Balk – *Greek Mysteries*, Carl Abrahamsson – *The Economy of Magic*, Stephen Sennitt – *The Book of the Sentient Night: 23 Nails*, Henrik Dahl – *We Ate the Acid: A Note on Psychedelic Imagery*, Jason Louv – *Robert Anton Wilson's Cosmic Trigger and the Psychedelic Interstellar Future we need*, Carey Hodges & Chad Hensley – *New Orleans Voodoo: An Oddity Unto Itself*, Alexander Nym – *Kabbalah references in contemporary culture*, Zaheer Gulamhusein – *Standing in Line*, Carl Abrahamsson – *As the Wolf Lies Down to Rest*, Vanessa Sinclair & Ingo Lambrecht – *Ritual and Psychoanalytical Spaces as Transitional, featuring Sangoma Trance States*, Hagen von Julien – *Listening to the Voice of Silence: A Contemporary Perspective on the Fraternities Saturni*, Erik Davis – *Infectious Hoax: Robert Anton Wilson reads H.P. Lovecraft*, N – *II. Land*, Cadmus – *Neo-Chthonia*, Kadmus – *A Fragment of Heart: A contribution to the Mega-Golem*, Stojan Nikolic – *The One True Church of the Dark Age of Scientism*, Miguel Marques – *The Labors of Seeing: A Journey Through the Works of Peter Whitehead*, Renata Wieczorek – *The Conception of Number According to Aleister Crowley*, Orryelle Defenestrate Bascule – *Fragments of Fact*, Derek Seagrief – *Conscious ExIt*, Kasper Opstrup – *By This, That: A spin on Lea Porsager's Spin*, and Genesis Breyer P-Orridge – *Greyhounds of the future*.

The Fenris Wolf 7 (2014)

Carl Abrahamsson – *Editor's Introduction*, Sara George & Carl Abrahamsson – *Fernand Khnopff, Symbolist*, Sasha Chaitow – *Making the Invisible Visible*, Vanessa Sinclair – *Psychoanalysis and Dada*, Kendell Geers – *Tu Marcellus Eris*, Stephen Sennitt – *Fallen Worlds, Without Shadows*, Antony Hequet – *Slam Poetry: The Warrior Poet*, Antony Hequet – *Slam Poetry: The Rebel Poet*, Genesis Breyer P-Orridge – *Alien Lightning Meat Machine*, Genesis Breyer P-Orridge – *This Is A Nice Planet*, Patrick Lundborg – *Psychedelic Philosophy*, Henrik Dahl – *Visionary Design*, Philip Farber – *Higher Magick*, Kendell Geers – *Painting My Will*, Carl Abrahamsson – *The Imaginative Libido*, Angela Edwards – *The Sacred Whore*, Vera Nikolich – *The Women of the Aeon*,

Jason Louv – *Wilhelm Reich*, Kasper Opstrup – *To Make It Happen*, Peter Grey – *A Manifesto of Apocalyptic Witchcraft*, Timothy O'Neill – *The Gospel of Cosmic Terror*, Stephen Sennitt – *Sentient Absence*, Carl Abrahamsson – *Anton LaVey, Magical Innovator*, Alexander Nym – *Magicians: Evolutionary Agents or Regressive Twats?*, Antti P Balk – *Thelema*, Kjetil Fjell – *The Vindication of Thelema*, Derek Seagrief – *Exploring Past Lives*, Sandy Robertson – *The Fictional Aleister Crowley*, Adam Rostoker – *Whence Came the Stranger?*, Emory Cranston – *A Preface to the Scented Garden*, Manon Hedenborg-White – *Erotic Submission to the Divine*, Carl Abrahamsson – *What Remains for the Future?*, Frater Achad – *Living In the Sunlight*, Genesis Breyer P-Orridge – *Magick Squares and Future Beats*

THE FENRIS WOLF 6 (2013)

Carl Abrahamsson – *Editor's Introduction*, Frater Achad – *A Litany of Ra*, Kendell Geers – *Tripping over Darwin's Hangover*, Vera Nikolich – *Eastern Connections*, Carl Abrahamsson – *Babalon*, Freya Aswynn – *On the Influence of Odin*, Marita – *Runic Magic through the Odinic Dialectic*, Aki Cederberg – *Afterword: The River of Story*, Shri Gurudev Mahendranath – *The Londinium Temple Strain*, Gary Dickinson – *An Orient Pearl*, Derek Seagrief – *Aleister Crowley's Birth & Death Horoscopes*, Tim O'Neill – *Shades of Void*, Nema – *Magickal Healing*, Nema – *A Greater Feast*, Philip Farber – *Sacred Smoke*, Robert Taylor – *Death & the Psychedelic Experience*, Michael Horowitz – *LSD: the Antidote to Everything*, Alexander Nym – *Transcendence as an Operative Category…*, Carl Abrahamsson – *Approaching the Approaching*, Renata Wieczorek – *The Secret Book of the Tatra Mountains*, Sasha Chaitow – *Legends of the Fall Retold*, Sara George & Carl Abrahamsson – *Sulamith Wülfing*, Robert C Morgan – *Hans Bellmer*, Genesis Breyer P-Orridge – *Tagged for Life*, Carl Abrahamsson – *Go Forth and Let Your Brain-halves Procreate*, Anders Lundgren – *Satanic Cinema is Alive and Well*, Anton LaVey – *Appendices*

THE FENRIS WOLF 5 (2012)

Carl Abrahamsson – *Editor's Introduction*, Jason Louv – *The Freedom of Imagination Act*, Patrick Lundborg – *Such Stuff as Dreams are Made of*, Gary Lachman – *Secret Societies and the Modern World*, Tim O'Neill – *The War of the Owl and the Pelican*, Dianus del Bosco Sacro – *The Great Rite*, Philip H Farber – *Entities in the Brain*, Aki Cederberg – *At the Well of Initiation*, Renata, Wieczorek – *The Magical Life of Derek Jarman*, Genesis Breyer P-Orridge – *A Dark Room of Desire*, Genesis Breyer P-Orridge – *Kreeme Horne*, Ezra Pound – *Translator's Postscript*, Stephen Ellis – *Poems for The Fenris Wolf*, Hiram Corso – *Mel Lyman*, Mel Lyman – *Plea for Courage*, Gary Dickinson – *The Daughter of Astrology*, Robert Podgurski – *Sigils and Extra Dimensionality*, Frater Nigris – *Liber Al As-if*, Peter Grey – *The Abbey Must be Built*, Vera Mladenovska Nikolich – *A Different Perspective of the Undead*, Kevin Slaughter – *The Great Satan*, Lionel Snell – *The Art of Evil*, Phenex Apollonius – *The Quintessence of Daimonic Ipseity*, Phanes Apollonius – *Infernal Diabolism in Theory and Practice*, Anonymous – *Falling with Love: Embracing the Infernal Host*, Lana Krieg – *Sympathy with the Devil: Faust's Infernal Formula*, Carl Abrahamsson – *State of the Art: Birthpangs of a Mega-Golem*, Carl Abrahamsson – *Hounded by the Dogs of Reason*

Smith 1923-1991, Andrew M McKenzie – *Outofinto*, Beatrice Eggers – *Nature: Now, Then and Never*

GENESIS BREYER P-ORRIDGE: SACRED INTENT
– CONVERSATIONS WITH CARL ABRAHAMSSON 1986-2019

Sacred Intent gathers conversations between artist Genesis Breyer P-Orridge and longtime friend and collaborator, the Swedish author Carl Abrahamsson. From the first 1986 fanzine interview about current projects, over philosophical insights, magical workings, international travels, art theory and gender revolutions, to 2019's thoughts on life and death in the the shadow of battling leukaemia, *Sacred Intent* is a unique journey in which the art of conversation blooms.

With (in)famous projects like C.O.U.M. Transmissions, Throbbing Gristle, Psychic TV, Thee Temple Ov Psychick Youth (TOPY) and Pandrogeny, Breyer P-Orridge has consistently thwarted preconceived ideas and transformed disciplines such as performance art, music, collage, poetry and social criticism; always cutting up the building blocks to dismantle control structures and authority. But underneath the socially conscious and pathologically rebellious spirit, there has always been a devout respect for a holistic, spiritual, magical worldview – one of "sacred intent."

Sacred Intent is a must read for anyone interested in contemporary art, deconstructed identity, gender evolution, and magical philosophy. The book not only celebrates an intimate friendship, but also the work and ideas of an artist who has never ceased to amaze and provoke. Also included are photographic portraits of Breyer P-Orridge taken by Carl Abrahamsson, transcripts of key lectures, and an interview with Jacqueline "Lady Jaye" Breyer P-Orridge from 2004.

GENESIS BREYER P-ORRIDGE: BRION GYSIN – HIS NAME WAS MASTER

Brion Gysin (1916–86) has been an incredibly influential artist and iconoclast: his development of the "cut-up" technique with William S. Burroughs has inspired generations of writers, artists and musicians. Gysin was also a skilled networker and revered expat: together with his friend Paul Bowles, he more or less constructed the post-beatnik romanticism for life and magic in Morocco, and was also a protagonist in an international gay culture with inspirational reaches in both America and Europe. Not surprisingly, Gysin has become something of a cult figure.

One of the artists he inspired is Genesis Breyer P-Orridge, who collaborated with both Gysin and Burroughs in the 1970s, during his work with Throbbing Gristle and C.O.U.M. Transmissions. The interviews made by P-Orridge have since become part of a New Wave/Industrial mythos. This volume presents them in their entirety alongside three texts on Gysin by P-Orridge, plus an introduction. This book is an exclusive insight into the mind of a man P-Orridge describes as "a kind of Leonardo da Vinci of the last century," and a fantastic complement to existing biographies and monographs.

CARL ABRAHAMSSON: MOTHER, HAVE A SAFE TRIP

Unearthed plans and designs stemming from radical inventor Nikola Tesla could solve the world's energy problems. These plans suddenly generate a vortex of interest from various powers. Thrown into this maelstrom of international intrigue is Victor Ritterstadt – a soul searching magician with a mysterious and troubled past. From Berlin, over Macedonia, and all the way to Nepal, Ritterstadt sets out on an outer as well as inner quest. Espionage, love, UFOs, magic, telepathy, conspiracies, LSD, and more in this shocking story of a world about to be changed forever…

"It's a thrilling roller coaster ride through psychedelic adventures, juicy romantic interludes, metaphoric dreamscapes, high Himalayan yoga enclaves, telepathic portals, 60's flashbacks, magical constructs, secret government pursuits and many more twists that kept all three of my eyes open. It's a story that you'll definitely want to keep non-stop reading, which I enthusiastically recommend."
> – George Douvris, Links by George

"*Mother, Have A Safe Trip* is a highly entertaining and thought-provoking novel. Chock-full of psychedelia, the book is also a much welcome addition to the far too few fictional works published dealing with psychedelic culture."
> – Henrik Dahl, Psychedelic Press

"The dialogues are great. But it's too short. I wanted more."
> – Genesis Breyer P-Orridge, Artist

"It's a wonderful read. A lovely book."
> – June Newton/Alice Springs, Photographer

Vanessa Sinclair: Switching Mirrors

Switching Mirrors is an amazing collection of cut-ups and mind-expanding poetry by Vanessa Sinclair. Delving into the unconscious and actively utilising the "third mind" as developed by William S Burroughs and Brion Gysin, Sinclair roams through suggestive vistas of magic, witchcraft, dreams, psychoanalysis, sex and sexuality (and more). Causal apprehensions are disrupted by a flow of impressions that open up the mind of the reader. What's behind language and our use of it? What happens when random factors and the unconscious are given free reign in poetic form? *Switching Mirrors* is what happens.

Vanessa Sinclair (ed.): Rendering Unconscious
– Psychoanalytic Perspectives, Politics & Poetry

In times of crisis, one needs to stop and ask, "How did we get here?" Our contemporary chaos is the result of a society built upon pervasive systems of oppression, discrimination and violence that run deeper and reach further than most understand or care to realize. These draconian systems have been fundamental to many aspects of our lives, and we seem to have gradually allowed them more power. However, our foundation is not solid; it is fractured and collapsing – if we allow that. We need to start applying new models of interpretation and analysis to the deep-rooted problems at hand.

Rendering Unconscious brings together international scholars, psychoanalysts, psychologists, philosophers, researchers, writers and poets; reflecting on current events, politics, the state of mental health care, the arts, literature, mythology, and the cultural climate; thoughtfully evaluating this moment of crisis, its implications, wide-ranging effects, and the social structures that have brought us to this point of urgency.

Hate speech, Internet stalking, virtual violence, the horde mentality of the alt-right, systematic racism, the psychology of rioting, the theater of violence, fake news, the power of disability, erotic transference and counter-transference, the economics of libido, Eros and the death drive, fascist narratives, psychoanalytic formation as resistance, surrealism and sexuality, traversing genders, and colonial counterviolence are but a few of the topics addressed in this thought-provoking and inspiring volume.

Contributions by Vanessa Sinclair, Gavriel Reisner, Alison Annunziata, Kendalle Aubra, Gerald Sand, Tanya White-Davis & Anu Kotay, Luce deLire, Jason Haaf, Simon Critchley & Brad Evans, Marc Strauss, Chiara Bottici, Manya Steinkoler, Emma Lieber, Damien Patrick Williams, Shara Hardeson, Jill Gentile, Angelo Villa, Gabriela Costardi, Jamieson Webster, Sergio Benvenuto, Craig Slee, Álvaro D. Moreira, David Lichtenstein, Julie Fotheringham, John Dall'aglio, Matthew Oyer, Jessica Datema, Olga Cox Cameron, Katie Ebbitt, Juliana Portilho, Trevor Pederson, Elisabeth Punzi & Per-Magnus Johansson, Meredith Friedson, Steven Reisner, Léa Silveira, Patrick Scanlon, Júlio Mendes Rodrigo, Daniel Deweese, Julie Futrell, Gregory J. Stevens, Benjamin Y. Fong, Katy Bohinc, Wayne Wapeemukwa, Patricia Gherovici & Cassandra Seltman, Marie Brown, Buffy Cain, Claire-Madeline Culkin, Andrew Daul, Germ Lynn, Adel Souto, and paul aster stone-tsao.

Sir Edward Bulwer Lytton: Vril – The Power of the Coming Race

Sir Edward Bulwer Lytton's cautionary tale of occult super-powers and advanced subterranean cultures have fascinated readers since 1871. Part early science-fiction, part educational tract, part occult romance, *Vril* keeps spellbinding readers thanks to its wide range of themes and emotions, as well as its thrilling sense of adventure.

A curious man descends into a mountain through a mine and experiences far more than he bargained for. Deep inside the mountain lies a completely different world. Its inhabitants, the Vril-ya, are human-like but physically superior and philosophically more advanced. They live in harmony made possible by their wisdom but also by the powerful and potentially destructive magical energy they call "Vril."

The impressed yet terrified visitor is allowed to stay and learn more about their ancient and advanced culture, something very few visitors have – it seems that all the previous adventurers have been mercilessly disposed of by the Vril-ya...

This edition includes an introductory essay by Swedish author Carl Abrahamsson.